The Gazetteer
1735-1797

THE

GAZETTEER

1735 - 1797

A Study in the Eighteenth-Century
English Newspaper
by
ROBERT L. HAIG

SOUTHERN ILLINOIS UNIVERSITY PRESS

Carbondale

LIBRARY OF CONGRESS CATALOG CARD NO. 60-5071
© 1960 BY SOUTHERN ILLINOIS UNIVERSITY PRESS
PRINTED IN THE UNITED STATES OF AMERICA BY
VAIL-BALLOU PRESS, INC., BINGHAMTON, N.Y.
DESIGNED BY ANDOR BRAUN

Preface

THIS STUDY constitutes, I believe, the first attempt ever made to record in detail the history of a single eighteenth-century daily newspaper. That fact alone may partially justify the undertaking, but the contemporary significance of the *Gazetteer* provides further justification. In the early years of its existence it was the most famous daily newspaper published in England—or the most infamous, depending upon the political sympathies of its individual reader. Parson Adams, who had never heard of it, was informed by his host that it was "a dirty newspaper which hath been given away all over the nation for these many years." Thirty years later, long detached from the service of government, it was probably the most widely circulated daily paper in London. Historians of the press have naturally emphasized the circumstances of its early career; they have been almost unaware of its later importance. The success of a newspaper in the eighteenth century is to be estimated pretty accurately from the length of its life. The life span of the *Gazetteer* as a separate publication extended over a period of sixty-two years and three months. Its length was exceeded by the career of only one other daily newspaper.

The immediate purpose of my work has been to present as complete an account as possible of the *Gazetteer* in its progress through six decades, and of the persons most directly concerned in its production. More generally, I hope that the history of the *Gazetteer* may be considered in two respects as an acceptable contribution to the history of British journalism which Mr. Stanley

v

Morison observed nearly thirty years ago was urgently needed and
which has still to be written. First, as a comprehensive study of a
single newspaper, it may ultimately serve as one stone in the
foundation of that monumental edifice. Secondly, inasmuch as the
Gazetteer corresponds in many respects to other newspapers of its
time, a number of the facts here presented should have general
application to the history of the English newspaper in the eighteenth century. "Of the inside of any newspaper-office in those days
we have still much to learn," Professor Nichol Smith wrote in
1933. The statement remains distressingly accurate, but I should
like to hope that a few of the facts previously lacking are supplied here.

The principal sources employed have been the surviving issues
of the *Gazetteer* itself and a unique group of manuscript materials
relating to the production and management of the paper from
1774 which are preserved in the Public Record Office. Two invaluable sources of information, tantalizing references to which
are found among the Record Office manuscripts, are unfortunately
beyond recovery. One is the marked office file of the *Gazetteer*
(each volume of which was sewn in blue paper at a cost to the
publisher of four shillings annually); the other is a group of publisher's accounts deposited for safekeeping in 1772 at the Fleet
Street bank of Gosling and Giles and apparently destroyed in relatively recent years by their successors.

A narrative of the sort here attempted is beset by a number of
practical difficulties. In the first place, if one resists the temptation to chronicle the political and social history of the period as
reflected in the pages of the newspaper, it is almost impossible to
maintain a consistent degree of emphasis upon every period of the
paper's career, for the quantity of evidence and the intrinsic interest of the paper itself vary widely at different periods. An analyti-
cal study, for example, of Walpole's *Daily Gazetteer* as an organ
of political propaganda might well occupy more space than is here
devoted to the paper's entire history. Moreover, a coherent treatment is made difficult by the many-sided nature of a daily newspaper at a time when there was no editorial page to serve as a focal
point. The perfect synthesis of all elements is to be found only in
a single day's issue of the *Gazetteer*, and the ideal history, perhaps,
only in the sixty-two annual volumes.

The length of the paper's life precludes an organization on
purely topical lines, for the *Gazetteer* published in 1735 was not
the same as that published in 1765, and both differed essentially

from the paper published under that title in 1795. Chronological
arrangement has made it necessary to treat portions of a single
topic at several points in the paper's history. The problem of
organization is by no means novel; I have been comforted in the
knowledge that it was encountered a century ago by Alexander
Andrews in a pioneer study of the English newspaper press. "The
adoption of a chronological arrangement," Andrews wrote in 1859,

—necessary, it seemed to us, in all other respects—rendered this a less
easy task than it might seem, for we had got our anecdotes parcelled, and
lotted out, and classified in distinct branches of the subject . . . ; and
when we came to pick out facts as they had occurred in the order of
time, they looked to us very forlorn, detached from the companion facts
of the same order with which they had been associated, and which they
tended either to illustrate or contrast.

I have tried to minimize the difficulty to which Andrews referred
by the use of cross references in the notes and the inclusion of a
comprehensive index.

For both the general reader and the student of eighteenth-
century England to whom newspapers of the time are not readily
accessible, I have sought to convey the particular flavor of the
paper and of the period as it is reflected in the paper by allowing
the *Gazetteer* to speak for itself whenever that has seemed appropriate.

*

IT IS A PRIVILEGE to record my obligation to the teachers, colleagues,
and friends who have contributed in various ways to the comple-
tion of this study. Professor James Sutherland, of University College, London, and Professors Philip B. Daghlian and John Robert
Moore of Indiana University are jointly responsible for my immer-
sion in eighteenth-century England; their guidance and encouragement have, on embarrassingly numerous occasions, prevented my
drowning.

To Professors George Sherburn, Robert W. Rogers, and Richmond P. Bond, I am indebted for careful readings of the manuscript and for a number of valuable suggestions that have been
incorporated. Others who have contributed indispensably by their
learning and counsel are my colleague Professor G. Blakemore

Evans, the late Professor Arthur W. Secord, Professor Irvin
Ehrenpreis, and Professor Robert R. Rea.

My research is a pleasure to recall because of the kindness and
co-operation shown by the staffs of the University of Illinois Library, the British Museum Reading Rooms, Somerset House, and
the Victoria and Albert Museum. Particular thanks are due to
Mr. E. K. Timings, whose learning and interest greatly facilitated
my work at the Public Record Office. A grant in aid from the University of Illinois Research Board has enabled me to complete my
work much earlier than would otherwise have been possible.

Finally, because in every list of acknowledgements that name
stands last which should stand first, I record here the debt that is
beyond definition—to my wife, Lois.

R. L. H.

Champaign, Illinois
March, 1959

Contents

Illustrations

The Gazetteer
1735-1797

And monumental brass this record bears,
"These are,—ah no! these were, the Gazetteers!"
—Alexander Pope, *The Dunciad*

No, madam, I have enough to do to read the Daily Gazetteer.
My father has six of 'em sent him every week, for nothing;
they are very pretty papers, and I wish you would read them,
miss.
—Henry Fielding, *Pasquin*

A Statesman's Logic unconcern'd can hear,
And dare to slumber o'er the Gazetteer.
—Samuel Johnson, *London*

. . . after being at considerable pains to study the subject, he
wrote three several letters in the *Gazetteer* . . . .
—James Boswell, *The Life of Samuel Johnson, LL.D.*

"What, give up liberty, property, and, as the Gazetteer says,
lie down to be saddled with wooden shoes!"
—Oliver Goldsmith, *The Vicar of Wakefield*

And what if I bring my last letter to the Gazetteer on the
encrease and progress of earthquakes?
—Oliver Goldsmith, *The Good Natur'd Man*

This man is printer of the Gazetteer, and if a ghost is to be
raised, or a minister to be roasted, no body seems to have a
nobler contempt for his ears.
—Arthur Murphy, *The Auditor*

All the commonplace lamentations upon the decay of trade,
the increase of taxes, and the high price of labor and provisions, are here retailed again and again in the same tone with
which they have drawled through columns of Gazetteers and
Advertisers for a century together.
—Edmund Burke, *Observations on a Late Publication
intituled 'The Present State of the Nation'*

I

THE GAZETTEER LEGION

1735-1742

WHEN in the autumn of 1797 the proprietors of the *Morning Post* announced that they had purchased the copyright of the *Gazetteer*, they referred to that paper as "the oldest established Morning Newspaper in London." The claim of seniority was open to some dispute,[1] but there was a definite note of pride in the announcement, for the *Morning Post* had purchased, besides a new subtitle and a few subscribers, the prestige of a name which through two generations of London life had become a tradition. To most who read the announcement, the origins of the *Gazetteer* were obscure. A paper of that name had appeared in the coffeehouses every weekday morning for sixty-two years, and there was by now a certain respectability about it which discouraged curiosity.

Few readers of 1797 could have recalled the ascendancy of Sir Robert Walpole and the bitterly partisan controversies which then occupied the newspapers almost exclusively and were, in fact, their chief excuse for being. Sir Robert's youngest son, who in some measure had continued to represent the spirit of those times, had died at eighty, just six months before the end of the paper which originated as an instrument of his father's power. Daniel Stuart, the editor of the *Morning Post* in 1797, might have made his announcement more impressive had he been disposed to exert a further claim to distinction for the *Gazetteer* on the basis of its antecedents. The paper was not only one of the oldest dailies in London at the time; it was also a direct descendant of the first daily newspaper established in England.

3

The Daily Courant, *"confin'd to half the Compass, to save
the Publick at least half the Impertinences, of ordinary News-
Papers,"* was first published on 11 March 1702. During the early
years of Walpole's administration it became an important vehicle
of ministerial opinion, enjoying after 1731 regular government
subsidies.[2] On 28 June 1735 a brief notice on page 2 of the *Courant*
announced the birth of the *Gazetteer:* "The Authors of the several
Political Letters in the *London Journal, Free Briton,* and this *Paper,* will, for the future, publish their Dissertations on Publick
Affairs in a New Paper, entitled THE DAILY GAZETTEER;
the first Number of which will make its Appearance on *Monday*
next." [3] The first issue of *The Daily Gazetteer* was duly published
on Monday, 30 June 1735.

In appearance the new paper was neat but in no way novel. Its
format corresponded to that developed by the weekly journals of
the preceding decade.[4] The prospectus, which nearly filled page 1
of the first issue, sought to introduce the paper "with such Accounts
of the Design, and of the Persons who undertake it," as might "at
once gratify every Man's Curiosity, and interest him in the Success of the Undertaking." The *Gazetteer,* it began, could not "have
a better Recommendation, than that it is owing to the amicable
Agreement of several Authors, who having, for many Years past,
been embarked in the same Cause, have at length resolved to unite
in the same Paper, and by the most extensive Circulation, to publish their faithful Endeavours in Support of the general Interest."
"Fra. Walsingham," who signed the introduction and who had
previously written the *Free Briton,* was to continue his regular
Thursday essays in the *Daily Gazetteer,*

And the *Author of the* LONDON JOURNAL is likewise determined to
proceed in this Paper every *Saturday,* as usual. For the rest, there are
other Gentlemen, particularly those of the DAILY COURANT, who will
choose for themselves, such days as may be convenient to them; and if
there are any Vacancies, they will be supplied with such Papers, as our
Correspondents shall be pleased to communicate to us.

Readers of the period required no more specific introduction to
the writers who were to collaborate in the new publication. Francis
Walsingham was the name with which William Arnall (or Arnold)
had signed his essays in the *Free Briton* since its inception in 1729.
In that paper Arnall, originally educated as an attorney, had
brought his far from contemptible talents to bear against the writ-

ings of the opposition *Craftsman*.[5] The Treasury records for the period show him to have been the most highly paid writer in government employ, and the report of the secret committee to enquire into Walpole's financial management revealed that he had received almost £11,000 from the secret service funds during a period of only four years.[6]

The author of the *London Journal* was James Pitt. Formerly a Norwich schoolmaster, and characterized in the *Dunciad* notes as "the eldest and gravest" of the government writers, Pitt wrote under the pseudonym of "Francis Osborne," which the *Craftsman* transmuted to "Mother Osborne" because of the heaviness of his style. Pitt's contributions to the ministerial journals, for which he was eventually rewarded with a post in the Customs House, were almost entirely defensive, as distinguished from the counter-attacking methods of Arnall. To the *Gazetteer*, wrote James Ralph, who may himself have been contributing to the paper at this time, "Mr. *Osborne* was to give solid Reason, Mr. *Walsingham* Wit, and the occasional Gentlemen Humour or Secret History, as the Exigencies of the Patron might require." [7] Among the occasional Gentlemen were those who had contributed to the *Daily Courant*. They included such highly placed statesmen and divines as Horatio Walpole, brother of Sir Robert, Dr. Henry Bland, Dean of Durham, Francis Hare, Bishop of Chichester, and Benjamin Hoadly, Bishop of Winchester.[8]

Such were the men whose pens and energies would be devoted to the success of the new paper. "The Cause," Arnall continued in his introduction,

The Cause which we have undertaken is, to vindicate Publick Authority from the rude Insults of base and abusive Pens; to refute the Calumnies, and the injurious Clamours, of factious dishonest Men; to expose the Insincerity of Mock Patriots the little Arts and mean Practices of which they are notoriously guilty, in seducing Mankind, and misleading the People from their Duty to their Destruction: To set the Proceedings of the Administration in a true and faithful Light; to inculcate the most affectionate Zeal for the *Sacred Person* of the KING: the just Regard which every *Englishman* ought to have for all the Branches of his illustrious Royal Family; and the most vigorous Resolution to transmit the Crown in the *Protestant Line* to the latest Posterity, as the only Security which we can have, under GOD, for our Religion and Liberty.

These were noble-sounding aims indeed, but there were less idealistic features to recommend the venture as well:

It is not the Intention of this Undertaking to increase that Burden of *Weekly* and *Daily Papers,* which every *Coffee-House* complains of, but to ease it as much as lies in our Power. . . . Our Readers will have these Benefits from the Nature of this Institution, that the Vindication of publick Authority will be regularly carried on, in one distinct Paper; that the Hands which contribute to this Work, will succeed to each other, Day after Day; and that no more than one will require Attention on any particular Day. To this we may add, that whilst we lessen the Charge of our Readers, we increase their Entertainment, and, on the whole, we can have no Cause to doubt their intire Approbation.

Certainly, the design proposed represented an innovation in political journalism. The exposition and defense of government measures could now be carried out with greater efficiency than ever before. There would be a variety of talent, the best available, with but a single theme, and openly identified with a single publication. The *Craftsman* speculated facetiously on the minister's motives for the project: "Perhaps, he had a mind to try what *Clubbing of Wits* would do, after They had all fail'd in their *separate State;* and as *nine Taylors* are generally allow'd to make a *Man,* He might suppose that *twenty* or *thirty Scribblers* would, at least, make *one tolerable Writer*."[9]

Besides the galaxy of political essayists, the coverage of foreign news promised in the introduction would have interested prospective readers:

. . . tho' the Article of publick Intelligence cannot fall within the Province of any who write amongst us on Matters of higher Concern, yet I am authorized to say, that those of our Friends, who have the best Opportunities of knowing the most early and most authentick *Foreign News,* will furnish constant Supplies of it in this Paper; as also, that the *Domestick News* will be collected without sparing Expence, and with the greatest Care.

Such friends as had the earliest and most authentic intelligence of this sort could hardly have been other than Walpole's Secretaries of State, who supplied it to the official *London Gazette.* Thus, the *Gazetteer* was to have a monopoly with which no unsponsored paper could compete.

Even the name chosen for the new paper was not without its significance. Reviving an old Mercury title, it was responsible for giving the words "Gazette" and "Gazetteer" a new lease of secular life.[10] The adjective "daily" referred, of course, to the frequency of publication, but it also applied, as Arnall remarked, to the succession of essayists which would give the paper a different character each day: "Where so many different Hands are engaged, it will be equally impossible to preserve any Form of Character upon the whole, as it must be to confine particular Persons to the same Way of writing, or which is still more difficult, to the same Way of thinking." [11] "Gazetteer" to readers of the 1730's signified neither a newspaper nor a geographical dictionary. It referred to a person who wrote "gazettes," or newspapers, just as the names "Post-Man," "Post-Boy," and "Mercury" referred to the bearers of news. More particularly, it was the title applied to the government appointee who conducted the *London Gazette*.[12] According to Arnall, the *Daily Gazetteer*'s title had been chosen "to relate to the Intelligence which it contains," and the similarity it bore to the name of the traditional official publication was more than coincidental. Arnall and the other essayists who wrote "in Defence of the Justice of this Government" now became, each in his turn, gazetteer for a day; the implied access to government sources of foreign news made the parallel even more striking. These features, with the title, left as little doubt of the new paper's essential nature as if it had taken over the time-honored motto of its near namesake—*Published by Authority*.

The original plan of the paper did not long survive. Less than a year after the foundation of the *Gazetteer* there were sweeping alterations in its staff of contributors. After March 1736 James Pitt ceased to contribute his weekly essay and continued to appear only at infrequent intervals. He was replaced by Ralph Courteville, organist of St. James's Church, who became, after the retirement or death of Arnall in May,[13] the chief regular writer for the government. Courteville wrote under the pseudonym of "R. Freeman," but the disguise does not seem to have been carried out very scrupulously. A nodding editor allowed the signature "R. Courteville" to appear after an essay in the *Gazetteer* of 12 May 1738; on the following day an italicized notice pointed out that "the Letter published in some of our Yesterday's Papers should have been sign'd FREEMAN." [14]

Clues to the identity of two other ministerial contributors after 1736 occur in a pamphlet published in 1740 entitled *An Historical View of the . . . Political Writers in Great Britain*.[15] The signature "Algernon Sidney," which was appearing in the *Gazetteer* as early as 1738, is there attributed to a "M[urra]y" who is described as "a Lawyer of good Reputation." [16] "Another Gentle-

man," continues the *Historical View*, "who is a Clergyman at
H——y, whose name is N[ewcom]b, is concern'd in the *Gazetteer*.
He is the Author of some very pretty Pieces of Poetry, and I am
inform'd keeps a large Boarding-School in that Place." [17] This
must have been the Reverend Thomas Newcomb, rector of Stop-
ham and chaplain to the Duke of Richmond, who conducted an
academy at Hackney. He published in 1742 "An Ode to the Right
Hon. the Earl of Orford, in Retirement," and three years later
an ode inscribed to Walpole's memory.

It would be gratifying to know the name of the *Gazetteer*'s
editor during this early period—that is, the name of the man
responsible for selecting and synthesizing the materials that went
into each day's paper, and for preparing the copy for the press.
The author of *An Historical View* apparently had this information, for he wrote that the paper was "under the Direction of one
W——ly in Gray's-Inn," but I have failed to identify with certainty the person so designated. The most plausible assumption is
that he was Stephen Whatley, a Whig journalist who had earlier
edited the *Flying Post* and who received semiannual payments of
fifty pounds from the Treasury until the end of Walpole's administration. He is designated as a writer for the government in
the issue of the *Hyp Doctor* for 10 July 1739.

Whoever "W——ly" may have been, he was undoubtedly well
known to Samuel Richardson, in whose printing house the *Gazetteer* was produced.[18] Richardson and the booksellers John Peele
and John Walthoe were among the proprietors of the paper, a
group distinct from those who, like Arnall, were preoccupied with
"Matters of higher Concern." Another partner may have been
Thomas Woodward, a bookseller associated with Peele in the
London Journal, and Thomas Cooper, the publisher of the paper,
was possibly a fifth. The organization of the *Gazetteer*, apart from
its connections with the government, appears to have been simple
enough. The property in what may be most simply described as
the copyright was probably held in shares by the partners, as was
certainly the case a decade later. A contract for printing the paper
would then have been made between them and Richardson, who
seems at the time to have been specializing in periodicals.[19] The
payment of contributors for copy, the printing costs, and the
arrangements for sale of the paper were the proprietors' joint
responsibilities. Their profits, normally, would have consisted of
the difference between these expenses and the income from advertisements and sales of the paper.

But the situation was not a normal one since the proprietors held what amounted to a government contract for the production of their paper. The subsidies paid from the Treasury for sustaining a campaign of ministerial propaganda in the *Gazetteer* were indirect, and their nature was twofold. In the first place, while the proprietors of the paper paid for some of the copy which went into it (like the domestic intelligence which Arnall was authorized to say would be "collected without sparing Expence"), the greatest amount was supplied by the government, and paid for either in pounds or preferment, according to the rank and condition of the writers concerned.[20] Thus the contributions of Arnall, Pitt, Courteville, and the other "gentlemen" who wrote for the *Gazetteer* cost its owners nothing.

The second and more important way in which the paper was subsidized was in the matter of circulation. This took the form of purchases with Treasury money of large quantities of *Gazetteers* to be distributed throughout the country, free, through the agency of the Post Office. The practice evoked Pope's reference to

gratis-given Bland,
Sent with a Pass, and vagrant thro' the land; [21]

and Fielding, writing in the *Champion*, bore witness to its efficacy among provincial readers, who "by the help of a comment upon the text, by the exciseman or parson, believe every man who dips a quill against the administration, is descended in a right line from Guido Faux, or one of the Papishes who began the Fire of London."[22]

Payments for *Gazetteers* sent to the Post Office, as recorded in the Treasury minutes, were made quarterly by one of the secretaries to John Walthoe, who seems to have been the chief representative of the paper in transactions with the government. They averaged about £900 per quarter and were made regularly between October 1735 and November 1741 though after 1738 specific mention of the *Daily Gazetteer* was omitted from the records, and the payments were recorded as being "for printing work delivered to the Post Office by John Walthoe." [23]

The papers supplied for government distribution were a special edition of the *Gazetteer*, differing in form from the two-page quartos published daily in London. Each copy of this edition consisted of the issues for two days imposed in folio on a half-sheet of paper, with the title and date line of the second issue replaced by a line of intertwined double loops, and the imprint omitted from the verso of the first issue. This arrangement and the numbering of the second issue in every copy as pages 3 and 4 allowed each of the double *Gazetteers* to circulate as one newspaper, requiring only a single stamp.[24]

The first page of each double copy bore the same date as its single daily counterpart of Monday, Wednesday, or Friday. Page 3, corresponding to the first page of the single issues for Tuesday, Thursday, or Saturday, was undated. *The Daily Gazetteer* distributed by the Post Office was thus ostensibly a thrice-weekly publication issued on Monday, Wednesday, and Friday, but in reality it was published, like most thrice-weeklies, on the post days—Tuesday, Thursday, and Saturday.

Some details of the typographical procedure involved may be deduced from a comparison of single and double issues. The type from the daily single issue of Monday, for example, was left standing, and the imprint "for T. Cooper" removed. On Tuesday morning, after the single issue for that day had been worked off, the title and date were removed from the type for page 1 and replaced by the line of ornamental loops. The page numbers 3 and 4 were then inserted in their respective positions, and the two pages of type for Tuesday's paper imposed with those of Monday's in folio formes. The printing was done on specially stamped half-sheets, since for the single issues each quarter-sheet required a halfpenny stamp. It has been estimated that after the government concentrated its financial interest exclusively in the *Gazetteer*, about 3,000 copies of each double issue would have been purchased for distribution.[25] With two presses operating concurrently, one for each of the two formes, it would have taken about twelve hours to turn out this number.[26] Richardson's pressmen would have had such interval, since on post days the country carriers did not leave London until late at night.[27]

What the *Gazetteer*'s circulation may have been apart from government purchases cannot be estimated with accuracy. Two indirect suggestions, however, offer some basis for speculation. A document among papers of the Audit Office [28] estimates the circulation of the *Daily Courant* for 1704 or 1705 at about 800 per day. This figure would represent, presumably, only direct sales, since the practice of government distribution had not yet been introduced. If this estimate is accepted, it may be assumed, I think, from the thirty-year subsequent life of that paper, and with recognition of the growth in the newspaper-reading public which took place over the interval, that the direct circulation was not less than

800 at the time of the *Courant*'s absorption of the *Gazetteer*. There is a strong possibility that it had increased, and that the *Gazetteer* when it replaced the *Courant* as the single daily ministerial newspaper would have been able to capture a large majority of the *Courant*'s readers. Besides the *Courant*, the *Gazetteer* replaced two weekly political essay papers, the *Free Briton* and the *London Journal*.[29] Their circulations apart from sales to the government are not known, but it is probable that they claimed some purchasers who did not buy a daily paper, but who would, after 30 June 1735, have purchased the *Gazetteer* at least on Thursdays and Saturdays to read the regular essays by Walsingham and Osborne. From these considerations, it may not appear too rash a conjecture that the *Gazetteer* had an average direct sale to the public of not less than 1,000 copies per day.

A writer in the *Gazetteer* of 4 July 1737 provides another but perhaps even less reliable indication. He is describing some estimates of the public loss arising from time wasted in the daily perusal of newspapers. The statistics presented, he says, were supplied "by a Political Arithmetician of my Acquaintance, a great Studier of *Grant, Petty, D'Avenant*, and *Daniel Foe* . . . [who] makes it stand thus: He supposes 10 News and Political Papers to be published daily, one Day with another, and that 1,000 of each of them, one with another, is dispersed, amounting in all to 10,000, which are each read and heard by 20 Persons only. . . ." The writer finally concludes that £400,000 in labor valued at 3*d*. per hour is lost annually in reading newspapers. The essay in which these figures appear is unsigned, but its length and style preclude the assumption that it was contributed by an unknown casual reader. While there is not the slightest basis for assuming, on the other hand, that the writer knew the circulation of the *Gazetteer*, his estimates possess the undeniable virtue of having been made in 1737, possibly from a conception formed either at first hand or by hearsay of prevailing conditions in the world of journalism. The figures are admittedly averages formed for the purpose of illustration, and they are conveniently rounded in multiples of ten, but one feature about them is striking, and that is their modesty. The writer's aim was to impress readers with the magnitude of the annual loss. He might have doubled that loss by simply suggesting an average daily circulation for each paper of 2,000, a figure which does not appear fantastic in light of circulation statistics for later in the century. But a 2,000 average may have seemed incredible to readers of 1737, and the writer had to appear credible if his final conclusion were to be impressive. Therefore, he may have felt that an estimated circulation average of 1,000 copies for each paper had the quality of credibility, as well as that of convenience, to recommend it.

If the figure of 1,000 seemed to contemporary minds a reasonable estimate, and if it is assumed that the *Gazetteer*, as a daily paper and as the unique ministerial paper, would have sold more than the over-all average, one may perhaps venture a tentative estimate of the paper's direct sale at somewhere between one and two thousand copies per day. The maximum figure of 2,000 would have required at least eight hours for printing from a single setting of type, and a comparison of duplicate copies of the *Gazetteer* for 1737 reveals no indication that there were two settings at the time.

From a financial point of view, the *Daily Gazetteer* must have proved highly successful. With a guaranteed circulation of perhaps 3,000 besides the number sold in London through Thomas Cooper, and with the exclusive and unpaid services of the most eminent ministerial writers and a monopoly on official information, the partners would have found themselves in an enviable position among newspaper proprietors, with virtually all financial risk removed. Politically, however, the paper as it progressed appears to have been a disappointment.

Bolingbroke's retirement to France in 1735 had significantly diminished the force of the *Craftsman*'s attacks, and the energy of the minister's defenders decreased proportionately. The writer of *An Historical View* in 1740 offered an enlightening explanation for the decline in quality of political journalism, and for the *Gazetteer*'s weakness at the time. It was "very observable," he said, that the writers

seldom enter into the Discussion of political Points in the same manner as they used to be handled in the end of the last and beginning of this Reign. This manner was highly prejudicial to the national Interest, as it obliged the Writers for the Government to lay open the secret Motives of the Conduct of the Ministry, which was often attended with the worst Consequence; that of putting the Enemies of the Nation on their Guard. This Method is now turn'd entirely out of Doors, by the profound Secrecy with which all the Affairs of the Public are conducted. So that when a Malcontent Writer attacks a Measure of the Ministry, the latter wisely avoid any *Eclaircisement* even though it might clear up their own Conduct, because it is enough if the Objections against it are answered by the Event. Hence it is, that in the *Gazetteer* we meet with very few or no Papers relating to Foreign Affairs, or undertaken in Defence of any particular Step of the Ministry. This is a very mortifying Conduct, as it deprives the other Party of a great many Opportunities of triumphing, which they had formerly.[30]

Writers on both sides had become preoccupied with the personalities of the minister and his friends. Between 22 July and 21 October 1737 Courteville contributed each Friday an impressively footnoted installment of the *Memoirs of William Cecil Lord Burghley*, in which flattering parallels were drawn between Walpole and Elizabeth's Lord Treasurer,[31] and from time to time the first page of the *Gazetteer* was given over to poetry of a type which, from its theme and form, seems to have presaged later acknowledged works by the Reverend Thomas Newcomb. On 24 April 1738 nearly half of page 1 was occupied by an imitation of an Horatian ode the concluding lines of which were:

> This is the Sovereign Man, Compleat;
> Hero; Patriot; glorious; free;
> Rich, and wise; and fair, and great;
> Generous WALPOLE, Thou art He.

Sometime during the first half of 1738 Samuel Richardson suggested that the *Gazetteer* should admit a wider variety of subject matter. It was this suggestion, perhaps, that resulted in such features as an essay on cider-making,[32] and in Courteville's efforts "to digress a little from Politicks, in order to discourse on Subjects more nearly allied to the Scenes of Common Life," which bore fruit in moral essays like those on the virtue of generosity and the education of young men.[33] Aaron Hill wrote to Richardson in July 1738 that he was "very much pleased that the good advice you have given seems to have had its due weight in the variation of subject, which that paper appears to be opening itself into." Hill promised to submit an occasional piece of his own that would "flatter no side, misrepresent no intention, nor disoblige any person," but he was keenly critical of the political writers' "tiresome and servile pursuit of those tracks which are opened for them, by anti-ministerial, more popular, outstarters." If they would take the initiative more often, and at least show a pretence of impartiality, Hill felt, "it would quicken their reader's curiosity, and multiply the enquiries after the paper." Even the defense of Walpole seemed to him but halfhearted. "Their patron would certainly have a good deal more reason to thank them, if they considered his dignity as part of his interest; and in place of endeavouring to prove him no criminal, took pains to find arguments which might call for respect on his conduct."[34] The criticism had no perceptible effects; it would have been as applicable to the paper in 1741 as it was in 1738.

The justice of Aaron Hill's observation that the *Daily Gazetteer* was politically lacking in vigor is undeniable. In the final analysis, however, the paper was probably quite as dynamic as the administration which it had undertaken to support. By 1730, five years before the *Gazetteer*'s foundation, Sir Robert Walpole had reached the zenith of his personal ascendency. The history of his administration during the decade that followed is an account of a struggle, against increasing opposition, to maintain the *status quo*. After the accession of George II in 1727, political initiative had largely passed into the hands of Walpole's Parliamentary opposition. "The Patriots," a group composed of discontented Whigs in alliance with both Hanoverian and Jacobite Tories, had by 1733 attained to an influence on public opinion sufficient to induce the minister to abandon his famous Excise Bill, the last significant piece of domestic legislation he was ever to initiate. In 1735, the year of the *Gazetteer*'s origin, a general election left Walpole with a markedly decreased majority in the House of Commons, and this despite great personal exertion in the campaign and the expenditure of an estimated £60,000 from his private funds. Two years later, the death of Queen Caroline deprived him of his staunchest supporter at the court.

The most important issue of the years immediately following the foundation of the *Gazetteer* was one perfectly adapted to the uses of the opposition. The British merchants' determination to break a Spanish monopoly on colonial trade enabled the Patriots and their partisans in the press to take the initiative in demanding a war to defend the honor of the nation and the prosperity of its people. The minister, seeking to settle international differences by treaty, and his gazetteers were clearly on the defensive, with no positive basis for a counterattack. As the clamor for war mounted, Walpole found himself nearly alone in his resistance to it. While the Spanish exercised their right to the search and seizure of English ships smuggling contraband to South America, and British merchants petitioned Parliament for the redress of grievances which they had largely provoked themselves, the opposition skillfully exploited its many opportunities for influencing public opinion. The violence and indignities suffered by English seamen at the hands of the Spanish coast guard were dwelt upon in Parliament and in the press; the sailors who had suffered them were publicly exhibited and their stories given the widest circulation. In March 1738 Captain Robert Jenkins stepped before the bar of the House of Commons and displayed a severed ear, carefully preserved in cotton wrappings, which he claimed to have lost seven years before at the sword of a Spanish coast guard captain.

While the minister's partisans might cast doubt on Jenkins' story, they had nothing remotely comparable in effectiveness with which to counter it. Faced with the alternatives of war or resignation, Walpole chose war. By the end of 1740 England had become involved in yet a second war, that to settle the question of the Austrian succession, and the minister was being blamed publicly for events over which he had no control. Admiral Vernon's defeat at Cartagena in 1741 was a boon to the opposition, as were the heavy commercial losses inflicted by the Spaniards on English shipping.

Early in 1742 Walpole's party was defeated in the Commons on a petition relating to a disputed election. The minister's resignation from office on 28 January 1742 put an end to the wholesale government subsidization of the press and to the *Gazetteer*'s rather brief career as a ministerial organ. It marked the real beginning of the paper's life in a world of competitive journalism, where patronage was to be sought only among readers and advertisers.

II

OBSCURITY

1742-1753

"WE hear," declaimed the *London Evening Post* on 20 February 1742, "that *the Gazetteer Legion* are disbanded, and those Wretches, that have prostituted the *Honour* and *Interest* of the Nation to the Vilest Purposes, publickly defended *Bribery* and *Corruption*, and *ridiculed* and *despised* the Merchants and Traders of this City, are *turn'd adrift*, to live in that Obscurity, from whence they were brought, for such *dirty Purposes.*"

"As the *Gazetteer-Legion*," replied the *Daily Gazetteer* of 22 February 1742, "never had any other Existence than in the *Imagination* of our Brother *News-Writers*, so they had certainly a Right to *disband* the *Troops* they had *rais'd*, whenever they saw fit. . . ." Then, for the first time, the paper's voice was raised in vindication not of the "publick Authority" but of itself. "With respect to the other *Reflections* upon this Paper"—the statement that it had despised merchants and traders—"we must take the Liberty of saying that they are very *ill founded*, our Pains and our Expence in Procuring *Intelligence* useful to the *Mercantile* Part of the World having been much greater than that of our Neighbors."

The defeat of Sir Robert Walpole had significant effects among those concerned in the *Gazetteer*, though there was no indication of this in the paper itself. January 28 had passed without political incident so far as the news columns were concerned, but readers would have noticed the absence of a major theme from the essays of the ensuing weeks. A correspondent in the *Daily Post* certainly noticed it. "I much wondered," he wrote, "that the Press had been

16

so long freed from Vindications of the late *Grand Corruptor;* not from an Opinion that his Crimes were capable of Vindication, but from being well acquainted with the callous Impudence of his prostitute Hirelings." [1] The hirelings, like many another of Walpole's adherents, found themselves without employment. The fact that there was now no market for their productions does not imply any disloyalty on the part of the *Gazetteer*'s proprietors, for their support of the government had been purely a business arrangement which automatically came to an end with the change of ministry.

That the paper continued to be published at all is a clear indication that it was capable of producing a profit without assistance from the Treasury. Perhaps the revenue from direct sales and advertisements alone had been sufficient, even during Walpole's administration, to justify its publication. At any rate, no anxiety was perceptible in the month following the change of government. There was neither lamentation nor apology for what had passed. Instead, there seems to have been a concerted effort to pretend that nothing unusual had occurred, and while the political tone of the paper was changing radically, there was no acknowledgment that it was changing at all. On 18 February an anonymous essay called for the extinguishing of "private Prejudices" and an assertion of national unity in prosecuting the Spanish war which Walpole had sought in vain to avoid. Only the concluding paragraph of the essay referred to past unpleasantness: "We know . . . that the Minds of Men have been lately in a great Ferment, that the Causes thereof are now taken away, and that consequently there is no Excuse for our not attending to the Care of the Publick now . . . since if we relapse into our former Disputes a Coalition may come too late, the Time for Action will be over."

This attempt to live down the past was to be partially successful, though there were some former political foes, like those already quoted, who could not resist gloating a bit over what they considered the downfall of an enemy. The *Gazetteer*'s policy-makers refused to be goaded into recrimination or protestations of injured innocence. They realized, however, that some reply to the attacks was necessary so that readers would not be left in uncertainty about the course the paper intended to follow. With a wise restraint, therefore, they rather condescendingly labeled the outburst in the *London Evening Post* as ill founded, and seized the opportunity to state, in a few words, a policy calculated to win readers of every shade of political opinion: "As to the Conduct of the *Gazetteer* for the future, we hope, that if we deserve *better* of the Publick than *most* of our *Brethern,* we shall not be *worse* received; and in a just Confidence of this, we shall continue to use our utmost Intelligence and best Endeavours to *please all Parties* and to *offend none.*"

Caleb D'Anvers, the inveterate enemy of Walpole's "scribblers," received the announcement with unusual good humor. "I heartily forgive," he declared,

all the Writers in the *Gazetteer,* and elsewhere, from the highest to the lowest, as far as their Labours have been personally aim'd at Me. . . .

Some of Them, I find, intend to continue the same Paper, and promise very fairly only to deal in the ordinary *News Occurrences,* and assure the Publick that They will be very industrious to get the earliest Account of *Facts.*

If I find They proceed in this honest Undertaking, I shall be so far from being desirous of hurting Them, that I do assure Them every Morning at *Squire's,* after I have drank my Dish of Coffee, smoak'd one Pipe of Captain *Jeane's* best *Virginia,* after having fixed on my Spectacles, I will always call first for the *Gazetteer;* for I will never be wanting to encourage an honest Industry either in *Friend* or *Foe.*[2]

Having said this much half seriously, D'Anvers proceeded to indulge in a pleasantly ironic consideration of the writers' plight which could not have evoked much resentment. An ordinary newspaper, he observed, would not support even a fourth of their numbers. He hoped those who had other occupations would return to them, and that the *Gazetteer's* printer would show gratitude for the profits they had brought him by continuing to employ as many as possible. Those among them who were not intellectually qualified "to collect and digest *News Articles*" might be employed as compositors, "and so in Subordination, as their Capacities and Industry will enable Them . . . and if such who cannot be taken in, will apply to Me, I will speak favourably for them to my Printer, or will give any of them a Recommendatory Letter to my Brother Common-Sense [3] for the like Purpose." He was certain, he continued, that the writers would find compensation for the hardships of poverty and labor in "that Peace of Mind, to which in their late Course of Life, They must be Strangers." The concluding paragraph was an apology for having thrown doubt upon the gender of Francis Osborne by references to him as "Mother" and "Goody," and a solemn assurance to the public that Osborne was a *"Male."*

After these parting thrusts from the *Craftsman,* writers of the time were content to allow the *Gazetteer* to proceed unmolested in its reformed state. *The Daily Gazetteer* continued, in its established two-page format, to be printed by Samuel Richardson "for T. Cooper" until 3 February 1744, when the latter was replaced in the imprint by his widow, "M[ary]. Cooper." It usually contained two and a half to three columns of news on page 1, classified in the traditional order of foreign news, "Home Ports" and "London," and followed by periodic extracts from the *London Gazette* and the latest stock prices. The whole of the back page and frequently part of the third column of page 1 were taken up by advertisements. Essays still appeared, including a number by Richardson's friend Aaron Hill,[4] though with much less frequency than in the days of Walpole, and on much less controversial themes. Often the subjects were literary, usually dealing with a book in which one of the paper's proprietors had an interest. Thus, on New Year's Day 1743, half of page 1 was occupied by a discussion of a new translation of Fenelon's *Telemachus,* which was later advertised as printed for John Walthoe. By 1745 essays had become still less frequent, and in the autumn of that year, possibly in the interest of economy, several extracts from the works of Joseph Addison were reprinted in the *Gazetteer.*[5]

Financially, the paper must have been successful for a time at least. In 1744 it attracted enough advertising so that on one or two days each week it was extended to four pages, the additional space being occupied entirely by advertisements. In the following year four-page issues became rare, a fact which probably indicates that profits were declining. In 1746 they appear to have declined to the point where most of the proprietors lost interest, and in the summer of that year Samuel Richardson gave up his share, apparently because financial responsibility for the paper had fallen exclusively upon him. A letter written by Aaron Hill to Richardson at the time reveals that the *Gazetteer*'s past had not, after all, been obliterated by the reformation of 1742. "As to the *Daily Gazetteer,*" Hill wrote, "since it had been thrown wholly upon your own Charge and Hazard, and wou'd have always had a *Prejudice* to make way against, from the Original partiality It was suppos'd to have *sett out* with, I am not sorry you determin'd to drop it."[6] The reading public had a tenacious memory, and Hill's tone seems to imply that Richardson might yet have blushed at recalling John Walthoe's deliveries to the Post Office.

It is impossible to trace in detail the fortunes of the *Daily*

Gazetteer for the period between Richardson's withdrawal and December 1748, when a thorough reorganization took place. There are extant, so far as I have been able to determine, only about two dozen issues of the paper as it appeared during the two and a half year interval.[7] From those issues, from clues provided by a book published in 1748, and from a consideration of later developments, a few relevant facts do, however, emerge. First of all, Richardson was replaced as printer of the paper, and Mary Cooper as its publisher, by John Griffith, "at the *Crown*, in *Green-Arbour-Court*, in the *Little Old-Bailey*." At the same time, despite whatever prejudice still clung to the *Gazetteer*'s title, it was retained and augmented by a subtitle. *The Daily Gazetteer: Or, London Advertiser*, as it was now called, became the third morning paper in London to include the word "advertiser" in its title, thereby openly declaring its entry into competition with Matthew Jenour's highly successful *Daily Advertiser*, founded eighteen years before.[8]

A change in the paper's format showed clearly a desire to imitate the *Daily Advertiser* as far as possible. Its size was increased to a single folio half-sheet, in three columns as before but with a type area now measuring 10 by 15 inches; and the royal arms factotum was replaced by one of a flying Fame. A notice at the foot of page 1 announced: "ADVERTISEMENTS are taken in for This Paper at the following Coffee-Houses; *viz. Sam*'s, near the *Custom-House; Royal-Exchange*, Threadneedle-Street; *Old Slaughter*'s, the Upper End of *St. Martin's-Lane;* and *Conduit-Street*, near *Hanover-Square*," and the imprint contained the further information that advertisements "of a moderate Length" were inserted "at Two Shillings each." From the specimen copies it appears probable that a length of one to one and a half column inches was considered moderate, though most of the advertisements ranged from two to five, with auctioneers' and booksellers' lists occasionally extending to eight inches. The Stamp Act of 1712 had imposed a duty of one shilling, payable by the printer, on every advertisement inserted in a newspaper regardless of length, so that booksellers, for example, found a single long ad[9] much more economical than the corresponding number of a "moderate Length."

In its content, too, the *Gazetteer* of 1746–48 bore a strong resemblance to the *Daily Advertiser*. The first two columns, more or less, of page 1 were occupied by news, and the rest of the page entirely by advertisements. A unique feature of the *Gazetteer*, however, was an essay series entitled "The Fool," which occasionally occupied half of page 1. "The Fool" dealt in turn with political, moral and humorous topics, appearing dullest, perhaps, in the last named, though its style at best was hardly brilliant. A collected edition of the essays published in 1748 indicates that the first number appeared in the *Gazetteer* on 10 July 1746; [10] the change in the paper's title and format, therefore, probably occurred during the four weeks following Hill's letter to Richardson on 13 June. "The Fool" appeared irregularly about three times a week, and expressed the paper's editorial policy insofar as there may be said to have been one. Number 67 for 3 January 1747 affords a revealing sidelight on the attitude toward the *Gazetteer*'s origins in a mocking allusion to "sixty thousand Pounds thrown away on Hackney writers" during Walpole's administration. Number 164, which appeared on Wednesday, 22 July 1747, had as its theme the blessings of mercantilism. "We have gone on," it declared "from Thing to Thing, to the Attainment of something like Human Perfection; and the Means towards this Attainment [the interchange of knowledge and ideas] has been entirely opened to us by *Commerce*." To the same agency were attributed the glories of the Elizabethan age, when "all concentering in the Love and Pursuit of Commerce, there was a universal Agreement in the making the Nation, rich, glorious, and happy." The *Gazetteer* could not have been accused of despising merchants and traders in the summer of 1747. Six days after the essay first appeared, a notice announced: "There having been an extraordinary demand for the *Fool* Nº 164, to oblige the Public we here Re-print it."

The identity of the author of "The Fool" remains in some doubt. Mr. Stanley Morison has attributed the essays appearing in 1749 under that title to Sir John Hill,[11] who conducted the *British Mazagine* from 1746 to 1750 and contributed "The Inspector" to the *London Daily Advertiser* (1751–53); I have been unable to trace his source for the attribution. A copy of the 1748 edition of "The Fool" in the Hope Collection of the Bodleian Library contains a note that the essays are "by William Horsley, according to a manuscript memorandum in Mr. Alex. Chalmers' copy." [12] Chalmers (1759–1834) probably did not have firsthand information, but his extensive biographical researches lend some authority to the statement. If it is correct, then the author of "The Fool," at least during 1746–47, may have been William Horsley, the economist, who published in 1753 a translation of *The Universal Merchant*.[13]

The proprietorship of the *Daily Gazetteer: Or, London Advertiser* is still more doubtful. Richardson's withdrawal from the paper in 1746 does not necessarily imply that the other partners gave up their interest at the same time. The assumption that they did not is strengthened by the continued use of the original title, and, less substantially, by the apparent continuity of issue numbers.[14] But the identity of the remaining partners can only be speculated upon. The absence of copies of the paper for the period at which the change took place deprives us of any statement that may have been published then, and the only indications I have found are in the imprint of the 1748 collection of "The Fool," and in advertisements published in the *Daily Gazetteer* of 1744 and 1747.

The Fool, in two volumes duodecimo, was published by (i.e., sold by) a conger of thirteen booksellers, three of whom are definitely known to have been connected with the *Gazetteer* at one time or another. They were Mary Cooper, who published the paper from February 1744 until the summer of 1746 while Richardson still printed it; John Griffith, its printer and publisher in the years 1747 and 1748; and William Owen, who first appears as a proprietor in a contract of 1753, to be discussed presently. It appears probable, therefore, that these three held interest in the paper during the interval when it bore the subtitle "London Advertiser."[15] Another bookseller, Thomas Osborne of Gray's Inn, is also listed as a proprietor in the 1753 contract. The extent of his advertising in the *Gazetteer* of 1744,[16] chiefly in connection with the sale of the Harleian library, and in the surviving issues for 1747 makes it seem not unlikely that he held an interest in the paper at both those times as well.

The early career of the *Gazetteer* as an "advertiser" could not have been very encouraging to the proprietors. Possibly the lack of surviving copies of the paper for the years 1746–48 is a result of small circulation and the attendant commercial failure which must have overtaken the venture in the winter of 1748. On the fifth of December in that year, articles of agreement were drawn up for the foundation of a daily paper to be called the *London Gazetteer;* the title and a number of the contracting parties were to be the only vistiges of the *Daily Gazetteer: Or, London Advertiser.* A copy of the agreement now in the British Museum provides the earliest detailed information that has thus far come to light on the organization of an eighteenth-century newspaper.[17]

By the terms of the contract, the property of the *London Gazetteer* was to be divided into twenty equal shares, of which each proprietor was entitled to hold only one. No individual, therefore, or small group, would be able to gain controlling stock in the paper. Such shares as remained unsubscribed, or would in the future be relinquished, became common property to be disposed of by majority vote. It was agreed also that no one who held interest in any other daily paper could become a partner in the new paper, and that any partner who should later acquire such interest automatically forfeited his share in the *Gazetteer*. The proprietors' authority was to be exercised at general meetings held quarterly. There the treasurer's accounts would be examined, and such orders made and recorded as were necessary for the admission of new partners, "the Methodizing or Management" of the paper, or "otherwise however relative to the Support and Conduct of the same." The book in which the orders were entered was to be kept in the custody of the treasurer.

Robert Wilson, a stationer and one of the partners, was appointed treasurer of the paper for the first year, but the office was to be elective annually thereafter. His duties were set forth in some detail. First, he was to take charge of the 200-guinea common fund, made up of a ten-guinea contribution by each shareholder, which was the initial working capital of the organization. Secondly, he was to obtain a monthly statement of accounts from the printer and settle with him on behalf of the proprietors. At the quarterly meetings, he would present his own accounts for approval, together with a statement of profit or loss for the preceding three months. If the statement were unfavorable, he would then be authorized to call for a contribution from each shareholder to meet the deficit. Finally, if the profits were sufficient, he would once a year distribute a dividend.

The London Gazetteer's direct succession to the *Daily Gazetteer* was made clear by two clauses in the contract. According to the ninth article, a number of the contracting parties "were and are concerned in another Daily paper, entituled the Daily Gazetteer or London Advertiser . . . which, for the better carrying on of the said London Gazetteer, they have agreed to lay down." It was therefore agreed that "all such Sum or Sums of money that they . . . shall appear to have been out of Purse on Account of carrying on . . . the said now declined Paper" would be fully refunded out of the profits of the *London Gazetteer*, before any general dividend should be paid. The tenth article appointed a printer and publisher. He was to be John Griffith, who had held the same position in the *Daily Gazetteer*. Griffith was to remain in the situation so long as a majority of the proprietors should "think proper," on terms which would, when settled, be entered in the order book and signed by "a majority of the Subscribing Parties."

Unfortunately, the surviving copy of this agreement contains none of the partners' signatures, so it is certain only that Robert Wilson was one of them, and highly probable that John Griffith was another. For the rest, some may have been among the group suggested earlier as proprietors of the *Daily Gazetteer: Or, London Advertiser,* and others among the proprietors of 1753 to be named in the next chapter. It has been pointed out that this contract is the earliest known "direct documentary evidence . . . of the application of the joint stock principle to the establishment and control of a newspaper," [18] but a pamphlet published two decades earlier, containing proposals for the establishment of several coffee-houses by newspaper proprietors, suggested a method of organization apparently based on newspaper practice. The proprietors of each participating newspaper were to elect two or three persons from among themselves to a committee for managing the coffee-houses. Moreover, it was suggested that "the meetings of the Proprietors of Papers &c. in relation to the Concerns thereof, shall be, as often as possible, held at those Coffee-houses, in their Turn." [19] There is little reason to suppose, then, that the partnership arrangement which had existed in 1735 between Richardson, Walthoe, Peele, *et al.* differed significantly from that set forth in the contract of 1748.

In format the *London Gazetteer* was a four-page folio, the sheet measuring 16 by 23 inches. In appearance, it differed little from what had been published previously. The focal point of a three-column page one continued to be the flying Fame factotum block which was part of the equipment of John Griffith's press. The title was set as before in canon upper and lower case, followed by the date between horizontal rules.

A new notice, running across the top of all three columns and set off by another rule, announced: "ADVERTISEMENTS In this Paper have the Advantage of others, as they are seen by being stuck up in all the most Public Places of the Town." A correspondent in Colman and Thornton's *Connoisseur* (No. 85) two years later claimed to have become "completely grounded in politics by stopping at *Temple-Bar* every morning to read the *Gazetteer,* which used to be stuck up there to the great emolument of the hackney-coachmen upon their stands."

The numbering of issues was recommenced, with Number 1

appearing on Monday, 5 December 1748, the date of the contract, and the early issues were distinguished by a prevalence of leaded type in the text. The practice of leading resulted in a contrast which made the text and advertisements both attractive and highly legible, but it may have been symptomatic of a shortage of matter. When news and advertisements were plentiful, as, for example, in the autumn of 1752, there was little or no leaded type, and the front page generally appeared as a dull grey mass. Essays by "The Fool" were still an important feature, and one gains the impression that their frequency and length were determined partly at least by the need for filling up space. On Saturday, 24 December 1748, two such essays (Nos. 350 and 351) appeared on page 1, each occupying a column and a half. Whoever may have been writing them, it seems probable that the voice of "The Fool" was that of the paper's "author" or editor. Much of the correspondence printed, even as late as November 1751, was addressed "To the Fool" rather than "To the Printer" as was customary at the time.

The printer and publisher of a mid-eighteenth century newspaper were held responsible both by the public and by the law for whatever appeared in the paper. The anonymity of most of the matter made it difficult, or at best inconvenient, to fix responsibility for any single item on an individual author, but the printer or publisher or both were readily identified by the paper's imprint and by the accounts kept at the Stamp Office. Consequently, their titles had come to stand for the paper's authority, whether or not another person was engaged to carry out the editorial functions. In the case of the *Gazetteer,* as later evidence will show, and undoubtedly in most other papers as well, this basic printer-publisher responsibility was recognized by the proprietors and compensated by regular payments on account of the duties involved. If a "conductor" was employed to perform the editorial duties, he would at this time have been directly responsible to the printer. The office of publisher implies duties distinct from those of the printer. The most significant of these for the *London Gazetteer* of 1748 were probably arranging for the supply of paper to the printer and supervising the circulation. But as the *Gazetteer* progressed, the publisher's duties expanded to include some of those originally carried out by the treasurer, so that he became finally the paper's general business manager, acting as secretary to the body of proprietors, and liaison officer between them and the printer. The functions of the offices of publisher and printer will become more

clearly evident later in the *Gazetteer*'s history. It has been necessary to anticipate matters here in order to account for changes which
occurred in the imprint of the *London Gazetteer*.

John Griffith, we have seen, was appointed both printer and
publisher of the *Gazetteer* by the contract of December 1748. The
dual appointment was expressed in the paper's imprint by a notice
identical to that which had appeared in the *Daily Gazetteer* of
1748: "LONDON: Printed for J. Griffith, at the *Crown*, in
Green-Arbor-Court, in the *Little Old-Bailey;* where Advertisements of a moderate Length are taken in, at Two Shillings each."
Slightly less than three months after Griffith's appointment, however, the imprint changed. On 27 February 1749 the *London
Gazetteer* first appeared as "Printed for J. Brown, at J. Griffith's."
This, of course, meant that Griffith had relinquished the office of
publisher, but the reason remains obscure. Since the majority of
proprietors had to authorize such a change, one suspects that they
were dissatisfied either with Griffith's performance of the duties
or with the thoroughness of the check kept upon his performance by
the treasurer, Robert Wilson. Brown must have represented exclusively the proprietors' interest as distinguished from that of the
printer in the actual process of publication, and his appointment
may be considered, I think, as the first step in the development of
the *Gazetteer*'s publisher as an executive exercising the proprietors'
authority. There were to be further changes in the imprint during
the five-year life of the *London Gazetteer*. One of the changes,
and the relative brevity of that life, may have resulted in some
measure from an event that occurred early in 1750.

During the first days in January of that year, a disturbing rumor
was circulating through the trading district of London. As in all
such cases, there were variations in the rumor, and the version a
man heard depended, probably, upon which coffeehouse he fre-
quented. But all versions agreed in the most essential particular:
the plague had broken out on board a ship at Bristol. There seems
to have been no concrete expression of the story until Saturday,
6 January. On the morning of that day the *London Gazetteer*,
believing no doubt that it was publishing news of singular importance for the entire nation, announced that letters from Bristol
reported an outbreak of the plague on a ship lately arrived there
from Smyrna. A number of deaths were said to have taken place
within the past several days.

Those who were alarmed by the paragraph—and it was certainly
just cause cause for alarm—might have found comfort in the

contradiction published the same afternoon in the *Whitehall Evening Post.* "By some Letters received from Bristol," it said, "we can assure the Publick, that the Report of a Ship coming in there, deserted by the Crew, and having the Pestilence on board, which has prevailed in Town some Days, is altogether a Mistake, the Ship from the Levant, which was stopped till her Bill of Health was delivered, having been under Quarantine some Days in Stangate-creek." [20] But one person to whom all Bristol news was important did not see the *Whitehall Evening Post,* or was not reassured by it. That was Mr. Justice (later Sir Michael) Foster, a judge of the King's Bench, who had been appointed Recorder of Bristol fifteen years before. Foster, after reading the *Gazetteer* paragraph, showed his concern by at once communicating its contents to the Mayor of Bristol, Thomas Curtis, who in turn was sufficiently alarmed to begin a thorough investigation of all ships then in the port.

On Monday morning, 8 January, the *General Advertiser* assured its readers, in the first item of news under the *London* heading, that "the Report in one of the Papers, of the Plague's being broke out in Bristol, is entirely groundless; several People having arrived from thence since the Date of the Letter, who positively assert the contrary." Still the rumor, which since its publication in the *Gazetteer* had become prevalent throughout the country, had not been authoritatively denied. Mayor Curtis, on 8 January, was at some pains to see that it should be, and that without delay. When his own investigations had revealed no foundation for the report, the mayor's feeling of anxiety was replaced by one of considerable irritation at those who had propagated it. He therefore wrote on that Monday to the Duke of Newcastle, then Secretary of State for the Southern Department in the ministry of his brother, Henry Pelham:

Bristol, January 8, 1749[/50]

My Lord,

I was greatly surpriz'd to hear, by a Letter which I this Day receiv'd from Mr. Justice *Foster,* that it had been inserted in the *London Gazetteer* of Saturday last; that there was certain Advice by Letters from this Place, that the Plague was broke out on board a Ship in King-road, lately arrived from Smyrna, several of the People having died within these few Days. On receipt of this Letter, I immediately applied to the Collector of the Customs here, who directly order'd the proper Officers to make diligent Search and Inquiry, whether any Distemper is, or lately had been on board any Ships arrived at this Port. And those Officers have certified under their Hands, that no Sickness whatsoever has been on board any such Ships.

Altho' there is not the least Foundation for this Rumor, nor any Ship arrived here from Smyrna for many Years past; yet I find by several Gentlemen, who have receiv'd letters from their Correspondents in the Country, that the Alarm is become general, and likely to be of the greatest Detriment to the Trade and Interest of this City, and very alarming to the Publick in general, if not speedily put a stop to.

I therefore take this Liberty of informing your Grace of it by Express, not doubting but you will take all proper Methods, that this false and villainous Report, be contradicted in the most publick and authentic Manner, as soon as possible; and the Publishers of it brought to their due Punishment.

The Collector of the Customs has, by the same Conveyance, wrote to the Commissioners, and certified to them, that there is not, nor has been, any Sickness on board any Ship lately arrived at this Port.

I am, &c.

THOMAS CURTIS, Mayor

The mayor's letter was printed, apparently at Newcastle's desire, in the *General Advertiser* of Wednesday, 10 January. On the following day it was reprinted in the *London Evening Post*, and on 12 January in the *Penny London Post*. Its publication must have gone far toward counteracting the rumor. Meanwhile, the Duke wondered what action might be taken against the *Gazetteer* and requested advice from Mr. Justice Foster. Foster, who had been out of London for several days, did not receive the request until late afternoon of the tenth. By that time the full effects of the *Gazetteer* paragraph were being felt in Bristol, and Mayor Curtis wrote once more to the Duke:

I find the false report I wrote your Grace an Account of on Monday continues to spread itself Our Merchants and Tradesmen receiving great Numbers of Letters from their Correspondents who appear to be greatly alarmed by it. Altho' I can assure Your Grace there is so little foundation for this false piece of Intelligence that this City has not been in a better State of Health for many years than at Present.[21]

The next day, Foster replied to Newcastle's request for advice. He was sure, he said, that the citizens of Bristol were deeply obliged to the Duke for the care he had already taken to put a stop to the false reports "raised by yᵉ Publication of yᵉ London Gazeteer," and begged acceptance of his "Humble acknowledgments in their behalf." This referred, probably, to the publication of Mayor Curtis' letter of 8 January. Foster was honored that Newcastle had requested his opinion "touching any further Measures to be taken on this Occasion," but he feared that his "near Relation to ye City of Bristol" and his "present Station in Westm^r hall" might render it improper for him to interpose. Nevertheless, the course he advised revealed a prudence which would have been useful in some of the government's later dealings with the press:

I make no doubt [Foster wrote] y^t ye Raising Reports of this Nature without foundation is a very high Misdemeanor, worthy of ye Animadversion of ye Publick. But considering ye difficulty, in point of Legall prooff, y^t may attend a Prosecution of this kind, and how much ye Hon^r of ye Administration is concern'd in ye Success of every publick prosecution, I dare not advise to that Measure.

If ye Author of ye London Gazeteer could be brought, from ye Apprehension of a publick prosecution, to Acknowledge his Temerity in publishing that Article of Newes, and to ask pardon in a proper form of words to be inserted in ye publick papers, I Hope two valuable Ends would be answer'd by it. The News writers would be taught to use more Caution for ye future, and ye falsity of ye Report, which must have given an Alarm to ye whole Kingdom, would be Once more intimated to ye Publick.[22]

In this suggestion, Foster added, "I Entirely submit to your Grace."

Once again, as with disturbing frequency it happens, there are no known surviving copies of the *Gazetteer* for the period under discussion. It is impossible, therefore, to discover how the paper reacted to the tempest it had raised. Judging from the practice of the time, there would probably have been, after the original paragraph appeared, some form of retraction or explanation and an assurance of the paper's zeal to serve the public with the earliest and most authentic intelligence. Whether this would have satisfied the conditions for atonement suggested by Foster cannot be known. If the *Gazetteer* ever did acknowledge its temerity, or "ask pardon in a proper form of words," the gesture went unnoticed by the other papers of the day. The Duke of Newcastle had Mayor Curtis' letter of the eighth inserted in the *London Gazette* on Saturday, 13 January. With that official contradiction of the *Gazetteer* report, he seems to have let the matter rest.

The earliest known issue of the *Gazetteer* following the misfortunes of January 1750 is one for 5 March 1751. The imprint of that issue reveals that a change in printers had occurred during the interim, and the paper was now printed "by J. Brown, at Charles Say's, in *Newgate-Street*, near the *Gate*." The change in the preposition before Brown's name from "for" to "by" may mean that he was to be considered from a legal point of view as the paper's printer, but contemporary usage of the two forms was far from consistent, and "printed by J. Brown" in this case almost certainly includes the sense of "at the behest of"—signifying that Brown was still the publisher. The actual printing of the paper was being done in the shop of a twenty-nine-year-old master printer named Charles Green Say.

Say was the second member of a family of eighteenth-century newspaper printers who were less prominent than the famous Woodfalls only, perhaps, because they were less numerous. His father, the son of a gentleman and the younger brother of Queen Caroline's principal librarian, was Edward Say, who had served an apprenticeship under Swift's printer Benjamin Motte. From 1737 until his death in 1769 Edward Say was printer of the *General Evening Post;* in 1763 he was Master of the Stationers' Company.[23] Of Charles's early years nothing is known except that he was bound apprentice to James Bettenham of St. John's Lane in November 1735. He probably set up his own shop, with assistance from his father, sometime in the late 1740's.

There is no evidence that Say's replacement of John Griffith as printer of the *London Gazetteer* was directly connected with the Bristol affair of 1750. A statement made by Say some years later suggests, however, that the change took place shortly after the publication of the Bristol news. In January 1758 Charles Say gave evidence in a chancery suit involving the printer of the *Westminster Journal*. He was "better able to depose" in the case because, at that time, he had "printed the Gazetteer for about 8 years." [24] If "about" eight years means "almost" eight years, as I think it does, then Say must have begun to print the paper in the early months of 1750. During the quarter of a century that followed, his history and that of the *Gazetteer* were to be inextricably linked.

The appearance of the *London Gazetteer* as printed by Charles Say differed little from that of the issues John Griffith had produced. The most outstanding change was in the factotum initial wood block that adorned page 1. Griffith's flying Fame was replaced by an ornamental garland bearing the initials F. H., which

identify the work of Francis Hoffman, engraver, versifier, political pamphleteer, and inventor of "Shipping with Three Bot-
toms." [25] In its general content the paper remained unchanged,
but an announcement published on 5 March 1751 showed clearly
that, notwithstanding the absence of the word "advertiser" from
its title, the *Gazetteer* was competing earnestly for a share of the
advertising revenue that was indispensable to the success of a daily
newspaper. The announcement occupied the most conspicuous position in the paper. It was the first item in the column of news headed
"London":

As many People have Occasion to advertise in the Publick Papers, and
cannot send their Advertisements in the usual Time for being inserted,
whereby they are greatly disappointed, we take this Opportunity, for
the Publick, of assuring them, that all Advertisements will be taken in
that are *Temporary,* particularly Things that are Lost, Stolen, or Found
coming out of the Playhouse or elsewhere, &c. &c. till Eleven o'Clock at
Night, at Mr. Charles Say's Printing Office in Newgate Street.—They
will likewise be taken in at Mr. Barnes's Pamphlet Shop . . . , and at
Old Slaughter's Coffee-House . . . till Nine o'Clock; at Seagoe's
Coffee-House . . . , and at Mr. Owen's, Bookseller, at Homer's Head,
Temple Bar, till Half an Hour after Nine; at the Royal-Exchange
Coffee-House . . . and at the New Jamaica Coffee-House . . . till
Ten o'Clock; at which Places there is a proper Person calls every Night,
to receive and take Care of the Advertisements left, and carry them to the
Printer's.

Several interesting facts are revealed by the announcement. First,
it describes a feature of the routine involved in the production
of an eighteenth-century daily newspaper. The employment of a
"proper Person" to make daily rounds of the advertisement receiving stations—usually coffeehouses or booksellers—seems to
have been a practice adhered to by most of the daily papers published in London during the second half of the century. There is
evidence that the *Public Advertiser* did so in 1774, and the *Gazetteer* continued to employ such a person until 1795.[26]
The second revealing feature is the time limit imposed for the
receiving of advertisements. The elaborate variations in the deadline among receiving stations is of little significance, but the 11:00
P.M. deadline at the printing office means that at least two pages
of the paper cannot have gone to press until almost midnight.
Since the usual hour of publication for a morning paper was six

o'clock, and the standard capacity of a two-man press was 250 sheets an hour, the maximum daily circulation of the *Gazetteer* in March 1751 would appear to have been 1,500 copies or less.

The third significant point in the announcement is the name of Owen. William Owen, bookseller at the sign of Homer's Head, No. 11 Fleet Street, was one of the most extensive publishers of newspapers and periodicals in London.[27] I have already suggested that his connection with the *Gazetteer* may date from as early as 1748, although his designation as a receiver of advertisements for the paper in 1751 is the earliest direct evidence for such a connection. Two years later, his name had replaced those of both J. Brown and Charles Say, and stood alone in the imprint of the *Gazetteer* as that of the paper's publisher. A notice at the head of page 1 advised: "All Persons who chuse to take in this Paper, may be supplied early in the Morning, by giving Orders to any of the News-Carriers, or to W. Owen . . . , near Temple-Bar, where THIS PAPER is published, and Letters to the Author and Advertisements are received." [28] Owen was to retain an interest in the *Gazetteer* until his death forty years later.

III

THE GAZETTEER AND
LONDON DAILY ADVERTISER

1753-1764

THE advent of William Owen as publisher, like that of Charles Green Say as printer, was an important milestone in the *Gazetteer*'s history. With the assumption of joint authority by these two men, the paper emerged from a phase of rather erratic development and began a course of steady progress which was to bring it after a dozen years to full maturity and an undisputed place as one of the leading daily papers published in London. The earliest sign of that progress was made apparent at the beginning of November 1753 when *The London Gazetteer* became *The Gazetteer and London Daily Advertiser*.

The vicissitudes of title had come nearly to an end. "The Gazetteer" was by 1753 a well-established designation for a particular newspaper, and the qualifying "London" which had done service in 1748 by displacing half of a stigmatized title, and possibly by increasing the similarity to the title of the *London Gazette*, had become redundant. The subtitle was of dual significance. It indicated the paper's position in a class with the *Daily Advertiser* and the *Public Advertiser*, and at the same time identified it as the product of a merger between the *London Gazetteer* and the short-lived *London Daily Advertiser*.[1] The partnership contract drawn up on the occasion of the merger set forth a plan of organization and control for the paper which was to remain in effect for more than forty years.

Proprietors who ratified the contract included "Eight Persons who represent the Partners that were Concerned in the London Daily Advertiser." Among them were Thomas Payne, Lockyer Davis, and John Whiston, three of the most substantial booksellers of the age. Payne—"honest Tom," Nichols called him—kept a shop at the Mews Gate which became known as the "Literary Coffee-House." He remained, as did Lockyer Davis, a partner in the *Gazetteer* until the 1790's. Other proprietors from the *London Daily Advertiser* were Charles Davis, Daniel Browne, and Richard Ware, also booksellers; John Ward, who abandoned that calling for the wool and hosiery business; and Samuel Baker, the eminent book auctioneer of York Street, Covent Garden. The names of six other partners appear in the contract. They are William Owen and Charles Say; Robert Wilson, who had served as treasurer for the *London Gazetteer;* Thomas Osborne, the quasi-legendary victim of Dr. Johnson's folio volume; John Nourse, a bookseller to the Society for the Encouragement of Learning; and Thomas Trye, a theological bookseller near Gray's Inn Gate.[2]

The conditions for partnership differed little from those imposed by the *London Gazetteer* contract five years before. The property was divided into twenty equal shares, each partner being limited to the ownership of one and excluded from holding an interest in any other daily paper. General meetings were to be held semiannually, instead of quarterly, within one month after Lady Day and Michaelmas. Any partner not present "within one Hour by the House Clock, of the Time named in the . . . Summons" was subject to a fine of half a crown; the fine was increased to five shillings if he were not in attendance "by Ten of the Clock at Night." At each general meeting the proprietors were to "Sign their Accounts when Ballanced, make a Valuation of the Shares in the . . . Paper," and change or add to the articles of partnership when necessary. They were also empowered "to raise Money upon the Partners in equal Proportions, for the use of the . . . Paper, to be paid to a Treasurer by them Chosen, and to declare Dividends of Profit, in such a manner as the Gain arising . . . will fairly Permit." Any partner who did not pay the money called for within a month automatically forfeited his share in the paper.

The most outstanding change in organization was the provision for a committee of proprietors to be appointed at each general meeting. The committee assumed some of the authority previously vested in the treasurer and publisher, thereby placing executive responsibility on a broader foundation and affording the proprietors a more direct control in the paper's management. Members were to meet once every month "or oftener if they find Occasion," an allowance being made for refreshment at the coffeehouse or tavern where the meetings were held. The committee was authorized to contract for paper required by the printer, "to regulate the Prices of Advertisements, to contract with the Author, Collectors, Printer and Publisher, and Summon them to Attend, . . . to examine their Accounts, . . . to call a General Meeting, and to report to the General Meeting the State of the Paper, and offer such Alterations or Matters, as . . . shall seem Conductive to the interest of the Paper." The first committee was to have ten members, namely, Browne, Osborne, Wilson, Nourse, Whiston, Baker, Trye, Lockyer Davis, Ward, and Owen. Thereafter, each committee would consist of seven members, at least three of whom must be chosen from the eight representatives of the defunct *London Daily Advertiser*. The attendance of five members was necessary to transact business. Minutes of the proceedings of both committee and general meetings were to be taken and signed by the partners present. The committee book was to be kept in the possession of the "Senior Person of the Committee," and that for general meetings by the chairman of each, who would be elected by ballot.

The ninth article of the agreement provided "That Charles Green Say be the Printer and William Owen the Publisher of the said Paper" until removed by majority vote of a general meeting. Owen's administrative duties as publisher were clearly defined. He was to summon general meetings, giving at least two days' notice to each partner "under the Penalty of Five Shillings for every Partner neglected to be Summoned." Committee meetings were likewise his responsibility. Members were to be notified "to meet . . . by Eight o'Clock in the Evening the last Wednesday of every Month from Lady day to Michaelmas, and at Seven from Michaelmas to Lady day, or oftener if any three Members shall direct. . . . And the Publisher omitting to summon any Person on the Committee shall forfeit One Shilling for each Person so Omitted." The publisher and printer were to be "respectively and separately" responsible to the partners for all advertisements inserted in the paper. They were to extend no credit to advertisers "but at their own respective Risque," and to account "well and truly . . . for all Paragraphs or Letters that shall be paid for to be inserted in the said Paper."

That the immediate management rested with Owen and Say appears from the fact that both were authorized to collect money for advertisements and to make disbursements for literary contributions. The committee was to contract with the "Author" and "Collectors," but the eleventh article of the agreement made it clear that direct editorial authority lay with the printer:

And the Printer of the said Paper shall bear one half of the Expence of any Prosecution, arising from any Letter Paragraph or Advertisement inserted in the said Paper, Unless such Letter Paragraph or Advertisement be signed by Two of the Committee to some of whom he shall Apply for Advice upon any Doubt. But it shall be in the power of a General Meeting by a Majority, to remit this Penalty on the Printer, when they shall see fit.[3]

This editorial responsibility, with his other duties, made Charles Say's position in the *Gazetteer* organization analogous to those of the modern managing editor and production manager combined, hence the wide and not always consistent connotations of the title "printer" with reference to an eighteenth-century newspaper. The ambiguity of the term was recognized and a remedy sought in the application of the title "manager," which became current long before the title of editor was introduced. Say is thus most accurately referred to as the *Gazetteer*'s printer and manager.[4] For seven years following the contract of 1753, the division of responsibility between him and Owen was explicitly set forth in the paper's imprint: "Printed by C. Say, in Newgate-Street; and sold by W. Owen (the Publisher) at Homer's Head, Temple-Bar. . . ."

The reorganization and change of title effected no immediate changes in the makeup of the *Gazetteer*. It continued to appear as a three-column four-page folio of a size with the *London Gazetteer*, two-thirds occupied by advertisements. The news content was in no way distinguished from that of the other daily papers. Indeed, the *Gazetteer* only escaped classification as a somewhat inferior copy of the *Daily Advertiser* by admitting to every issue several letters to the printer on political and other topical subjects. All such letters were either unsigned or bore fictitious signatures. Some were written by paid correspondents or by Say himself, but the majority appear to have come from readers. Merchants, lawyers, moral reformers, politicians, and military strategists of both the genuine and coffeehouse varieties began to make known their views on conditions and events of the day in the

columns of the *Gazetteer*. Perhaps the most distinguished contributions during the fifties were three letters which appeared on
December 1, 8, and 15 of 1759, expounding the architectural
advantages of semicircular arches over elliptical arches for the
new Thames bridge to be built at Blackfriars. The author was
Samuel Johnson.[5] The letters are in the finest manner of contemporary newspaper controversy, and though Say may have been
influenced in inserting them by a knowledge of the author's identity, their publication, like that of other controversial letters, served
to illustrate the basic editorial policy professed by the *Gazetteer*
for nearly forty years after its liberation in 1742—a policy expressed and frequently reiterated in a single word—"impartiality."

It was during this period, too, that the printer began to display
unmistakable signs of initiative. Between 1753 and 1759 a notice
in the *Gazetteer* imprint advertised the accommodations of Say's
printing office "where Gentlemen, either in the Law, Physic, or
Divinity, Merchants, Brokers, Shop-keepers, &c. &c. may have
any thing in the Printing Business executed as elegant and reasonable, as any where in England, he having a very great Variety of
curious NEW TYPES, all cut by Mr. CASLON." At the same office,
during at least a part of the period, it was possible to purchase
for two shillings ("or one Guinea the Dozen") a bottle of *Dr.
Boerhaave's Pectoral Drops,* for asthmas, consumptions, shortness
of breath and "Hooping Coughs in Children." [6]

In the autumn of 1752, Say apparently decided to extend his
activities by printing another newspaper solely on his own account,
this time a weekly. The advantages of the plan were obvious.
Materials assembled for six daily issues of the *Gazetteer* would
yield more than enough news for a compilation such as the weekly
papers then were. To these need only be added some original
matter in the form of an essay or two, and a postscript containing
whatever news was current on the day of publication; there was
little need for advertisements. The result was a paper "particularly
calculated for the Use and Entertainment of all Private Families,
and such as do not chuse to purchase a Paper oftener than once
a Week." It would appeal strongly, of course, to readers in the
country, and would be "extremely proper for Merchants and
Gentlemen to send to their Correspondents Abroad; and for all
Captains of Ships to take with them." The selection of a title displayed considerable ingenuity. From the point of view of historical significance, what better complement to a daily *Gazetteer* than
a weekly *Craftsman; or Gray's Inn Journal?* Published on Friday

afternoons, the paper was to have an enduring success. Sometime during the first dozen years of its existence, the subtitle was altered to *Say's Weekly Journal,* and it continued to be published until 1810.[7]

With this project launched, Say openly set about raising the status of the *Gazetteer* in competition with the other papers of the day. It had become usual to distinguish the most significant letter to the printer each day by placing it first among such letters on page 1 and adorning its initial paragraph with a factotum block.[8] Late in 1758 a particularly well written series thus appeared over the signature "Probus," dealing with political and commercial subjects, and obviously written by a professional connected with or paid by the *Gazetteer.* The essays seem to have been popular, for a number of them were reprinted in other papers, as was the practice at the time. But the *Gazetteer's* manager resented the fact that his paper was not receiving due credit for the excellence of this contributor. Indication of the resentment was given in a letter by Probus published on 3 January 1759. Certain evening papers, it said, had copied a number of his letters without acknowledging their source, so that readers in the country had the impression that Probus was original with those papers. He declined to name the most flagrant offender, but would do so, he said, if the practice were continued. The indictment was followed by a brief discussion of the moral issues involved, and then the legal aspects were taken up. One of the evening papers had also copied essays from the *Monitor* (a weekly essay-paper), but had acknowledged the source. The implication was that it had done so through fear of a prosecution for piracy, and had omitted acknowledgment to the *Gazetteer* because by its nature that paper could not be entered at Stationers' Hall. The letter concluded with an analogy between an increase in newspaper stamp duty which had occurred eighteen months before and the raising of import duties. As the latter, said Probus, always resulted in an increase of smuggling, so the former had obliged some papers to filch from their neighbors, and retail the materials so acquired as their own. The character of the protest and the knowledge of contemporary journalism it displayed show that it was editorially inspired, and not the work of an unknown correspondent concerned for his own literary laurels. The concern was manifestly for the literary reputation of the *Gazetteer.* It is the earliest overt display of such concern I have encountered in surviving files of the paper.

A week after the protest was published, an effort was made to increase the content of foreign and shipping news by setting up a system of receiving stations and enlisting the co-operation of mariners. Previously, the main sources of such news (to be discussed more fully later) had been newspapers arriving in the foreign mails and private letters from abroad received by the London merchants. On 10 January 1759 Say announced the beginning of an attempt to develop a practical auxiliary source. The notice was prominently displayed in a three-column banner at the head of page 1:

The Printer of this Paper, begs leave to inform all Captains of Ships, Masters, Lieutenants, and other Officers and Gentlemen using the Sea, who may be willing to communicate to the Public any Intelligence that may occur during their Voyage, or elsewhere, That he will be much obliged to them for their Information, which he begs the Favour they would direct, for Him, to be left at either of the following Coffee-Houses, *viz.* Lloyd's in *Lombard-Street;* the Jamaica Coffee-House in *St. Michael's Alley;* the Pennsylvania Coffee-House in *Birchin-Lane;* the New-York and Cape Breton Coffee-House in *Swithin's Alley;* the New-England and New-York Coffee-House in *Threadneedle-Street;* or at Sam's Coffee-House near the *Custom-House;* at which Places a Messenger will call every Evening at Six and Eight o'Clock, for any Thing that may be left for the *Gazetteer.* . . . Advertisements, and Letters of Intelligence concerning every other Sort of Business, are also received for the Gazetteer at the above Coffee-Houses.

The notice was repeated daily for almost a month; thereafter, only the substance of the final sentence continued to appear. While it is impossible to determine the success with which the idea met, the fact that it was attempted, presumably with a full knowledge of contemporary circumstances, indicates that a reasonable hope of success was entertained. The interest of the plan lies in its novelty at the time. Nearly two years were to elapse before a sense of urgent competition called forth more striking innovations in the *Gazetteer*'s policy, content, and appearance. In the meantime, there occurred the first of several episodes in which the printer of the *Gazetteer* became a source of annoyance to the Commons of England.

A House of Commons resolution of 1660 banning the publication of votes and proceedings had been evaded with varying success by writers of newsletters late in the seventeenth century.[9] The prohibition had been formally restated by a Commons resolution passed in 1723. Thereafter, only the *Gentleman's Magazine,* with its famous Gulliverian subterfuge, and the *London Magazine* had succeeded in consistently evading it so as to publish monthly reports of the most important Parliamentary business. The *Gazetteer*, like the other newspapers of the time, had regularly published only three kinds of intelligence relating to Parliament. These were the dates on which sessions began and ended, the King's speech and the Commons' reply at the opening of each session, and at its close, a list of the acts passed. The last two items of information were readily available, since they were published by the King's Printing Office and circulated freely.[10] Occasionally, other items concerning the proceedings had appeared in the newspapers, but they were nearly always derived from external sources, seldom from eye-witness accounts of a session. A specimen from the *Gazetteer* of 25 May 1759 illustrates their general nature: "The mail which arrived last week from New York brought the following answer from Major-General Amherst to the Right Hon. the Speaker of the House of Commons, who, in obedience to the commands of that house, had transmitted to the Major-General their Thanks, for the services he had done to his King and country in North America." Amherst's formal acknowledgment of the Parliamentary gratitude followed. The item seems to have attracted little attention, and there is no indication that it was noticed at all by the House of Commons.

Eight months later, on Thursday, 31 January 1760, a very similar item appeared in the *London Chronicle*, a thrice-weekly evening paper. It reported that the thanks of the Commons had, on the previous Monday, been tendered by the Speaker to Sir Edward Hawke for his victory over the French fleet at Quiberon Bay in November 1759. There followed an ostensibly verbatim report of the Speaker's address and Hawke's reply. The source of the news was not given, but the vote of thanks was probably a current topic of social conversation among members of the House. On the following morning the same report was published in the *Daily Advertiser*, the *Public Advertiser*, and the *Gazetteer*.

When the House of Commons met on that day (Friday, 1 February 1760) complaint was made of all four papers "as containing printed Accounts of the Proceedings . . . in Contempt of the Order, and in Breach of the Privilege, of this House." [11] The papers were delivered in at the table and the offending paragraphs read. Then four separate orders were made, one for each paper. W. Eglesham for the *Public Advertiser*, J. Wilkie for the *London Chronicle*, and Matthew Jenour for the *Daily Advertiser* were to appear before the House. In naming a representative from the *Gazetteer,* the House avoided a perplexing choice by making a clean sweep of the paper's imprint: "*Ordered.* That . . . *C. Say, W. Owen,* and *F. Knight* do attend this House upon Monday Morning Next."

On Monday, 4 February, the House went through a considerable amount of other business before it came to deal with the culprits. Finally, being informed that they "attended, according to Order," it proceeded to call in the representative of each paper in turn. The excuses given for having printed the report varied only slightly. Eglesham of the *Public Advertiser* "confessed that he printed the said Paper; and expressed his Sorrow for his printing therein an Account of the Proceedings of this House; declaring that he did not know the same to be an Offence. And then he was directed to withdraw." Wilkie's apology and excuse followed the same form. Matthew Jenour of the *Daily Advertiser* showed some slight originality. He "expressed his Sorrow for his printing . . . the Proceedings . . . ; declaring that the same were inadvertently copied by his Servant, when he was out of Town, from One of the Evening Papers." Representatives of the *Gazetteer* came last:

Then the said *C. Say, W. Owen,* and *F. Knight* were called in; and the printed News Paper, intituled "The Gazetteer, and *London* Daily Advertiser, Friday, Feb. 1, 1760" . . . (which Paper was, upon *Friday* last, delivered in at the Table) being, at the Bar, shewn to them, the said *C. Say,* confessed that he printed the said Paper; and acknowledged that his having printed therein an Account of the Proceedings of this House, was a great Fault; and expressed his Sorrow for the same.

The position of Knight in the affair was unique, but there was no provision for equity in the ceremony to which the House was subjecting its victims: "Then the said *F. Knight* said, he had no concern in the said Paper; but that he only took in Advertisements for it; which he said he had done about a Week; and acknowledged himself sorry that an Account of the Proceedings . . . had been printed in the said Paper. . . ." Owen followed, declaring "he knew nothing of the . . . Proceedings . . . being printed in the said Paper, till he saw the said Paper; but confessed himself sorry it had been done." After they had withdrawn, a separate resolution was passed for each of the six. The resolutions were identical in form; I quote the one pertaining to Knight: "*Resolved* that the said *F. Knight,* having printed the Proceedings of this House, in

Contempt of their Order, is guilty of a Breach of the Privilege of this House." How heavily Knight's guilt lay upon him is not recorded. It was ordered that he, with the others, should "be brought to the Bar of this House," and that all should be "upon their Knees, reprimanded by Mr. Speaker, for their said Offences.

"They were brought in accordingly; and, upon their Knees, reprimanded by Mr. Speaker; and discharged, paying their Fees."

It is hardly to be imagined that such treatment as these men received would inspire a genuine submission and respect for the House of Commons. Humiliation, some fear, perhaps, and distress at the extortion of fees must have produced resentment in any self-respecting individual. The case in which the *Gazetteer* figured early in 1760 was not an isolated one.[12] Other printers had already abased themselves at the bar, and still others would do so in the decade to come. The resentment being built up among them might have come to nothing but for the activities in 1771 of a group of "patriots" led by a notorious demagogue. Those activities must later be treated in some detail, for the *Gazetteer* was to have a prominent role in them.

But there were more immediate problems in 1760. On 6 July 1757 "An act for granting to his Majesty several rates and duties" had doubled the tax on both newspapers and advertisements. Every paper sold was required to bear a penny stamp, and a duty of two shillings was payable on every advertisement published. As a result, the basic advertisement rate for all papers had increased from two to three shillings, and most papers had added the stamp increase to their selling prices, raising them from twopence to twopence-halfpenny. The London coffeehouse keepers had felt the new taxes severely. At a general meeting early in July they agreed unanimously "to represent to the Gentlemen, frequenting their respective Houses, the great Increase in the Expence of all kinds of Intelligence by the Number of, and additional Duty upon News-Papers" as well as other rising costs, and "to express their Hopes that Gentlemen will not think it unreasonable to pay threepence for the usual Accommodations, to take place from the Commencement of the New Stamp Duty." [13]

The *Gazetteer* committee had been compelled at the time to raise advertisements to three shillings each in order to maintain the actual price of one shilling, but the selling price of the paper had remained twopence as before. This meant that the receipts from circulation had been cut by one-third (from $1\frac{1}{2}d.$ to $1d.$ on each paper) and a substantial loss of profit had resulted. The purpose of such a policy was clearly to increase the paper's circulation by underselling a number of competitors, and the plan may have been successful for a time, since the *Gazetteer* provided every feature that was to be found in the rival papers. An indication of its success may perhaps be inferred from the fact that in 1760 Charles Say was given publishing responsibility along with Owen, and his printing office replaced Owen's bookshop as the chief distribution center for the paper. The altered imprint announced: "This Paper is sold by C. Say, Printer, in Newgate-Street, where Advertisements, Letters of Intelligence, Letters for the Service of our Country, and Letters of Entertainment (Post paid) will be received, and proper Notice taken of them." Owen and the half-dozen coffee-houses designated in January 1759 continued as receiving stations for advertisements and letters. Such an extension of the news service had probably increased production costs somewhat in the face of reduced profits, but much more serious pressure was brought to bear in January 1760 by the foundation of a new daily paper whose competition was to produce a number of significant changes in the *Gazetteer.*

The most immediately striking feature about the *Public Ledger; Or, Daily Register of Commerce and Intelligence,* when it first appeared on 12 January 1760, was certainly its makeup. Besides being the first daily paper to appear with a title in blackletter,[14] it introduced the four-column page which was to become a standard form in the succeeding decade.[15] More important to the *Gazetteer* than the new form, however, must have been the class of readers which the *Ledger* was designed to attract. As the subtitle implied, the paper was aimed at appealing to commercial London, a public with which the *Gazetteer* had long sought favor. The methods adopted by the *Ledger* were unique. It was published in conjunction with a "Register Office" in St. Paul's Churchyard, conducted on the pattern of John and Henry Fielding's "Universal Register Office" founded in 1749.[16] Persons wishing to buy or sell any commodity, those seeking employment or desiring services of any kind, would have their requirements registered at the office when they advertised in the *Public Ledger.* In this manner it was possible for an advertiser who wished "to conceal any part of his proposal from the public eye" to insert only "a short hint in the paper." The files of the Register Office were accessible to "every Enquirer, on paying Three-pence." There, he would either find what he required "or be convinced that he requires what is no where to be found." The last page of the *Ledger* comprised a

"Complete Index to all Advertisements, Proposals, Schemes, Orders, Meetings, Subscriptions, Transactions, Invitations, and Amusements published in the *Daily, Evening,* and *Weekly* Papers
throughout the Kingdom; brought into one Point of View as they
are published, or arrive by the different Posts; and which may
be seen at our Register-Office. . . ." This compilation, protected
by a royal license which forbade others to reprint it, devoted a section to summarizing the most important advertisements contained
in each of the other papers. That for the *Gazetteer* was headed,
anachronistically, "Daily Gazetteer"; a specimen will best show
the method:

DAILY GAZETTEER, October 30

Notice given that there are to be SOLD
1. Four Geldings and a Mare
Notice given that there is to be LETT
2. A Coal-Wharf
Notice given that there is LOST
3. A single Brilliant in a Ring

The catalogue was followed by lists of ships recently entered or
departed from the various seaports, letters unclaimed at the Post
Office, and the latest stock prices. Essays by Oliver Goldsmith—
among them the long and justly renowned series of "Chinese
Letters"—provided a literary counterpart to the commercial excellence of the *Public Ledger* during the first two years of its
existence. A threat to the circulation of long established dailies
must have been felt almost at once.

Absence of surviving copies of the *Gazetteer* for the first nine
months of 1760 makes it impossible to determine the paper's early
reaction to the new competitor.[17] By the autumn of that year, one
possible aspect of the reaction had become apparent in an increased
display of editorial energy. Part of a column was frequently devoted
to summaries of unpublished letters from readers with appropriate
editorial comment, and, for the first time, the opening paragraph
of the news column headed *London* assumed a character not unlike that of the modern leading article. The most striking news
of the day, foreign or domestic, was subjected to a brief interpretation and comment of the sort previously confined to letters
"To the Printer." An effect of such comment was on at least one
occasion pointed to with considerable pride. In the *Gazetteer* of
Saturday, 4 October, the *London* news was headed by a report of

an impending combination among brewers to raise the price of beer. The report was accompanied by a discussion of the hardships that would result, and an expression of the hope that "the people will be rescued from such an unsufferable avaricious intention, either by the interposition of parliament, or by a resolution in the people to substitute some other liquor in lieu of it." On the Saturday following, a rather triumphant announcement occupied the same prominent position:

> In consequence of our representation against the combination of brewers for raising the price of beer, inserted in this paper of last Saturday; we now have the pleasure to inform the public, from UNDOUBTED AUTHORITY, That ORDERS are issued from the Treasury to their Sollicitor, to prosecute any persons that may be concerned in the combination for raising the price of beer and ale.

Whether the influence claimed by the *Gazetteer* in the matter was real or imaginary—and there is little reason to doubt so bold an assertion when it was apparently unchallenged at the time— it would probably have had a negligible effect upon the paper's circulation. *The Gazetteer and London Daily Advertiser* in the autumn of 1760 had little obvious claim to preference over its competitors aside from the halfpenny difference in purchase price. Badly worn types and a coarse grade of paper rendered its physical appearance a poor advertisement for the elegance with which Charles Say still announced his readiness to execute "any thing in the Printing Business." By the middle of September the proprietors had become convinced of an urgent need for renovation to meet the competition of the *Public Ledger*. The step would necessitate a rise in price which they had avoided for more than three years, but experience had probably shown that economy was not an all-important consideration with the reading public.

On Wednesday, 29 October 1760, three days after George III was proclaimed king of Great Britain and Ireland, the *Gazetteer* made its first appearance in the sixteen-column form introduced by the *Public Ledger*.[18] Readers on that day must have been pleasantly surprised at the metamorphosis, for there had been no warning. Columns were reduced in width by ⅝ of an inch to 2½ inches, set off by single vertical rules. New types had been used throughout, and a whiter, finer grade of paper displayed them to the best advantage. In general appearance the paper was strikingly attractive by comparison with its own previous issues and with most of the other dailies. But improved appearance and legibility were not the only significant changes. In content, too, the *Gazetteer* displayed the results of extensive planning. An address to readers, occupying more than a column of page 1, explained the innovations in some detail. The explanation is of unusual interest, and it can be adequately conveyed only by a rather full transcription:

To the Publick.

The Proprietors of the Gazetteer having received frequent intimations how agreeable an Amendment in Paper and Print would prove to their Readers; and being extremely desirous of meriting, from the Publick, that Favour and Indulgence they have long enjoyed; they became anxious to comply with the general Desire, in this Particular. The late heavy Tax, however, of a double Stamp laid on all Publications of this Kind, and the Effects of an additional duty of a Shilling on every Advertisement, were invincible Obstacles to such an Improvement while their Paper continued to be sold at the usual Price. With the Consent and Advice, therefore, of many of their Readers, as well as several of those Gentlemen, who are so obliging occasionally to favour them with their Correspondence, they have taken a Resolution to enable themselves to effect the required Improvement, by making such a small Addition to the Price, as may indemnify them in the Attempt: a Resolution, to which they flatter themselves, none of their Readers will have the Least Objection, when they are informed, that, besides an Improvement in Paper and Print, they have taken every other Measure that suggested itself, to render their Paper more instructive, entertaining, and useful.

In Confidence, therefore, of the Approbation of the Publick, they propose the following Sketch of their future Plan.

In the first Place, there will be inserted, in every Day's Paper, one, or more, Letters or Essays, on popular or interesting Subjects; in the Discussion of which, the utmost Regard to Truth and Impartiality will be constantly observed. Of these Essays, a Part will constitute a regular Series, on the Topicks, of Policy, Commerce, and other Matters of Importance to the Nation; and will be distinguished under the Title of

THE BRITISH COMMONWEALTHSMAN.

Another Series of Letters and Essays, respecting the Progress of the useful and polite Arts, both at home and abroad, with such Discoveries in Nature, or Improvements in Science, as may tend either to public Utility or Entertainment, will be occasionally inserted. To these will succeed such Essays, or Letters, on miscellaneous Subjects, as have hitherto been addressed to the Printer; who hereby invites as well his former

Correspondents as every other ingenuous Observer that may not have yet done him that Honour, to communicate their Sentiments, or Remarks, on such Matters, as may, from Time to Time, become the Objects of their Attention, and merit that of the Publick.

In the next Place, with Respect to the principal Department of a Newspaper, that of *Intelligence;* the Readers of the Gazetteer may depend not only upon having the usual foreign Advices communicated as early as possible, but they will sometimes, by means of a Correspondence, very lately established, have the advantage of Articles not easily to be acquired. In regard to domestick Intelligence, as it is impossible that every Article of News published in these Kingdoms, can be communicated immediately to the Printer of any one Paper; all those which may be found in other News-papers, and are not the same Day in the Gazetteer, shall be inserted therein, *after the other News,* on the day ensuing. By this means, such private Families, or Houses of publick Business or Entertainment, as take in this Paper *only,* may be certain of having every particular of Intelligence contained in *all others;* a Circumstance, which, joined to the preceding, is intended to render the Gazetteer the best family News-paper ever yet published.

The Proprietors, ever attentive to the trading Interests of these Kingdoms, and equally desirous of being useful to those who are concerned in their Promotion, have added to their Improvements, under the Sanction of Royal Authority, a most useful Compilation, called the COMMERCIAL REGISTER; which will regularly comprise in it the following important Articles.

First, A Price Current of Merchandizes; from which Dealers and others will be enabled to remark the utmost Extent of the Variation of the Price of any Commodities, and the Times when it usually happens; whereby, Experience assisting to trace out Causes from Effects, the Trade may be instructed in the most difficult Secrets of Business, *viz.* those of Buying and Selling at Seasons the most advantageous.

Secondly, An Alphabetical Account of all Goods, and the Quantities of them, that are Exported and Imported: From which all People will be made judges of the true State of our national Commerce, and of course know when the Rates of Commodities may be expected to rise and fall.

Thirdly, A Daily Account of the Arrival of British ships at, and their Departure from, the several Ports of the habitable World. By which Merchants and Insurers may know how their several Engagements go on, and all other Persons become acquainted, from Time to Time, with the Progress of their respective Friends, who are absent on Sea Voyages.

Fourthly, There will be regularly inserted the several Courses of Exchange; the Prices of Gold and Silver; of Stocks; of Corn; and all other Commodities sold at Bear-Key; of Hay, at its several Markets; and other Articles of a like Nature.

Fifthly, A Bill of Mortality.

Sixthly, A List of all Letters left at the Post-Office, directed to Persons unknown.

Seventhly, All Notices given in the Gazette, with Lists of Bankrupts, and such other Matters as may be useful to the Publick.

The concluding paragraph expressed the hope that, in view of these many improvements and the added expense they entailed, the public would not consider unreasonable a small advance in the price of the *Gazetteer*. It was to remain at twopence for three days following, and to be increased to twopence-halfpenny on Monday, November third.

That the elaborately outlined "Commercial Register" owed its suggestion to the *Public Ledger* is obvious. Like the *Ledger*'s daily "index" it occupied nearly all of page 4, and it was headed by a royal license made out to William Owen:

George R.

Whereas our Trusty and Well-beloved WILLIAM OWEN hath represented unto Us, that he hath, at a very considerable Expense, engaged several Gentlemen, of great Knowledge of the Trade and Commerce of these Kingdoms, to Write and Compile A COMMERCIAL REGISTER, which he most humbly apprehends will be of singular Advantage to all the Trading Part, more especially of our Subjects . . . We being willing to give all due Encouragement to this his Undertaking, are graciously pleased to condescend to his Request. And we do therefore, by these Presents, grant . . . our Licence, for the Sole Printing and Publishing of the said COMMERCIAL REGISTER, strictly forbidding all our Subjects, within Our Kingdoms and Dominions, to reprint, abridge, or publish the same, as they will answer the Contrary at their Perils. . . .

The date on which the license was granted, 16 September 1760, indicates that changes in the paper had been some time in preparation. It seems probable that the chief of Owen's "Gentlemen of great Knowledge" was Joseph Massie, a statistician and a prolific writer on trade and finance. Signed contributions by Massie appeared with some regularity in the *Gazetteer* during the winter of 1760–61. They frequently took the form of statistical tables, occupying as much as half of page 1, and relating to such subjects as the average yearly profit of a typical English merchant, a list of the specialized occupations included in or dependent upon the woollen manufactory, and the state of exports and imports from the British sugar colonies.[19] Occasional letters signed "J. Massie" continued to appear in the paper until late in the 1770's.

The unique feature of the Commercial Register, and certainly the most difficult to compile, was the "Price Current of Merchandizes." Regular publication of current London prices had been attempted with varying success since shortly after the Restoration, but the *Gazetteer* appears to have been making the only effort to supply that information in 1760.[20] The *Public Ledger,* which contained no such feature, was quick to display its reaction to the *Gazetteer*'s attempt. On Saturday, 1 November, three days after the changes had taken effect, a long editorial note expressed its attitude toward Price Currents in general. There was no mention of the *Gazetteer,* but the implication could not have been overlooked:

We have received a letter signed Mercator, desiring us to insert a PRICE CURRENT in the Public Ledger; to which we reply, that the plan has been often attempted, but as often discontinued; as its effects on trade have been too experimentally felt, by misleading the reader with erroneous accounts of prices, which, from the nature and quality of the articles, cannot be sufficiently ascertained. Hence, as the inutility of the project, not to say its pernicious influence on commerce, has been proved by introducing daily error and confusion in the most important branches of business, we hope to stand excused from a publication which must necessarily bring discredit upon its author, and give offence to every judge in trade.[21]

Subjoined to the note was an anonymous letter purporting to have come from an "eminent merchant" who had heard rumors that the *Ledger* intended publishing a Price Current. There is something faintly comic in his almost suppliant request that the paper refrain from doing so, a request supported by the same arguments contained in the editorial note—that a Price Current would be not only useless and inaccurate, but highly injurious to trade.

It is possible, of course, that the *Public Ledger*'s strictures on Price Currents were motivated as strongly by a zeal for public service as by the threat of competition from the *Gazetteer.* Whatever the motives, the implicit prediction of failure for the *Gazetteer*

Price Current was destined to be fulfilled. By March 1761 the
Commercial Register had shrunk to two columns, and by May it
was down to one; the Price Current, whether as a result of
mercantile opposition, the difficulties of compilation, or the undoubtedly "very considerable Expence" of carrying on the project,
had ceased to appear.[22]

If the commercial features introduced in October 1760 were,
as the royal license seems to indicate, largely the responsibility of
William Owen, the proprietors' address to the public justifies the
assumption that the paper's literary content was under the supervision of the printer. During the two months immediately following the address, the volume of editorial work must have increased
considerably. Notices from the printer to his correspondents acknowledging receipt of letters appeared with greater frequency and
at greater length than during any earlier period. In the beginning
of the following year, Charles Say felt he needed an assistant
in carrying out his duties. The man he selected for the position
was John Almon, then a young journeyman printer lately returned from an extended tour of the continent.

Almon had completed his apprenticeship at Liverpool in 1758
and had come to London in 1760 seeking employment as a printer.
There he had rapidly become acquainted with a number of booksellers, who had employed him as a compiler and pamphleteer,
and it is not improbable that he had contributed occasional essays
to the *Gazetteer* during the final months of 1760. The "extraordinary success," as he himself recorded, which attended some of
his pamphlets, "induced Mr. *Say*, printer of the daily newspaper
called the Gazetteer, in the month of January, 1761, to engage
him at a fixt salary, as an assistant to him in the conduct and
management of his paper." [23]

Say must have recognized great promise in his assistant from
the beginning. Indeed, later developments make it appear that
he must have been unusually dull had he not recognized it. Less
than a year after Almon began working on the *Gazetteer*, the
resignation of William Pitt provided him with an opportunity of
which he took full advantage. A lack of copies of the paper for
the period precludes the careful study which Almon's own version
of events makes desirable, but from his version the main outlines
are clear. The resignations of Pitt and Earl Temple in October
1761, as a result of court opposition to Pitt's war policies, were
followed by what Almon termed "prodigious streams of abuse
. . . in all the channels of conveyance to the public." Pitt's

friends, it seemed, were "unaccountably indolent and indifferent" in endeavoring to answer the flood of criticism, and Almon's "volunteer pen, was the only one exercised" in defense of the ex-minister for several months. To this end, Say's assistant "wrote many letters in the *Gazetteer,* in support of . . . [Pitt's] character and measures, under different signatures; but several of them under that of an Independent Whig, which, and Lucius, were his most usual signatures." The epistolary efforts were followed by a sympathetic review of Pitt's administration which Almon dedicated to Earl Temple.[24] As a result, he soon began to enjoy Temple's friendship and patronage.

When Newcastle, who had abjectly clung to office after Pitt's resignation, was finally forced out in May 1762, Almon rendered similar service; whereupon "Lord *Temple* carried him to the Duke of *Newcastle,* to make known to his grace the author of some letters which Mr. Almon had written in the Gazetteer, at the time of the Duke's resignation." Newcastle's reaction, as recorded by Almon, displayed no trace of the pique he had felt for the paper twelve years before. He thanked Almon, and "acknowledged the great pleasure he had received every day in reading those letters." Through Temple, the *Gazetteer*'s assistant manager became widely acquainted in Whig political circles. He met such diverse and outstanding figures as William Pitt and John Wilkes, as well as "many gentlemen who were at that time in opposition to the court."

Almon's connections must have been of value to the *Gazetteer* in attracting contributions from important members of the opposition. Political controversy became in 1762, and remained for the decade that followed, the most outstanding feature of the paper aside from its news content. Almon's letters of "An Independent Whig" were frequent and prominently placed throughout 1763, along with the contributions of "Pro Patria," "True Whig," and "A Moderate Whig," but the policy of impartiality was carefully maintained by admitting letters from the other side as well, notably those of "Simplex" and "G. T." And the printer—or his assistant—was never hesitant in reminding disputants of certain limits imposed by both typography and propriety. Insertions of two- and three-column political letters, quite probably influenced by the exalted rank of their authors, were usually followed by a reminder that "as every gentleman claims an equal right to a place in the *Gazetteer,* we must beg this correspondent, and all others, to shorten their letters as much as possible, for the sake of room." [25] The paper was never in danger of becoming the instrument of a single faction. If opposition letters were more prevalent than those favoring the Bute ministry, it was primarily because their authors were more articulate, and shades of opinion varied even as the adjectives preceding "Whig" in a great many of the signatures. "We do not allow ourselves," declared an editorial note of 1763,

to interfere with public disputes, but for the sake of keeping them within bounds: and that we must and will do for the public service as well as our own credit and security. . . . Impartialis must become more impartial, more temperate, and more knowing in what he writes of than he appears to be, before we shall admit his opinions to have place in this paper on this subject.[26]

Concern for the printer's security had been heightened in the preceding autumn when Charles Say, with apparent reluctance, had accepted an invitation from Newcastle's successor, Egremont, to take chocolate with his Lordship. Say's assistant, we may suppose, informed John Wilkes of the event, and the fifteenth *North Briton* made capital of it. "I should not hesitate a moment," Wilkes wrote,

to prefer *pledging* PATRIOT *toasts* with a set of sensible and spirited friends of their country . . . to the drinking *chocolate* with a weak, passionate, and insolent secretary of state, on the very expensive terms that it was given, together with wonderful good advice, last week, by lord *Egremont*, to Mr. *Charles Say*, the printer of the Gazetteer. I will only tell his lordship, that if he means to give *chocolate* to every *Englishman*, who declares his suspicions of what the ministry are doing, all the sugar islands together . . . will not hold out a single month in furnishing that commodity.[27]

Possible evidence of John Almon's editorial activities is found in two new departments which were added to the *Gazetteer* during 1762. The first of them represented the development of a feature that had occasionally appeared since the change of title and organization in 1753. It was the compilation of summarized correspondence received by the printer which, for one reason or another, could not be published at length. In 1762 a half-column or more of such summaries was appearing almost daily, indicating the general increase of correspondence which was taking place, and the feature was granted, for the first time, the dignity of a special heading: "Observations from our Correspondents." [28] By far the most interesting portions of the observations are the occasional remarks addressed by the printer to correspondents concerning their opinions and literary style, and the excuses given for not having printed the texts of their letters. The tone of the remarks was generally very courteous, but at rare times a note of impatience crept in. Here is an example from the paper of Tuesday, 29 June 1762:

C. H. in several letters, recommends to people great care, that their children, when they eat fruit, do not swallow the stones. . . . He is likewise a remonstrator against the suffering of Hogs to be kept in the streets. . . .

These important observations our correspondent required should appear in our paper on certain prescribed days, under the penalty of our losing his assistance, by his bestowing it elsewhere, and is highly offended that his injunctions were disregarded. But we must take the liberty to inform him, that it is not always convenient to us to be so very obedient even to more valuable correspondents, and that if he has nothing better to communicate to us than what every old woman is already apprized of, he may put his menaces in execution as soon as he pleases.

The considerable labor that these columns must have involved together with their increased frequency in 1762 suggests that Almon performed the task of compilation while the general policy expressed was laid down by Say. The observations were to become an increasingly popular feature of the *Gazetteer*, and they are an invaluable source of information on the paper's policies in the years that followed.

The second department inaugurated in 1762 which suggests the work of Almon was an occasional column on page 4 replacing a part of the curtailed Commercial Register and headed "Articles of Literature and Entertainment." Its content was derived from "the Morning and Evening Papers, from New Books, and other Publications." Frequently, entire essays were copied from Say's weekly *Craftsman* and other papers, but most often it contained one-paragraph summaries and extracts from "the weekly political papers," and current pamphlets.

During the period of Almon's connection with the *Gazetteer*, the popularity of the paper increased significantly. An indication of this was the opening of a new distribution center, announcement of which first appeared on 2 October 1762:

As the Inhabitants of the Eastern Part of this City, and particularly the Gentlemen who frequent the Royal Exchange, have often been disappointed of having the Gazetteer; and as there have been frequent

Disappointments in Advertisements . . . for want of a regular and particular Office to take Care of what may be left for the Same, C. Say, the Printer, begs leave to inform the Public, that, to prevent any of the like Inconveniences for the future, he has opened a Shop at the Corner of Pope's Head Alley, opposite the Royal Exchange, as an office for receiving whatever may be sent for the GAZETTEER, and where the said paper is SOLD:

N.B. Nothing received at the Office on Sunday.[29]

The expense of renting and staffing such an office, while retaining the numerous coffeehouse receiving stations, could only have been justified by a substantial growth in the paper's circulation. For this growth a number of factors seem to have been responsible. The improvement in typography and content which occurred in 1760 was certainly one of them, and the continued pressure of competition from the *Public Ledger,* as well as from Woodfall's *Public Advertiser* and other papers undoubtedly stimulated efforts by the printer and proprietors toward increasing the *Gazetteer*'s appeal to readers. Probably the most significant over-all factor, however, was the political condition of England at the time. Culmination of a war with France and the accession of a young king with definite ideas of his prerogative and definite favorites among politicians excited greater interest, perhaps, and more discontent than had been known since the time of Walpole. *North Briton* No. 45 and the General Warrant episode of April 1763 were at once symptoms and causes of such popular concern, and daily newspapers were its nourishment and the vehicles of its expression. Almon's popularity among leaders of the opposition, as I have suggested, probably heightened the quality and significance of political essays in the *Gazetteer;* and it may in some instances have gained favor for the paper in the publication of important news. Though it is impossible to adduce any specific examples of such favor, two items which appeared shortly after Wilkes's arrest in 1763 may be worthy of consideration. The first, which appeared on Friday, 6 May, headed the *London* news and was labeled "the GENUINE letters and speech of John Wilkes, Esq." It included Lord Egremont's letter to Temple ordering Wilkes's dismissal as a Colonel in the Bucks Militia; Temple's letter to Wilkes conveying the message; Wilkes's reply to Temple, and his speech "when he was brought to the bar of the Court of Common Pleas, on Tuesday the 3d of May." [30] A second item of interest occupied the same position on the following day. It was in the form of an editorial note: "The Paragraphs and a Letter, received yesterday from a person who has frequently favoured us with things of importance, have been some-how mislaid: we should take it as a particular favour, if the gentleman would oblige us with another copy for Monday's paper." An examination of "Monday's paper" reveals, prominently displayed, the news of Temple's dismissal as Lord Lieutenant of Bucks, and a copy of a letter composed by Wilkes in the Tower to his daughter.

Whatever direct influence such news may have had on the paper's sale, much of its prosperity must be attributed only to the fact that "the spirit of party" was, in Almon's phrase, "at this time . . . advanced to a considerable height." In view of that very circumstance, the *Gazetteer*'s assistant conductor thought it "a good opportunity to emancipate himself from his subaltern situation with Mr. *Say,* and to create a more permanent property for the support of himself and family." With heartening encouragement from Temple and other leading Whigs, he therefore took a house in Piccadilly at Michaelmas, 1763, and converted the lower part of it into a bookshop. In succeeding years, Almon was to become one of the most eminent booksellers and publishers in London; but, at least at the outset of his new career, "he preserved a connexion with Mr. *Say,* which was of mutual service." [31]

The precise nature of the connection and the length of its duration cannot be determined, but it is probable that Almon's services to Say would have consisted chiefly in furnishing essays and news paragraphs for the *Gazetteer,* arising from his wide acquaintance as official bookseller to the opposition *Coterie.* Possibly he contributed the series of about sixty letters entitled "The Contrast," which began appearing in the final months of his tenure on the paper and continued into the summer of 1765. These letters, signed "B. X. P.," contain a number of Almon's favorite themes, including defenses of Wilkes and Chatham and attacks on Bute and the Scotch nation; some of them provoked answers from "Simplex," a leading antagonist of Almon's acknowledged "Independent Whig." In 1765 they were collected and published as a volume by G. Kearsley, who had published Almon's *Review of Mr. Pitt's Administration* in 1762.[32] Another interesting coincidence was the publication by Almon himself in 1767 of *A New and Impartial Collection of Interesting Letters, Essays, &c. from the Public Papers,* which included letters by a number of pseudonymous correspondents whose signatures were familiar to readers of the *Gazetteer.*[33]

Almon's resignation in the autumn of 1763 had no perceptible effect on the paper, and Charles Say continued to extend his business activities. In October 1763 he printed and published *The Englishman at Bordeaux*, a comedy translated from the French, and in 1764 he began to print the monthly *St. James's Magazine; Or Literary Chronicle.*[34] In view of his expanding concerns and the *Gazetteer*'s growing popularity and increased diversity of content, it is probable that Say engaged another assistant to succeed Almon. The identity of the new assistant, if there was one, is unknown.

The two years following Almon's departure witnessed further gains in the circulation of the *Gazetteer;* during those years it reached a position of eminence among London newspapers which was to be maintained for nearly a decade.

IV

THE GAZETTEER AND NEW DAILY ADVERTISER

1764-1769

THE earliest statement that the *Gazetteer* had attained a circulation outstanding among the London dailies appeared on 16 April 1764, when a notice "To the Public" declared that the paper's sale had "since a late public declaration" so far increased as to equal that of the *Daily Advertiser*. As a consequence, the paper was put to press "at an earlier Hour," and advertisements which required immediate insertion "must be sent to the Printer before seven in the Evening," or there could be "no Certainty of such Advertisements appearing in the next Morning's Paper."

The circulation of Jenour's *Daily Advertiser*—never, it seems, explicitly stated—was employed throughout the latter half of the eighteenth century as a criterion for measuring the popularity of other papers. Not infrequently an editor or printer in representing his paper's circulation to the public described it as "exceeded only by the *Daily Advertiser*," [1] and that paper had become long before 1764 the acknowledged leader in its chosen field: the "advertiser" *par excellence*. The chief reason for its popularity among advertising customers was obviously its superior circulation, but that, paradoxically, resulted from its almost exclusive concentration upon advertising. The news content of the *Daily Advertiser* was generally confined to about two columns on page 1, and essays or correspondence were rarely to be found. The simplest explanation for its success seems to be that it was a pioneer in the process of specialization—the first daily paper to acknowledge advertising as its primary function, and to label itself accordingly. By 1764 space in the *Daily Advertiser* was at such a premium that the paper could not, it was said, "insert one-third of the advertisements they receive in any reasonable time." Competitors like the *Public Advertiser* and the *Gazetteer and London Daily Advertiser* normally devoted slightly more than half of their space to advertisements and by their titles solicited consideration as commercial counterparts of Jenour's paper. But they never pretended to the exclusive specialization of the *Daily Advertiser*.

Several historians of the press have classified such papers as "advertisers," thereby distinguishing them from actual newspapers and implying that their news content was, like that of the *Daily Advertiser*, of secondary importance.[2] The classification is partially misleading. The fact seems to have been that until the last decade of the century every daily newspaper published in London was necessarily an "advertiser." Advertising was an important kind of commercial intelligence, and it was one of the few features of an eighteenth-century newspaper which encouraged daily publication. Merchants, auctioneers, estate agents, and persons seeking employment, among others, required a medium providing frequent publication and admitting frequent variations in their notices. Moreover, the morning papers drew a great number of their readers from the commercial classes in the city, and such readers were probably attracted in large measure by the daily portion of advertisements. The thrice-weekly evening journals might have conveyed an adequate and timely enough quantity of news and essays during the period before Parliamentary debates became an essential feature, but it would have been practically impossible to fill a daily publication of four large folio pages exclusively with such matter.

These factors shaped the development of the eighteenth-century daily into an organ of a twofold nature. It was certainly a bona fide newspaper in every sense of the term as then understood; it was, besides, an "advertiser." Evidence of this duality is to be found in the title of nearly every daily newspaper founded in the second half of the century: *The Morning Chronicle and London Advertiser* (1769); *The Morning Post and Daily Advertising Pamphlet* (1772); *The Morning Herald and Daily Advertiser* (1780); *The Aurora and Universal Advertiser* (1781); *The World, Fashionable Advertiser* (1787); *Stuart's Star and Evening Advertiser* (1789). Even *The Times* began as *The Daily Universal Register* (1785) with the statement that one of its "great objects" was "to facilitate

the *commercial* intercourse between the different parts of the community, through the channel of *Advertisements*" which would not
be "sacrificed to the rage for parliamentary debates." [3] The limited
utility of advertising confined the development of dailies to London and was at least partially responsible (with the difficulty of
communications) for the fact that none was published in provincial
England until the nineteenth century.

The *Gazetteer* announcement of 16 April 1764 marked the beginning of a serious attempt by the printer and proprietors to raise
that paper's status as an "advertiser." They sought to bring it to the
level of commercial popularity enjoyed by the *Daily Advertiser,*
while at the same time maintaining its claim to be "the best family
News-paper ever yet published." The first important step in the
campaign was taken on 27 April, when the paper's subtitle was
altered to *New Daily Advertiser.* It was to remain thus for thirty-
two years.

No editorial statement accompanied this obvious imitation of
Jenour's title,[4] and it was over a month before a correspondent
complimented the printer upon the change and obligingly asked
what the future plan of the paper was to be. "To our correspondent's request of knowing our plan," came the reply,

our design is to insert every important and entertaining letter we receive; to throw into the class of Observations, all such letters as contain
useful hints and good thoughts, but whose inaccuracy, or extraordinary
length, will not permit us to insert the letters themselves: to furnish a
sufficient quantity of such intelligence, as seems to be authentic, . . .
and lastly, always to leave room for Advertisements; that as there are
now (in the Gazetteer and New Daily Advertiser, and in the Daily
Advertiser) two equally extensive channels for conveying the business
or wants of individuals to the public eye, those who have occasion to
advertise, may not be disappointed or delayed.

There followed the statement that the *Daily Advertiser* had been
unable to accommodate even a third of the advertisements sent
in. Finally, the printer thanked the public for the encouragement
already received, "which is obvious by the great encrease of miscellaneous advertisements since the alteration of our plan and
title"—the public being, it seemed, "already in part convinced of
the utility thereof." [5]

The success of the new plan became increasingly apparent in
the year that followed. On 15 January 1765 the printer announced
"by way of satisfaction to those who favour this Paper with their
Advertisements . . . that the Number circulated of THE GAZ-

ETTEER AND NEW DAILY ADVERTISER, exceeds that
of ANY OTHER NEWS-PAPER (either Morning or Evening) in *this*
kingdom"; two months later, on 16 March, it was more explicitly
stated that "the Number printed" was "now superior" to *The Daily
Advertiser*. On 22 April 1765, as though to substantiate the claim,
the sheet on which the *Gazetteer* was printed was increased in size
from 17½ by 22½ inches (the standard demy) to 18 by 24 inches,
and the column width was enlarged by an eighth of an inch to
2⅝ inches. An "Advertisement" set forth the reason for the en-
largement: "THE GAZETTEER having frequently been obliged
to postpone, and sometimes to reject Advertisements, for want of
room to insert them; it became necessary to procure a Paper to
be made of a size larger than common, which might be sufficient
to contain the various matter of which the *Gazetteer* consists" [6] In
the following month the physical appearance of the paper was
further altered by the insertion of double rules, vertical between
columns and horizontal above and below the date line, in place of
the single rules previously employed. The change was a simple
one, but it imparted a distinction which made the *Gazetteer*'s appearance strikingly unique among daily newspapers for more than
a decade.[7] On the day of this innovation—16 May 1765—a rather
long announcement at the head of the *London* news explained
more fully than any previous notice had done the position of the
Gazetteer as an "advertiser" and the chief reason for its success.
"Attempts have at several times been made," it began,

to establish a News-paper, that might serve as an Assistant Register of
the business of this metropolis with the Daily Advertiser; but such
attempts have always hitherto proved fruitless, and for this plain reason,
that the *papers* so intended to be established, could never be brought
up to that *extensive circulation of sale*, without which the reciprocal
wants of mankind, however carefully *exhibited*, must needs fail of being
supplied. This desirable circumstance is at length obtained, and, it remains only to apprize the public, that the GAZETTEER and NEW DAILY
ADVERTISER, is, by popular favour, arrived at so great a sale, as to be
equal to the Daily Advertiser; and now offers to the trading part, more
especially, of London and Westminster, its joint services with THAT,
which, as an advertising paper, has hitherto been considered by the
public, as being superior to any other; and to this must be attributed, the
prejudicial necessity the Daily Advertiser is often laid under, of leaving
out a great part of its advertisements, for want of room to insert
them.

The moderation of this statement of circulation, as compare─
some of those preceding it, may indicate a decrease in the Ga
teer's sale. Equally reasonable, it should be noted, is the implic.
tion that the sale of the *Daily Advertiser* had increased. The announcement continued in more specific terms:

> Among many others, the Brokers and Auctioneers, in particular,
> have frequently experienced that the Daily Advertiser is often in want
> of room to insert their advertisements of Sales by Auction and the Can-
> dle, so soon and so often as they could wish; on which account several
> of those Gentlemen have come to a resolution to send their adver-
> tisements to the Gazetteer . . . as well as to the Daily Advertiser.—
> We beg leave therefore to inform the Public, that the advertisements of
> Sales by Auction shall always be placed together, that they may be seen
> at one view. At the same time, we beg the Auctioneers, and the Public
> in general, to send all advertisements that are designed for immediate
> insertion, as early as possible; which is the more necessary, since when-
> ever we fixed any particular hour, as the latest for receiving advertise-
> ments, there have frequently been a great number delayed till then,
> which rendered it impossible for us to comply with their orders.
>
> *N.B.* Servants wanting places suitable to their abilities (as well as
> masters and mistresses who are in want of servants) may soon be con-
> vinced that advertising in the Gazetteer . . . is a much more likely
> method to answer their purposes *expeditiously,* than giving their money
> to Register-Offices, &c. &c. &c.

The contemptuous reference to Register Offices may have been
aimed at the *Public Ledger.* That paper had provoked open hostility in the preceding January by printing a letter in which, as the
Gazetteer described it, *"a nameless writer"* was "very unjustly and
indecently *suffered* to attack *by name* the Printer of the Gazetteer."
The attack had accused Charles Say of reflecting on the character
of the clergy by misrepresenting, in the Observations column, a
letter on the accuracy of parish registers. Say had felt that some
defense was necessary, and had printed the controverted letter in
full to justify the earlier summary of it, even though the action
represented a departure from one of his most firmly held policies.
"We have long despised," he said, "the low arts of the malevolent
. . . and should have treated the insinuations of the Public Ledger,
as usual, with the silent contempt they deserve," had the attack
not involved "so respectable a body" as the clergy.[8] But this later
revenge, if it was intended as such, is irrelevant to present concerns. The immediate problem is to trace some of the factors re-

sponsible for the *Gazetteer*'s attainment of the preeminence it claimed.

Of these the most obvious (diversity of content and the public interest created by opposition to court policies) have been indicated in the preceding chapter. Another cause was undoubtedly the increased emphasis placed upon advertising in 1764–65. Daniel Stuart described the effect of such emphasis much later as he had perceived its action on the *Morning Post*. "Numerous and various advertisements interest numerous and various readers," he wrote. "Advertisements act and react. They attract readers, promote circulation, and circulation attracts advertisements." [9]

More observable in retrospect than any other cause for the circulation increase was the monopoly on police news and advertisements acquired jointly in 1764 by the *Gazetteer* and the *Public Advertiser*. The "late public declaration" referred to at the beginning of this chapter as responsible for the *Gazetteer*'s growing sale was a statement by the renowned Bow Street magistrate Sir John Fielding, first published in the paper on 3 April 1764. It appeared as a banner at the head of page 1, daily for a time, and thereafter at irregular intervals:

From the POLICE

The extensive Sale of THE GAZETTEER AND NEW DAILY ADVERTISER[10] (joined to the Variety of Channels through which it passes) has lately been the Means of detecting so many ROBBERIES, and of apprehending so many OFFENDERS, that it may be proper to give this PUBLIC NOTICE, That for the Future, all Informations of this Kind, sent to BOW-STREET, will be constantly inserted in THIS PAPER (as also in the Public Advertiser): [11] and if SUCH INFORMATIONS are properly attended to by PAWNBROKERS, JEWELLERS, SILVERSMITHS, STABLE-KEEPERS, BUYERS OF SECOND-HAND CLOATHS, &c. few Robberies will scape Detection; especially if ALL PERSONS ROBBED make use of the same Paper to advertise their Losses in.

J. FIELDING

From the first appearance of this notice the columns of the *Gazetteer* testified to its efficacy. Hardly a day passed without the publication of several advertisements from Bow Street, and there was a growing incidence of private notices concerning objects lost or stolen, runaway apprentices, and, on occasion, runaway wives. In addition, more space in the *London* news was given to robberies and other crimes than had been customary in the past, and ac-

counts of persons being brought before Fielding and committed or
discharged by him appeared almost daily. The salutary effect of
such a monopoly on the paper's circulation, human nature being
what it was and is, admits of no doubt. By the beginning of 1765
the name of Sir John Fielding had become so closely associated
with those of the *Gazetteer* and the *Public Advertiser* that the magistrate, and possibly the printers as well, were feeling some em-
barrassment. On 2 January 1765 Charles Say addressed the following announcement "To the PUBLIC":

Being acquainted by Sir John Fielding, that it has been frequently
thrown out and insinuated, as well publickly as privately, That the
Management, Conduct, and Compiling of This Paper is under his
Direction; and that he has been often blamed for Things published
in it, which have given Offence to Individuals: in Justice to that Gentleman, I do publickly declare, That HE HAS NOT, NOR EVER HAD, ANY
THING TO DO IN ANY RESPECT WHATSOEVER, either with the Management, Conduct, or Compiling of this Paper; and that he only favours it
with all Advertisements relative to his Office as a Magistrate, long Experience having proved to him, that confining Advertisements of Frauds
and Felonies, and other Matters tending to preserve Peace and good
Order, to particular Papers, has been productive of most essential
Benefits to the Public.   C. Say.[12]

This monopoly and the benefits it produced were not without
their price. In 1773 William Augustus Miles criticized Sir John
Fielding for accepting fifty guineas a year from two morning
papers for the puffs and advertisements with which he favored
them. The criticism has recently evoked from Sir John's biographer, R. Leslie-Melville, a characterization of Miles as a "very
backward young man" and a "fool" whose "nonsense . . . hardly
needs refutation." Leslie-Melville appeared to find Miles offensive
chiefly because of his tender age; he was "nineteen or twenty
when he had the impertinence to publish *A Letter to Sir John
Fielding,*" and "when John became a magistrate Miles was neither
born nor thought of." Nevertheless, Sir John's biographer stooped
to contradict this "young idiot" with the statement that "of course
John paid the papers, not the papers him; the accounts are in
existence to prove this." [13] The accounts referred to are Sir John's
statements to the Treasury recording expenditures for advertisements.

In 1850 F. Knight Hunt first published the financial accounts
of the *Public Advertiser* for 1774. They contain an entry record-

ing payment of £50 to Sir John Fielding,[14] and Hunt wondered what service Sir John might have rendered. Nine years later Alexander Andrews found the same entry "rather puzzling." "Could it," he asked, "have been paid . . . for reports of the police cases that came before him?"[15] Neither seems to have noticed the prominently displayed endorsements by Fielding of the *Public Advertiser* and *Gazetteer*, or the frequency with which police news and advertisements appeared in those papers after 1764. The earliest financial accounts of the *Gazetteer* which have survived begin in June 1774. On 22 May 1775 and in April or May of each year until 1780 the publisher's accounts show a payment of £50 to Sir John Fielding.[16] There can be little doubt that the payments began at the time of Sir John's first "public declaration" in 1764. They ceased at about the time his notice was finally discontinued, in the year of his death.

The value of the *Gazetteer*'s Bow Street connection is impressively indicated by the size of these payments. Fifty pounds was a considerable sum, and the proprietors must have been certain that the benefits of such a connection more than offset the expense. Numerous private and official advertisements of robberies and other crimes (along with a priority, no doubt, on reports of police affairs) and a growth in circulation definitely ascribable to these features must have yielded an increase in profits comfortably exceeding £50 annually. Notwithstanding Leslie-Melville's anxiety to protect Sir John Fielding from charges of having been a trading justice, there is little basis for criticism of the magistrate's role in the arrangement. Without invoking the standards of political morality accepted in the eighteenth century, it may be pointed out that the favors he bestowed upon the *Gazetteer* in no way lessened the value of his public service; on the contrary, a system of concentrating "Advertisements relative to his Office" undoubtedly heightened the efficiency of that service. It was simply his good fortune to encounter a situation in which rectitude and prosperity were not incompatible.

The flourishing condition achieved by the *Gazetteer* in the first half of the 1760's probably owed a great deal to the management of Charles Say. Late in 1764 he became publisher of the paper as well as its printer and manager. The imprint from 4 December stated that the *Gazetteer* was printed for rather than by Charles Say, thereby investing him with full legal responsibility for everything that appeared in it. During the five years which followed there were no significant changes in the content or makeup of the paper, and no indications of any decline in its prosperity. The *Gazetteer* in that period of relative tranquility lends itself to a more general consideration of content than has hitherto been possible. And since such a consideration may be most clearly organized with reference to the paper's physical makeup, the discussion which follows is based, insofar as possible, upon a typical issue of the *Gazetteer and New Daily Advertiser* for 1764–70. Most of it, however, is applicable to the paper from the inauguration of its sixteen-column form in 1760.

Page 1 was about equally divided between advertisements and text. The first column was the most favored position for advertisements, and it was headed from September to June by announcements of the evening's performances at the Theatres Royal in Covent Garden and Drury Lane. These were replaced during the summer by the playbills of Samuel Foote's theatre in the Haymarket.

The *Gazetteer*'s general policy with respect to the theatres may be more clearly seen later in the paper's history, in the period for which some documentary evidence is available. The most significant development of the 1760's was the announcement which began to appear after the playbills in September 1767, to the effect that the "Entertainments" at the Theatres Royal would, thenceforth, be advertised "By Authority of the Managers."

Following the current theatre programs on page 1 were advance notices of benefit performances and advertisements for such other forms of entertainment as exhibitions, lectures, and masquerades. During the summer season advertisements for the pleasure gardens at Vauxhall and Ranelagh were frequent. The remainder of column 1, and one-half or more of column 2, were composed of advertisements given preferential treatment probably in consideration of increased charges. The basic rate of three shillings effective in 1757 may still have applied, but it was no longer explicitly advertised in the paper. Often a number of publication notices appeared on the front page, usually announcing books printed for the bookseller-proprietors of the *Gazetteer*. Patent medicines, too, were frequently included. Below the advertisements in column 2 appeared the factotum initial block used to highlight the first—and nearly always the featured—letter "To the Printer" for each day. This varied in length and was carried over into column 3, sometimes even into column 4. It was usually brief enough, however, to be followed by several other letters extending into, or entirely filling the last column. When correspondence did not occupy all of column 4, the lower portion of it contained either extracts from the *London Gazette* (usually foreign news and a list of bankrupts, on Mondays and Wednesdays) or several paragraphs of foreign news. On rare occasions the beginning of the news headed *London* appeared there.

The first column of page 2 continued whatever feature had begun in column 4 of page 1. Thus correspondence, *Gazette* extracts, and foreign news alternated. At some point in column 1 the *London* news began and extended through most of column 3. It must be noted here that the locations described for each of these features are those which they most often occupied. Variations were frequent of a half or even a full column resulting from day-to-day differences in the length of each item. Intelligence which appeared under the heading of *London* was by no means confined to events of the city, or even of Great Britain. That heading (throughout this study distinguished by italics) identified what Henry Sampson Woodfall referred to as the "Column of formal Intelligence," [17] and was properly considered as the heart of the newspaper. The first item placed under it was considered the most important news of the day, and when the printer had something to communicate to the public at large rather than to a particular correspondent, it was always placed there. Other matters occupying that prominent position varied from the brief editorial leaders described in the preceding chapter [18] to the latest piece of foreign news, from reports of a royal levee to the latest activities of Lord Clive. The articles of intelligence were unclassified, but there was a generally consistent order in their arrangement. Foreign news or news of the court was placed first, followed by arrivals and departures of ships. Important city news, such as meetings of the aldermen or of the East India Company directors, came next. Police and legal news—accidents, crimes, trials, sentences, Tyburn speeches, and executions—were followed by notices of appointments and promotions, civil, military, and ecclesiastic. The *London* news concluded with reports of births, marriages, and deaths. It was followed in column 3 by "Articles of Intelligence &c. From the other daily Papers of Yesterday," in accordance with the plan set forth in 1760. This extended into column 4. Then came a list of stock prices followed by newsworthy advertisements such as notices of meetings and announcements by the Post Office, Commissioners for Paving, and other official bodies.

Page 3 consisted entirely of advertisements. The first column usually contained those relative to Sir John Fielding's front-page recommendation, followed, there or in column 2, by miscellaneous notices of positions or dwellings vacant or desired, money to lend, and the appeals for charity by destitute widows, invalids, and prisoners for debt which Sheridan was to satirize in *The Critic.* Columns 3 and 4 were regularly devoted to sales of real estate, auctions, and "Sales by the Candle."

The Commercial Register of page 4 had gradually contracted to a single column and then disappeared altogether in 1763. Readers of the time had probably shown a greater interest in politics than in commerce, though the most important features of the Register— stock prices, bankruptcies and shipping news—now appeared elsewhere in the paper. The first two columns of page 4 contained several more letters "To the Printer." They were often original, but occasionally a particularly significant one was reprinted from the *Public Advertiser* or some other paper. The longest letters were generally relegated to page 4, and the column of summarized letters headed "Observations" was included there on an average of two or three times a week. Column 3 contained advertisements which are almost unclassifiable. Tailors, wine merchants, peruke-makers, dancing-masters, and vendors of patent medicines were but a few of the artisans and tradesmen whose notices appeared there. This column and the second of page 3 probably displayed the greatest variety in the paper. Most of the booksellers' advertisements, each, with rare exceptions, headed "This Day is Published," appeared together in column 4. This last page of the paper, it would appear, was of all the most readily adaptable. Under pressure of last-minute advertisements the printer could easily have omitted a portion of the correspondence prepared for page 4, and in the event of an advertisement shortage, another letter or two might have filled the necessary space.

Before proceeding to some of the more general topics raised by this description, it should be noted that the *Gazetteer*'s content was subject to seasonal variations. The quantity of news and advertisements noticeably decreased during the summer months when Parliament was not in session, and the printer may not have found it easy at such times to maintain a diversity of matter. One result of this variation was apparent in the use of leaded type, which was confined almost exclusively to the summer season. Throughout the rest of the year the columns were set in minion type, ten lines to the inch (as was much of the advertising), in contrast to the brevier, nine lines to the inch, employed for the news and front-page correspondence. Circulation, too, declined in the summer, and an effort to offset this by a system of post subscriptions was inaugurated in 1764:

This Paper, on account of the number printed, being under a Necessity of going to Press early in the Evening, the NOBILITY and GENTRY, who are Members of either House of Parliament, may be supplied with it, during their Recess in the Summer Season, by the following very easy Method, viz. They will be pleased to cause the Persons who served them in Town, to be honoured with their proper Address in the Country; upon the Delivery of which address to the Printer . . . he will take care that the Paper shall be regularly given in at the General Post-Office in Lombard-Street, under cover, every Evening preceding the Publication.

The price of each paper under these circumstances was threepence, "in consideration of the additional Expence and Trouble," and gentlemen who were not in Parliament might have the *Gazetteer* on the same terms by supplying the printer with an order from an M.P. or "a proper number of . . . Franks." In 1766 the price of each paper so dispatched ("whereby a gentleman or lady may have the Gazetteer forty miles off at breakfast, on the same morning it is published in London") was increased to fourpence.[19]

The principal sources of foreign news throughout the eighteenth century were Continental newspapers. The announcement "yesterday arrived a mail from Holland," for example, which so often headed the columns of foreign intelligence in the London papers, referred to the thrice-weekly arrival of packet boats bearing mails from the Continent. The packets were scheduled to arrive in the forenoon of the "bye-days"—i.e., Monday, Wednesday, and Friday; hence, most of the news they brought appeared first in the London dailies on Tuesday, Thursday, and Saturday mornings and was copied into the evening journals published on those days. Since the schedule was subject to frequent disruptions, chiefly by adverse winds, the printers could not always depend upon having translations from the foreign papers ready by press time on Monday, Wednesday, and Friday nights, and the nature of the source precluded any possibility of one London paper gaining priority over its competitors in news of this kind.

Individual competitive enterprise with regard to foreign news was confined to the exploitation of other sources. Charles Say's effort of 1759 to enlist the co-operation of ships' officers and other "Gentlemen using the Sea" has already been described,[20] but the most important source aside from the foreign "prints" was the private correspondence of London merchants with their agents and customers abroad. The first issue of *Lloyd's Evening Post* [21] explained that such intelligence spread "from the Coffee-Houses, to a small Circle round the Exchange," and access to it seems to have depended largely upon personal contacts and the initiative of the "collectors" employed by each paper. It is not improbable that some of the items headed "Extract of a Letter from . . ." were obtained by payments to the recipients of such letters.

As the century progressed, the methods of obtaining foreign news became more elaborate, and details of the *Gazetteer*'s activities in this sphere will be taken up in due course. Long before the decade of the sixties, however, some of the London papers were including Continental news from private correspondents abroad. There is no evidence that such correspondences were arranged at this time by the papers themselves. It is quite likely that in most cases they were the result simply of a paper's having obtained exclusive access to a correspondence already established for other purposes, and they yielded, generally, only the counterpart in European capitals of the topics discussed "round the Exchange" at home. At least two of the *Gazetteer*'s proprietors may have been able to supply this kind of correspondence. Paul Vaillant, son and grandson of booksellers with important foreign business connections (who was certainly a proprietor in 1775,[22] and had probably become one much earlier), had gone to Paris in 1759 to arrange for a new edition of Tacitus by the Abbé Brotier, and in 1760 the *Gazetteer* promised readers an occasional supply "by means of a Correspondence very lately established" of "Articles not easily acquired." [23] There is evidence also that William Owen was engaged in rather extensive concerns on the Continent. In 1771 he advertised for an assistant who not only understood "the bookselling trade, in the large way," but who had "been used to carry on correspondence abroad, in France, Italy, &c." [24]

Provincial news was obtained in much the same way as foreign, from newspapers and private correspondence. "Letters from all the Sea-Ports and every City and Town in Great Britain" arrived in London on the same days as the foreign mails, Monday, Wednesday, and Friday.[25] The most important source of shipping news was *Lloyd's List,* published twice weekly from 1740, but this was supplemented by merchants' letters containing notices of arrivals and departures from various ports.

Collection of the London news was carried out independently by each paper, but the general procedure seems to have been the same for all. Charles Say's daily reminder in the *Gazetteer* imprint, that "Articles of Intelligence" were taken in at the printing office, was an invitation to the public at large to report any event which might be considered interesting; the notices to correspondents during the 1760's testify to the willingness of considerable numbers to accept his invitation with accounts of everything from mistreatment of a horse to "a glaring instance of neglect in the officers of a certain parish . . . in their suffering a poor man to lay dying at an ale-house door." Reports of births, marriages, and deaths, Say frequently reminded his readers, would not be inserted without proper authentication. But the coffeehouses remained, as they had become in the preceding century, the most important centers of information on local and national affairs. To the coffeehouses in Covent Garden and the City, to the courts and gaols, the market at Smithfield, and the taverns where servants of the nobility and gentry took their recreation, collectors daily made their rounds seeking news of the latest event or opinion. Their reports, each single item constituting a paragraph of intelligence, were conveyed to the printing office and were paid for, if published, at the rate of a penny a line. Particulars of the *Gazetteer*'s news staff in the 1760's have not survived. Alexander Andrews wrote in 1859 that Hugh Kelly, the dramatist and sometime editor of the *Public Ledger*, supplied the *Gazetteer* with news at "five-and-twenty shillings a week, as per his contract," [26] but I have been unable to find authority for the statement. The connection is not improbable, since Kelly was contributing "The Babler," an essay series, to William Owen's *Weekly Chronicle* between 1763 and 1767.

Essays in the form of letters to the printer were the feature which more than any other imparted a distinct personality to a daily newspaper in the first two decades of the reign of George III. There was some diversity, of course, in the news and advertisements to be found among the papers published on any given day. But the really significant difference between them, and the reason that keepers of coffeehouses were compelled to subscribe to nearly all of them, was the variety provided by the many correspondents who favored the printers with animadversions on conditions and events of the time. The *Gazetteer* of the sixties, there can be no doubt, owed a great deal of its increasing popularity to the letters it printed. The subjects with which they dealt almost exclusively were politics and the manners of the age. Some of them, perhaps most of those appearing first on page 1 and set off by the factotum initial, were paid for by the printer and composed by men like

John Almon and Hugh Kelly—men whom Paul Hiffernan referred to as

> the grubs, in pay
> By the two Woodfalls, Faden, and Charles Say. . . .[27]

Others, undoubtedly, were written by distinguished members of the court and opposition parties, almost all now unidentifiable from the pseudonyms they employed.[28] Many of the letters appearing in the *Gazetteer,* however, were contributed by the "ingenuous Observers" whom Say had invited in 1760 to "communicate their Sentiments or Remarks" on subjects which had become "the Objects of their Attention." Some of them displayed classical learning; most were familiar with the writings of Addison and Steele; and nearly all were deeply read in the newspapers and pamphlet literature of the day.[29]

The volume of correspondence received by the printer of the *Gazetteer* is indicated to some extent by the brief acknowledgements which frequently appeared at the head of the leading letter on page 1. The number of pseudonyms ("Pro Patria," "Philo-Britannicus," "Antigallicus," etc.) designated as having "come to hand" each week averaged several dozen and sometimes exceeded fifty in the winter months. An apparently unique announcement by the printer in the first issue of the paper under the new subtitle gave the following impressive totals for the first four months of 1764:

> The following fact needs no animadversions, since it will shew, at first sight, the great extent of our REAL correspondence, and our endeavours to oblige.
> Since the first day of January to this day, we have received EIGHT HUNDRED and SIXTY-ONE letters:
> Of which FIVE HUNDRED and SIXTY have been inserted at length:
> TWO HUNDRED and SIXTY-TWO have been taken notice of under the article of *Observations of our Correspondents:*
> And THIRTY-NINE now remain in hand; to which due attention will be paid.[30]

By its nature the correspondence placed considerable responsibility on the printer, and by its volume considerable labor. Both were strikingly manifested in the columns of Observations which included frequent expressions of editorial opinion relevant to the letters there summarized. These remarks afforded the reading public its only glimpse of the guiding intelligence behind the *Gazet-*

teer's anonymous formality, and by the autumn of 1764 they had become popular enough to require an addition to the title of the feature:

SEVERAL of our correspondents having hinted to us, that the articles in our paper, which we have entitled, *Observations of our Correspondents,* do not properly come under that head, because we have frequently not only given their observations, but have added such remarks and comments of our own, as have seemed to be requisite either to explain, enforce, answer, or confute their hints. This we have indeed constantly done, and as we shall continue the same; not by making ourselves parties in any cause or dispute, but only by endeavouring to represent it in what we take to be the true light. In compliance therefore with the advice of our friends, who have thought that part of our paper, not the least entertaining, we shall give it to the public in future, under the title of OBSERVATIONS of our CORRESPONDENTS with OCCASIONAL REMARKS.[31]

The "Occasional Remarks" were indeed not the least entertaining part of the paper. Correspondents who submitted moral observations, theological disquisitions, or bits of scandal might be confident of evoking an editorial reply ranging in manner from indulgent commendation to frigidly dignified statements of policy:

S.B. has returned her thanks . . . for our having given the substance of one of her letters in our paper of the 13th instant. We can only say, that we wish her remonstrance may have the good it deserves, as it seems to proceed from a very compassionate heart.[32]

T. BOLUS's account of a young man who was deeply smitten at a dancing assembly, could only answer the ends of private scandal, which we are ever unwilling to admit: and if we may judge the style, Engglish, and spelling, such attacks are generally made by those, who if we should print their letters as they are written, would have reason to blush themselves.[33]

We shall never give the least room, in this paper, to any reflections on female reputations . . . as we are determined not to insert any thing which may stain any woman's character, or that would raise a blush on the cheeks of a vestal.[34]

Observator's Letter on a certain Vicar of a parish is inadmissable—none should correct preachers who are ignorant of common orthography.[35]

Poetic efforts found in the writer of these remarks a sympathetic but exacting critic:

D.C.'s acrostic is very pretty, but the last two lines are entirely out of measure . . . ; however irregular verse may be admitted in pindarics and odes, no delicate ear can suffer it in acrostics.[36]

ADOLESCEN's Poem . . . wants nothing but a little correction to make it acceptable to the public. . . . We recommend particularly to his consideration, the tautology in the 5th and 7th lines; the bad rhimes [*sic*] of the 13th and 14th, the 49th and 59th lines; the too warm expression in the 26th; and the want of measure in the 48th.[37]

On one occasion there appeared a noteworthy discussion of amateur poets in general and their relation to the newspaper press:

A LOVER OF GENIUS has sent us some verses written by a lad of 14, upon his companion, which he earnestly desires us to insert, that so rising a genius may not lay concealed in embryo. We are sorry to declare, that we do not find one single requisite for a poet in this youth, if we may judge by his verses, which are as lame as can possibly be conceived. We heartily wish our correspondents would not put us to the disagreeable necessity of rejecting what they certainly design as favours, by sending poetry which can have no pretention whatever to public approbation. They should consider that partial friendship often blinds judgment, but that the public who know not the authors nor their ages, circumstances or connections, will not too readily approve, or even excuse, poems which are not really good and harmonious. It is not measuring a number of lines with equal syllables, and ending one with a word which will jingle with another, that constitutes a poem. Imagination, description, justness of thought, strength, dignity of expression, and harmonious cadence must all unite to make any piece of poetry acceptable to the public. And he, who upon mature reflection, or from the opinion of such his friends (who may have a competent judgment) does not find the greatest part, or all of the above requisites in his works, had far better stifle them. . . . We know that poetry is very enticing, and if once the youth is stung by the tarantula of Parnassus, he thinks the harmony of his own verses can please others as well as it does himself; he is angry with all who do not approve his labours . . . , insomuch that we dare say we have never refused to insert one poem, but it has made us one enemy: But if these gentlemen would consider, that as we know not from whence they come, we can have no partiality, nor any one motive for rejecting them but the fear of disgusting our readers. We do not mean by this to discourage such productions, as are really good, or those in which a sufficiency of wit may render even the want of some poetical graces excusable; to such the Gazetteer will ever be open, and for such our judicious readers, as well as ourselves, will ever think themselves obliged.[38]

These pleasantly oracular pronouncements almost certainly gained popularity for the paper. One imagines that a number of readers turned first to the "Occasional Remarks" on the back page, and some of the letters described there seem to presage the "fan mail" attracted by syndicated columns of advice six generations later. "If I am walking with a lady," asked T. N. in 1770, "and a gentleman comes to, and strikes her for being with me, is it legal for me to give him an hearty drubbing with my cane for his insolence?" [39] The personality which the public associated with the title "printer" of the *Gazetteer* became for some a guardian of truth and morality, a wise and impartial arbiter of literary and social decorum.

The basic policy expressed continued to be that of impartiality, but it was no safeguard against the remarkable flexibility of interpretation to which the libel laws of the time were susceptible. Discretion was at least as vital a quality for the editorial head of a newspaper in the eighteenth century as it is for one in the twentieth, and Charles Say appears to have possessed it in full measure. When three correspondents accused "the people at a certain fish-stall" of selling stale mackerel for fresh, he "sent to enquire the truth" of the charge from the accusers, but was unable to find such persons at the address given.[40] And when a political correspondent, "Misanthropos," complained of alterations and suppressions made by the *Gazetteer* in some of his published letters and insisted upon his future contributions being printed "*verbatim et literatim,*" considerable pains were taken to explain the printer's position. While he "should be sorry to displease so valuable a correspondent as Misanthropos," there could be no "promise to insert whatever he may send":

If this gentleman (with several other of our correspondents) would consider, that it is our interest, as well as our pleasure, to pay due attention to what is sent us; he would doubtless agree, that nothing but a prudent regard to ourselves could influence us to suppress one tittle. We have been occasionally accused of partiality by all parties, which is certainly the greatest proof of our impartiality to all. The Gazetteer is neither a ministerial nor an anti-ministerial paper; and we can boldly call upon any person to show one mark of a bias. . . . Experience hath made us, in some measure, better judges of what is safe or unsafe; and that experience has taught us caution. —If with this restriction we can be favoured with the continuance of this gentleman's correspondence, we shall gladly embrace it, and shall never omit, or alter any thing therein, but what we are morally certain would subject us to a prosecution. . . .[41]

There were important distinctions to be observed between the criticism of public measures and unfavorable reflection upon the basic institutions of government or its members. "We cannot help applauding our correspondent's wit," the *Gazetteer* once announced, "though we disapprove of the application of it. The legislative body, ought never to be considered as objects of satyrical raillery; . . . but the measures of administration are almost always ample field for remarks, in which the greatest talents of wit and humour may be exercised, with safety to themselves, and advantage to the public. . . ." [42]

Such discretion was not acquired, however, without some rather unpleasant practical experience. Three times in the course of the preceding four years Say had appeared at the bar of the House of Lords to answer for what their Lordships termed "gross and insolent" breaches of privilege. The first of these episodes had occurred in March 1764, after Say had copied from the *London Evening Post* a paragraph "highly reflecting upon the Earl of Hertford, His Majesty's Ambassador to the Court of *France.*" [43] The second, and more serious, breach of privilege had taken place in May 1765, when the *Gazetteer* had reported a message delivered from the Lords to a group of weavers rioting in support of John Wilkes. Say's defense on this occasion, submitted in writing and read by a clerk of the House is of some interest:

My Lords,
    The Paragraph, which I have been so unfortunate as to insert. I heard mentioned by many Persons in the Court of Requests; and I inserted it, in Hopes of being instrumental in preventing any future Mob: This was the true Motive, my Lords; and I most humbly hope your Lordships will consider my unhappy Situation in having inadvertently incurred your Lordships Displeasure. I have a Family of Six Children.[44]

Finally, in the *Gazetteer* of 27 January 1767, less than two months before the sagacious advice to correspondents quoted above, Say had printed some paragraphs containing reference to a matter then before the upper house. When asked how he had come to publish the paragraphs, and whether he did not know it was a breach of privilege to print "any Thing relative to the Proceedings of the House," the printer had replied that the paragraphs had been sent him, by whom he did not know, "and that he [had] published them by Way of Argument; but did not think there was any Harm in so doing." [45] His punishment on this occasion, as on the two preceding, had been to pay a fine of £100 and to be taken into custody by the Gentleman Usher of the Black Rod, and confined to Newgate, until the fine was paid. Experience had, indeed, qualified Say as a judge "of what is safe or unsafe."

The general election of 1768 naturally increased the volume of correspondence, and the printer found himself "under the disagreeable necessity of leaving out a great number of advertisements, and other matters of much advantage"; but some compensation was obtained by charging for the insertion of "all letters in favour, or disfavour, of the respective candidates," since such letters were "of the nature of advertisements." [46]

On Thursday, 4 February 1768, the following "non-political" advertisement appeared inconspicuously on page 1 of the paper:

AN ESTATE for seven years to be SOLD. To prevent trouble, none need apply who cannot deposit four thousand pounds, five hundred of which to be advanced on making out the title, which is a very good one, and the remainder not to be paid till the deeds are executed. Enquire of C. D. at Baker's coffee-house, Exchange-alley.

Innocent as the notice appears, the estate for sale was really a seat or seats in the House of Commons, and it was immediately recognized as such. Charles Say and the "Person who keeps Baker's Coffee-House" were ordered to attend the Commons on the day after the advertisement appeared and were finally called in and examined on Tuesday, 9 February.[47] Say, when questioned, declared that the advertisement had been delivered to a clerk in the printing office by Robert Withy, a stockbroker in Exchange Alley; Samuel Purney, keeper of the coffeehouse, testified that Withy had received several letters addressed to "C. D." Two days later Withy appeared. He had published the notice, he said, on behalf of a John Reynolds, to whom all prospective purchasers had been referred. Withy had heard Reynolds tell Mr. Hickey, a St. Albans Street attorney acting for one "Mr. Nightingale," that there were "some Boroughs which would come reasonable," namely, "*Mil-*

borne Port, Reading, and *Honiton,*" and a deposit had been made for the borough of Reading.[48] Further examinations during the fortnight which followed culminated in a House resolution that Hickey was guilty of "a corrupt Attempt to obtain a Seat . . . for a Client," and the attorney was taken into custody. John Reynolds could not be found.[49] Happily for Charles Say, the House of Commons seems to have appreciated his ready co-operation in the matter, for no action was taken against him.[50]

In the celebrated Middlesex election of 1768 the *Gazetteer*'s reputation for impartiality may have suffered from a single exhortation that appeared in the column of *London* intelligence: "May every true Englishman . . . do their best . . . to support Liberty and Wilkes." [51] In view of the Commons' attempt to disenfranchise the Middlesex electors, however, the sentiment may have been motivated by a concern for justice rather than political bias. On that basis it has been fully vindicated by posterity.

Any general consideration of the *Gazetteer* in the 1760's must take into account a statement made in 1887 by H. R. Fox Bourne, whose work *English Newspapers* remains one of the most valuable on its subject. Of the London daily newspapers published early in the reign of George III, he wrote that the *Daily Advertiser* and the *Gazetteer and New Daily Advertiser* were the oldest:

> But both of these had come to be little more than advertising sheets, containing a few columns of news, but of no political importance. They were far surpassed by 'The Public Advertiser,' which offered, along with a good summary of foreign and domestic intelligence, original articles, and sometimes smart pieces of verse. Its chief attraction to many readers, however, was the ample supply of letters on all sorts of subjects, and from writers of all shades of opinion, which were printed in it.[52]

My description of the *Gazetteer* in the sixties will make unnecessary, it is to be hoped, a detailed contradiction of this statement. Nevertheless, if the subtitle assumed by the *Gazetteer* in 1764 served its purpose with advertising customers, the statement quoted illustrates how well it has continued to do so with historians of the press. Fox Bourne's collective description of the *Gazetteer* and the *Daily Advertiser* as "little more than advertising sheets . . . of no political importance" was more facile than accurate. In 1769 the vendors of London newspapers circulated a printed handbill "complaining of the hardship of not being supplied with the Gazetteer, at so early an hour as with the Daily Advertiser." In reply, the *Gazetteer* published a statement which clearly set forth the fundamental difference between the two papers. "We beg leave, by way of apology," it said,

to remind the friends of this paper that the Daily Advertiser, from the uniformity of its contents, being able to keep its stated hour of going to press in the evening, is, in consequence, published with great regularity, very early in the morning. Whilst the Gazetteer, being open to political and other discussions, which frequently come to hand late at night, and being also connected with the Theatres, the Police, and other Public Offices, has not, it must be confessed the advantage of the favourable circumstances above mentioned; to say nothing of its superiority in point of numbers, which is very considerably encreased this winter, and must therefore proportionally encrease the number of hours in which it is working off.[53]

A comparison of the *Gazetteer* with Henry Sampson Woodfall's *Public Advertiser*, on the other hand, reveals a striking similarity between the two papers throughout the decade. Makeup and content were basically similar, and the joint arrangements with Sir John Fielding have already been described. A number of the signatures of political correspondents are duplicated; and while the "Simon Meanwell" and "Philanthropos" letters in both papers, for example, were probably written by the same person— perhaps a writer employed occasionally by both printers—there appears to have been no duplication of the letters themselves, except when one paper reprinted a particularly significant letter the day after it had appeared in the other. The *Public Advertiser* had no regular feature comparable to the *Gazetteer*'s "Observations of our Correspondents."

The most readily apparent difference between the two papers was in their typography. Throughout the sixties the *Public Advertiser* continued to be printed on the smaller demy sheet abandoned by the *Gazetteer* in 1765. It was made more attractive to readers by the use of upper-case headings for each section of the paper— "FOREIGN INTELLIGENCE," "COUNTRY NEWS," "SHIP NEWS," etc.—and by a consistent use of leaded type in the news and correspondence, which were set eight lines to the column-inch in contrast to the *Gazetteer*'s nine. As a result of these differences the *Public Advertiser* contained appreciably less printed matter than the *Gazetteer*. Its advertisements were generally fewer, and I have encountered no statement of a deadline for receiving them imposed by the necessity of an early press time.

Junius obscured for Fox Bourne, as he has for nearly every writer on the period, the importance of newspapers other than the *Public Advertiser* as represented by their contemporary popularity. The measure of that popularity is to be found only in the circulation which they enjoyed. A surviving account book of the *Public Advertiser* for the years 1765 to 1771 shows that in the period preceding January 1769, the month in which Junius first appeared, the average number printed of that paper was between 2,800 and 2,900 copies per day.[54] From January 1769 to December 1771 the average daily impression during the winter seasons was about 3,400. On only three occasions did the number exceed 4,100, and the greatest number ever printed was 4,800 copies of the issue for 19 December 1769, which contained the uniquely famous letter from Junius to the King.

The claims made by the *Gazetteer* of being the most widely circulated daily newspaper in London from 1765 to 1769 have already been set forth. In December 1770, when an average of 3,238 copies of the *Public Advertiser* were printed daily, the number of the *Gazetteer* printed was announced as being "five thousand daily; a number much superior to that of any other morning paper in London." [55] This statement, like preceding ones, appears to have gone unchallenged; it was also, admittedly, unsubstantiated. Credibility is imparted to it, however, and in a lesser degree to earlier claims, by actual circulation figures for the first four months of 1772. In a sworn statement submitted to the Court of Chancery, Charles Say declared that 427,500 copies of the *Gazetteer* had been printed from 1 January to 6 April 1772, inclusive.[56] Eighty-three issues of the paper were published during that period,[57] for an average of 5,300 copies of each issue. In December 1771—a month before the Junius letters ceased to appear and a month before the *Gazetteer*'s circulation is known to have exceeded 5,000 daily—the average number of the *Public Advertiser* printed daily was 3,229.

But this discussion has led far beyond the events of 1769. In the spring of that year the *Gazetteer* was once again complained of in the House of Commons, this time for reflecting on the character of Sir William Meredith, Baronet and M.P. for Liverpool. Meredith had declined a challenge to a duel and had taken advantage of his Parliamentary privilege to have the challenger confined to Newgate. On 8 May 1769 the *Gazetteer*'s front page carried a letter signed "A Clergyman and Freeman of Liverpool" in which the writer sarcastically professed a deep concern for the baronet's safety when, on the prorogation of Parliament, the challenger should be released. Sir William, it was suggested, might insure his permanent safety by taking Holy Orders. On the day following the publication of this letter, complaint was made in the House of the *Gazetteer* and of the *Liverpool Chronicle* for 9 March, which had offended in a similar manner. The House ordered the complaints referred to the Committee of Privileges and Elections for an opinion.

Whatever apprehension Charles Say may have felt at the time proved unfounded, for no action was ever taken.[58] Nearly two years were to elapse before there occurred the final test of Parliamentary privilege in relation to the newspaper press. Meanwhile, the career of the *Gazetteer and New Daily Advertiser,* if unspectacular, was not wholly uneventful.

V

THE INDUSTRIOUS APPRENTICE

1769-1771

IN content the *Gazetteer* throughout most of 1769–70 was basically the same as it had been during the preceding five years. The productions of Junius, reprinted from the *Public Advertiser* by every other newspaper of the time, gave rise to a number of imitators, and there was an increased incidence of serial essays in the *Gazetteer*. *The National Mirror* (twenty-four numbers from December 1769 to February 1770) was aimed at "humbling the power of four and twenty tyrants" who controlled the East India Company, though it was asserted that the author "neither had, nor is to have, by any promise or agreement with any Minister, the value of 1s." for writing the essays.[1] *The Constitutionalist* (twenty numbers from July 1769 to May 1770), moderately Whig in tone, disavowed sympathy with Junius and professed agreement with the principles of Burke as set forth in *Thoughts on Causes of the Present Discontents*.[2] *The Volunteer* (No. 1, 31 October 1770) was dated from "Tom's Coffee-House" and sought to follow *Spectator* tradition by correcting morals, assisting judgment, improving taste, and providing half an hour's entertainment while readers were taking their morning chocolate. Correspondents were invited to assist in "carrying on a sort of chit-chat paper, as a kind of relief or light to the dark laboured pieces of the *disappointed* politician, the *rigid* philosopher, and *unideal* Alderman, who have of late so engrossed the whole papers, and been so very dull, that it scarce answers calling for a dish of coffee to have the liberty of reading them into the bargain. . . ."

But the *Volunteer* shortly expired, for politics was the favored journalistic fare of the day and Junius the supreme figure. Although his pseudonym was imitated by "Junius Junior," and with more distinction by "the American Dr. Lee," whom John Wilkes identified as "the Gazetteer's Junius Americanus" [3] and whom Junius himself admitted to be "plainly a man of abilities," [4] care was taken that the name should never be usurped by a lesser writer. The real Junius was too valuable an asset to be trifled with by the printers. "We commend the good intention *of our correspondent* under the signature Junius," the printer of the *Gazetteer* once wrote, "whose letter will be inserted but the signature omitted, because it will be deceiving the expectation of our readers." [5]

Junius' letter to the King, printed in the *Public Advertiser* on 19 December 1769 and in most of the other morning papers on the following day, resulted in one of the most renowned legal causes of the century. The letter was eventually reprinted in nearly every periodical publication in England, but the Attorney General instituted proceedings for libel against only six printers—"a *select few*," according to a writer in the *Gazetteer*, who had been marked out for "ministerial vengeance." [6] The group consisted of Henry Sampson Woodfall, who had published the letter originally; John Miller, printer of the *London Evening Post;* George Robinson of the *Independent Chronicle;* Henry Baldwin, printer of the *St. James's Chronicle;* John Almon, publisher of the *London Museum;* and Charles Say of the *Gazetteer.* [7] Only four of these—Almon, Woodfall, Baldwin, and Miller—were ultimately brought to trial, and Almon alone was formally convicted. The results of the prosecutions are too well known to be treated here in detail, [8] but the documents prepared by the Treasury Solicitor for the action against Charles Say are of interest because they provide a view of government methods in dealing with newspapers of the time and throw light upon several of the routine procedures carried out in the printing and publishing of the *Gazetteer.* [9]

By 1769 it had become a received doctrine of the courts that in an action for libel the court had the sole power of determining whether the offending publication was libelous; the jury could decide only whether the defendant was actually the publisher. Theoretically, for a verdict of guilt to be returned, the Attorney General had only to prove that each defendant had published a paper containing the letter to the King. The brief for the Crown prepared against Say reveals that the prosecution was to be based entirely upon the testimony of three witnesses who could prove that Say was publisher of the *Gazetteer* for 20 December 1769, the issue which contained the offending letter.

Nathaniel Crowder, who was employed "occasionally" by the government's Messenger of the Press "to buy up the daily papers" was prepared to prove that on 20 December 1769 he had bought at Say's shop in Newgate Street about "18 Gazetteers for that day each of them containing the Libel in Question." He had bought them of one William Anthony, described as Say's "Servant in the Capacity of his publisher." Anthony appears, therefore, to have been responsible for distributing the paper from Newgate Street to the news vendors and other retailers. Of greater interest, perhaps, for the governmental vigilance it reveals, is Crowder's statement that he had "bought the Gazetteer at the same place almost every Morning for two years past," and that he had frequently seen the papers "bro^t. down stairs in the . . . house wet, as coming immediately out of the press," from which he concluded that Say was the printer of the paper as well as its publisher. Say's servant William Anthony could, it was noted, prove "if . . . thought necessary to call him" that Say was "both printer and publisher."

The third witness was to be Robert Harris, registrar for newspapers and pamphlets at the Stamp Office. His evidence related entirely to Say's transactions with the Stamp Office as printer and publisher of the *Gazetteer,* and described them in some detail. Large quantities of paper, it was stated, were brought to the office "to be stamp'd" and the duty was paid each time by "the person bringing it." That the procedure was sometimes retarded and that sufficient quantities of stamped paper were not always in reserve at the printing office is suggested by a notice which appeared in the *Gazetteer* for 3 November 1770: "A CONSTANT CUSTOMER is informed, that the cause of our Paper not being sometimes so well printed as we could wish, is, that, by some unaccountable neglect at the Stamp-Office, we cannot get the paper from thence in time to have it properly wetted before it is worked off." Unsold papers were returned to the Stamp Office where the printer appeared personally to swear that he had "made no profit or advantage of them, in order to obtain an equal Number of fresh Stamps."

The duty on advertisements was "accounted for generally once a month," on which occasions Say "frequently" attended himself. The amount of the duty was determined by an official count of the advertisements published, and a copy of the *Gazetteer* was sent daily to the Stamp Office for the purpose "and there filed." Harris was prepared if necessary to produce "the paper in Question."

The evidence prepared against Say on this occasion was of pre-cisely the same nature as that compiled for the other five pros-ecutions. On 18 May 1770 the printer petitioned the Attorney General for a stay of proceedings, pleading that "he was absolutely ignorant both of the printing and publishing . . . [of Junius' letter] being at that time unable to transact any business through an apoplectic or paralytic fit," and that the letter had been "inad-vertently and without his knowledge copied by his servants from the other newspapers. . . ." Moreover, Say continued, "sincerely disapproving of the former letters signed 'Junius,' he had actually engaged, at a considerable expense, a writer of well-known abilities to supply the *Gazetteer* with proper answers to . . . 'Junius'; which answers were first printed in the *Gazetteer* under the signa-ture 'Modestus,' and were received by the public with great appro-bation." [10]

"Modestus" was identified by an early editor of Junius as one Mr. Dalrymple, a Scotch advocate.[11] The "well-known" abilities attributed to him by Say were, however, unacknowledged by Junius himself, who declared in a letter of 19 October 1769 that he would "never descend to a dispute with such a writer as Modestus."

Reaction to Say's impending trial became apparent in the *Gazetteer* only after Miller and Baldwin had escaped conviction. A series of eleven essays published on consecutive Thursdays be-tween 9 August and 25 October 1770 put forth a comprehensive and well-reasoned argument condemning the prosecutions as illegal. Under the title of "The King's Fool," the series began with the narration of a dream vision in which George III had appointed the writer "censor general of the plumatique corps" and commanded him to "lay before the public, in a continued series of essays, *the History and Law of Libels.*" The purpose of this assignment, the King was made to say, was "that my present doubts, in regard to the legality of these *ex officio* Informations may be entirely re-moved." Later essays set the scene of Say's expected trial in the court at Guildhall and introduced the legal and historical argu-ments into speeches made by the prosecuting and defending lawyers.

The outcome of Woodfall's trial in November 1770 (he was found guilty of printing and publishing "only") [12] seems to have discouraged further government proceedings,[13] but a note in the Crown's brief against Say reveals that the printer's denial of guilt had made little impression upon the prosecution. "This may be very proper evidence," the memorandum runs, "to be given in mitigation of the sentence, . . . but we apprehend it is not sufficient to entitle the Def^t. to an Acquittal, he being answerable . . . for the Mischief done by his Servant."

Although Say's illness was considered no defense in the prosecution of 1770, he sought to employ it again two years later as part of his defense in a Chancery suit. In December 1769, he testified, he had suffered a stroke of palsy and had been for a long time "confined" and in "great danger." The suit which evoked this later testimony was responsible for the preservation of unusually detailed information about the persons engaged in the production of the *Gazetteer* during the period of its greatest prosperity and influence. It was instigated by the same "servant" who in 1769 had allegedly published the Junius letter without Say's "Knowledge or Privity." That servant was Roger Thompson, a journeyman compositor in the *Gazetteer* printing office.[14]

Roger Thompson, son of Henry Thompson, merchant, of Bury Street, St. James, had been bound apprentice to Say on 7 December 1756. On 1 May 1764 he had been admitted to the freedom of the Stationers' Company,[15] and thereafter had continued to be employed by Say as a compositor on the *Gazetteer* and the weekly *Craftsman*. It is probable that, during the period between the end of his apprenticeship and December 1769, Thompson's activities had not been confined exclusively to the composing room. John Almon had resigned as assistant to Say in the autumn of 1763, and it should be noted that Thompson was just completing his apprenticeship at the time. He may, therefore, have had opportunity to become acquainted with Almon's duties. Moreover, as a journeyman printer, his professional qualifications in the spring of 1764 would have been similar to those of Almon when he had become Say's assistant. If Thompson had not succeeded Almon directly, it is almost certain that he had acquired some editorial experience under Say in the five years that followed, for when Say was stricken in December 1769 Thompson was able to take full charge of printing and publishing the *Gazetteer* and *Craftsman* and to carry out the "conduct and management" of those papers to the full satisfaction of both Say and the *Gazetteer* proprietors.

The progress of Thompson's career in the period immediately following would have served well to point a moral, or adorn a tale designed to illustrate the eighteenth-century ideal of an Industrious Apprentice. When Say partially recovered from his illness, he placed Thompson formally in charge of both papers, and an agreement was reached whereby the younger printer was to be rewarded for his diligence by receiving one-eighth of the profits arising from the printing of the *Gazetteer* and one-eighth share of the property in the *Craftsman,* in addition to a salary of one and one-half guineas per week from the proprietors of the *Gazetteer* and half a guinea from Say in consideration of his managing the *Craftsman.*[16] Sometime in 1770, apparently after Say had fairly recovered from his illness, a deeper and more far-reaching verbal agreement came into effect. Thompson was to have one of Say's daughters in marriage, if he could "procure her consent thereto," and was to succeed to his master's business after the marriage, Say turning over to him the entire profits from printing the *Gazetteer.* In the meantime, the original agreement was to remain in effect.

If the concessions made to Thompson seem unduly liberal, there is evidence that Say was fully satisfied with the plan. In several conversations with Miles Penfold, a neighbor in Newgate Street, he mentioned having left the management of the *Gazetteer* entirely to Thompson, and spoke of him "as being a very diligent active sensible man and one whom he intended to introduce into the business and into his own family." [17] James Dixwell, a printer who for a time received advertisements for the *Gazetteer,* and William Phillips, a Newgate Street tobacconist and Say's acquaintance of thirty years, were also informed of the arrangement.[18]

The courtship appears to have gone smoothly enough. The house at No. 3 Newgate Street,[19] where the *Gazetteer* and *Craftsman* were printed, was also the residence of Charles Say, his wife, and at least one of his six children—a daughter.[20] During Say's convalescence, it became necessary for Thompson, as manager of the printing office, to be "upon the spot to take care of the apprentices and business." [21] Consequently, he was provided with board and lodging in the household, and, there can be little doubt, with opportunities for advancing his suit with the favored daughter. According to Thompson's later statement, he endeavored with his master's approval to obtain her consent to a marriage, and, "after much solicitation and attention," succeeded. Say was "apprized" of the fact, and "watched and marked the progress of . . . [Thompson's] and his said daughter's affections." [22]

For the first seven months of 1770 the situation remained unchanged, and the *Gazetteer* revealed no marked effects of the new management. By August of that year Say had nearly recovered his health, and preparations were made for a trip to Weymouth in order that he might try the benefits of bathing in the sea. The preparations would normally have been a simple matter and Thompson would not have been involved, but there were complicating factors. Edward Say had died in May 1769 and had left to his son the house at No. 10 Ave Maria Lane, where the *General Evening Post* was printed.[23] Charles Say now decided to move his family into the house of his late father, leaving the Newgate Street house and printing plant in the custody of Thompson, probably with a view to the projected marriage. The change of residence was to be made shortly after the return from Weymouth, and a housekeeper was meanwhile to be installed at Newgate Street to manage domestic affairs for Thompson. The person engaged for that purpose was Mary Morris, a spinster, 56 years of age, who had known Charles Say "from his childhood." [24] The choice, from our point of view, was a fortunate one. Miss Morris was observant, and if her housekeeping was as efficient as her memory, Roger Thompson can have had no cause for complaint.

Mary Morris was engaged early in August 1770. On the ninth of that month she assumed her duties, receiving final instructions from Charles Say, and "charge of the linen" from his wife. Thompson was to board and lodge at the house, Say told her, "he as master and she as mistress," and she was to "provide a pint of porter for Mr. Thompson every Night." Money for housekeeping expenses was to be supplied by Mr. North, the clerk who kept Say's *Gazetteer* accounts. To him the household accounts were to be submitted periodically.

Production of the *General Evening Post,* which after Edward Say's death must have continued for some time at the house in Ave Maria Lane, was transferred to the Newgate Street printing office sometime in 1770, probably in anticipation of the Say family's change in residence. When, therefore, on the evening of 9 August, Charles Say with his wife and daughter set out for Weymouth, Roger Thompson was left in complete charge of the conduct of three prominent London newspapers—one published daily, one thrice weekly, and one weekly. The general physical arrangement of the house in which they were produced may be inferred from later statements by persons who were familiar with it. A part or all of the ground floor was occupied by the *Gazetteer* office, or countinghouse, where advertisements were received and records kept, and from which distribution of the papers was carried out. Possibly, though there is no definite indication, this office was also the center of editorial activities. Above the office, on the first floor, were the kitchen and dining room, and perhaps other living accommodations as well. There are no details concerning the other floors, except that the composing rooms and press rooms were located above the kitchen and dining room; it is probable that the upper floors contained living quarters also.

During the Says' absence at Weymouth, Thompson apparently managed the papers without undue difficulty. His responsibilities would obviously have included general supervision of both the editorial and the typographical department of the newspapers, and Mary Morris, who took a definite interest in his work, described two details of his activities which are illuminating. Thompson, she said, "was at the head of the management of all the three newspapers . . . and used to look at the letters and things which were sent to be inserted . . . and to give directions about their being inserted . . . and used to correct the proof sheets. . . ." The official titles applied by Thompson to his position were "manager and publisher"; [25] John Cooke, a clerk in the office, referred to him as "manager or editor." [26] These designations, with Mary Morris' description of his duties, leave no doubt that Roger Thompson was *de facto* editor of the *Gazetteer*. The assumption is thus justified that Charles Say, as manager in the years preceding, had carried out the same functions, and had been directly responsible for the paper's general personality and for the often revealing "Observations . . . with Occasional Remarks" described in the preceding chapter.

Some two months after their departure, the Says returned from Weymouth. The excursion seems to have had a favorable effect on the printer's health. To his neighbor Miles Penfold he gave "an account of the amusements he had met with . . . and the benefit he had received . . . and told . . . [him] that he had received so much benefit that he believed he should go annually to Weymouth." John Cooke, the clerk, heard him declare that "he was as well as ever he was in his life." At Newgate Street, Mary Morris said, the family "stayed a short time till their House in Ave Maria Lane was got ready for them." Then they moved, taking with them "such part of their household furniture as they thought proper." None of the printing equipment, however, was transferred to the new house.

Say's activities for the next few months are well documented, but their motive remains somewhat ambiguous. Generally, they consisted in making Thompson independently responsible for the publication of the *Gazetteer* and *Craftsman* and legally liable for any difficulties which might arise. His first action was to arrange that his own name should be removed from the parish rate books as occupant of the Newgate Street house, and Roger Thompson's substituted. This, according to Mary Morris, was "publickly talk'd of" at the printing office, and the parish books revealed that it was accomplished sometime during the quarter beginning in October 1770.[27] In the litigation that produced so much detailed information for the years 1770-72 it was claimed by Thompson that Say sought to escape the "great danger and hazard" involved "in the printing and publishing such papers." [28] Miles Penfold believed that Say wished to "screen" himself "from any trouble that might arise on account of any thing that might be inserted" in the papers, and George Abraham, Say's senior apprentice at the time, also believed that his master was interested in avoiding "any bad consequences which might arise" from matter published in the *Gazetteer*.[29] John Gibson and William Brinkworth,[30] two of the printers employed on the *Gazetteer*, and Mary Morris, were of the same opinion. Say himself did not wholly deny this motive, claiming later that his health at the time was so poor that he would not have survived a prosecution. But there was not, he insisted, any greater risk involved in publishing the papers in 1770 than there had been at any other time.[31]

It is curious that none of the other persons whose statements have been cited appears to have considered the state of Say's health as in any way connected with his fear of a prosecution. There may indeed have been no greater risk in the autumn of 1770 than there had been previously, but it must be observed that Say's earlier editorial indiscretions had resulted in some rather serious consequences: a reprimand and fine in the House of Commons in 1760; three fines of £100 in the House of Lords in 1764, 1765, and 1767; a narrow escape in the Commons in 1768; and sizable legal fees, probably, in the Junius affair. Worthy of consideration also is the anxiety he must have suffered on those and a few other occasions. The sum of these factors may, perhaps, be considered sufficient cause for the apprehension that Say felt in 1770. In November of that year, however, there occurred an event of the most vital significance for the *Gazetteer* and, indirectly, for English journalism in general. Its occurrence at the beginning of Say's almost complete withdrawal from the *Gazetteer* may have been only coincidence; or it may have been, in the light of later developments, the chief cause of the apprehension that motivated his withdrawal. The event in question was the commencement of publication of brief accounts of the proceedings in the House of Commons.

The innovation was daring indeed, and though the *Gazetteer* was not the first paper in London to undertake the venture, it was apparently the first daily paper to publish speeches and accounts of the debates with any approach to regularity. Initiative in the matter was taken originally by Charles Say's former assistant, John Almon, who has left an account of his motives and methods. "When the spirit of the nation was raised high," Almon recalled, "by the massacre of St. George's-fields, the unjust decision upon the Middlesex election, &c. . . . [he] resolved to make the nation acquainted with the proceedings of Parliament." To this end, he

employed himself sedulously, in obtaining from different gentlemen, by conversation at his own house, and sometimes at their houses, sufficient information to write a sketch of every day's debate, on the most important and interesting questions; which he printed three times a week regularly in the London Evening Post. At this time the late printer, *Meres,* was dead, and the paper was now printed for *J. Miller,* a young man.[32]

The intrepidity of young Mr. Miller was to be displayed several times in the next few years. It is of special interest here because, at least as early as 1771, Miller was a son-in-law of Charles Say.[33] Moreover, Say, it will appear, had an interest in the *London Evening Post* in 1769 and may even have printed it for a time.

Reports of the debates were published by Miller "during two sessions . . . without any notice being taken," and Almon

furnished them constantly, from the best information he could obtain. Though they were short, they were in general pretty accurate; and their accuracy was perhaps the cause of the printer's security. The proprietors of the St. James's Chronicle, . . . observing the impunity with which these accounts . . . were printed, and perhaps being a little jealous of the success of their rival, resolved upon deviating into the same track. And for this purpose, they employed one *Wall,* who went down to the House of Commons every evening, to pick up what he could in the lobby, in the coffee-houses, &c.

"It was impossible," Almon continues, that Wall's reports could be accurate at first, but "by perseverance and habit, and sometimes by getting admission to the gallery, he improved; and judging, in a little time, that he could supply two newspapers as well as one, he amplified his accounts for the Gazetteer, after having published the heads in the St. James's Chronicle. This encouraged the printers of the other papers to follow the example." [34] On Almon's authority, Wall may be considered the first special Parliamentary correspondent employed by an English newspaper; his connection with the *Gazetteer* was to become increasingly important in the decade that followed.

The manner in which Wall's earliest efforts were presented in the *Gazetteer* reveals a justly exercised caution on the part of Roger Thompson. In imitation of the famous "Senate of Lilliput" device employed earlier by the *Gentleman's Magazine,* the Commons' proceedings were reported as "Intelligence from the Lower Room of the Robinhood Society," a popular London debating club, and speakers were at first designated by transparent pseudonyms. Thus, Onslow became *"One Slow";* Charles Fox was "Young Reynard"; Conway "General Goneaway"; and Burke "Edmundo." For a short while the proceedings themselves were veiled in a rather ingenious allegory. For example: "Mr. Dowell [Dowdeswell] moved for papers that would show the 'Squire's Groom [Prime Minister] had received intelligence of the horse-stealers' intentions time enough to have shut the door before the steed was stolen, if he had not been an idle, neglectful fellow" [35]—this, with reference to Spain's seizure of the Falkland Islands. Such reports would have been clear only to readers well versed in the political issues of the day, and the labor of translating them into a sufficiently transparent and consistent allegory must have been considerable. Though Parliament continued to be referred to as the "Robinhood Society" or, more simply, as "a great assembly," throughout the remainder of 1770, the elaborate puns and allegories were discontinued soon after they had begun, and brief, straightforward accounts of the proceedings replaced them, with members' names being represented by initial and final letters connected by dashes. An interval of three or four days usually elapsed between a debate itself and the publication of its report in the *Gazetteer,* and often the accounts of two sittings were combined in a single report.

The reports appeared in various forms. Sometimes they were printed as letters to the printer from a correspondent; [36] at other times they were headed simply "Intelligence from the . . . Robinhood Society"; and not infrequently a few paragraphs descriptive of the proceedings were included in the columns of *London* news, without special distinction of any kind. The brief general accounts were augmented at irregular intervals by longer reports of single speeches made by members in the course of particular debates. These sometimes filled as much as two columns, and while some of them were the products of Wall's memory, the texts of others were undoubtedly supplied by the members who had made them, and who had no objection to personal publicity, or who were, as some later revealed themselves, favorably disposed toward the publication of the proceedings.

In spite of the rapid social and professional rise of Roger Thompson—he was admitted to the Livery of the Stationers' Company on 6 November 1770 [37]—and the domestic reorganization at Newgate Street, the *Gazetteer* imprint throughout November and most of December 1770 continued to proclaim that the paper was "Printed for C. Say." Late in December, however, a written order from Say to Edward Benson (who was responsible for such details at the time), directed that Thompson's name should replace Say's "at the foot of the . . . Gazetteer, Craftsman, and General Evening Post." [38] Accordingly, on Thursday, 27 December 1770, the *Gazetteer* made its first appearance as "Printed for R. Thompson."

No formal announcement accompanied the change, and nothing in the paper called attention to it. Charles Say had now, ostensibly, no further interest in the *Gazetteer;* more significantly, he was immune from all legal liability. Sometime in the month following, at a "public feast or entertainment" which Say gave for his journeymen and apprentices, he announced "openly to them all that they were to look upon Mr. Thompson as master." [39] By the terms of Say's agreement with Thompson, which was not reduced to writing until four months later, the younger printer was subject to punishment "by pillory and imprisonment and liable to pay fines and damages" [40] arising from any prosecution in which any of the three papers might be involved. Though Say continued to call as often as two or three times a day at the Newgate Street house, and occasionally took his dinner with Thompson and Mary Morris,[41] he was at some pains to dissociate himself, publicly, from any concern in the newspapers printed there. One morning when he and his apprentice George Abraham were in the Newgate Street counting-house, a gentleman entered and asked for Say, who acknowledged his identity. But when the caller inquired "about some thing which was to have been inserted in the . . . Gazetteer," Say told him that he "was not the printer of the . . . paper and had no business with it" and that he must "apply to Mr. Thompson." "After the gentleman was gone," Say instructed the clerk "that if any body should come to inquire for him . . . with regard to any thing that might be inserted in the . . . papers he should tell them that . . . [Say] had no business with them and that Mr. Thompson was the printer." [42]

That the proprietors of the *Gazetteer* approved of the new arrangement is certain, for the guinea and a half which they allowed Thompson weekly was, Say later declared, in the nature of a "present or compliment," paid to encourage "diligence" and partially a result of the good reports Say had given them of his prospective son-in-law. The proprietors of the *General Evening Post*, however, were apparently not consulted before the management of their paper was transferred, and they were much less satisfied with the plan. For this and other reasons, a public dispute ensued which, while its description here may appear irrelevant to the history of the *Gazetteer*, provides one contemporary view of the character of Charles Say and some details of his professional career not found elsewhere.

Until March 1771 Thompson's management of the *General Evening Post* seems to have been a matter of indifference to the paper's proprietors. At the beginning of that month, the imprint gave no indication of who the printer might be, announcing only that the paper was sold by the publisher, S. Bladon, in Paternoster Row, and that advertisements, letters, and news items would be received, among other places, at the printing office in Newgate Street. On Saturday, 9 March 1771 a conspicuous notice on page 4 of the *Post* declared that "On Tuesday next" the paper would be "printed and sold by R. THOMPSON, (at No. 3 Newgate-street) to whom all Gentlemen in Town and Country, Masters of Coffee-Houses, and News-Carriers" were requested to send their orders. On the following Tuesday, 12 March, the *Gazetteer* carried a similar announcement at the head of its *London* column.

No little confusion must have resulted when, on that same evening, the news carriers offered their customers two versions of the *General Evening Post*. The cause of the duplication could hardly have been mystifying; disputes among proprietors, or between them and the printers of their newspapers, had resulted in similar phenomena on several occasions since 1709, when such a quarrel had given rise to the publication of two *Post Boys*.[43] But the choice between *General Evening Posts* would have been difficult. Typographically, the two papers were nearly identical, though an observant customer might have noticed that in the version printed by R. Thompson, the factotum wood block on page 1 displayed in its background the dome of St. Paul's, as usual, while in the paper "Sold by S. Bladon," the Tower of London was shown behind the horse and rider common to the blocks in both. Charles Say, it was later revealed, had been discharged as printer of the *General Evening Post* at a proprietors' meeting of 7 March. His decision to continue publishing a version of the paper independently had been quickly made, and the notice published in the original *Post* on 9 March (quoted above) was in fact an advertisement for the unauthorized publication which he intended to bring out.

For several weeks the dispute was carried on privately, neither version of the *General Evening Post* making overt reference to the other. In the proprietors' paper the imprint, in which the name of S. Bladon was prominently displayed, was moved from page 4 to a banner at the head of page 1, and a long notice, without reference to the rival publication, thanked the public for past patronage and promised a continuation of "the strictest and most vigorous Attention to improve this Paper in all . . . Particulars." The Say-Thompson paper gave no hint of any change in its proprietorship aside from the imprint, but new initiative was displayed in a method of distribution inaugurated in mid-March. Bladon's paper continued, apparently, to be circulated only through the usual channels; Thompson's, it was announced in the *Gazetteer* of 14 March, would circulate through the same channels, but would be "also published, between two and three o'clock . . . at the Pamphlet Shops at the Royal Exchange, and at the Gates of the 'Change; by which means Gentlemen will have an opportunity of taking them home when they go to dinner."

On Tuesday, 26 March, the Bladon *General Evening Post* gave the first direct notice of its dissociation from Say, still without mentioning the unauthorized paper: "The Proprietors having removed the Printing of this Paper (which has been established upwards of forty years) from C. G. Say . . . to J. Cooper, in Drury-lane, such Persons as are disposed to favour them with Advertisements, or Letters . . . are requested to direct thither or to S. Bladon. . . ." The following Saturday, Say made a striking bid for public support, anticipating the proprietors' arguments by accusing them of his own transgression. The statement appeared not, as might have been expected, in Thompson's *General Evening Post* nor in the *Gazetteer* but on the last page of a rival evening paper, the *London Evening Post,* published by Say's son-in-law John Miller.

"Some Gentlemen having thought proper," the notice began, "to print a General Evening Post, sold by S. Bladon, it becomes necessary to inform the Public, that the General Evening Post is continued to be printed as usual, and is now sold by R. THOMP-SON, at No. 3, in Newgate-street." This was followed by a statement designed to convince readers that the pirated paper was really the genuine one, carried on in the tradition established by Charles Say's father:

The readers of the General Evening Post (sold by R. Thompson) both in Town and Country, are to be acquainted, that the Editor is the same Gentleman, many years employed to compile the General Evening Post for Mr. EDWARD SAY, who printed that paper from its first institution (near forty years since) to the time of his death; and which has been since that time, and now is, continued in the family.

The General Evening Post, printed by Mr. EDWARD SAY, was always esteemed the most decent paper in England, with respect to its compilation; and was therefore much admired by many sensible private families, in the country in particular.

Those readers who were "inclined to favour the General Evening Post, which was printed by Mr. EDWARD SAY," were asked to send their orders "to his Son, Charles Say, who now lives in his worthy Father's house, . . . in Ave Maria-lane, near St. Paul's; or to R. THOMPSON." Should such readers by "any mistake" receive the wrong paper, on sending a line to Charles Say, "who always pays postage," they might depend on having it rectified.

This amounted to an open declaration of hostilities; the appeal of family tradition was well conceived, and the proprietors of the original paper had no choice but to sacrifice dignity, submitting their grievances to the judgment of their readers. With the issue of Thursday, 11 April, they undertook to do this in a notice on page 1 addressed "To the PUBLIC":

Whereas Charles Green Say, late Printer of the GENERAL EVE-NING POST, was discharged from that employment by a General Meeting of the Proprietors thereof, on Thursday the 7th of March last, which was afterwards confirmed at a subsequent Meeting on Thursday the 21st of the same Month, the said C. G. Say having acted in direct opposition to the sense of the Partners and the interest of the said Newspaper.

The conduct of the said C. G. Say has been so distinct and foreign to the articles of partnership, that the Public are desired particularly to take notice in what manner he has been treated by the Proprietors, and how little he has deserved their lenity.

By the articles of partnership, the proprietors explained, no share-holder was permitted to have an interest in any other evening news-paper.

The charge against the said C. G. Say will now appear in the clearest light. —In the year 1749 he was admitted a partner—In the year 1761 he committed a breach of covenant, by printing another Evening Paper, entitled The Royal Chronicle, and for which . . . his share was re-solved to be forfeited; but,—out of respect the Proprietors had for his father Mr. Edward Say, he was restored to his share and dividend in the said paper. —His father was a witness to, and attested this con-viction of his misbehavior. But yet in the year 1769, he persisted in the same unlawful manner, and again printed and published another Evening Paper, called the London Evening Post; [44] and at a General Meeting of the Proprietors in that year, it was resolved, that for so doing, he had ferfeited his share in the . . . [*General Evening Post*], agree-able to the articles of Partnership. However upon the death of his father, this same C. G. Say, was appointed Printer of this Paper, and a share given him—as an encouragement to him to exert his abilities for the service of this Paper. So much reward for so little merit, and so much pity and compassion for his infirmities, produced the most ungrateful returns to such proofs of generosity; that he has ever since studied to reduce and abridge the value and credit of a Paper, which for a series of years has been established on the firm basis of public approbation. —For these and a variety of other reasons he was discharged from the further printing of this Paper, and has since insolently presumed to print and publish an anonymous, spurious, and pirated News-paper, under the fictitious name of the General Evening Post, whereby his share in the Genuine and Real GENERAL EVENING POST is again forfeited, and his property in the said News-paper is lost, void, and dissolved.

Having set forth their grievances, the proprietors proceeded to an examination of Say's personal character:

The Advertisement in the London Evening Post of Saturday the 30th of March last, relative to this Paper, is false, imposing and nugatory; but in every respect similar to the said C. G. Say, who has afforded the Public so many repeated proofs of his truth and veracity, that his char-acter is indisputably known, and the uprightness of his actions visible to those only, who ever experienced the benefit of it.

These infamous proceedings will not pass with impunity, the Proprietors being resolved to have redress for the damage already committed by the daring and flagrant behaviour of the said C. G. Say; and will not suffer their property to be invaded by the undermining efforts of a man, who has violated the Articles of Partnership, and corrupted the faith they were intended to preserve.

The charge was reprinted in succeeding issues of the proprietors' *General Evening Post*, with the added promise that "Some further particulars respecting Mr. Say" would be presented to the public "in a few days." In Thompson's *Post* for Thursday, 18 April, Say replied to the above statement with some countercharges of his own. I have failed to locate a copy of the reply. It was sufficiently provocative, however, that the proprietors answered it immediately, apparently in a high state of anger:

Charles Green Say having on Thursday last set forth, in a spurious and pirated News-paper published by R. Thompson, a most false, scandalous, and impudent Account of the Proceedings of the Partners of the General Evening Post; the Public are particularly desired to take Notice, That in the course of the next week, a Reply will be given to the said Account, in a Hand-Bill, which will be dispersed and circulated throughout the Trade, and all the Coffee houses and public Places in the City of London, whereby the Fallacy of the said C. G. Say will be fully and clearly detected, and his unjust treatment of the Proprietors of this Paper exposed to the Judgment of the World.

The threat was published on Saturday, 20 April. For more than two months thereafter, both Thompson and the proprietors seem to have continued publishing their respective *General Evening Posts* without further reference to the dispute.[45]

Whether the promised handbill was ever published is not known, but in the proprietors' paper of Thursday, 4 July 1771, there appeared a detailed two-column indictment of Say, the content of which might well have been prepared originally for handbill publication. The proprietors had been reluctant to trouble the public with their private concerns, they said, and had therefore delayed replying to Say's representation of the state of their differences. They had believed that "the impracticability of carrying on a spurious News-paper with any prospect of success" would have reduced "even the excentric Mr. Say within the compass of reason and justice." Their patience had gone unrewarded, and they now proposed to set forth the true state of affairs.

Up to the end of 1768, it was stated, the *General Evening Post* had been printed and published by Edward Say to the full satisfaction of the proprietors, to whom he had "regularly accounted for the profits, and paid their respective dividends." Tracing again the history of Charles Say's connection with the paper, the proprietors filled in details not given in the earlier announcement. In the early part of 1769 Say had, in violation of his contract, begun to print the *London Evening Post*, and his share in the *General Evening Post* had been revoked. Prior to the death of his father in May 1769, however, he had discontinued the printing of Miller's paper, and had been made printer of the *General Evening Post*, in succession to his father, "at his earnest request." [46]

Say had previously asserted that he gave up an annuity of £80 per year arising from his interest in the *London Evening Post* to become printer of the *General Evening Post*. Actually, the proprietors claimed, he had merely signed over the annuity to his daughter—a "palpable collusion" at which they had "winked," since the two papers were conducted, as they truly understated it, "on different principles."

Say's authority over the *General Evening Post* had been at first far less extensive than his authority over the *Gazetteer*. Two "Editors" had been appointed "at stipulated salaries, to manage the different departments of the paper," and "Mr. Say was restrained from inserting anything contrary to . . . [the editors'] opinion."

In 1770—the first year of Thompson's management—there had been no cause for friction until November, when Say as executor of his father's estate had presented a bill to the proprietors for £710 10s. "on account of outstanding debts due for advertisements." The partners, "astonished at this unexpected demand," had "represented the improbability of its being justly founded; Mr. Edward Say . . . having ever maintained the appearance of the paper's being in a flourishing state, and regularly paid them . . . their dividends; a thing hardly creditable for him to do, had the Partners been so deeply in his debt." After their representation, Charles Say had agreed to give them a receipt in full for the debt claimed if they would assist him, when necessary, to "get in the debts really outstanding." This condition, Say claimed, had never been complied with; but the proprietors declared that they had "so far complied" with it, "that on application to several persons, supposed to be indebted to the *General Evening Post* for advertisements, they have produced written receipts of the late Mr. Edward Say proving their discharge." This statement gave rise to a number of interesting questions, but the proprietors refrained from asking them publicly.

At the same time, they continued, Say had presented another bill for £90 "which he pretended to have been laid out in procuring extraordinary intelligence and recompencing other secret service; notwithstanding the salaries of the Editors were limited." When the proprietors had objected, Say had reduced this claim to £46 14s. 6d., which they had paid. To prevent future disputes of the like nature," Say had been offered "the editorship and management of the Paper at a certain stipulated price, which he himself proposed; and it was immediately allowed him."

"It was soon apparent" to the proprietors, however, "that the composition of the *General Evening Post* was subservient to that of the *Gazetteer*," and the presswork had been often "so slovenly executed, as to render the paper . . . unintelligible." When they had complained to Say, "so far from correcting the abuse," he had "referred them to Mr. R. Thompson," to whose care, he told them, he had resigned the management of the paper. "Nay, so far did Mr. Say proceed, that, without obtaining, or even asking, leave" he had "withdrawn his name from the paper, and substituted that of R. Thompson in its stead." On the assumption that Say was retiring from business the proprietors had discharged him as printer of their paper and arranged to pay his "bill for printing." Curiously enough in the light of evidence already set forth, Say had complained that "the insinuation of his retiring from business" was "injurious" and "known to be false"—a complaint that lends weight to the assumption that he wished to retire only from the legal responsibilities. He had begun to print the spurious *General Evening Post* "to his own manifest loss" and the "common detriment" of both himself and the proprietors, "justifying this extravagant act under colour of his being hardly used, and the specious pretence of submitting his cause to arbitration." In May 1771 the proprietors had agreed to appoint arbitrators in the dispute, but Say had once more brought up for consideration his claim for £710 and his resignation of the *London Evening Post* annuity, to which the proprietors could "by no means submit," though they were ready to submit nearly anything else to arbitration. There the matter stood on July fourth.

The "impartial public" before whom the proprietors laid their case must have seen little hope for a settlement outside the courts, and no possibility of personal reconciliation. What surprise must the public have felt, then, when only five days later the *Gazetteer* published the following announcement at the head of its *London* column: "The late disagreement between the Proprietors and Printer of the General Evening Post, . . . being now adjusted, there will, for the future, be only One General Evening Post printed, which will be sold by S. Bladon, No. 28, in Pater-noster Row." [47]

Fortunately, the key to this settlement has survived. A memorandum preserved in the British Museum [48] and dated 2 July 1771 contains Say's proposals, submitted to the proprietors of the *General Evening Post,* for the adjustment of the dispute. In it Say imposed three conditions on the proprietors and offered an equal number of concessions. He was to be reinstated as printer, and his share in the paper was to be restored. Profits or losses which had accrued during the period of the dispute were to be brought to the "General accompt," and Say was to have "no demand or claim for the Paper he has publish'd, for his Law Charges or any other Expenses from the time of his Separation. . . ." The partners were to pay him an outstanding printing bill of £525 "in three months," and were to settle with him thereafter every six months. The name of neither Say nor Thompson was to be included in the imprint—Bladon's name alone to appear there—and Say was not to receive any advertisements for the paper. Finally, Say agreed that J. Osborne, through whom he was submitting these proposals, should be authorized to settle any further disputes which might arise.

The apparent simplicity of the settlement is surprising in view of the vehemence with which the dispute was carried on, and several aspects of the affair seem worthy of attention. Most striking, perhaps, is the tenacity of purpose displayed by Say in continuing to finance the publication, for a period of four months, of a paper which must have run at a deficit. More significant, however, is the value that he attached to the contract for printing the *General Evening Post,* a value sufficient, it would appear, to offset the loss incurred by the publication of his "spurious and pirated Newspaper." On the other hand, the fact that Say was finally reinstated indicates first that, although we have been able to consider only the proprietors' side of the argument, Say must have had claims of his own sufficiently justifiable to provide an incentive for compromise; secondly, his independent publication had been capable of seriously damaging the circulation of the original *General Evening Post.* For the public estimate of Say's character, there is no evidence that the proprietors ever apologized.

During a part of the time in which Say was engaged in the dispute over the *General Evening Post*, Roger Thompson was involved in another dispute of far greater magnitude. On 9 March 1771, the day on which the first issue of the *General Evening Post* "printed for R. Thompson" was advertised in the *Gazetteer*, a reward of £50 was offered by royal proclamation for the arrest of the same R. Thompson. That, however, constitutes a chapter of its own in the history of English journalism; it can be accorded no less in the history of the *Gazetteer*.

VI

THE PRINTER PROCLAIMED

February-March 1771

FOR more than a month after Thompson's name replaced that of Say in the imprint, the *Gazetteer* continued to publish reports of the Parliamentary debates with impunity, and by January 1771 most of the other London papers were providing similar fare, though the reports given by the majority of them were either copied or adapted from the *Gazetteer*, the *London Evening Post*, and a few other of the more enterprising papers which cultivated their own sources of such information.

No official notice was taken of the reports in either House until 5 February 1771, when, on the motion of Colonel George Onslow, the House of Commons resolution of 1728 which forbade publication of the proceedings was read and thereby reaffirmed. Three days later the Colonel entered a specific complaint against the *Gazetteer* of that day (Friday, 8 February) and the *Middlesex Journal* of the evening before, printed by John Wheble. The two papers, Onslow protested, had been guilty of misrepresenting the speeches and reflecting on the characters of several members, in contempt of the order (as the formula ran) and in breach of the privilege of the House. He moved that both of the offending papers be delivered in and read, and that Thompson and Wheble be ordered to attend the House on the Monday following.

In making his motion Onslow claimed to be pursuing the mildest course possible against the two printers, who had seemed to defy openly the House resolution against publishing debates. The immediate cause for his deep concern with the honor of the House was soon revealed. The papers named had ventured to report his motion of 5 February for the reading of the very resolutions designed to prevent such publication, and they had implied that he was a tool of the ministry, seeking to cover its iniquities by prohibiting reports of the proceedings. Sometimes, the Colonel declared, he had been made out as a villain, at other times as an idiot, and on occasion, as both. Today they had called him *"little cocking George,"* but they would find him a cock not easily beaten, for he was determined never to give up on this point. He then read the offending paragraph:

It was reported, that a scheme was at last hit upon by the ministry, to prevent the public from being informed of their iniquity; accordingly, on Tuesday last, little *cocking* George Onslow made a motion, that an order against printing Debates should be read, and entered on the minutes of that day. Mr. Charles Turner opposed the motion with great spirit; he said, that not only the debates ought to be published, but a list of the divisions likewise; and he affirmed, that no man would object to it, unless he was ashamed of the vote he gave. Mr. Edmund Burke supported Mr. Turner's opinion; he said, that so far from its being proper to conceal their debates, he wished they would follow the ancient rule; which was to record them in the journals.[1]

A debate followed, in which the Colonel's motion for calling in the printers was supported by his cousin George Onslow, member for Surrey, but opposed by a number of other speakers on several grounds. Captain Constantine Phipps and Lord John Cavendish felt that for the House to show such concern would only promote the sale of the papers, which would be read with greater avidity, and believed with greater credulity. Other members invoked the right of constituents to know what their representatives were saying, and objected to the breadth of the proposed measure. If a printer had libeled an individual member, he should be subjected to the censure of the House, and to prosecution at law, but there was no reason to forbid the printing of debates generally. This was the view taken by Edmund Burke, who addressed himself, he said, to the prudence of the House. If it forbade all printing of debates, he thought, it would surely lose the good opinion of the public; and even in spite of such prohibition, as long as the public felt an interest in examining the proceedings of Parliament, so long would a man be found who would print them. When the House divided, the vote was 90 to 55 in favor of Onslow's motion. The offending passages were read by a clerk

and an order made that the printers attend the House on Monday,
11 February.

The paragraph which Colonel Onslow found offensive, and
which he quoted in the House, had appeared in the "Postscript"
of the *Middlesex Journal,* Number 289, from Tuesday, 5 February,
to Thursday, 7 February 1771. The *Gazetteer,* on the morning
of the eighth, had repeated the substance of the report, but with
an obvious effort to render it less exceptionable to the House. The
"little cocking George" epithet had been omitted, the House of
Commons had not been mentioned by name, and the names of the
members had been presented in the conventionally transparent
camouflage of letters and dashes:

A correspondent belonging to the Lower Room of the Robinhood Society informs us, that "it was reported a scheme was at last hit upon by
the Ministry, to prevent the public from being informed of their iniquity;
accordingly on Tuesday last Mr. O——w made a motion in the Lower
Room, 'that an order against printing the debates should be read, and
entered in the minutes of that day.'

"Mr. Ch–rl–s T–rn–r opposed the motion with great spirit; he said,
that not only the debates ought to be published, but a list of the divisions
likewise; and he affirmed that no man would object to it, unless he was
ashamed of the vote he gave.

"Mr. Ed——d B——ke (ever a friend to the liberty of the press!)
supported Mr. T–rn–r's opinion; he said, that so far from its being
proper to conceal their debates, he wished they would follow the ancient
rule, which was to record them in the journals."

Reflection upon any member except Colonel Onslow is not apparent here; misrepresentation could be claimed only in the "reported" interpretation of his motive.

Onslow's resentment, however, was not ill-founded. There is
evidence that the paragraph as originally published in the *Middlesex Journal, Or Chronicle of Liberty*—a paper founded by the
"democratic" Lord Mayor Beckford which served as an organ
for the City "patriots"—had been composed for the specific purpose of provoking the Colonel to a motion such as he had made.
The ultimate design was to test legally the privilege of the House
of Commons to prohibit the publication of its proceedings. The
movement appears to have been sponsored chiefly by the Supporters
of the Bill of Rights, a society formed originally "to support John
Wilkes, Esq.; against ministerial oppression, by discharging his
debts, and rendering him independent." [2] John Wheble, the printer

of the *Middlesex Journal,* revealed later that a few weeks before the offending paragraph was published, a gentleman had come to him, foretold that the House would take notice of such a paragraph, explained the unjust nature of the privilege claimed by the Commons, and "asked him if he had courage to refuse obedience" to the House "and trust to the laws of the land." Wheble had replied that he "would suffer any extremity" rather than obey any power except the law.[3]

After the paragraph had been published, and the House had ordered his attendance, the same person called again on Wheble and conducted him to a meeting with the Reverend John Horne, then a leading ornament of the Bill of Rights society. Horne advised the printer "not to obey the summons, but to keep out of the way." If Wheble would follow his directions, Horne assured him, he would stand by the printer "in all . . . consequences"; and if, "in any part of the progress of the business, Mr. Wheble repented, or was afraid," he was directed to "go down to the House, and declare Mr. Horne to be the author of the obnoxious paragraph, and tell them that Mr. Horne advised him not to obey their summons." "For the rest," Horne told the printer, "they must be governed by circumstances, and he would let . . . [Wheble] know from time to time what he should do."

Wheble obeyed instructions. The House did not again take up the business of the printers until 19 February, eight days after Thompson and Wheble had been scheduled to appear.[4] When the orders were read out that day in the House, neither was in attendance. The messenger who was to have served the orders reported that he had done so, but had served the printers with no further order for their appearance on the nineteenth. Thompson, the messenger added, had appeared on the date specified (11 February), but had gone away again. Colonel Onslow moved that "R. Thompson, not having attended this House this day, in obedience to the orders of this House, is thereby guilty of a contempt of this House." In the debate which followed, several members sought to defend Thompson on the claim that he had attended as ordered, and had not been given notice of the postponement of the matter by the House. Richard Whitworth, member for Stafford, said that he knew Thompson had intended to obey the order, and that on 11 February the printer had waited in the lobby of the House but had received no further orders. "I myself," Whitworth added, "who have been in Parliament a great while should not know whom to apply to . . . [in Thompson's circumstances]." [5] At length a motion was passed ordering both Thompson and Wheble to attend the House on the Thursday following.

During the ten days between Roger Thompson's compliant appearance in the lobby and the date upon which he was ordered to appear a second time, it is almost certain that he, like Wheble, had been persuaded to resist the orders of the House. On 21 February, when the orders for attendance were again read in the House, neither printer appeared. The messenger reported that he had been unable to find either of them at their respective houses, and that after several attempts, he had left copies of the orders with the servants of each.

The Speaker observed that the journals were lacking in precedents for matters of this sort, and suggested that the House might justifiably set a new one. It was finally agreed that, for the third time, orders should be issued for the printers' attendance on Tuesday, 26 February, and that thenceforth "the service of the said order, by leaving a copy of the same at the usual place of abode . . . be deemed equal to personal service, and be good service." [6]

The messenger of the House was to fare no better on this occasion than he had previously. Thompson and Wheble were not in attendance on the twenty-sixth, either. The messenger explained that he had gone to Thompson's house in Newgate Street after receiving the new orders on Thursday evening. The shop had been shut up, but he had been let in by a boy who told him that Thompson was not at home, though he was in town. The messenger had then asked to see John Cooke, the clerk, whom he had encountered on a previous call, but was told that Cooke had gone home for the night. Finally, he had asked the boy to call for one of Thompson's men, if there were any about. Apparently, a person had been found who fulfilled the qualification, and the messenger had proceeded to read the order to him, and had given him a copy to be delivered to Thompson. Things had gone much the same at Wheble's, and Colonel Onslow moved that the printers, for their contempt of the order, should be taken into the custody of the House's Serjeant at Arms or his deputy. After a debate in which it was suggested with some discernment that the House should "aim at higher individuals, and not begin with a milkman, or a printer," the motion was carried. [7]

By March first Roger Thompson had committed himself wholeheartedly to the support of the constitutional experiment which he had, perhaps unwittingly, played a part in originating. In the *Gazetteer* of that day he acknowledged the receipt of "several letters respecting the *constitutional rights* and *legal power* of Parliaments," and assured his correspondents that it was "his utmost ambition to merit their and the public favour, by a ready adherence, *at all events,* to the CONSTITUTIONAL RIGHTS of an ENGLISHMAN." [8]

On Monday, 4 March, the deputy Serjeant at Arms made his report to the House of Commons. In the course of a dozen calls at Wheble's between Thursday, 28 February, and Sunday, 3 March, he had received conflicting and evasive reports from servants of the times when he might expect to find their master at home, and at least one of the servants had been unable to suppress his mirth at the frequency and futility of the deputy's calls. His first call at Thompson's had not been made until the morning of Friday, 1 March, because some confusion had arisen concerning the Christian name of the *Gazetteer*'s printer. The deputy had heard, he said, of two R. Thompsons—a Richard and a Robert— and had wanted to be certain of apprehending the proper one. To this end he had inquired at the Stamp Office and found that, although in the House debates the printer had been referred to as "Richard Thompson," [9] the name of the man he sought was really "Robert." [10] He had later sent a messenger to the office again to make certain that there was no other newspaper printer of that name. Three calls at the house in Newgate Street had yielded only the information that the structure containing Thompson's printing office was also his dwelling-house.

For Colonel Onslow this, assuredly, was the climax of contempt. He moved "that an humble address be presented to his Majesty, that he will be graciously pleased to issue his royal proclamation for apprehending . . . John Wheble and R. Thompson, with a promise of reward for same." [11] In the *London Gazette* of Saturday, 9 March, the printers were duly proclaimed.

The proclamation recited their original offence and recounted the unsuccessful efforts of the House of Commons to deal with the matter, at the same time charging all "loving subjects" as they would "answer the contrary at their perils," to "discover . . . the said John Wheble and R. Thompson, to the end he or they may be secured." For the encouragement of care and diligence, the proclamation further declared,

who ever shall discover and apprehend . . . them, within three weeks
from the date hereof, and shall bring . . . them . . . before some
Justice of the Peace or Chief Magistrate as aforesaid, shall have and receive, as a reward for the discovery . . . the sum of fifty pounds for
each; which our Commissioners of our Treasury are hereby required
and directed to pay accordingly.

John Wheble was becoming apprehensive. A dispute between
Horne and John Wilkes, then Alderman for the ward of Farring-
don Without, had resulted in a struggle for the personal allegiance
of the printer. Shortly after the first interview with Horne, Wheble
had been visited by Wilkes, who told the printer that he had been
shamefully treated, and even abandoned, by Horne. Thereafter,
Wilkes had "with frequent daily applications and earnest importunity" intreated the printer to "apply" to him, threatening
that if Wheble "did not come to him now . . . , if he should
apply to him afterwards, he [Wilkes] would do nothing in the
matter."

In this dilemma Wheble sought reassurance from Horne, who
told him only to "be patient, be cool, be quiet; that he should . . .
be told how to act" at the proper time. They had gained greatly,
Horne assured him, by the delay; it was sufficient for Wheble,
"having engagement of support, to know what he was to do at
the time of execution, and . . . it was not proper he should know
it before or otherwise than step by step. . . ." In view of the in-
definiteness of Horne's advice, it is not surprising that the printer
had doubts. "In this situation," Wheble stated later, he was "at
length persuaded, by the earnest repeated importunity and in-
treaties of Mr. Wilkes, to apply to him at Guildhall, without Mr.
Horne's knowledge or consent." [12]

Although definite evidence is lacking, there can be little doubt
that Roger Thompson, too, was in communication with Wilkes
at this time. Whatever may have been Thompson's personal reaction to the proclamation, he gave no sign of submission in his
paper. On Monday, 11 March, the proclamation from the *Gazette*
was reprinted in the first column of page 2 of the *Gazetteer*. There
was no editorial comment, nor was any to be expected; but in
column 2 of the same page, side by side with the proclamation,
appeared the fourth in a series of speeches on the *Nullum Tempus*
bill. This was the "GENUINE Speech of Mr. Serjeant L[ei]gh,"
avowedly received by the printer from a member of the House
of Commons. There followed a notice assuring readers, though

without direct reference to the situation in which the printer found himself, that further "GENUINE Speeches" on the bill would be "printed in this paper in the exact order in which they were delivered." The implicit defiance could not have been overlooked.

It is unfortunate that we cannot know what the proprietors of the *Gazetteer* felt about the situation in which their printer had become involved. If the clause in the contract of 1753 which made him liable for half the legal costs resulting from editorial actions not sanctioned by the management committee remained valid, Thompson, by proceeding independently, was running no inconsiderable risk with his own, or Say's, financial assets. The fact that he continued to print the debates, however, and to defy both the Speaker's warrant and the proclamation, argues that the policy had the support of the proprietors. They would certainly have had legal advice, and they must have been convinced that the possible benefits to be derived from such a policy could more than compensate for the dangers that were involved.

A series of ten letters to the *Gazetteer* between 11 and 28 March, signed "A Citizen," sought to refute on legal grounds the course taken by the Commons. The first letter protested that the proclamation published in the *London Gazette* was illegal. It did not contain R. Thompson's Christian name, the name of the county or parish in which he resided, or a description of his person. On the following day the writer admitted that Lord Chief Justice Mansfield might discount such omissions as "only formal inferences of the law, but what answer," he wondered, "will this subtle disciple of Justinian, this ambidexter interpreter of our laws give, when I tell him the proclamation is published without the sanction of the Great Seal." The proclamation had not, in fact, passed the Great Seal until Monday, 11 March, two days after its publication. The writer of these letters was concerned exclusively with the case as it affected Thompson; John Wheble was never mentioned in them. It would be absurd to believe that they were the work, simply, of a public-spirited citizen.

Other heartening considerations were at hand. Only a few months before, Henry Sampson Woodfall had been effectually rescued from the consequences of Mansfield's interpretation of the libel law by a jury of his countrymen. The memory of *North Briton* Number 45 and its aftermath was undoubtedly prominent in the public mind at a time when John Wilkes, the elected member for Middlesex, was still prohibited from taking his seat in the House. From a practical point of view there was the effect on circulation to be considered. It is difficult to conceive of any form of publicity that would have served better to increase the sale of a newspaper than the proscription of its printer in a royal proclamation. It had become the declared duty of every "loving subject" in the realm to interest himself in the activities of Roger Thompson, and by far the most salient of those activities was the publication every morning of the *Gazetteer*. Moreover, Wheble and Thompson did not stand alone. The London newspaper press was presenting a united front, and reports of Parliamentary proceedings continued to appear in nearly all the papers. In making their stand against the privilege of Parliament, the printers were attempting to gain a right that would make them better able to serve their readers, and such a motive could not have failed to enlist public sympathy. Edmund Burke had, in effect, pointed this out to the House of Commons.

On Tuesday, 11 March, Colonel Onslow brought to the attention of the House "three brace" more of culpable printers.[13] The opposition could not defeat his motion for proceeding against them, but it did succeed in protracting the debate until four in the morning, and in forcing no less than twenty-three divisions. Two days later four of the printers attended and made their submission to the House. Richard Whitworth, who seems to have had a considerable acquaintance among the printers, reported that a fifth, William Woodfall of the *Morning Chronicle*, had wished to appear out of respect for the order of the House, but had found himself unable to do so because of a previous commitment; for a similar offense he had been detained at Newgate by order of the House of Lords. Henry Baldwin, printer of the *St. James's Chronicle*, explained to the House that he had been compelled to copy the debates into his paper because his readers had complained of the omission. A member of the House had himself told Baldwin that several of his friends had discontinued taking the paper because the debates did not appear in it; and, said Baldwin, "many other instances of like kind might be produced, to prove the necessity the Printer was under to give the Debates, or materially injure the Paper."[14]

On Wednesday, 13 March, Robert Morris, an attorney who acted as Wilkes's contact with a number of the printers, called upon both Wheble and Thompson and was favorably impressed by the attitude of the *Gazetteer*'s young printer. "I saw Wheble and Thompson this day," he wrote to Wilkes. "The direct opposites of each other in patience; & the hasty one is the former. I gave your message to the latter. He thanks you, as he has much reason, for your alacrity to serve him. . . ." [15] And on the day of Morris' call, Thompson himself wrote to Wilkes:

R. Thompson presents his most respectful Compliments to Mr. Wilkes, and, agreeable to his desire, informs him, that not the least Objection is at present seen to the adoption of the plan proposed.

Newgate Street,
March 13, 1771.[16]

Meanwhile the proclaimed printers remained at large. On Thursday, 14 March, John Wheble sent notice to the Speaker, Sir Fletcher Norton, that he had laid his case before counsel (Robert Morris) and would yield no obedience but to the laws of the land. He enclosed a copy of Morris' opinion, which held the proclamation illegal, and advised Wheble to institute proceedings against "the Counsellors, Promoters, Aiders, Abettors, and Publishers thereof." [17] Thompson maintained silence, except for an occasional indirect reference to the affair in the *Gazetteer*. On Friday morning, 15 March, readers of the paper were assured "from good authority," that at a general meeting of the Justices of the Peace in the County of Hertford, "it was unanimously agreed not to *secure* either of the two printers described and proscribed in a late Proclamation, should they, or either of them, be brought before any of the Justices of that County. . . ." On the afternoon of the same day matters reached a climax.

At 12:20 P.M. Edward Twine Carpenter, himself a printer, carried John Wheble before the "sitting Alderman" at the Guildhall, who at the time happened to be John Wilkes. Carpenter was promptly asked (somewhat unnecessarily, one imagines) whether he was a constable or peace officer, and whether Wheble was guilty or suspected of any felony, or charged by Carpenter with any crime, all of which he was compelled to answer negatively. By what authority had he brought Wheble before the Alderman? By the authority of the proclamation. Wilkes then proceeded to address Carpenter, according to the report published in the next morning's *Gazetteer*, as follows: "As you are not a peace officer, nor constable, and you accuse not the party of any crime, I know not what right you have to take his person; it is contrary to the chartered rights of this city, and of Englishmen." Wheble requested to be heard, and began to protest the unconstitutional nature of the affair from beginning to end. The Alderman, interrupting, declared that he had nothing to do with such matters, and asked whether Wheble "accused Carpenter of any thing." Wheble picked up the cue with alacrity. He charged Carpenter with assault and breaking the peace. Wilkes could not bind over the captor on the second charge, since Wheble had not been in fear of his life, but the charge of assault seemed valid enough. "You," Wilkes said to Carpenter, "have no authority for making this arrest, contrary to the rights of Englishmen and Citizens; therefore I do release Mr. Wheble, and shall commit you, unless you can find bail to answer for your behavior at the next sessions." Bail was immediately forthcoming from "Mr. Kearsley and Mr. Smith," both London booksellers, who seem to have been present in anticipation of just such an exigency. Kearsley, indeed, had earlier been prosecuted with Wilkes in the matter of *North Briton* No. 45. After the necessary arrangements had been made, Carpenter asked about claiming the reward promised in the proclamation. A certificate was made out, designed to satisfy the Treasury that Carpenter had complied with the requirements of the proclamation. The *Gazetteer* reported later that "Mr. Carpenter, as soon as the certificate was signed, took coach to the Treasury, to demand the reward promised," but that he had been there put off, and "desired to attend on Tuesday next." Surviving Treasury records for the period do not reveal that Carpenter's services were ever rewarded.[18]

The arrest of Wheble raised the curtain on a sort of comedy which was to be played out at intervals during the day. About two hours after Twine Carpenter had gone to seek his reward from the Treasury, a messenger of the House of Commons, acting on a warrant from the Speaker, attempted to take custody of John Miller, printer of the *London Evening Post,* who had failed to appear before the House on the day before. Miller was well prepared to receive the messenger, having previously taken counsel with Wilkes and John Almon[19] in anticipation of his visit, and the messenger was immediately given into the custody of a constable who was obligingly near at hand. Miller charged that the messenger had assaulted him, and the company proceeded to the Mansion House, where the Lord Mayor, Brass Crosby, appointed the hearing of the case for six o'clock that evening.[20] The interval seems to have been calculated to allow for a marshaling of forces on both sides. At six the Lord Mayor was flanked by Aldermen Wilkes and Oliver, while the House of Commons was represented

by a deputy Serjeant at Arms. "The Attorney General, as Coun-
sellor *behind the scenes*, Mr. Francis, Deputy Solicitor of the
Treasury, and several Members of Parliament," were, according
to the *Gazetteer*, "also at the Mansion House on Friday evening." [21]
Miller was discharged by the Lord Mayor as having been illegally
seized without a warrant signed by a City Magistrate, and three
witnesses testified to assault by the messenger. The deputy Serjeant
at Arms refused to offer bail, or to allow anyone else to do so,
until he had seen the warrant for the messenger's arrest signed by
the magistrates. But having been satisfied of their earnestness, he
supplied bail and adjourned with the messenger to make his report.[22]

If the episode involving Wheble may be viewed as a prologue,
the part taken by Roger Thompson in the events of the day made
a fitting epilogue. About an hour after Miller's case came before
the magistrates, Thompson was arrested, and the routine established by Wilkes at noon was repeated yet again, though with
several minor variations. The *Gazetteer* for Saturday, 16 March,
gave this account of it:

Last night, about seven o'clock, R. Thompson, printer of this paper, was
apprehended at his own door, in Newgate-street, and carried before
Mr. Alderman Oliver, at the Mansion-house, as being the person described in his Majesty's proclamation; but not being accused of having
committed any crime, he was discharged and set at liberty. The man who
had apprehended him then desired a certificate of his having acted in
pursuance of the proclamation, in order to obtain the reward of fifty
pounds; which was immediately granted him.

The restraint and brevity with which the report was presented
seems to indicate a realization on Thompson's part that he could
expect to gain little credit by pulling the tail of a dragon that
others had already slain. Several features of the report, however,
deserve consideration. In defying on three successive occasions both
a royal proclamation and a Speaker's warrant, nothing was to be
gained by spacing the acts of defiance over a long period of time,
and there was a risk that the powers defied, if given the opportunity, might have found a way to forestall such acts after the
first one. There was, in fact, an advantage to be gained from carrying the thing off quickly, and with something of a flourish. None
would have realized this more fully than John Wilkes and his co-
operative defenders of "the liberties of Englishmen." The "cap-

tures" and appearances of Wheble and Thompson on the same day that Wilkes, Almon, and John Miller sprang their trap on the House of Commons messenger were obviously the results of something more than coincidental diligence by two reward seekers. Thompson had undoubtedly had immediate intelligence of the magistrates' treatment of Wheble and Miller. Indeed, the participants in the Miller episode cannot have been long departed from the Mansion House before Thompson arrived there with his captor. It is probable that Thompson had been instructed as to when he should appear, and that he knew exactly what would be the result of his appearances.

The second interesting feature about the *Gazetteer* report is that Thompson's captor is unnamed. Whoever wrote the paragraph for the *Gazetteer* could hardly have been ignorant of the name while the paper carried the name of Wheble's captor and even that of Mr. Towns, the constable who had arrested the House messenger. Finally, unlike Miller and Wheble, Thompson did not file a charge against "the man who apprehended him." With these features in mind, the admonition of Sir Joseph Mawbey to the Commons seems especially pointed. If the present course were pursued, Mawbey had said, all the printers in London would be printing and passing out debates, and their wives would be turning them in for £50 each. "If only a hundred printers are so employed," he had reminded them, "the rewards to be offered for their apprehension will amount to £5,000." The Treasury accounts record no application for a reward by Thompson's captor, but there can be little doubt that the printer was apprehended by a friend; not improbably by one of his own men; possibly by John Cooke, whose loyalty to his master was to be shown rather dramatically a year later.

The restraint with which Saturday's *Gazetteer* treated the successful if anticlimactic outcome of Thompson's visit to the Mansion House was displaced during the following week by a growing boldness in which the printer's hand is clearly apparent. There was no scurrility in the new tone; it was a boldness tempered by discretion. For the most part, it took the form of lengthy encomiums on the City officials who had opposed Parliamentary tyranny, but the temptation to an occasional thrust at their opponents was not entirely to be resisted.

On Monday, 18 March, Thompson headed a column of matter bearing upon the events of the preceding Friday with a letter set in leaded type. It was addressed to "RICHARD OLIVER, *Esq;*

ALDERMAN *of* BILLINGSGATE WARD, *and* REPRESENTATIVE *in* PARLIAMENT *for the* CITY *of* LONDON":

SIR,

WHEN a Magistrate of the City of London faithfully discharges the duties of his high office, he merits *at all times* the thanks and approbation of his fellow citizens; but in a singular manner is he entitled to those thanks *in these days,* when an upright discharge of his duty might expose his life, his person, or his fortune to all the malice, rancour, and rage, of the enemies of our laws and constitution. What an exalted notion, Sir, must the city then entertain of your justice, firmness, and intrepidity, in nobly daring, even at your own peril and imminent danger, to set at liberty a *captive* Freeman and Citizen of London, who had committed no other crime against Government, but that of *not* betraying the *chartered* rights and free customs of his native city, and which he must have betrayed, as much as in him lay, had he implicitly obeyed either the arbitrary mandate of Sir Fletcher Norton, or that other equally despotic command illegally issued against him, *by* and *with* the advice of his Majesty's Privy Council. If the Citizens of London *in general,* Sir, gratefully extoll and admire the dignity and uprightness of your conduct on this trying, this critical occasion, how much greater must *my* debt of gratitude be, seeing I am the identical Citizen, who owes *perhaps* his life (for confinement in a loathsome dungeon might have occasioned the loss of it) *certainly,* what is still more valuable than life to an Englishman, his LIBERTY, to your unshaken virtue and exemplary patriotism? The voluntary effusions of my heart, and the fear of offending where I would wish most to please, permit me only to assure you, the deep sense of the obligation shall forever remain indelibly impressed on the memory of, Sir,

Your most obedient,
Most devoted,
And most humble Servant,
R. THOMPSON.

This was followed by several paragraphs extolling the heroic actions of the Lord Mayor and aldermen, whose memories would "be ever revered by the Citizens of London for the spirit they have shewn in defending their rights and privileges," and it was hoped that a Common-Hall of the City Livery might be called to return thanks to the three magistrates for their "spirited, manly, and constitutional conduct." The "noble intrepidity" with which Towns, the constable, had taken charge of the House messenger was not overlooked; it likewise deserved the gratitude of every citizen.

And the entire episode was considered "of as much consequence as the late affair of general warrants." Finally, having distributed his praise with such profusion, Thompson could not ignore the side which had been vanquished. "We hear," the column continued, "that the present O—— family intend to apply for an Act of Parliament for leave to change their names, since some recent transactions." Two further columns on page 4 gave a detailed account of the Commons' proceedings on the previous Thursday against three of the six printers who had been ordered to appear, and reprinted the Speaker's warrant for apprehending John Miller, together with a letter from Wilkes to the Earl of Halifax explaining his refusal to hold Wheble on the authority of the proclamation.

On the following day (Tuesday, 19 March) news was sparse. Monday the House had debated the City Magistrates' actions, but the report of this debate was not ready by press time and had to be postponed until Wednesday morning. The issue was kept alive, however, by a lengthy letter from "Vigilator" addressed to the two Onslows "On the advantages and propriety of publishing SPEECHES made in PARLIAMENT." Thompson allowed himself another thrust at the ministry in an "ADVERTISEMENT EXTRAORDINARY": "Dropt out of the LONDON GAZETTE, No. 11,126, last Saturday evening, about six o'clock, A PROCLAMATION. —If any LOVING subject has found it, and will *dare* (AT HIS PERIL) to carry it to the Mansion-house, he will be rewarded with a *genteel* and *wholesome* apartment in Newgate for his trouble."

Wednesday's *Gazetteer* carried an account of Monday's debate, and of the Lord Mayor's triumphal procession, Tuesday, from the Mansion House to Westminster in compliance with a summons from the House of Commons. There were reports, too, that Evans, the publisher of the *London Packet*, had stated his intention to ignore an order for his appearance in the House, since the City Magistrates had declared such orders illegal, and that Mr. Alderman Sawbridge had resolved to follow the precedent set in the Miller case, should Evans be brought before him on a Speaker's warrant. The matter had now become a jurisdictional dispute between the House and the City of London. The *Gazetteer* and other papers continued to devote much space to it, but the issue of publishing debates was almost obscured by the larger question.

Early in the following week, the Lord Mayor and Alderman Oliver, who, in the House, had outspokenly defended their actions, were ordered committed to the Tower. There, they were to hold court for their friends until Parliament was prorogued in May, and they were released to the roar of a twenty-one cannon salute, and conveyed to the Mansion House in a state coach, escorted by fifty-three carriages. When Parliament convened again in July, the ministry made no attempt to reopen the issue. It was probably just as well, for Wilkes and his group would have liked nothing better. By January 1772, they were preparing another campaign, this time against the House of Lords. The victim was to be one of the Lords Pomfret, Denbigh, or Talbot. "Are there more furious wild beasts to be found in the upper den than the three I have named," Wilkes asked in a letter to Junius. And Charles Say's son-in-law, qualified both by temperament and experience, was selected for bait. "Miller, the printer of the *London Evening Post* . . . is the best man I know for this business," Wilkes continued. "He will print whatever is sent him. He is a fine Oliverian soldier." [23]

From this period John Almon wrote some two decades later, "the debates in both houses have been regularly printed, with more or less accuracy, according to the ability of the writers, in every diurnal publication of the metropolis." [24] An important concession had been tacitly made by Parliament, and a significant milestone in the history of English journalism had been passed. The name of Wilkes shone forth with new lustre as the champion of freedom of the press.

The role of the *Gazetteer* in the events of March 1771 must not be overestimated. The dispute involved a principle of which Wilkes and his adherents could make capital. Thompson and the proprietors of the *Gazetteer*, however, were perhaps more deeply concerned with circulation and dividends than with "Wilkes and Liberty," and the public had shown a distinct preference for newspapers which reported the debates in Parliament. The *Gazetteer* was distinguished by being one of the first papers chosen for prosecution by the House of Commons, and its printer by being one of the first to resist. Thompson achieved further distinction by being officially proclaimed as a fugitive. He allowed himself to be used by the City democrats to try a point with the government, but by no stretch of the imagination can he be made into a martyr or a hero. It is, however, undeniable, that he was a shrewd and able managing editor. Resistance to the proclamation and co-operation with the Patriots were certain to improve the sale of the *Gazetteer* by virtue of the publicity gained and the right to publish debates which stood to be won. Charles Say seems to have nominally relinquished his business to Thompson because he wished to avoid the discomforts of such crises. Thompson, eager to improve the business, felt that the risk involved was worth while. That the paper gained by the part he played in the affair is certain. It continued to gain throughout the tenure of his management.

VII

NO. 3. NEWGATE STREET

April 1771-April 1772

THOUGH they were the most important, the Parliamentary debates were not the only new feature of the *Gazetteer* under Roger Thompson's management. In general the paper during 1771 became more of a miscellany than it had been during the decade of the sixties. The department of observations from correspondents was discontinued, and in its place appeared only an occasional note acknowledging the receipt of a letter, giving notice of a rejection, or apologizing for a postponement. But readers to whom the observations had appealed were not forgotten. Instead of the two or three lengthy political essays which had normally been included each day, there appeared shorter but more numerous letters to the printer. While politics remained the staple of content, space was allotted to include a greater variety of subject matter than ever before, and special attention was given to the selection of interesting articles from the other papers. The larger format adopted in 1765, Thompson reminded readers, enabled the *Gazetteer* "to comprise much more in quantity than any other daily paper can," and allowed for the inclusion of "whatever may be thought essential in *the other papers*, either . . . literary articles, or paragraphs of intelligence: whereby we have long endeavoured to gratify the curiosity of those readers, who, confining themselves to the perusal of a single News-paper, wish to be acquainted with every thing that appears in the rest." [1]

Of original, nonpolitical matter two series of letters were outstandingly popular. The first was the ostensible production of a

"fair correspondent" who styled herself "Hortensia." It consisted
of essays on manners and morals obviously designed to appeal to
feminine readers, and eschewing the fictionalized problem situa-
tions propounded by the occasional "female correspondent" of
"Mr. Spectator" and the "Rambler." Hortensia was sometimes
assigned the most prominent position of page 1, a position previously devoted almost exclusively to political topics. There, for
example, appeared "Hortensia, to her country friend," a graceful
dissertation on the lack of shame, fear, and modesty in contemporary womanhood, with appropriate quotations from Halifax's
Advice to a Daughter.[2] With this opinion a "Camilla," steeped in
Pope's *Moral Essays*, mildly took issue, blaming men for the faults
attributed to women, of whom she thought Hortensia expected too
much, considering the treatment they received from their husbands.
But a great majority of the replies which the letters evoked expressed only admiration for their author, praising her nobility and
virtue, and often proposing special topics for her future essays. "I
find, Madam," wrote a gallant admirer, "it is as much the fashion
to pay respects to you, as to visit Tunbridge Wells . . . . Junius
has not more admirers. As he remains unrivalled in politics, so do
you in ethics . . . . It is to you, and your indefatigable labours,
we men hope to be indebted for prudent, for sensible, for affectionate wives . . . ."[3]

Even more popular than "Hortensia" was the "Attorney General
to the Gazetteer," who first appeared in the paper in the autumn
of 1771. The writer, a person learned in the law, dispensed free
legal advice through the columns of the paper to readers who applied for it. This kind of feature, a commonplace of twentieth-
century journalism, had originated in the question-and-answer departments of such early periodicals as John Dunton's *Athenian
Mercury*; its occurrence in the daily newspapers of the eighteenth
century was, however, rare, and its popularity in the *Gazetteer* of
1771 was immediate. The Attorney General began by treating in
some detail each case submitted, citing precedents and expounding
statutes; but the volume of requests soon made detailed replies
impossible, and the method was adopted of treating half a dozen
cases of the widest interest at one time, each in a single paragraph.
There were frequent recommendations, where the problems stated
were unusually complex and apparently genuine, that the readers
submitting them should consult a solicitor. Most often, the cases
submitted were couched in hypothetical terms involving "A" and
"B," and many of them concerned wills and contracts. Occasionally,

however, there were more abstruse matters, as when a group of twenty-five law students requested an interpretation of a term from a statute of Edward I "promulgated in the Norman-french tongue," and received an impressive etymology of the term beginning with the code of Athelstan. By late September the printer was compelled to request the "*Law Querists* . . . not to send any fresh queries to the *Attorney-General,* until those . . . already come to hand shall be Answered . . . ." [4]

> *R. Thompson* informs the Law Querists, that he has almost a hundred different cases upon his table for the *Attorney-General,* to each of which an immediate answer is requested; but that néither the Attorney-General has leisure upon his hands to give opinion upon more than two or three cases *per diem,* nor can he crowd his paper with too much matter of one kind only. The infinitely numerous readers of the GAZETTEER expect to be daily entertained with a variety of literary amusements, as well as a few individuals expect to be gratified in their personal requests. For this reason the *Few* must in some measure give way to the *Many.* However the Querists may be assured, that cases, the answers to which will convey information any way serviceable to the Public, shall in convenient time be noticed; but the general plan and extensive utility of this paper must always be primarily considered by the Printer.[5]

Thompson did consider the utility of the paper, and sought earnestly to improve it. Early in October he announced that he had "settled a correspondence with certain Gentlemen at *Paris,* the *Hague,* and other parts of the Continent; by which means he will in future be enabled frequently to lay before his readers earlier *Foreign Intelligence,* than can be received by the usual channel, the foreign prints." [6] Thereafter sources of foreign news were classified as the "mails," or as extracts of letters "from our correspondent."

Politically, there can be no doubt that the *Gazetteer* of 1771, especially after the contest with Parliament, favored the opposition. The allegiance is in no way remarkable, for the newspaper press of this period, unsubsidized by government, was by nature an instrument of criticism, and, as Professor Laprade has observed, "there was never an opposition in the century but advocated its freedom." [7] Nevertheless, the strength of the *Gazetteer*'s Whig inclination could be measured, if at all, only by statistical methods— that is, by a comparison of the column lineage occupied by pro-ministerial and anti-ministerial essays. For the paper's editorial voice, when it was heard, declared itself to be impartial, and care

was taken that all expression of partisan sentiment should be confined to letters from ostensible correspondents. An accusation of
bias, based apparently on memories of the Walpole era, was re-
pudiated by Thompson as "both mistaken and unjust." "We are
gratefully sensible from the favours of different correspondents,"
he declared, "that men of worth, probity and sense, are to be found
in every party." [8] More than a decade was to elapse before the paper openly declared an attachment to any party.

Political essays of the early 1770's represented no perceptible
departure in form or style from those of the preceding decade.
The printer still insisted, for his own safety and in deference to
readers, upon a moderation of tone, and anonymity was carefully
maintained. One of his occasional correspondents at this period was
probably Richard Whitworth, who had recognized Thompson in
the lobby of the House of Commons and had subsequently spoken
in his defense.[9] Whitworth was identified by Junius in 1769 as
the "Veridicus" of the *Public Advertiser*,[10] and in May 1771
Thompson was restricting the use of that pseudonym in the *Gazetteer* to a favored correspondent: "We have taken the liberty to
alter our correspondent's signature [to "Veritas"], that of VERI-
DICUS having been adopted by a Gentleman, who sometimes
honours this paper with his productions." [11]

Letters to the King, inspired by the Junius prototype, became
a fashionable form for political essays. The conditions surrounding
publication of one such letter illustrate a significant *Gazetteer*
policy. In the *Public Advertiser* of Saturday, 3 August 1771, the
leading essay was Part I of a letter to the King by "Brunswick."
The *Gazetteer* reprinted this on the Friday following, and on the
next day, Saturday, 10 August, a letter from the author appeared
on page 1 of the *Gazetteer:* "The Author of 'BRUNSWICK' presents his compliments to R. Thompson—having come to a resolution of henceforward sending his sentiments always to the *Gazetteer*, he now encloses him the Second Part of the letter from
BRUNSWICK to the 'KING'—which the Author begs may be
inserted immediately." The letter was obviously the production
of someone whom both printers considered a valuable correspondent, for Thompson published it immediately, as requested. In
acquiring it he had profited by Woodfall's loss, but in an editorial
note he apologized for having omitted a part of the author's cover-
ing letter, "as it seemed to convey a reflection on the conduct of the
Printer of another daily paper." This consideration for competitors

was a basic *Gazetteer* policy, several times reiterated,[12] and it appears to have been reciprocal.

Typographically, so far as may be judged from a single file of the paper, the *Gazetteer* printed by Thompson displayed a marked improvement. Throughout 1771 notices of errata in preceding issues were less frequent than before, the inking was more consistently even, and the presswork in general, hurried though it must have been, appears to have been more carefully executed than in the years immediately preceding. Perhaps steps had been taken to guard against the delays at the Stamp Office which prevented a proper wetting of the paper. In September 1771 the purchase of new type was heralded by this announcement: "R. Thompson informs the readers of the GAZETTEER, that Mr. *Caslon* has finished a new set of types for this paper, and that the *Essays* and *News* will be printed on it on Monday next [16 September 1771]." [13]

The abilities of Roger Thompson as a manager and editor were rated highly by a number of the men best qualified to judge them. William Brinkworth, a printer who had worked under both Say and Thompson, testified in 1774 that, in his judgment, Thompson conducted and managed the *Gazetteer* in "a more regular and methodical manner than ever . . . [he] had known . . . [it] managed before," [14] and Thomas Ferebee, who was completing his apprenticeship in 1771, was of the same opinion. "It was the common talk of the printing house," Ferebee declared, "that the proprietors of the . . . Gazetteer were mightily satisfied with . . . [Thompson's] management of that paper." [15] There was just cause for their satisfaction. In September 1771 Thompson claimed for the *Gazetteer* a sale of "above FIVE THOUSAND daily (a number much superior to that of any other morning paper printed in London)," [16] and there is good reason for allowing full credit to the claim. Joseph Dunball and Samuel Turlington, two more of the printers employed on the paper, testified to an increased sale during the period of Thompson's management, though "in what proportion . . . or how many more" were printed, they were unable to say,[17] and John Cooke, the clerk, heard "the person who distributed the . . . Gazetteer to the hawkers say that the . . . paper had increased . . . ." [18]

Publication at an early hour of the morning was throughout the century one of the factors most directly influencing the circulation of a daily newspaper, and it gave rise to a dilemma; for as the circulation, and consequently the period of working off, increased, the difficulty of maintaining an early publication time became more acute. The hour at which a paper went to press was partially determined by a desire to include the latest news possible, but the most definite limitation was imposed by the necessity of publishing daily playbills, which could not be obtained from the theatres until late in the evening.[19] The *Gazetteer*'s difficulty in this respect had undoubtedly been increasing for a number of years, and throughout 1770–71 Thompson had put forth his best efforts to cope with it. Richard Birtles, a compositor who admired Thompson's "care skill and assiduity" and considered his management "the most indefatigable . . . that he . . . ever saw either in town or country," believed that the *Gazetteer*'s circulation increase "was in a great measure owing to . . . [Thompson's] judicious choice of the paragraphs and essays inserted in the . . . paper and the regard he had to the truth of the paragraphs inserted . . . and to the great care and pains he took that it might be published early before the other news papers." "So particularly careful" was Thompson "that it should be published early," Birtles said, "that if he found the business behind hand he would himself assist to get it forward . . . ." It was reported, and Birtles believed truly, that under Thompson's management there were more copies of the *Gazetteer* printed daily "than of any other news paper whatever." [20]

Perhaps the most eloquent testimony to the paper's increased circulation was that of Thompson himself, in the *Gazetteer* of 28 December 1771:

The superior demand for the paper having, for several years, rendered it almost impracticable to supply the requisite number, at an hour sufficiently early in the morning, whereby our readers have been liable to the disappointment of receiving from the News-carriers other Papers instead of the GAZETTEER; it becomes necessary to give this public information, That proper measures, attended with a very great deal and constant expence, are now taken, in order effectually to prevent any such disappointment for the future; and that on *Monday* next THIS PAPER will be published at *Six* in the morning, and will continue to be so published regularly and without intermission.

Four days later the columns of formal intelligence were transferred from the second to the fourth page, and readers were informed that "the London News will in future be inserted in the Last Page . . . that we may not be obliged to omit, by reason of the very great Number printed of this Paper, any Intelligence which may be interesting to the Public." [21]

Thompson's "proper measures" were the setting of the *Gazetteer*'s outer forme in duplicate, and the "constant expence" consisted, at least in part, of £7 13s. per week paid to the compositors who set the extra forme.[22] Thomas Ferebee the apprentice said that "there were so many more of the . . . [*Gazetteer*] printed . . . that they were obliged to employ an additional number of compositors as well as press men about the . . . paper in order to get it published in time[,] and for that purpose the first and last pages . . . were set twice over so as to enable two presses to work on them at the same time . . . ." Duplicate composing, Ferebee added, had never been done before "during . . . [his] knowledge of the . . . paper or that he . . . ever heard of." [23] I am aware of no evidence that the procedure had been employed by any daily paper prior to this time.

Although sales of the paper had undoubtedly benefited from the dispute with Parliament, much credit for the increase must be given to Thompson's talents as editor and manager. During the first three months after duplicate setting was inaugurated, the number of *Gazetteers* printed averaged 5,300 daily [24]—a number which, even with one forme duplicated, would have required at least eleven hours in working off.[25] The figure was apparently never again attained by the *Gazetteer*. It is of interest, however, that more than two decades later *The Times* stated its own circulation as "near 4000 daily, a number which was never before attained by any Morning Paper under any circumstances," and in the following year (1794) began "printing the Paper at three Presses instead of two." [26]

Acknowledgment of Thompson's abilities was not confined to the men who worked under him. Late in 1771 Dryden Leach, a printer, and William Palmer Davis, a bookseller, two of the principal proprietors of the *Middlesex Journal*, had apparently become dissatisfied with the performance of John Wheble as printer of their paper. Considering Roger Thompson as a "proper person to be the printer and publisher thereof," and that such a position would not be incompatible with his printing of the *Gazetteer*, Leach proposed to him, about November, that he become printer of the *Middlesex Journal*, and assured him that he might expect a profit from the arrangement of £100 to £150 per year. Thompson, after taking some time to consider the offer, was compelled to refuse it, because, he said, he was under exclusive contract to Say, and "could not be concerned in any other news paper." [27]

If Thompson's successful management of the *Gazetteer* in 1771 is itself impressive, it appears even more so in view of the conditions under which it was carried out. The contract which compelled him to refuse the *Middlesex Journal* offer was entered into less than a month after his difficulties with the House of Commons, and it may have been a direct result of his success.

On 2 April 1771 there was executed a memorandum of agreement whereby Say and Thompson stated their intention of entering into a formal contract as soon as Say's contract with the *Gazetteer* proprietors should be renewed, or at the expiration of six months, whichever should occur sooner. The terms of the memorandum were those of the unwritten agreement which had been in force for more than a year. Thompson assumed full legal liability for whatever he published. In return he was to have an eighth of the profits from printing the *Gazetteer*, an eighth interest in the property of the *Craftsman*, and was automatically to become manager and printer, on the same terms, of any other paper in which Say might eventually acquire interest.[28] Say promised not to discharge Thompson from his position as manager and publisher of any paper without the latter's written consent, or without just cause, to be ascertained by arbitration. Thompson, for his part, promised to be "faithful diligent and just in the discharge of his duty," and not to become concerned "directly or indirectly" in any other newspaper. A mutual penalty of £500 was imposed "for the true performance of the . . . covenant intended," and the memorandum was duly signed and witnessed.[29] Those portions of the agreement which related to the projected marriage alliance and to Thompson's future receipt of full profits from printing the *Gazetteer* remained, perhaps from a sense of delicacy, unwritten, but they were mutually understood.

Precisely when Charles Say became dissatisfied with the agreement he had made is unknown. Probably it was not before October, six months after the April memorandum, when the obligation to execute a formal assignment to Thompson became due. Say's dissatisfaction, first expressed, it appears, to James Dixwell, printer, stationer, and receiver of advertisements for the *Gazetteer*, arose neither from Thompson's management nor from the terms of the April memorandum. Rather it sprang from what he felt to be his own ill-considered generosity in having promised that as a marriage portion for his daughter he would assign to Thompson the entire profit from printing the *Gazetteer*.

When Say made known the change in his sentiments, he "did not make the least objection to any part of . . . [Thompson's] conduct but spoke of him with the utmost respect . . . ." Thompson, he told Dixwell, was to marry his daughter, and Say had "promised him . . . the printing of the *Gazetteer*." Now, however, Say "thought that too much," feeling that "by his . . . promise he should give too much away from his other children"; he expressed himself "desirous of retracting" the promise. Dixwell was to convey, at Say's request, an alternative proposition to Thompson, whereby Say offered to "allow him a fourth part of the profit of printing the . . . paper" and to "give the girl one hundred pounds to buy her cloaths." If Thompson accepted the offer, Say promised to call a meeting of the *Gazetteer* proprietors, and to settle the matter at once.[30]

Thompson's reaction to the offer was hardly surprising. According to Dixwell, the young printer "rejected the same and was greatly affected at hearing the . . . proposal as not expecting any such thing." The immediate result, we may suppose, was a cooling of the friendship between the two printers, and the breach must soon have become serious. After Thompson had rejected the new offer, he said, Say "took occasion to quarrel" with him, and "without any reason whatever directed his . . . daughter not to see . . . [Thompson]." Thereafter, exercising the prerogative of a father, Say sent his daughter "into the country to avoid . . . [Thompson] and . . . refused to consent to her intermarriage with . . . [him] or to assign any reason whatever for . . . his refusal . . . ." [31]

Charles Say, whatever his motives, had carefully burned every legal bridge when he made Thompson nominal printer of the *Gazetteer*. The manner in which he went about attempting to rebuild one of them is highly interesting. William Carter, a silversmith who knew Thompson only by sight but had been a neighbor of Say "for many years," was in 1771 a churchwarden of Christ Church, Newgate. During that year and certainly after the rift between Say and Thompson had occurred, Say informed Carter that he "had given . . . [Thompson] a part of his business and that . . . [Thompson] now wanted to oust him and wanted it all . . . ." In order to frustrate Thompson's alleged design, Say asked Carter "to erase . . . Roger Thompson's name out of the parish books" as occupant of the Newgate Street house, and to reinsert Say's own name. When Carter explained that the books in question were in the possession of the parish overseers, Say asked him to "speak to the overseers for that purpose and told . . . [Carter] that if he and the overseers would do it he [Say]

would meet them in any tavern and give them a genteel supper . . . ." Carter declined, advising Say to apply to the Vestry
which was soon to meet. Say, however, preferred more direct
methods, and Thompson's name remained in the parish books.[32]

By December 1771 relations between the two printers were
openly hostile; Say, according to Thompson, had become determined "at all events" to regain possession of the Newgate Street
premises, and Thompson, it appears, was equally determined that
the original agreement should be adhered to. He had, he said,
made frequent applications to Say, asking if the contract with the
Gazetteer proprietors had been renewed, and requesting the formal
assignment of the shares agreed upon.[33]

On Monday, 9 December, Charles Say ordered Edward Benson,
once more, to alter the *Gazetteer* imprint. Thompson's name was
to be omitted and that of Benson was to appear in its place,[34] the
change to be carried out without Thompson's knowledge. On the
following morning (Tuesday, 10 December) the paper appeared
as printed for Edward Benson, and on that day matters reached a
climax. By coincidence or as a result of the changed imprint, a
meeting of the *Gazetteer* proprietors was held in the evening at
the King's Head tavern in Holborn. John Cooke, the clerk, attended on behalf of Thompson, apparently to protest the substitution of Benson's name in the imprint.[35] Charles Say was not present; he was engaged in more absorbing matters.

From early in the day, Roger Thompson had been apprehensive
that Say would "cause some disturbance" at the house in Newgate
Street in an effort to evict him from the premises. Whether the
fear was founded on positive information, or was simply a reaction
to the surprising imprint borne by the *Gazetteer* of that morning is
not known, but it was a feeling genuine enough that Thompson
confided it to two of his friends, Charles Surmont, a jeweler, and
John Russel, a goldworker. He asked both of them to come to the
printing house "on his behalf," and they did. Throughout the
evening they remained in the first-floor dining room while their
host was engaged, presumably, in preparing the next morning's
issue of the *Gazetteer*.[36]

Say, his wife, his son-in-law John Miller, and a group of workmen from the printing office in Ave Maria Lane arrived at Newgate Street early in the evening and established themselves in the
kitchen, also on the first floor. There, according to Mary Morris,
Thompson's housekeeper, the group "were entertained with bread
and cheese and strong beer and other liquor," and "some of the

. . . people smoaked their pipes." Say, in the course of the festivities, sent upstairs for some of the *Gazetteer* workmen, among whom
was George Abraham. He complained to them of Thompson's
faithlessness, asked them to stand by him, and invited at least one
of them to drink with him.[37] Sometime during the evening Say and
North, the chief *Gazetteer* clerk, went into the dining room, where
Say informed Thompson's friends Russel and Surmont that the
house belonged to him, not to Thompson, and asked them to
leave. They refused.[38]

How long the gathering in the kitchen continued to imbibe
resolution is uncertain, but Mary Morris stated that "about nine
or ten o'clock at night or sometime thereabouts the people who
were in the kitchen went down stairs," and she "heard a great
noise."

More specifically (according to George Abraham the apprentice), John Miller, the clerk North, Abraham himself, and "three
or four more went down to the counting house." There, after "some
dispute" between Thompson and Miller, "Miller gave the word
for them to push . . . [Thompson] out which they accordingly
did . . . ." But their success was a fleeting one. North, "one of
the persons who assisted in pushing him out," became incon-
veniently "jambed between the door and the post," and Say's
partisans "were obliged to open the door to let him loose."
Thompson, seizing the opportunity, "rush'd in and ran into the
counting house." Abraham followed him, whereupon Thompson
"took up a knife and told . . . [Abraham] he did not want to
hurt him, but he must stand in his own defence . . . ." [39]

Of the sounds of contention that alarmed the house, by far
the most nerve-shattering was "a cry of murder" uttered by
Thompson and clearly heard by the people upstairs. Mrs. Say,
who, Mary Morris said, was "either in the kitchen . . . or at the
top of the stairs" was "greatly alarmed at hearing the . . . cry of
murder and was in a great fright lest Mr. Say should be hurt." [40]

She need not have worried. Say at the time was in the dining
room with the door closed. Russel and Surmont, who had remained
there, heard the cry and tried to go to Thompson's assistance,
but Say "kept the door in his hand to prevent . . . [them] from
going out of the room . . . ." "Oh tis nothing nothing nothing,"
he assured them, "or expressed himself to that effect." [41]

For the remaining events of the night no clear chronology
emerges. Apparently Say went downstairs and attempted to give
Thompson into the custody of a constable, but without success.

The constable refused the charge.[42] Soon after, Thompson joined Russel and Surmont in the dining room. They found him "in a great confusion and found by his appearance that he had been greatly pull'd about[,] one of the sleeves of his coat being torn off and his hair much ruffled and his face red as scarlet . . . ." Later Russel heard John Miller report to Say that "the business of the house went on as he would have it." This remark referred, Russel learned, to the exclusion of Thompson's name from the *Gazetteer* imprint; probably Thompson had restored it that day. It was finally decided that Say and Miller, with Thompson and a friend, should be left together in the dining room to see if they could reach an agreement. Russel and Surmont went into the kitchen, where Say's men had again assembled. After a time Say emerged from the dining room, dismissed his supporters, thanked them "for the assistance they had given him and told them that if they had a mind[,] to go any where and get a supper and he would pay for it . . . ."[43]

At some time during the evening John Cooke returned from the meeting at the King's Head bearing a letter from the *Gazetteer* proprietors to Say. Cooke thought the letter contained an order to restore Thompson's name to the paper's imprint, and it may have been instrumental in bringing about the temporary truce which appears to have been reached in the dining room.

The entire episode crystalized the unpleasant atmosphere in which a highly successful—perhaps the most successful—newspaper of the day was produced. Three weeks after it occurred, the *Gazetteer*'s circulation made necessary the setting of duplicate formes. Thompson's name was restored to the imprint on 12 December, and his competence as a manager seems to have remained unimpaired. The outcome of the dispute between Say and the proprietors of the *General Evening Post* nine months earlier indicates that a reconciliation between Say and Thompson was not impossible even in December 1771. But Say's determination, though less forcefully displayed thenceforth, remained unabated, and Thompson, having proved his capability, would accept nothing less than what he considered to be his due.

While in the following four months the *Gazetteer* flourished, the dispute between the two printers progressed to its final climax. On 11 December 1771, the day after the attempt to evict Thompson forcibly, Say sent a written notice to the younger printer ordering him to remove his name from the *Gazetteer* imprint and to quit the house in Newgate Street. This Thompson refused to do. Several offers of compromise on each side followed, but none was found acceptable to both men. In February 1772 Thompson notified Say that he was submitting their original agreement, together with Say's most recent offer, to a conveyancer at the bar in order that a new draft might be made which conformed to the earlier agreement. As an alternative to this procedure Thompson offered to submit the disagreement to arbitration. When Say refused to agree to either course, Thompson consulted "an eminent Counsel attending the Court of Chancery," who advised him to have the matter settled by a conveyancer.[44]

Say's patience was, however, exhausted. Near the end of March, before Thompson's conveyancer could present a basis for settlement, Charles and Mary Say returned to the house in Newgate Street and there took up residence. The household, under the circumstances, was far from harmonious. For one thing Roger Thompson seems to have deviated for a time from the patience and deliberation which had characterized his behavior throughout most of his tenure as editor and manager. He acted, Say later claimed, in a brutal manner—forcing locks, throwing Mrs. Say's blankets, sheets, and clothing about on the floor of her bedchamber, and even, according to Say, "assaulting" the lady and "throwing her down upon the stairs on her endeavoring to go into the parlour." [45]

On the night of Saturday, 4 April 1772, Thompson, returning to Newgate Street about midnight, found himself locked out of the house. At some time on the following day, however, he gained admittance, and, being compelled to go out again on business, arranged for two of his servants to readmit him when he should return. That evening the servants—"two dirty shabby fellows," Say called them, whom he feared were "secreted" in the house for "some bad and dangerous purpose"—were themselves expelled from the premises. When Thompson returned, he was again unable to enter the printing office.

Early the following morning (Monday, 6 April) Thompson returned to the house accompanied by his friends Charles Surmont and Jabez Goldar to find the doors locked and "the people within . . . delivering the news papers out of the window." [46] When he knocked, "a person looked out of the counting house window and . . . refused him admittance." Thereupon, Thompson called out to the clerk, John Cooke, to open the door. Cooke, who remained loyal to Thompson throughout the affair, attempted to comply but was prevented "by some people who were in the office." Surmont and Goldar, outside with Thompson, heard noises in the passage which they interpreted as "some persons preventing . . . Mr. Cooke from opening the door." [47]

In the imprint of the *Gazetteers* which were that Monday morning passed out of the window at No. 3 Newgate Street, Roger Thompson might have found a formal notice of his own defeat. After an interval of more than fifteen months, the paper was once more avowedly "Printed for" Charles Say. The outcome remained, however, in some doubt. Thompson proceeded to lay an information against Say, his son-in-law John Miller, and Miller's servant Joseph Stockdale, based on the statute of forcible entries, and a hearing was scheduled before Alderman John Sawbridge and a jury at the Queens Arms Tavern, Newgate Street, on Saturday, 11 April.[48] Whether Sawbridge's sympathy with Thompson's defiance of Parliament a year before [49] or simply the methods employed to oust the younger printer made Say apprehensive that the decision would go against him cannot be determined; that he felt such apprehension admits of little doubt.

At about nine o'clock on the night (Friday, 10 April) before the hearing was to take place, Richard Birtles, one of the compositors engaged in setting the *Gazetteer*'s third forme, descended from the garret of the Newgate Street house to procure some additional copy. In the lower composing room he found "all the cases and letter removed." John Miller, Birtles said, "was in the . . . lower composing room and refused to suffer . . . any of the people in the upper room to go out." Later, when Birtles asked Miller for more copy, he was told "that they would do without the third form that night," and was ordered, with the other compositors engaged in setting it, "to take down their cases and carry them" to Charles Say's house in Ave Maria Lane. The move was effected, Birtles understood, to prevent Thompson's "being enabled to carry on the Gazetteer in case he should be put into possession of the house . . . ." [50] Both his description of events and his interpretation of motives were fully substantiated by the statement of George Abraham, a partisan of Say:

. . . the night preceding the time for the Sheriff and jury to meet all the materials used in the printing business that could conveniently be removed were by the order of Mr. Miller taken away from the . . . house and carried to . . . [Say's] house in Ave Maria Lane and such things as could not conveniently be removed were mostly destroyed by the order of . . . Mr. Miller that in case the Sheriff should put . . .

[Thompson] into possession [of the Newgate Street house] he might be put into possession of an empty house. . . .[51]

Say's apprehension was well founded, for the jury at the Queens Arms next day returned a verdict favorable to Thompson. Later, however, the printer succeeded in moving the case to the Court of King's Bench, where the findings against him were set aside.[52]

With the removal of the *Gazetteer* printing office to No. 10 Ave Maria Lane, Thompson's active participation in the management of the paper came to an end. It is regrettable that the abilities which had distinguished his direction of the *Gazetteer* do not appear to have been employed to the advantage of any of the other daily papers that arose in London during the next two decades. Except as that of a plaintiff in a long and apparently futile suit in Chancery, Roger Thompson's name, after April 1772, disappears from the annals of English journalism into the obscurity from which it had so recently emerged.[53]

VIII

END OF AN ERA

1772-1775

THE removal of Roger Thompson's name from the imprint of
the *Gazetteer* in the spring of 1772 marks the end of a brief
but important era in the paper's history. Under Thompson's management the circulation and, it must be inferred, the popularity of
the *Gazetteer* had risen to heights previously unattained, so far as is
known, by any daily newspaper of the century. In broader perspec-
tive, however, the period of Thompson's management constitutes
but a small part of a much longer era—one which extended over
a quarter of a century and which ended in the summer of 1775
with the death of Charles Green Say.

The removal of the *Gazetteer* printing office from Newgate
Street to Ave Maria Lane and the change in the paper's imprint
were attended with as much publicity as could discreetly be given
them. On Saturday, 11 April 1772, the morning after John Miller
had supervised the transfer of equipment, a notice at the head of
page 4 restated the information given in the *Gazetteer* imprint; on
the Monday following, the notice was somewhat expanded: "C.
Say, the Printer of this Paper, having moved his business from his
house in Newgate-street, to his late father's house, No. 10 in Ave-
Maria-lane, The Gazetteer and New Daily Advertiser, and his
Weekly Paper, the Craftsman, or Say's Weekly Journal, will, for
the future, be printed and published there; and where Essays,
Articles of Intelligence, and Advertisements will be received." The
notice appeared daily for several weeks. During that period and
for some time therafter an effort was made to obliterate any

memory of Roger Thompson from the minds of readers. When reference was made to "the Printer" of the Gazetteer, an appositive construction was used identifying him as "C. Say." Frequently, too, letters from correspondents were given a more personal touch by being addressed to "Mr. Say" rather than to "the Printer" as had been customary.

Charles Say's actual participation in producing the *Gazetteer* appears, however, to have been negligible. In 1774 it was stated that Edward Benson was "commonly called in the . . . printing house the editor of the newspaper called the Gazetteer," and account books of the period revealed that he had immediately succeeded Thompson as the recipient of one and one-half guineas weekly from the proprietors of the paper.[1] For the most part, Benson seems to have been content to follow the editorial methods and policies he had inherited from Thompson, and the paper's history from the spring of 1772 to the outbreak of hostilities in America three years later was relatively uneventful.

Reports of the debates in Parliament remained, during the winter months, the featured form of intelligence, and they were nearly always accorded the prominence of a position on page one. In length the accounts varied from about two columns to four, depending upon the significance and length of the individual debates. Their form was paraphrastic, purporting to comprise only the "genuine substance" of what had been said and seldom including a verbatim transcript of any speaker's words:

We do not give the speeches in certain Assemblies *at length* [the printer announced] it being impracticable, but we endeavour, by an abridgment, to convey their sense, with a strict regard to truth, and as nearly as possible in the same words. —We have the pleasure to find, that our readers have expressed great satsifaction with our conduct, and not one speaker is offended at the liberty we have taken. . . .[2]

Generally, publications of these reports ran two or three days behind the actual debates, but Parliamentary business was frequently summarized very briefly at the head of the *London* column on the morning after it had taken place. There, for example, in the *Gazetteer* of Thursday, 22 February 1775, appeared this report: "Yesterday, pursuant to the notice given on Friday last in the House of Commons, the Lord-mayor [John Wilkes] moved to have all the Proceedings and Resolutions, relative to the Middlesex Election expunged out of the Journals. This produced a debate, which continued to be warmly supported on both sides till this account came away, which was after eleven o'clock." Five days later the *Gazetteer*, the *Morning Chronicle*, and the *Morning Post* each devoted an entire page to Wilkes's speech on the occasion. Since the texts were identical, it is probable that the Lord Mayor himself had supplied copies to the papers.[3]

The emphasis on Parliamentary news together with the limited space at his disposal often compelled the printer to be more highly selective in dealing with letters from correspondents than he had previously been.[4] While Benson professed to strive for variety in the letters he published and was firm in rejecting matter which "having already appeared in print, would not be pleasing and entertaining to our readers, who love novelty," [5] he departed from Thompson's practice of publishing numerous brief letters on a variety of topics and included fewer and longer ones whose subjects were almost exclusively political. In the winter of 1772 a notice of rejection explained, "The present season being appropriated to *politics*, is a sufficient reason, we hope, for not inserting the letters of the *Old Batchelor*, *Urbanus*, *Lucia*, and *James*, addressed to the Ladies. The present busy season of politics will not admit of letters on the subject mentioned by *Leonidas*." [6] Some compensation for the change in policy was afforded by a return to the practice of including an occasional column of remarks in which unpublished letters were briefly summarized. This feature, which had been so popular in the preceding decade,[7] may indicate that Charles Say continued to exert a direct editorial influence on the *Gazetteer*. "A Constant Reader, whose daughter's arms are remarkably covered with hair" could, at any rate, write to the printer in 1772 as in 1764 requesting "a receipt for eradicating them" [8] and expect that the request would be published. There, however, the similarity to the earlier feature ended, for the editorial comments of 1772 lacked both the edification and the entertainment value to be found in the patronizing benevolence and occasional moral indignation which had colored the observations of the sixties. A noteworthy exception, perhaps, was the announcement which headed a group of such comments on Monday, 12 October 1772: "The Printer of this Paper presents his Compliments to the House-breakers, and begs they would not attempt any more to break into his house, as his cash is always carried to the Bankers every day. They may alarm him and family, but cannot get any thing of consequence."

Periodic series of essays by a single writer were considerably less frequent between 1772 and 1775 than they had been in the five years before. Partially responsible, of course, was the fact that Parliamentary news was displacing the productions of political essayists in the interest of the newspaper-reading public; authentic statements by government and opposition leaders upon political issues of the time, when available, naturally held a greater attraction than anonymous commentary on such issues. Moreover, there was almost certainly an economic factor involved. Regular reports of Parliamentary proceedings entailed considerable expense on the part of the printer and publisher, and this must have made him less willing to pay for the works of professional essayists. A writer signing himself "Lucullus" proposed in the summer of 1772 to contribute for payment letters "in defence of Administration." "Lucullus may be possessed of the literary merit he claims," the printer conceded, "but we must be excused from paying the extraordinary compliment to it, which he insists upon. If he expects a reward, he must look for it only from those person[s], in whose favour he proposes to write." [9]

Essay series on nonpolitical subjects were most often published during the summer season, when Parliament was not in session and when news and advertisements were less plentiful. Of those appearing while Edward Benson conducted the *Gazetteer*, none was as outstanding as "Hortensia" or the "Attorney General," which Thompson had published, but two examples are perhaps worthy of note. Letters from "Ibrahim to Osman Effendi Hoje," of which six appeared in May and June 1774, discussed English manners and institutions with a pseudo-Oriental astonishment highly reminiscent of Goldsmith's *Citizen of the World*. *The Plagiarist*, in the summer following, proposed to furnish a weekly essay "in a great manner . . . extracted from the words of historic, philosophic, and other writers," and aimed at "the encrease or cultivation of a spirit of liberty, virtue, honour, courage, chastity, prudence, or goodness . . . ." The first number concluded with the writer's promise to cultivate brevity in future essays and to cease writing whenever the printer found that his observations were dull and "totally void of Attic salt." In all, seven numbers appeared.

One other editorial feature of the *Gazetteer* under Benson's management should be mentioned. That is the publication in January and February 1773 of a number of brief leading articles at the head of the *London* news column. The general theme of these paragraphs was the dire threat to British trade and commerce represented by the aims and measures of the incumbent ministry. In one instance, royal prerogative encroaching upon Parliamentary freedom through bribery and corruption was charged with threatening to deprive the East India Company of its legal powers;[10] two days later the writer decried the increasing number of bankruptcies which were destroying national credit and attributed them to the "luxury, corruption, extravagance and dissipation" which were stifling the "parents and nurses of trade and commerce," *viz.*, "Industry, Care and Frugality." On 20 January there appeared a sharp criticism of government sponsorship of lotteries whereby gaming was encouraged, bankrupts multiplied, and the nation's trade and commerce were jeopardized.[11] Articles in this form, it has been noted,[12] had appeared in the paper for a short time in the autumn of 1760, but with the change in makeup which had followed, the practice of commenting in the column of formal intelligence upon the news of the day had been discontinued. The significance of its temporary revival of 1773 is difficult to estimate, for the leading article did not become a consistent feature of the *Gazetteer* until the decade of the 1780's.

If the editorial management of the *Gazetteer* from 1772 to 1775 appears less than inspired, it may be largely due to the fact that in the three years following Roger Thompson's displacement there occurred no event of a significance comparable to that in which he had participated. That fact may also have been more responsible than any recession in the *Gazetteer*'s quality for the serious decline in circulation which the paper suffered in the twelve months following the move to Ave Maria Lane. Although documentary proof is lacking, such a decline must necessarily be inferred from evidence that within a year after Thompson ceased to manage the paper the setting of duplicate outer formes became unnecessary. William Haynes, a compositor employed in setting the extra forme, testified in 1774 that "some few months" after Thompson's name was removed from the *Gazetteer* imprint "the method of setting one of the forms twice was discontinued."[13] More specifically, at some time between 19 April and 8 May 1773[14] the *Gazetteer* reverted to the normal makeup in which it had appeared before duplicate setting began: the *London* news was returned to page 2 (inner forme) while the theatre programs, which were among the latest items to be received nightly, remained on page one (outer forme). Haynes's statement that the duplication of one forme ceased a "few months" after April 1772 may have been due to a bias in favor of Thompson or to a faulty memory, but it should be noted that the appearance of duplicate settings could easily have been maintained for some time after the practice was discontinued by simply retaining the columns of *London* news in an outer forme which was set only once.

A less noticeable but equally significant change occurred two years later, in the spring of 1775, when the *Gazetteer* imprint was altered to announce that the paper was printed "by" rather than "for" Charles Say. After more than a decade during which Say had been designated as both printer and publisher of the paper,[15] he now relinquished the duties and legal responsibilities which accompanied the latter title. A surviving account book for the period indicates that he was replaced as publisher by William Owen, who had preceded him in the office,[16] and who was to continue in it until 1793.[17] While a definite reason for the change cannot be advanced, it is probable in view of later events that by 1775 the printer's health had so far failed as to prohibit his taking an active part in the management of the paper. If that was the case, the proprietors may have ordered a change in publishers for their own financial security and for the comfort which Say might have found in a partial relief from legal liability.

Throughout the spring of 1775 the steadily growing hostility between England (as represented by the government of Lord North) and the American colonies was a topic of major importance in the *Gazetteer*. Considerable space was given over to political essayists like "Veritas" and "Mercator Americanus" who sympathized with American grievances and advocated conciliation. Opinions favoring current governmental policies were also represented, most notably perhaps by a writer signing himself ironically "A Bostonian Saint," but the paper's general attitude clearly coincided with that of its mercantile readers in favoring redress of the colonists' grievances and preservation of the commercial advantages which normal trade relations entailed. News from America, such as the resolutions passed by the Continental Congress in the autumn of 1774[18] and the proceedings of individual colonial assemblies, was published freely and without adverse comment. Even as late as the date of the battles of Lexington and Concord, 19 April 1775, the printer was refusing to publish an unflattering "anecdote of an American Officer, which was neither pleasing, laughable, nor credible, and was intended through the misconduct of an individual to convey a national reflection. . . ."[19] Ten days later, unaware that the battles had taken place, he admitted that there seemed no longer any basis for compromise: "The dispute must now be terminated by submission or arms. . . . We presume not to determine the rectitude of the proceedings of either party. It is, however, neither treason against the sovereign nor the people to pray, God give them both a safe deliverance from the impending calamities, and a speedy reconciliation." [20]

Although the calamities were by then no longer merely impending, no one in England could yet have been aware of it. Just one week later occurred what must be considered one of the most remarkable coincidences in the history of British journalism; the first item in the *London* column of the *Gazetteer* on Saturday, 6 May 1775 read as follows:

By a private correspondent we learn, that the Kings troops at Boston have attacked and defeated the Provincials, who lost a thousand men in the action. The loss of the former, it is said, is six hundred. We are not yet enabled to give our readers a more particular account of this unhappy event, but have reason to believe it must very soon be circumstantially known, an express with the above news to government being just arrived.

The item was by no means an accurate account of the April skirmish, but then it could not possibly have been. Only seventeen days had elapsed since the actual engagement, and news of it was not to reach London for another three weeks.[21]

The paragraph quoted was, as the *Gazetteer* implied, an exclusive one. It was reprinted on Monday, 8 May, in the *Morning Post* and the *Morning Chronicle*, and attributed by both to the *Gazetteer*. What, one wonders, could have been the source of the report? Satirists from Ben Jonson onwards had accused news writers of supplying reports which they knew to be fiction a good part of the time, but it is difficult to believe that the conductor of the *Gazetteer*, whether Say or Edward Benson, would have published such startling news unless he believed it to be true. One can only conjecture that the editorial head of the paper was the victim either of a deliberate hoax or of a trusted correspondent who had uncritically given credit to a wholly unfounded rumor. That such a rumor existed is quite probable, for increasing tension in America had raised expectations of an armed clash, and there is significance in the fact that the *Post* and *Chronicle*, when they printed the report, did not question it. Whatever its origin, the paragraph served the purpose, for those readers who gave credence to it, of announcing in timely fashion the outbreak of hostilities in America.

If the *Gazetteer* or any of the other newspapers learned that the report was without foundation, no indication of the fact was ever given. For nearly three weeks after it was published, it remained unsubstantiated and uncontradicted. On Monday, 29 May, a notice headed simply "Intelligence" appeared among the correspondence on page 1 of the *Gazetteer:* "All kinds of favorable intelligence to Government from America, *as given out by the Scotch cabal,* is entirely void of foundation, and calculated to support the drooping spirits of *their party;* the winds for three weeks past having been so contrary, as not to admit of a ship coming up the Channel." Did this statement refer, by implication, to the report of 9 May?

The day it appeared authentic news of Lexington and Concord reached London, and on the following morning (Tuesday, 30 May) every newspaper carried an account. The manner in which the news arrived and the treatment it received in the papers clearly illustrate some of the journalistic techniques and problems of the period.

In the first place, the main source for the account published in the London dailies on Tuesday, 30 May 1775, was a Massachusetts newspaper, the *Essex Gazette* of 25 April. The report published there, six days after the conflict, did not pretend to be definitive. "The particulars relative to this interesting event" the New England paper stated, "we have endeavoured to collect as well as the present confused state of affairs will admit." The particulars thus collected, strongly colored by a pro-Colonial bias, were reprinted in full by the *Morning Post* and *Morning Chronicle,* and they included such statements as that the British troops, "not content with shooting down the unarmed, aged and infirm," had "disregarded the cries of the wounded, killing them without mercy, and mangling their bodies in the most shocking manner."

But the *Essex Gazette* was not the only source of the news in London. *The Morning Chronicle,* which reprinted that text, referred to "many different accounts of the matter, sent us yesterday, by various correspondents." The *Gazetteer,* which did not reprint it, described the arrival of the news thus: "Sunday night [28 May], about nine o'clock, Captain Danby . . . from New York, arrived express from Southampton, where he left his ship, and has brought papers, dated the 25th of April last, which mention an engagement having happened on the 19th of the same month. . . ." Then it gave what it termed "the substance of the account of the . . . affair, which is handed about at Lloyd's and Garraway's":

General Gage having heard that the insurgents were drawing some cannon a few miles from Boston, he dispatched an officer, with some troops, to demand them to be delivered up, which the insurgents refused to comply with. —A second message was sent, when the officer informed them, that he must obey his orders, which were, in case of refusal to surrender them, that he must fire on those that surrounded them, but which he hoped they would prevent, by immediately relinquishing them. This they absolutely refused to do; on which the troops fired on them, and killed about sixty. On this the country arose, and assisted the insurgents to load the cannon, and they were directly fired upon by Gen. Gage's troops, which did great execution, near an hundred being killed, and sixty wounded. The noise of the cannon alarmed General Gage, who immediately sent Lord Percy, with a larger party of troops, to enquire into the matter. When his Lordship came to the place, he heard the Officer's account of the dispute, and then returned back with the troops to General Gage's intrenchments, as he did not find any authority he had to proceed further in it.

Yesterday stock fell one and a half per cent. on account of the above news.

The text of the report printed the same morning in the *Daily Advertiser* was nearly identical to that given in the *Gazetteer;* a *written* account must therefore have been handed about in the coffeehouses. But the reports in the two papers differed in the text of a single sentence: where the *Gazetteer* stated that the "insurgents . . . *were* directly fired upon *by* Gen. Gage's troops," [22] the *Daily Advertiser* omitted two words. The insurgents, it said, "directly fired upon Gen. Gage's troops." Which side had actually fired the first shot does not, happily, concern us here. The question is, which version of the report most faithfully reproduced the source? There can be little doubt, I think, that the one given in the *Gazetteer* did. The reports which Captain Danby had brought were directed, it was later stated, "to the several noblemen and gentlemen in the opposition, Mr. Lee, the Agent, Lord Dartmouth, &c. &c." [23] The first reports were, then, received and made public by a group definitely hostile to the North ministry and sympathetic toward the colonial cause; it is improbable that such reports portrayed the provincial forces as aggressors.

These accounts from opposition sources were also the earliest reports received in official quarters. *The London Gazette* on the afternoon of 30 May admitted as much:

Secretary of State's Office, Whitehall, May 30.

A Report having been spread, and an account having been printed and published, of a skirmish between some of the people in the province of Massachusett's Bay and a detachment of his Majesty's troops; it is proper to inform the public, that no advices have yet been received in the American department of any such event.

There is reason to believe, that there are dispatches from General Gage on board the Sukey, Capt. Brown, which, though she sailed four days before the vessel that brought the printed account, is not yet arrived.[24]

On Wednesday, 1 June, the official dispatches had still not arrived, but there was no reason for the public to doubt the report already so widely circulated. Arthur Lee, London agent for the Massachusetts House of Representatives, advertised in the *Gazetteer* as follows:

Tuesday, May the 30th, 1775.

As a doubt of the authenticity of the account from Salem, touching an engagement between the King's troops and the provincials in the Massachussets Bay, may arise from a paragraph in the Gazette of this evening, I desire to inform all those who wish to see the original affidavits which confirm that account, that they are deposited at the Mansion-house with the Right Hon. the Lord Mayor for their inspection.

By the following day the *Gazetteer* had heard of a corroborating account: "A letter from Lord Percy to his father is arrived at Northumberland-house, containing an account of the skirmish in America. It is said not to differ materially from the accounts already published."

Eight days more elapsed before the government made public its version of the affair. *The London Gazette* for Saturday, 10 June, carried the account given in General Gage's dispatches. According to this report, the Americans had been the first to fire, and earlier charges of atrocities by the British troops were fully reciprocated: "Such was the cruelty and barbarity of the Rebels, that they scalped and cut off the Ears of some of the wounded Men, who fell into their Hands." Four days later the *Gazetteer* reported (though not in its news columns): "The law of retaliation will take place in America. Abundance of scalping knives are getting ready, which are to be tried on American skulls in just revenge. . . ."[25] Seventeen years earlier, in *Idler* No. 30, Dr.

Samuel Johnson had observed: "Scarcely any thing awakens attention like a tale of cruelty. The writer of news never fails in the intermission of action to tell how the enemies murdered children and ravished virgins; and, if the scene of action be somewhat distant, scalps half the inhabitants of a province."

As was to be expected, reports of and comment upon the American Revolution dominated the columns of the London newspapers for many months after Lexington and Concord. In August 1775 "An Old Man," writing to the *Gazetteer*, complained that the "affairs of America engross so much of the attention of the public, that every other consideration seems to be laid aside, and nothing is seen in the newspapers but accounts of hostilities and slaughter in that part of the world." [26] Such accounts were not obtained, however, without some difficulty. Government, it appears, had instituted a form of censorship over such communications as those which had brought the first news of battle. The *Gazetteer* and the *Morning Chronicle* both reported on Saturday, 24 June 1775:

> An eminent American merchant had two thousand pounds worth of bills of exchange (which had been remitted him from his correspondents on the other side of the Atlantic) sent him on Thursday from the people in power, together with such extracts from his letters as referred merely to matters of business, but the letters themselves were kept back.

Extreme sympathy for America in the as yet undeclared war continued to be expressed in the London newspapers for some time after the earliest battles. The most striking examples of such sympathy were contained in two advertisements by the Constitutional Society (a group of London "patriots" in opposition to the North ministry) which resulted in serious consequences for a number of newspaper printers. The first of the advertisements appeared on Friday, 9 June 1775, in the *Gazetteer*, the *Public Ledger*, the *Morning Chronicle*, and the *Public Advertiser*, as well as in several evening papers of that day and the next:

> King's-Arms Tavern, Cornhill, June 7, 1775
> At a Special Meeting this day of several Members of the Constitutional Society, during an adjournment, a Gentleman proposed that a subscription should be immediately entered into (by such of the Members present who might approve the purpose) for raising the sum of One Hundred Pounds,
> "To be applied to the relief of Widows, Orphans, and Aged Parents,

of our BELOVED American fellow-subjects, who, FAITHFUL to the character of Englishmen, preferring death to slavery, were, for that reason only, inhumanly murdered by the KING's Troops, at or near Lexington and Concord, in the province of Massachusset's, on the 19th of last April."

Which sum being immediately collected, it was thereupon

Resolved, That Mr. Horne do pay tomorrow into the hands of Mess. Brownes and Collison, on account of Dr. Franklin, the said sum of 100 l. and that Dr. Franklin be requested to apply the same to the above mentioned purpose.

JOHN HORNE.

A little more than a month later (Saturday, 15 July) Horne again invited prosecution by a similar notice in which he deliberately repeated the most provocative phrases of that already quoted.

In the following year, after the American colonies had been officially proclaimed rebellious, prosecutions for libel were instituted by the Attorney General against John Horne and the printers of the newspapers which had carried his advertisement. The economist Joseph Massie, in a letter to the "Citizens of London" [27] printed on the front page of the *Gazetteer*, decried the proceedings as having their basis in *ex post facto* law, since Horne's statements had not been illegal at the time he made them. The prosecution had only to prove, however, as in the Junius case six years earlier, [28] that the defendants had in fact published the advertisements. Miller of the *London Evening Post*, Baldwin of the *St. James's Chronicle*, Randall of the *Public Ledger*, and Wilkie of the *London Chronicle* were accordingly found guilty in December 1776 and sentenced two months later to fines of £100 each. [29]

Charles Say, as printer of the *Gazetteer*, had been indicted for publishing both advertisements, but he was never brought to trial. An endorsement on each of the two briefs prepared against him, both of which are now in the Public Record Office, explains succinctly why. "Mr. Say," it reads, "is dead." [30]

Charles Say died in July 1775, not in November as John Nichols reported. [31] The exact date of his death is unknown, but it certainly occurred between 27 June, when a codicil was appended to his will, and 22 July, when the will was proved in the Prerogative Court of Canterbury. [32] Probably Say died on 19 July, for he had expressed in his will a desire that the *Gazetteer* and *Craftsman* should "immediately after . . . [his] decease be printed in . . . [his wife's] Name if she shall think fit," and the *Gazetteer* imprint proclaimed for the first time on Thursday, 20 July, that the paper was "Printed by M. Say." No other indication of the printer's demise was given in the paper on that date or subsequently, and no mention of it, so far as I have been able to determine, appeared in any other publication until the following year.

The provisions of Say's will were simple, and only those concerned with his profession need be mentioned here. To his wife, Mary, he left his shares of ownership in the *Gazetteer* and the *General Evening Post,* and one-eighth of the net profits from the printing business. The remainder of the profits were to be divided equally among his unmarried daughters. The *Gazetteer* and *Craftsman,* as has been mentioned, were to be printed in Mary Say's name until such time as she remarried or until the eldest of his sons who was trained as a printer should attain the age of twenty-four years. In the latter case the son was to receive all of the printing equipment which had belonged to his father, none of which was to be disposed of in the meantime. Say's widow was also to receive his share in the "English Stock" of the Stationers' Company.

Two other bequests are of incidental interest. Mary Say was to be given "the sum of two hundred Pounds South Sea Stock." This gift, Say explained in the will, was made "as a Consideration and to shew my Gratitude to her for the great uneasiness I have caused in her in consequence of my long Illness and notwithstanding all which she has been as careful and mindful of me and such of my Children as behaved well to her as if she had borne them herself." Finally, to his son-in-law John Miller, printer of the *London Evening Post,* Say bequeathed Miller's own promissory note for £300 and a "release and discharge . . . from all . . . sums of money due and owing."

Five days after the will was proved, the proprietors of the *Gazetteer* entered into a new contract by which Mary Say formally became printer of the paper. An era had ended.

IX

TRANSITION

1775-1779

THE general direction of the *Gazetteer*'s development between the summer of 1775 and the beginning of the year 1783 was largely determined by two factors. One was the absence, after twenty-five years, of the editorial influence of Charles Green Say. The other was the steady growth of competition in the sphere of daily journalism.

The influence of such competition had undoubtedly been felt by those concerned in the *Gazetteer* before 1775, and its effects are possibly to be traced in some of the relatively minor policy changes of the four years immediately following. Obvious results of that influence become apparent to the twentieth-century reader, however, only near the close of the decade, and a general discussion of the subject may be more profitably undertaken at that point in the paper's history. Meanwhile, the events of the period more closely following Say's death are not without interest.

The agreement by which Mary Say was formally designated printer of the *Gazetteer* is perhaps the earliest example known of a contract between the printer and proprietors of an eighteenth-century daily newspaper.[1] The "Articles of Agreement," signed and sealed on 27 July 1775, reveal that of the fourteen proprietors known to have been concerned in the paper in 1753[2] seven had retained their shares; the names of ten more partners, some of whose interests probably also dated from the 1753 contract, are included. The proprietors of 1775 who had certainly held shares in the *Gazetteer* for twenty-two years were (besides the late printer) Thomas Payne, Lockyer Davis, William Owen, John Whiston, Samuel Baker, Robert Wilson, and John Nourse. All were booksellers. Among the other partners at the time of the new agreement was Paul Vaillant, from 1750 an eminent publisher and dealer in Continental books, who had been Sheriff of London in 1760, Master of the Stationers' Company in 1770, and was to be known by the time of his death in 1802 as Father of the Company.[3] Vaillant was one of the three partners who signed the agreement as representatives of the other proprietors. It is probable that he, like William Owen and Lockyer Davis, who also signed, had held an interest in the *Gazetteer* since 1753.

Other proprietors whose names appear for the first time in the 1775 contract were Thomas Gardner, Benjamin White, William Johnston, David Wilson, Thomas Durham, James Fletcher, Charles Kemp, George Hayter, and John Twyman. Of these the first five were London booksellers, and James Fletcher was a bookseller in Oxford.[4] Hayter is described in the contract as "merchant"; John Twyman was a ship broker whose advertisements frequently appeared in the *Gazetteer;* and Charles Kemp, of Evesham, is designated only as "Gentleman."

By the terms of the contract Mary Say was appointed printer of the *Gazetteer* pursuant to a number of specific conditions. First of all, she promised never to "change or alter the Title Form Face or Appearance" of the paper without the consent of a majority of the proprietors at a general meeting nor to do anything that might injure the property or cause the proprietors to dismiss her as printer. She was not to dispose of her share in the paper "by way of setting herself at liberty to become the Printer or Publisher of any other Morning News Paper," and was prohibited from undertaking to print "any other Newpaper whatsoever." Exceptions were made for the two other papers which she already printed. She might remain printer of the *Craftsman* so long as it was published only once a week, and of the *General Evening Post* while it continued to be published only on Tuesdays, Thursdays, and Saturdays. Memories of the dispute between Say and Thompson perhaps caused the proprietors to introduce a clause which forbade Mrs. Say to "make over the profits of printing the . . . Gazetteer" or to print the paper in the name of anyone except herself without permission from a majority of the other proprietors.

Three separate provisions outlined in general terms the routine obligations of the printer toward the body of proprietors. She was to record in books provided for the purpose all receipts and disbursements on account of the *Gazetteer* "and everything incident thereto" and to produce such books at general meetings or meetings of the management committee whenever required. In addition to these accounts the books were to contain "the true Names Places of Abode and Professions of all . . . such . . . Persons as she shall employ to write for the . . . Gazetteer. . . ." At least once a month the new printer was to pay to the treasurer any balance due to the proprietors after deducting her expenses and the charges for printing. Finally, she promised to pay any fines which might be imposed upon her by a general meeting of the proprietors "as a Punishment for her Non Attendance as Printer of the . . . Gazetteer." To guarantee her performance according to the terms of the contract, Mary Say gave her bond for £2,000 to William Owen, Paul Vaillant, and Lockyer Davis, that sum to be forfeited should she fail in "a due Observance and Performance of the Covenant."

Mary Say's accounts for this period have not survived,[5] but a document of nearly equal interest, relevant to the period treated in this chapter, has been preserved in the Public Record Office. It is a book of accounts, apparently one of several, kept by William Owen. Briefly, the book records Owen's receipts and expenditures in connection with the *Gazetteer,* and while the accounts it contains are neither so complete nor so detailed as one might wish, they do reveal a number of facts concerning his functions as treasurer and publisher of the paper.[6]

By far the most numerous of the entries in the book are those which record payments received from *Gazetteer* advertisers. These entries, unfortunately, are also the least interesting. What proportion of the paper's advertising revenue was actually collected by Owen cannot be determined, but it appears that most of the advertisers paid their bills at the printing office. Owen's records indicate that his own dealings were chiefly with businessmen who advertised extensively in the *Gazetteer* and who ordinarily settled their accounts once every month. The majority of them were London booksellers and auctioneers, though receipts are noted from advertisers of a variety sufficient to include Samuel Foote the comedian, Jonas Hanway the eminent philanthropist, and Dutton Seaman, Esquire, Comptroller of the City of London.

Fewer, and of much greater interest, are the records of disbursements. The most regular of these were the payments incident upon meetings of the proprietors. Monthly meetings of the management committee entailed payments by the treasurer for refreshments which, since they sometimes cost as much as four pounds, probably included a dinner for each member of the committee. Semiannual general meetings of the proprietors, in April and October, were more expensive. They were usually held, it appears, at the King's Head tavern in Holborn, and Owen's disbursements on each occasion included a payment of five shillings to every partner attending. Once annually, in August or September, the proprietors and possibly the staff from the printing office gathered at Hampstead for an event which Owen recorded variously as "Annual Meeting at Hampstead," "Summer Meeting," and "Venison Feast at Hampstead." The cost of these assemblies ranged from about five pounds to just under ten, excluding, as the treasurer often noted, the venison, which seems to have been furnished in turn by each of the proprietors.[7]

A major responsibility of Owen as publisher was to provide the paper on which the *Gazetteer* was printed. The accounts include entries, generally monthly, recording payments for paper bought from William Flower, a stationer. Paper of double demy size, a half-sheet of which would produce a single copy of the newspaper, cost the publisher thirty shillings a ream in 1784, the earliest date at which the price is recorded. Payments to Flower usually ran about six months behind his deliveries, and they were sometimes made in irregular installments of varying amounts. The size and frequency of payments depended, apparently, upon the speed with which revenue from advertisements could be collected, and upon the size of Mrs. Say's monthly settlements with the proprietors. Consequently, it is impossible to estimate with any accuracy the quantity of paper used within a given period, from which approximate circulation figures might be deduced. From 1784, when Owen began noting occasionally the quantities of paper ordered, a single delivery usually consisted of fifty reams—enough to produce 50,000 copies of the *Gazetteer*. Papers remaining unsold were at this period returned to the Stamp Office, where the stamps were cut from them and credit was given to the printer on the purchase of new stamps.[8] Disposal of the waste paper that remained was another of the publisher's duties. Owen's accounts reveal that in 1774 he was receiving 3*s*. 6*d*. for a ream of waste; two years later the value had increased by sixpence, and by 1783 the price had reached five shillings.

For the most part, the *Gazetteer* accounts kept by the publisher concerned matters of simple business routine, but a number of entries relevant to editorial matters were also included. From the single ledger surviving it is impossible to draw any general conclusions about the extent of Owen's editorial authority, but the fact that between 1775 and 1779 his activities in this respect were relatively slight suggests that editorial control was still largely concentrated in the printer and that Owen's participation in it was confined to matters involving exceptional disbursements which the printer was not authorized to make. The annual payments of £50 to Sir John Fielding, for example,[9] as well as those to the Theatres Royal (to be discussed later) were made by Owen, and a number of payments for special contributions to the paper are found among his accounts.

Noteworthy among such special contributions between 1775 and 1779 was a series of essays by a writer who signed himself "Regulus." Letters from Regulus had begun to appear in the *Gazetteer* in January 1774, and about a dozen had been published by 29 December 1775, when William Owen recorded a payment of £20 for "Regulus by Mr. Davis." During the year 1776 forty-two Regulus letters were published in the *Gazetteer*, and Owen paid out in three installments [10] a total of £80 under the same cryptic entry. In 1777 thirty-four Regulus letters were published, and on 11 September £40 was recorded as having been "Paid Mr. Davis for Regulus." In 1778 thirteen of the letters appeared, but no payments were recorded until 14 January 1779, when Owen "Paid Regulus (by Mr. Davis)" the sum of £20. Friday, 19 February 1779, was apparently the final occasion on which Regulus favored the *Gazetteer* with his correspondence.

The general subject of the Regulus letters was contemporary politics, and their tone was decidedly anti-ministerial. The theme most frequently treated was the war with America, which Regulus thought had been brought on by ministerial blunders and the pernicious growth of the royal prerogative, but the letters of 1775–79 constitute a running commentary of sorts upon all the most outstanding political events and Parliamentary measures of their time, and in this respect they are reminiscent of Junius. In some cases a single letter was devoted to a single topic, but from 1776 groups of letters were published as numbered series of essays, each dealing with a general theme. Thus in April and May 1776 appeared five letters addressed to "Attilius," a pro-ministerial writer who had severely criticized Richard Price's *Observations on . . . the Justice and Policy of the War with America;* in the following month Regulus addressed three letters directly to Dr. Price praising his enlistment in the cause of liberty; in September the *Gazetteer* published in nine installments a reply by Regulus to

Dr. Johnson's *Taxation no Tyranny;* [11] in January 1777 seven letters were devoted to "Remarks on the Declaratory Act"; and
the following two months produced five letters "On Juries and
Libels."

Regulus wrote well. His letters display wit, learning, and a
considerable talent for the techniques of political controversy. He
was skilled in the use of irony and vituperation as well as in the
less emotional form of argument by logical analysis. In short,
Regulus was truly deserving of the designation frequently applied
by the printer to other political essayists, that of a "valuable correspondent," and Owen's payments to him, totaling £160 in just
over three years, indicate that he was so considered. [12]

Far less numerous than the letters of Regulus were the contributions of a "Roderic M'Alpin," largely confined to the theme of
royal influence in Parliament. In all, about a score of letters over
this signature were published in the *Gazetteer* between November
1775 and May 1779. The period of M'Alpin's most frequent appearance was the summer of 1778, when eight letters appeared
between 22 June and 2 September. Owen's account book records
a total of eight payments to this writer between 18 August 1778
and 1 November 1779, but the payments were apparently not
directly related to the publication of the signed letters. During
August and September 1778 Owen's payments to M'Alpin totaled
£1 6s. 6d. per month and may have constituted a regular salary
for contributions published anonymously; in the following year,
however, the writer was paid separately for each contribution. On
16 April 1779 Owen recorded a payment of five shillings to "Rod
M'Alpin for a Letter in April," and six days later another of 1s 6d.
"for 2 Para[graph]s." Similar payments varying from two shillings
to £1 3s. 6d. were made at irregular intervals between July 1778
and December 1779 to one George Tytler, all of whose contributions to the paper seem to have been anonymous. It is, of course,
impossible to determine the nature and extent of the anonymous
writing done by these men for the *Gazetteer,* but variations in the
amounts of Owen's payments to them and the irregularity with
which the payments were made indicate that they were occasional
contributors and probably "collectors" whose emolument depended
entirely upon the quantities of intelligence they submitted. Owen's
payment of them may have been a matter of convenience rather
than of administrative policy, for his bookshop and "Mineral Water
Warehouse" at No. 11 Fleet Street had long been, and continued

until nearly the end of the century to be, a receiving station for advertisements, letters, and "articles of intelligence."

Another series of entries in the publisher's ledger illustrates one more of William Owen's activities in connection with the *Gazetteer*. Between November 1776 and February 1778 there were published in the paper a series of thirty-four essays, ranging in length from two to four columns each, under the general title of "Characters." Each essay dealt with a single contemporary political figure, tracing his career in some detail and commenting upon his "parliamentary conduct." Their popularity was such that in the autumn of 1777 a collected edition, "Revised and corrected by the AUTHOR, Since the original Publication in the GAZETTEER," was issued at half a crown by John Bew, Paternoster Row bookseller and publisher of the *General Evening Post* which Mary Say now printed.[13] Payment by the *Gazetteer* to the author of the Characters must have been made by the printer, since Owen recorded no disbursements for the purpose. Financial negotiations for the collected edition, however, seem to have been his responsibility. From entries in the account book, it appears that the *Gazetteer* proprietors, as owners of the copyright, were paid a percentage of the profits on John Bew's sales of the volume. Between 8 April 1778 and 22 December 1779 Owen entered receipts from "Mr. Bew on Account of Characters" totaling £13 4*s.*, and on the latter date he received 127 books, which, at 2*s.* 6*d.* each, would have had a retail value of £15 11*s.* 6*d.* The proprietors' receipts from this edition, then, may have run as high as £28 15*s.* 6*d.*, though it is probable that the copies they received would have been disposed of, two years after publication, at less than the published price.[14]

A discussion of some of the materials found in the single *Gazetteer* account book surviving for the years 1775–79 has, it is to be hoped, indicated the general nature of William Owen's activities as publisher of the paper. It should be emphasized, however, that although the book throws some light on the background of the daily publication, the information it contains is mostly fragmentary, posing a number of problems in interpretation and leaving much to be desired in the way of detail. Reference to other items in the accounts will be made at appropriate points in the *Gazetteer*'s history.

Although sentiments favoring the cause of the American provinces continued to be expressed in the columns of the paper throughout the 1770's by writers like Regulus and Roderic M'Alpin, the general attitude of the paper, so far as it is perceptible, appears to have altered sharply, albeit temporarily, in the months immediately following Charles Say's death. On 25 August 1775 the *Gazetteer* published the royal proclamation for the suppression of rebellion and sedition which had been issued two days before. Six days later there began to appear in the *London* column expressions of approval for the punitive measures undertaken against the colonies by the British government. Members of the opposition—"patriots," they were called—were exhorted not to allow party animosities to blind them to their duties as Britons, and to support the government in the necessary steps it was taking to suppress the rebellion.[15] Such comparatively moderate Tory views continued to be expressed throughout September 1775, although the columns of correspondence allayed any suspicion that the paper was in danger of becoming an organ of Lord North's ministry.

Further indication of a change in editorial policy is to be found in an episode of September 1775. On Tuesday, 19 September, a paragraph in the paper implicitly accused John Wilkes, Lord Mayor of London, of "evading public justice and refusing to put the laws in execution on the clearest proofs." The following day Wilkes requested the printer to wait upon him at the Guildhall. Mary Say complied by sending a representative, "who was informed by his Lordship . . . that whatever abuse on his private character he might pass by unnoticed, he could never permit any reflection to be made on his majesterial conduct, without offering a justification." Wilkes therefore requested the printer to call upon the writer of the paragraph to state his complaint publicly, under his real name, in order that it might be answered in the same manner. On Friday, 22 September, the author of the offending paragraph replied in the *Gazetteer* offering to wait upon the Lord Mayor, or to "lay the whole transaction before the public." On the same day the paper published a letter professedly written by an unknown correspondent which took Wilkes to task for having usurped that authority, in summoning the printer, which he had formerly "denied to other public stations," and accused him of countenancing a meeting in the City "to consider the means to support his Majesty's rebellious subjects in America." The next day "two persons" from the *Gazetteer* waited upon the Lord Mayor at Guildhall. "His Lordship asked if the author of the paragraph was there. No answer was made." The "subject of complaint," they told Wilkes, had been merely his failure to punish a waterman for "taking more than his fare." The Lord Mayor protested that such matters were outside his jurisdiction, and the *Gazetteer* concluded, rather meekly, "It should seem now, that this virulent complaint against the Lord Mayor is, the not having exerted a power which he has not by law." On Thursday, 28 September, it was reported that Wilkes, once more conciliatory, had "appealed to the Printer, whether, in all the cards and messages, he had ever employed any other expressions than the *wishing, desiring,* or *requesting* any thing [i.e., the printer's attendance]." [16]

The tempest resulting from so trivial a motive (if the complaint actually reported to the Lord Mayor was indeed the true motive of the unflattering reference to him in the paper) was curious enough; the *Gazetteer*'s publication of such a reflection on Wilkes was a startling departure from the generally sympathetic view which it had previously taken of his activities.

Another obvious alteration in the paper's nature concerned the treatment of correspondents whose letters were not published at length. In place of the occasional, italicized paragraphs in which the printer had summarized or commented upon such correspondence, there now appeared only brief notices acknowledging receipt and acceptance of letters (e.g., "X.Y.Z.—A.B.—A SOLICITOR—Tomorrow"). As a substitute for the columns of observations from correspondents, comment upon letters received was introduced into the *London* news columns. On Saturday, 30 September 1775, a paragraph headed "Intelligence" described some allegedly dishonest transactions by one Mr. Blowers, a New England attorney. On the following Monday, another correspondent wrote in defense of Blowers to contradict the accusations of the first writer. Two days later, in the *London* column, appeared this paragraph:

The person who sent the [first] paragraph concerning *Blowers,* the lawyer at Boston, acquaints his *scoundrel friend and correspondent,* the paragraph writer of Monday, that the matter related, under the head of Intelligence on Saturday, is a TRUTH, which Blowers himself *dare not* deny. If he chooses to make a further replication, the whole affair shall be produced properly authenticated.

The tone of this paragraph was, to say the least, distinct from the impersonal objectivity which had characterized the *Gazetteer*'s *London* column for 25 years.

The obvious inference from these changes is that in the months immediately following Say's death the paper had acquired a new conductor (use of the title "editor" was still three years in the future), but any attempt to identify him must be based largely upon a process of elimination.

James Perry, the *Gazetteer*'s most renowned editor, is known to have succeeded to the position in 1783 "on the death of a Mr. Wall." [17] This, as I shall attempt to show later, was probably the same Wall designated by John Almon as the paper's first Parliamentary reporter in 1770.[18] Records of payments to him in William Owen's accounts indicate that he had become editor by 1780, and other evidence suggests a date sometime in the previous year. The years 1775 to 1779 remain, then, the only period of the paper's later history for which the name of its conductor is unknown. There was, however, a minor poet and writer of miscellaneous prose flourishing during this period who is said to have been "for a considerable time Editor of the *Gazetteer*." His name was John Huddlestone Wynne.

Details of Wynne's career as given in the very amusing and candid memoir of him written by his eldest son in 1806 [19] generally support the assumption that the period of his editorship fell within the three years following Charles Say's death. Born in 1743, Wynne attended St. Paul's School for a time and was apprenticed at thirteen to a printer. Shortly after completing his term, about 1763, he obtained a lieutenancy in the East India service, but "in less than two years from his departure returned to England," and "resolved on the expedient of trying his success as an Author." He was engaged in various literary tasks by a number of the London booksellers, and John Wheble hired him at a fixed salary to conduct the *Lady's Magazine,* which commenced publication in 1770, the year of Wynne's marriage. While the memoir is exasperatingly indefinite as to the chronology of his career from this point onward, the fact that the statement concerning his connection with the *Gazetteer* follows a rather lengthy discussion of his marriage seems to indicate that the writer of the memoir considered it chronologically as the next noteworthy event of his father's life. Mention of the editorship is also closely connected with a discussion of Wynne's political views at the time of the American Revolution. I quote the relevant passage:

Mr. Wynne was for a considerable time Editor of the Gazetteer, and was a well-known speaker at the Robin Hood and Coachmakers Hall Debating Societies; but, being unhappily a staunch supporter of an Administration whose measures were extremely unpopular, he got little good by his political speculations. In those days such topics were freely discussed, and often agitated with much warmth. Mr. Wynne in this respect acted the part of a champion and undertook to defend the Ministry in their War with America, and other ruinous measures.

Such sentiments certainly coincide with those occasionally expressed in the news columns of the *Gazetteer* during the late summer and autumn of 1775, and if Wynne was conducting the paper at this time, the fact may explain why the *Gazetteer* temporarily incurred the displeasure of the Lord Mayor, John Wilkes. Wynne's support of the Tory ministry, his son continues,

was done in the most disinterested and ingenuous manner possible, as he acted purely from the dictates of his own opinion. On his return from these heated debates, way-laid by some of the opposite party, many an unmerciful drubbing has he suffered, and once was so cruelly beaten that his life was endangered. It was in one of these rencounters that the lachrymal vessels of his right eye became contused, and occasioned him to undergo at times the most excruciating agonies, to alleviate which he frequently had recourse to large doses of opium. —But the most fatal accident happened at the time when he was in the zenith of his fame, about the year 1778, when, crossing Snow-hill on a dark night, he was run-over by a hackney-coach, and his leg broken in three places. . . . Owing to the terrible manner in which it was shattered, sixteen weeks elapsed ere it was judged proper to shift the leg from the cradle that encompassed it . . . and an instrument was obliged to be had to enable him to walk. . . .

During this confinement, Wynne was "obliged to remain nearly in a horizontal position."

More concrete information is lacking, but the emphasis placed on Wynne's martyr-like devotion to the Tory cause in the American war, and the date of his almost total physical disability fairly justify, I think, the conclusion that he edited the *Gazetteer* during at least a part of the three-year period following Charles Say's death. The evidence cited of changes in the paper during the latter part of 1775 seems to indicate that he began editing it at that time. If he remained in the position after 1775, however, he concealed his political views, for by the summer of 1776 comments in the *London* column favoring ministerial policies in the American war had ceased to appear.[20]

The autumn of 1775 witnessed, as well as the editorial changes already discussed, two minor events that are worthy of note. The first was the announcement on Saturday, 2 September, of the

establishment of a new receiving station for letters and advertisements at the shop of J. Marks, bookseller in St. Martin's Lane.
Several statements rendered by Marks to the *Gazetteer* proprietors
show that he received a commission of fourpence on every advertisement he took in, and that he was paid sixpence for each
letter or article of intelligence transmitted to the paper.[21] It is
probable that these rates were standard among the daily newspapers of the time. The second event—apparently an innovation
for the *Gazetteer*—was the installation of a letter box in the window of the printing office. "Many a Courtier and many a Patriot,"
the announcement read, "will drop a letter there, who would blush
to open the door and throw it on the counter, for fear of being
known another time. —For the convenience of all our correspondents, a hole is cut in the shutter, that letters may be conveyed into
the box either at night or on Sundays." [22]

On New Year's Day 1776 the most significant typographical
change in more than a decade occurred with the substitution of
single vertical rules between columns for the double ones which
had, since May of 1765, distinguished the *Gazetteer* from other
papers. These, with a new font of type, including ornamental de-
vices to set off advertisements and new factotum blocks, gave
the paper a cleaner, less cluttered appearance than it had presented
in previous years.[23] In July 1776 the government increased the
stamp duty on newspapers from a penny to three halfpence, and
the printer apologized to readers for a corresponding increase in
the paper's selling price:

The additional Duty of a Third Halfpenny on Newspapers, which
takes place Tomorrow, will oblige the Printer of this Paper from that
Day to raise the Price to Three-pence for each Paper. As this Advance
is no more than the additional Duty, and as it is evident, that a Capital
of One-Third more must necessarily be employed in Business, without
the Emolument of a single Farthing, it is humbly hoped that this
alteration will not be deemed unreasonable.[24]

The next four months passed without incident, but early in
December one of the *Gazetteer*'s contributors, and by implication
the paper itself, was subjected to criticism by a rival publication.
The criticism evoked the first allusion by the *Gazetteer* to the
death of Charles Say.

On Monday, 9 December 1776, the *New Morning Post* (a daily
publication issued for a short time by a disgruntled former printer
of the *Morning Post*) [25] remarked that, as there was that day no

news of any importance from the courts of law, the opportunity would be taken "of clearing up a few points outstanding between us and a brother intelligencer in another paper. . . ." "The man alluded to," it continued, "is the writer of parliamentary and law intelligence in the *Gazetteer*, be he who he will." The writer then proceeded to point out what he considered to be three incidents of error in recent *Gazetteer* reports of legal cases. The critique concluded with a number of interesting and pointed remarks:

To conclude, we hope every sensible candid reader will see the necessity of this expostulation. . . . If we [the newspapers] tell stories quite contradictory, who is to be believed? Say some people, The Gazetteer is an old paper, and the managers long experienced in the business; the Morning Post is new, we cannot so confidently rely upon it; therefore will suppose the Gazetteer most authentic. God knows, the Gazetteer may be very old, may be quite superannuated, and debilitated, having lost its late renowned printer and manager: but we trust, that *truth* is older and stronger than all that can oppose it. To the authentic records of these august and venerable judicatures, we refer the candid readers for judgment between us.

Aside from their direct application these remarks are of special interest as reflecting what may well have been a general public estimate of the *Gazetteer* in 1776—that it was old, and therefore venerable. The dignity of age was soon to be stressed directly by the paper itself; meanwhile, the reply it gave to the *New Morning Post* was a fair specimen of such dignity: "It was an invariable rule," the reply began,

with the late "renowned Printer and Manager of this paper," as he is with great justice stiled in a morning publication of Monday last, *never* to enter into any altercation with his brethren. —He said it denoted a lack of matter, but above all, silence on his part was the only sure means of *defeating* the grand *object* of those attacks, which was the desperate falling situation of the persons who made them, that of writing into *public notice,* a paper verging, perhaps, on the predestined state of eternal oblivion. This conduct did greater honour to the penetration and judgment of that worthy man. —Convinced of the wisdom of the rule, and the justice of the reasoning on which it was founded, his successors have inviolably adhered to it, and mean to observe it as religiously as he did, whenever the subject endeavoured to be *dragged* into the controversy, is merely personal between them and their brethren, or grows out of matter coming or supposed to come, directly within their own cognizance, in the way of their *business*. —Some of the observations, however, contained in the publication alluded to, *not* coming within that description, at the desire of the gentleman who occasionally sends the greatest part of our law intelligence, we have permitted him room for the following justification.[26]

The *Gazetteer*'s law reporter was less temperate in his scorn, and, in a point by point refutation of the *Post* criticisms, made use of such epithets as "pompous solemn blockhead" to describe his antagonist. The rejoinder of the *New Morning Post* expressed resentment that the *Gazetteer* had not deigned even to name the paper which had attacked it, indicating that the *Gazetteer*'s diagnosis of motives had not been greatly erroneous. "With pleasure we see, however," the *New Morning Post* consoled itself, "we have extracted the first tributary tear of esteem and gratitude, paid to the late renowned printer and manager of that paper, that we remember to have seen therein. How far his successors have inviolably followed his example, may appear by and by." Then the *Post* writer made sport of the rather stilted language in which the *Gazetteer*'s reply had been delivered: "As to 'matter growing out of matter, coming or supposed to come, directly within their own cognizance,' we leave to more learned readers than we are to explain or understand. . . ." Finally, replying to the "blockhead" epithet employed by the *Gazetteer* law reporter, the *Post* referred again to Charles Say: "This is not the politest language, and is a very awkward imitation of their late renowned manager, who studied decency and good sense; and always thought the want of decency implied the want of sense." The *Gazetteer*, in subsequent issues, maintained an aloof silence.

The year 1777 was for those engaged in the production of the paper relatively uneventful. While the essays of Regulus and the Parliamentary Characters were the outstanding political features of the paper, the only change in the general content during this year was the increased frequency with which poetry appeared. Henry Sampson Woodfall in the *Public Advertiser* had for some years featured occasionally a "Poet's Corner" on page four of his paper, and the practice had been adopted by a number of his competitors, notably the *Morning Chronicle*, printed by his brother William, and the *Morning Post*. The *Gazetteer* in this instance was undoubtedly following a trend which had proved its popularity in the other papers. Eulogistic verses on the celebrated clergyman and forger Dr. William Dodd, signed "J. H. W——NE,"[27]

and "Verses occasioned by the Death of Samuel Foote, Esq.,"
signed "W——." [28] were probably the productions of John Huddlestone Wynne. With these exceptions, however, all the poetry
in the *Gazetteer* was either unsigned or pseudonymous. While
some of the verse published was original and perhaps even paid
for by the printer, there was a considerable interchange of poetry
among the daily papers; a competent piece of verse appearing for
the first time in one of them was almost certain to be reprinted by
the others. [29]

Two noteworthy events in the paper's history occurred in 1778.
One was an innovation; the other had become by then almost a
matter of routine. On Friday, 19 June 1778, a letter signed "An
Honest Man" appeared on the front page of the *Gazetteer*. It was
occasioned, the writer said, by the bill in Parliament to relieve
Roman Catholics of some of the legal disabilities to which they
had been subjected since the time of William III. Moved by the
introduction of the bill to "enquire minutely into the causes which
brought about the Revolution" of 1688, the writer had concluded
that among them were the granting by James II of liberty of
conscience to the Papists and the "unbounded ambition of an artful
hypocrite," namely, William of Orange. In the course of his argument, "An Honest Man" strove to give the impression that he
was highly sympathetic to the Catholic cause and that he resented
the Revolution in which the English "with their usual sagacity, not
seeing an inch before their noses, perceived not that the crafty
Hollander was all along duping them, and only using them as
steps to mount the throne." The writer's efforts were eminently
successful. On the following day Roderic M'Alpin called him a
papist, a supporter of the Pretender, and an enemy to George III,
hoping that he did not represent the sentiments of all Roman
Catholics. Other replies to the letter were less temperate. A careful reading of the letter gives the impression that "An Honest
Man" was rather more clever than the writers who later attacked
him. No papist would have written so strongly on the matter as he
did, for the bill in question, introduced by Sir George Saville, had
the support of both ministry and opposition and was in fact passed
without even a division in the House of Commons. "An Honest
Man," in his immoderate condemnation of the Glorious Revolution, was almost certainly attempting to discredit the Roman
Catholics by too strongly supporting their cause. He had, however, gone too far.

A person employed by the government's Messenger of the Press and designated only as "John Boult's young Man" purchased a copy of the *Gazetteer* at the printing office on 19 June, and before the end of the following month Attorney General Wedderburn had filed an *ex officio* information against Mary Say.[30]

The terms in which the information was couched, though determined in large measure by routine legal formality, could hardly have been more formidable. Mary Say, to her surprise there can be no doubt, found herself described in part as

being a wicked malicious seditious and ill disposed person and being greatly disaffected to our . . . sovereign Lord the King . . . devising contriving and intending to traduce and vilify the late happy Revolution providentially brought about and effected under the wise and prudent conduct of . . . William the Third . . . [seeking] by most wicked cunning and artful Insinuations to represent suggest and cause it to be believed that the s^d. Revolution was an unjustifiable and unconstitutional proceeding. . . .

Thus characterized, it is hardly to be wondered at that Mary "with force of arms at London . . . did print and Publish . . . a certain false scandalous malicious and seditious Libel . . . intitled The Gazetteer and New Daily Advertiser." Even without the legal power it embodied, this information if printed in the *Gazetteer* might have been a more forceful answer to the letter of "An Honest Man" than any of the essays written specifically for the purpose.

The proceedings in the case were parallel to those of 1770 involving Junius' letter to the King; publication alone constituted guilt, and Mary Say, a lone defendant, did not attempt to fight the suit. In a memorial to the Attorney General she stated that the letter had been received by her servants "in the common course of business and by that means found a place in . . . [the] Paper." She had "done all in her power to discover the writer of the . . . Letter but not having succeded therein . . . [was] desirous of making the best Attonement in her power and not to put the Prosecutor to further expence and trouble . . . [had] submitted to Judgment by default. . . ." On 25 April 1779, she was fined £50.

Much more significant than the prosecution of Mary Say in 1778 was the first public application of the term "editor" to the *Gazetteer*'s conductor. Roger Thompson had been referred to by employees of the paper in 1771 as "manager or editor,"[31] and Edward Benson, between 1772 and 1775, had been "commonly called in the . . . printing house the editor of . . . the Gazetteer." [32] But the title had been confined to use within the printing house. Readers of the *Gazetteer* in the 1770's like those in the thirty years preceding, had been taught to look upon the printer as—what Charles Say in fact had been—the paper's guiding intelligence. On 14 September 1778 there was published in the *Gazetteer* the first letter from a pseudonymous correspondent addressed "To the Editor of the Gazetteer." From that date the term was employed consistently in the columns of correspondence, though for some time thereafter announcements concerning the paper's policy were still made in the name of the printer.

The introduction of the new usage was in effect a public acknowledgement that the editorial and typographical aspects of the *Gazetteer* were to be considered as separate departments. Once the fact had been acknowledged, the paper proceeded, in the two years following, to develop what may be most simply described as an "editorial personality."

X

ADVENT OF AN EDITOR

1776-1783

THE term "editorial personality," for want of a better one, has already been employed at several points in this study. The *Gazetteer* of the 1760's under Charles Say had revealed a personality chiefly through the columns of "Observations . . . with Occasional Remarks." [1] Under Roger Thompson the paper's personality had to be largely abstracted from the total of its contents; for though external evidence could provide a good deal of information about the personalities of Thompson himself and of Charles Say, the *Gazetteer* reflected none of the tension which existed between the two men, and in fact no part of their characters save perhaps Thompson's determination in the dispute with Parliament and Say's invariable rule never to enter publicly "into any altercation with his brethren." The paper did not, in short, speak directly to readers either of its printer or of itself. Of all its characteristics the most obvious was impersonality. Under Say's successors—John Huddlestone Wynne, Edward Benson, and perhaps others—a number of changes, described in the preceding chapter, occurred. They were, however, for the most part temporary. Without undue exaggeration, it may be said that the paper from 1776 to 1779 had no personality at all. Regulus, M'Alpin, the author of Characters and other writers employed by the *Gazetteer* each manifested in his works at least a political personality which was of considerable interest to readers; the paper itself functioned only as a silent vehicle for the works of such correspondents.

This function is not to be disparaged, for it conformed to a

widely accepted and highly valued concept of contemporary journalism which had become almost traditional, and which the *Gazetteer* itself, with such other leading papers as the *Daily Advertiser* and the *Public Advertiser*, had played a large part in establishing. *The Public Advertiser* after 1775 still had its "Mr. Woodfall," the printer, to whom correspondents addressed their remarks as they had previously, on occasion, to "Mr. Say." The *Gazetteer* from 1775 was without even a definite figurehead of this kind, until the title of editor was publicly introduced in 1778. The usage was then by no means unprecedented, and though its introduction may be clearly recognized as an important step in the development of the modern newspaper, the *Gazetteer* had been brought to take that step, so far as can be deduced, more by a process of gradual evolution than by any conscious attempt at innovation.

The decade of the 1770's marked the beginning of a period of significant growth in London journalism. By 1776 several new daily papers were competing strongly with the *Gazetteer* and other long-established publications. *The Morning Post*, founded in 1772, was by the middle of the decade specializing in "fashionable" intelligence designed to appeal to West End readers as distinguished from the commercial classes which the *Gazetteer* had long professed to serve.[2] *The Morning Chronicle*, established in 1769, achieved eminence when it was taken over by William Woodfall, the most famous theatrical critic and Parliamentary reporter of his day.[3] Finally, in 1776 was founded the *General Advertiser*, the paper on which James Perry a few years later was to gain his earliest experience as a journalist.[4]

The conductor of the *Morning Post*, from its commencement, had been designated in that paper as the editor, and while William Woodfall was actually the printer of the *Morning Chronicle*, and referred to himself as such, his chief activities were generally recognized as those of critic and debate reporter, and his frequent addresses to the public in the paper lent much to it of the personality which the *Gazetteer* acquired after 1778. Here, then, were at least two precedents for the introduction of editorial personality into the *Gazetteer*. The strength of their influence was determined largely by the pressure of the competition they brought to bear.

Among factors conducive to the foundation of a daily newspaper after 1770, by far the most outstanding was the public demand for reports of the Parliamentary debates. These had by 1775 replaced the animadversions of political essayists as the most

important single item of content in the daily papers,[5] and a corresponding importance was naturally attached to the abilities of the
various Parliamentary reporters. The result was that the relative
competence of these correspondents became, in the latter half of
the decade, probably the chief basis of competition among the daily
papers. Between 1775 and 1780 the growth of such competition
was made apparent in the columns of the *Gazetteer* through frequent assurances to the public that the reports given in that paper
were distinctly superior to those of any other. In November 1775,
for example, this notice was appended to a report of a debate in
the House of Lords:

The industry we have hitherto exerted to procure the most *authentic*,
as well as *important* PARLIAMENTARY INTELLIGENCE for the readers
of the GAZETTEER, has fully answered our most sanguine expectations,
and at the same time afforded an opportunity to the intelligent part
of the public, to give a clear, unbiassed testimony in our favour. Convinced of the superiority which the great objects of national consideration claim when thrown in the scale, and opposed to the mere inefficient
weight of *personal altercation* and *parliamentary anecdote*, we have
uniformly acted on suitable motives, and have frequently foregone our
own ease and convenience purely with a view of giving satisfaction to
our readers, and preserving our reputation in the great line of politics
by similar means to those by which we originally acquired it.[6]

The claim to superiority in this instance was based on the *Gazetteer*'s general method of giving the substance of the proceedings—
that is, of emphasizing "the great objects of national consideration" to the exclusion of verbal altercation between members of
Parliament. The statement contained an implied criticism almost
certainly directed at William Woodfall's *Morning Chronicle*,
which published by far the most lengthy and detailed Parliamentary
reports of any London newspaper. Woodfall, nicknamed "Memory," was renowned for his ability to report in the minutest detail
the proceedings of a long debate without having taken notes. This
talent and the notoriety attendant upon it, as well as the excellence of the resulting reports, made the *Morning Chronicle* the
paper most highly famed for Parliamentary intelligence and hence
the chief object of the *Gazetteer*'s rivalry.

A more pointed claim to superiority over competitors appeared
in the *Gazetteer* at the opening of the 1777 Parliamentary session:

The very favourable reception our endeavours for some years past to
furnish the most authentic and interesting Parliamentary intelligence

has met with, binds us, by every tie of duty and respect, to do all in our power to merit a like public encouragement on one hand, and friendly and important communications on the other. We take this opportunity, in *particular*, of returning our most *grateful* and *sincere* thanks to the two valuable Correspondents, who sent us the Debates on the Habeas Corpus Bill; the motion for paying off the Arrears in the Civil List; the Budget; and the Report of the Resolutions in the Committee of Supply of the 14th of May last, as *nothing* material, indeed worth public notice, relative to those very interesting Parliamentary proceedings, appeared in *any* contemporary print.[7]

In this case the emphasis was, of course, on the coverage of events not reported by Woodfall or any other competitor. The claim of assistance received directly from members of the House of Commons may be credited. It was repeated often, and in February 1778, when the gallery of the House was temporarily closed to "strangers," the *Gazetteer* continued to publish brief abstracts of the proceedings and expressed its gratitude to the "very obliging and respectable correspondent" who had furnished them.[8]

The most striking feature of the reports published by the paper was that from the beginning of 1776 they revealed an increasing tendency to favor, whenever possible, the members of the opposition in Parliament. The bias expressed was by no means extreme, and the tone of the commentary frequently interspersed in the reports was far removed from that employed by some of the regular political essayists. In general, the tendency took the form simply of seldom allowing the Tories to have the best of it; for example: "An altercation now arose between the Marquis of Rockingham and Lord Suffolk, in which the latter spoke with great violence and inconsistency." [9] A pro-ministerial writer signing himself "Detector" complained of the tendency and described the techniques employed:

Your very *candid* correspondent, who favors you with the Parliamentary Debates, is desired for the future to amend . . . the title which he generally prefixes thereto: and instead of "A short account of the debate in the House, on, &c." to introduce his parliamentary memoirs, by calling them, according to their true appellation, "Strictures on the debate, &c." He will then be justified in puffing the harangues of every minority declaimer, by the side-wind epithets of "ably, pointed, pertinently, sensibly, usual ability," and innumerable others. . . . He may then make his observations on the want of temper, modesty, reasoning, or even constitutionalism, in the speeches of the members on the side of government, may damn their most pointed expressions, by the assistance of Italics, and consign whole sentences to perdition, by the significant use of marks of admiration.[10]

It is significant that two days after the criticism appeared it was answered in a letter on page 1 by the debate reporter himself, who accused "Detector" of being a ministerial hack writing on behalf of Lord Mulgrave. Mulgrave, the reporter stated, frequently sent out "manufactured" speeches to be printed in the papers in order to puff himself. At the opening of the 1778 session a letter from "Candour" complimented the *Gazetteer* on its "very spirited and impartial" Parliamentary intelligence but suggested that all bias and coloring not inherent in the debates themselves be omitted from the reports published. This practice, Candour declared, would not cause the paper to lose any of the correspondents who supplied it with Parliamentary intelligence.[11] On the following day the *Gazetteer* declared: ". . . as we are promised the same assistance in parliamentary matters as formerly, [we] doubt not of being enabled to preserve that superiority above the other papers which has been hitherto universally allowed us."

The obvious inference seems to be that the *Gazetteer*'s friends in Parliament were all members of the opposition and that the paper's debate reporter had little sympathy for the policies of the North ministry. Since the debates were the most important feature of the paper, and since frequent declarations of their superiority had made them the feature most closely associated in the minds of readers with the voice of the paper, any distinction once made between the political sentiments of the *Gazetteer*'s debate reporter and those of the *Gazetteer* itself was gradually obliterated. As William Woodfall was both the debate reporter and the voice of the *Morning Chronicle*, the *Gazetteer*'s debate reporter, through the growing competition which emphasized his function, came to be considered the voice of the *Gazetteer*.

I have already remarked that between 1776 and 1779 the *Gazetteer* possessed no editorial personality. It may now be seen, however, that during the period such a personality, in a political sense, had been evolving in the columns of Parliamentary intelligence, and that by the end of 1778 readers may already have come to identify it with the personality of the paper itself. The frequent inclusion of Parliamentary reports within the columns of formal intelligence (i.e., the *London* columns) and the analogy to be drawn from Memory Woodfall's dual function in the *Morning*

Chronicle would have been conducive to such an identification. The final stage in the process was the transfer of the political opinions expressed in the debate reports from their subordinate position in those reports to a position of general authority in the paper. This occurred only after the *Gazetteer* publicly acknowledged itself possessed of an editor, and it did not occur suddenly even then.

During the three years following Charles Say's death the announcements which the *Gazetteer* had occasionally made directly to its readers had revealed some inconsistency. Before 1775 all such notices had been phrased as addresses from the printer; thereafter comparatively few, like the announcement of a new font of type in 1776, had been so phrased. The majority of announcements, like the reply to the attack of the *New Morning Post* and the recommendations of the paper's Parliamentary reports, had been unidentified with any one person connected with the paper and had employed the very indefinite nominative which has since come to be known as the editorial *we.* The adoption by the paper in the autumn of 1778 of the title "editor" to designate the recipient of letters from correspondents finally provided for this previously incorporeal voice, though without specific acknowledgment of the fact, a local habitation and a name. In the two years which followed, the pronouncements of the voice—now identified as that of the editor—became increasingly frequent and embraced an ever widening variety of topics. When, finally, they came to include the expressions of political opinion previously relegated to the Parliamentary reports, the *Gazetteer* had acquired a fully developed editorial personality. It is to the final stages of this development that we now direct our attention.

In the year 1779 three phases of editorial policy became for the first time clearly apparent. All were undoubtedly motivated in part by the increasing pressure of competition, but only two give unmistakable evidence of the fact. The first was the development of a less impersonal approach to readers shown by a tendency to explain directly some of the problems and policies that influenced the *Gazetteer*'s content. When, for example, the editor felt obliged to explain the absence, for some weeks before, of the column of news copied from the other papers, the mere acknowledgment of such obligation was a significant departure from previous practice:

Several correspondents having expressed a concern that the plan of inserting *Articles of Intelligence from the other Daily Papers,* has been for some time discontinued, it is become our duty to inform them that it was found impossible to continue it during the last session of Parliament on account of the multiplicity of important business then transacted, but they are assured that it will now be resumed, and that such articles will in future be inserted in the last page.[12]

This tendency is apparent again in an address to correspondents whose contributions had been condensed for publication,[13] and in the direct request which the editor made in December 1779 for assistance in gathering news:

We respectfully make our grateful acknowledgements to such of our correspondents as are so good as to send us any articles of intelligence. To give early and authentic intelligence has ever been, and will continue to be, the first object of our paper—and in return to those correspondents who contribute their share to fulfill our intention, we promise, *caeteris paribus*, to give a preference to their essays during the recess of Parliament.[14]

The second phase of the new policy was a candid admission of the *Gazetteer*'s role as a competitor among the London papers and the beginning of an appeal to the *Gazetteer*'s age as a basis for its claim to superiority. In July 1779 a letter addressed "To the EDITOR of the GAZETTEER" by one "Nestor" commented pointedly upon some growing fashions among newspapers of the day. Nestor considered a newspaper, he said, as a kind of House of Commons in which every British subject might express his political sentiments:

I hope your long-established and respectable paper will ever preserve that air of candour by which it is distinguished; and that you will continue to make it your first object to communicate . . . not only political intelligence, but also political reasonings and observations. . . . I am now an old man, and I was wont to read the Gazetteer, I suppose before you was born. In those days, Gentlemen in coffee-houses would have been very much disappointed, if they had not found in your paper something in the politic way; and would have thought you very impertinent, if you had amused them with stories concerning frail ladies, or other frivolous anecdotes. Strangers, in those good days, used to converse very sociably in coffee-houses concerning public affairs; but now there is nothing but whispering, or a total silence. In a word, there is too much whispering, both in the news-papers and elsewhere. And I confess I am afraid lest my old friend the Gazetteer should take a tincture of the times. . . . There are many of your old readers who are more concerned with the state of the nation than with the weaknesses and indiscretions of foolish women. . . .

The possibility that Nestor's remarks had been written to order cannot be ignored. Nevertheless, they evoked a lengthy reply. The immediate publication of the letter, said the editor, should prove to Nestor that his admonitions had been "taken in good part":

We cannot, however, admit his insinuation that the *Gazetteer* is deviating into that dirty, though fashionable path, of personal scandal. —We call the public to witness, that we never insulted their under-standings with the trifling tittle-tattle of an old maid's tea-table, and have ever scorned to profit by disturbing the peace of private families— we equally abhor the inventors and propagators of such tales. In answer to NESTOR's other remarks, we can only say, that for a period of more than forty years, the *Gazetteer* has been ever attentive to the points he so properly recommends to our present attention; and we flatter our-selves that the very original and authentic accounts of the proceedings of Parliament, printed in the *Gazetteer*, for the session just finished, will satisfy NESTOR that we have not relaxed in that attention.[15]

The reference to tittle-tattle and personal scandal was aimed pri-marily at the *Morning Post*. A few months later, in rejecting the offering of a correspondent, the editor again took occasion to stress "the multiplication of newspapers" and the "length of time that the *Gazetteer* has been established"; [16] in the following year, when the tax on advertisements was increased by sixpence, an address from the proprietors stressed both the paper's age and the increas-ing competition to which it was exposed:

The Proprietors of this Paper beg leave to remind their advertising Customers, that the new Tax of six-pence on every advertisement will take place on Thursday next the 1st of June; from which day the Proprietors, who propose no advantage to themselves, will be under the necessity of charging this additional duty.

The established credit of the Gazetteer, as a commercial and popular Paper, for thirty years past, and the superior sale it still preserves, amidst the encreased and *encreasing* number of News-papers (successful and unsuccessful) of the present day, may serve to convince its advertising friends of the advantages arising to them, from an extensive circulation of their advertisements, compared to a confined sale, within the narrow limits of a party.[17]

Two days before the close of 1779 the *Gazetteer*'s editor reminded readers of several specific "important articles of intelligence, which a correspondent announced through the *Gazetteer* . . . some weeks in all [cases] . . . many weeks, and some months in others, before they appeared in any other contemporary prints." [18]

The third aspect of the new policy in 1779 was an editorial emphasis—noticeably stronger than in the years preceding—upon the abilities of the *Gazetteer*'s debate reporter, not only as a reporter but as a political observer. On 10 June 1779 a letter addressed "To the Editor of the Debates in the Gazetteer" complained of the partiality shown in the accounts of Parliamentary proceedings:

Sir,

As no one admires more than I do the manner in which you almost *verbatim* give us the speeches of the noble Lords or Commons in the Debates, who are your favourites; so do I wish you would be as ingenuous and impartial in that part where yourself only are concerned.

When you speak of the Duke of Richmond, you say, he *ably, fully,* or in a *masterly* stile. The Duke of Manchester *took a large field, and supported his arguments in a masterly manner.* Lord Camden, *learnedly.* Col. Barre *very humourously:* and thus of every man in opposition whom you patronize.

Be impartial, my good Sir; give the speeches on both sides fairly, and never thrust yourself, or your italics, where you are not called upon.

If you take my advice, you will please the greater number of readers; if you do not, you will be called an *able* party writer; but no attention will be paid to your writings, as it will be supposed your account of the debates is not a true one.

You have filled four columns yesterday with the favourite Duke of Richmond; and given twelve lines to Lord Chesterfield, and nine lines to Lord Bathurst: their speeches must have been very bad indeed, to deserve so little of your attention. . . .[19]

The fact that this letter, like previous criticisms of a similar nature, was printed at all is one demonstration (there were many) that opinions favoring the government were by no means excluded from the *Gazetteer*. More striking, however, was the title chosen for the person to whom the letter was directed. The heading "To the Editor of Debates in the Gazetteer" was probably supplied in the *Gazetteer* office; but even if it was not, the use of it in the paper endowed the person responsible for Parliamentary reports with an authority comparable to that of "the Editor of the Gazetteer," thus encouraging an association of the two offices by the public while at the same time maintaining a distinction between them. The letter remained unanswered for almost a month. On 6 July, shortly after the close of the Parliamentary session, an address "To the Public" by "the person who executed that very arduous and laborious task" of reporting debates appeared on page 1. The writer took occasion "to return the most grateful acknowledgments to the Public, for the warm support and decided preference it has given to the Proceedings . . . which have appeared in this paper." He then asked leave to lay before the readers of the *Gazetteer* "some *particulars,* in order to shew, that this encouragement and support were not totally misplaced, either in point of execution, impartiality, or integrity." The justification which followed is of more than ordinary interest, for besides illuminating the techniques employed by the Parliamentary reporter, it treated the bias shown toward members of the opposition as a matter of qualitative selection rather than of party allegiance, though the writer admitted his personal dissatisfaction with the measures of the North ministry.

In discussing his execution of the debate reports, the writer insisted that it could be fairly judged only by members of Parliament or by others who had been present at the debates. A serious problem was created, he said, by a large group of figures each of whom was striving for the limelight, and it had "ever been his study to exercise his judgment to bring them forward, or throw them into the shade, according to the respective merits, and the particular part they took in the subject matter of debate":

For this reason, he avoided, as much as possible, the admission of closet speeches, written before-hand, or manufactured some days after, which long experience has convinced him contain more of what the *composer* of them *thought,* than what he said on the subject: and he had two very good reasons to be confirmed in this judgment: one, that the *first,* or even *second-rate* speakers, never send their speeches to the papers (a very few instances indeed excepted); and that, if way was given to this foolish itch of appearing in print, or of reporting what was so much altered in the closet, that space which ought to be occupied by speakers of *real* genius and abilities, would be filled up by those would-be candidates for parliamentary fame.

Taking up the charge of partiality which had been brought against him by two writers during the past session ("neither of whom he thought worthy of an answer . . . purely because he was convinced, how difficult it is to satisfy people, under the dominion of misinformation and party prejudice"), the *Gazetteer* reporter proceeded to state "the *principles* which . . . [had] hitherto directed his conduct":

Having the *honour, welfare,* and *prosperity* of his country solely at heart, he has all along endeavoured to distinguish those who were the promoters of them, from those perhaps with equal good intention; (for he does not pretend to develop the secret springs of human actions) who were manifestly hurrying it forward towards inevitable destruction. He . . . is persuaded, that the *best*-laid plans often miscarry, through intervening accidents, and unforseen incidents; for the prevention of which, *human wisdom,* however exalted, is totally unequal; but if, after nine years experience, much observation, and every possible attention he was capable of bestowing, he perceived that almost every one measure adopted by the present Administration, failed of its designed effect, and that every predicted consequence, foretold by those who differed in opinion from them, was fulfilled; he thought, from every principle of private or public judgment, he was fully justified in forming an estimate of the *political value* of such men. An estimate, he will be bound to say, fully justified by every rule of political or moral decision; a proof, indeed, little short of that species of demonstration, which, if admitted into discussions relative to *morals* or *politics,* would deserve to be classed next to that denominated mathematical.

If, in acting upon the judgment so formed, the writer had been guilty of prejudice or partiality, he was proud of the fact and would gladly, he declared, reverse his judgment whenever a series of wise measures by administration should prove by their results that the party in power was truly beneficial to the country. Nevertheless, the reporter continued, he rested his defense merely upon what he had done, not on "what were *his own* particular sentiments." He then proceeded to a discussion of the factors governing his presentation of the reports:

He submits to the unprejudiced public whether he has not on all occasions stated *impartially* and in *detail* the speeches of all the Cabinet Ministers and their friends in both Houses, and as far as his ear or memory served him, which they did *indifferently* [i.e., impartially], whether he has not at all times, when the argument *applied* to the subject matter, or to *personal justification,* brought forward *every* reason, *fact,* or exculpatory defence, into the most conspicuous point of view? It may be answered, why make *animadversions?* Why sometimes give in the *lump,* what ought to be brought out in detail? —To this he can return several answers, equally cogent and well-founded. . . . It is enough to say, that he *compressed* the speeches made by the Members in *Opposition* as frequently, and he believes more frequently, than he did those of Administration; and that when he commented, he was always provoked to it by some *law quibble,* some *trick* in debate, by *strings* of *paradoxes* entangling the question in subtleties and abstract reasonings; or . . . by far-fetched and irrelative allusions, by trite jests, worn-out topics, and fulsome panegyrics on the dead and the living.

On the question of integrity the writer declared that he had never courted favor with any man. If a speech was good, "no matter *which side* of the House it came from, he gave it, in the language of the bar, 'to the best of his recollection.' " More specifically, he insisted, he had never sought favor with the members of opposition in anticipation of their coming into power.

This apology by the "editor of the Debates" and the statement of policy it contained may be considered for all practical purposes a *Gazetteer* editorial. The identification of the debate reporter with the editor of the paper was, except in name, complete. In November 1779, shortly before Parliament convened, readers were reminded more emphatically than on any previous occasion of the exclusive priority to be accorded the debates and, incidentally, of the *Gazetteer*'s age and respectability as compared with those of its competitors.[20] In a note appended to that announcement the editor of the *Gazetteer* displayed unmistakably the same political sentiments expressed five months earlier by the paper's Parliamentary reporter: "We take this opportunity of calling to the recollection of readers of the Gazetteer, that this was the first, and for some months the only paper which announced the defection of the Bedford party from the ultimate views of the Court, that monster of political Quixotism the expectation of subduing America by the point of the sword."

A year later, in October 1780, the paper offered two and a half columns of instruction for the benefit of newly elected members of Parliament:

A correspondent, long conversant in the rules and customs of both Houses, and whose knowledge of the law of Parliament, and the application of it, in the course of ordinary proceeding is unquestionable, has favoured us with the following short abstract of the *nature* and *object* of the King's *Writ,* and so on till the House of Commons, in consequence of his Majesty's Speech, shall constitute the Committee of Supply and Ways and Means.[21]

Had the author of these observations been himself a member of Parliament, the editor would almost certainly have called him a "very respectable correspondent" or a "Member of the Legislature." [22] It is probable that the writer, with his "knowledge of the law of Parliament" was actually the paper's own debate reporter for whom, less than a month before, William Owen had purchased a copy of "Hale on the Jurisdiction of Parliaments." [23] The debate reporter, a Mr. Wall, was in the autumn of 1780, and may have been for some time previously, the editor of the *Gazetteer*.

John Almon, in a statement cited earlier,[24] declared that about 1770 the proprietors of the *St. James's Chronicle* "employed one *Wall*" as a reporter of Parliamentary debates, and that Wall, after "a little time," became proficient enough to supply "two newspapers as well as one," and "amplified his accounts for the Gazetteer, after having published the heads in the St. James's Chronicle." In William Owen's account ledger are recorded a total of nineteen payments to a Mr. Wall between September 1780 and January 1783. Of these, six entries indicate specifically that the payments were "on account of Parl[iamentar]y business," "for Lords Debates," or, simply, "for Debates." The name Wall is the only evidence for concluding that the debate reporter in 1780 was the same person who had held that position a decade earlier, but the possibility of such a coincidence in the names of two Parliamentary reporters within ten years seems remote enough. It is at least highly probable that the Wall who had begun reporting debates for the *Gazetteer* under Roger Thompson continued to perform that duty until 1783.[25]

The length of Wall's tenure as editor of the paper cannot be precisely determined. An undated memorandum in Owen's account book listing the "Private Signatures of Correspondents in Pay" gives that of Mr. Wall as "Edit." This certainly predates January 1783 when Wall was succeeded by James Perry. That he was editing the paper as early as the autumn of 1780 is attested by Owen's purchases "for Mr. Wall" of several reference books and a number of pamphlets, at least one of which was reprinted in the *Gazetteer*. The fact that Wall was not mentioned in the accounts before that time does not eliminate the possibility of his having become editor sometime previously, for Owen recorded no payments for Parliamentary reports prior to January 1781, some ten years after the *Gazetteer* had begun publishing them, nor were such payments recorded by the publisher after 1783. One can only conjecture from the general tone of the paper's editorial pronouncements, from the increased emphasis placed upon Parliamentary reports as manifested in the use of the title "Editor of the Debates," and by the long *apologia* quoted earlier, that Wall may have begun editing the *Gazetteer* in 1779. In thus combining the duties of editor and debate reporter, the *Gazetteer* was following a precedent apparently set by William Woodfall; the dual function was to be carried out by every one of Wall's successors to the end of the paper's life.

An effort to identify Mr. Wall otherwise than as editor of the *Gazetteer* makes it necessary to anticipate, for a moment, the chronology of the paper's history. A biographical article on James Perry which was published three years before Perry's death and which appears to contain information that only he himself could have supplied states that Perry became editor of the *Gazetteer* "on the death of a Mr. Wall." [26] The final payment to Wall recorded in Owen's account book was one of twelve guineas, made "by the hands of Mrs. Wall," on 16 January 1783. Two days later, Owen spent eighteen shillings for an "Extra Meeting" of the proprietors' committee at the King's Head. On Tuesday, 21 January 1783, five days after the final payment and three days after what may have been an emergency meeting, the *Gazetteer* and the *Morning Herald* published the following obituary: "Last night died John Henley Wall, Esq; of the Middle Temple, Barrister at Law." John Henley Wall was otherwise unidentified, but the notice of his death was considered worthy of repetition on the following day by two other daily papers, the *Morning Chronicle* and the *General Advertiser*, and it was included at the end of the month in the *Gentleman's Magazine*. John Henley Wall, third son of Patrick W. Wall of Tipperary, Ireland, had been called to the bar on 15 June 1781, only a year and a half before his death; [27] the legal eminence he might have attained in that length of time would hardly have commanded such relatively wide publicity for his demise. I suggest that in view of the coincidence between the dates of his death, of Owen's final payment to Mr. Wall, and of the proprietors' extra meeting, John Henley Wall the barrister was also the editor and debate reporter of the *Gazetteer*. The identification is consonant with the notice taken of his death by four daily newspapers, and it also accords with several inferences to be drawn from matter appearing in the *Gazetteer* between 1776 and 1780.

The New Morning Post in 1776 had criticized "the writer of parliamentary and law intelligence in the Gazetteer, be he who he will," with the apparent knowledge that one man was at that time supplying both kinds of report. The *Gazetteer* in reply had spoken of "the gentleman who occasionally sends us the greatest part of our law intelligence." [28] In 1777 the *Gazetteer*'s debate reporter had identified his critic "Detector" as an attorney's clerk, apparently with some certainty.[29] Two years later, in his address to readers, the debate reporter had consciously employed a legal phrase to describe his efforts; he reported the speeches of both government and opposition members, he said, "in the language of the bar, 'to the best of his recollection.' " [30] Finally, as has been noted, the correspondent who in October 1780 offered instruction to new members of Parliament was described as having "a knowledge of the law of Parliament, and the application of it," and William Owen, on 5 October 1780, paid out 3s. 6d. for "Hale on the Jurisdiction of Parliaments to Mr. Wall." None of these facts may be considered as proof that the *Gazetteer*'s debate reporter from 1776 to 1780 was, what John Henley Wall must then have been, a student of the law preparing for the bar; but they do not tend to diminish such a possibility. Reporting Parliament, and perhaps the courts as well, was an occupation perfectly suited to preparation for a legal career. In 1810 James Stephen, M.P. and a Master in Chancery, gave an eloquent defense of Parliamentary reporters before the House of Commons. In it he told of his own experience about 1780 reporting debates for the *Morning Post* and referred to five or six of his contemporaries "in the same employment" who had later become barristers. The experience so obtained, he declared, had "improved his qualifications for future success at the bar." [31]

Editorial procedures during Wall's tenure are more fully documented than during any previous period of the *Gazetteer*'s history. Information concerning sources of part of the paper's content during his editorship may be gathered from entries in William Owen's account book. The list of correspondents "in Pay" already referred to contains the names of ten contributors to the paper during at least a part of that period, together with some indication of the nature of their contributions. The memorandum is as follows: [32]

Private Signatures of Correspondents in Pay

Essays and Poetry W. H. Wynne	——————————	H.W.
Guildhall Intelligence &c. D Gunstan	——————————	X
Bow-Street Intelligence E. Cook	——————————	W
Court News &c. Mrs Odell	——————————	O
Commitments and Sessions News, Newgate, etc, Mr. Newman, Giltspur St	——————————	N.C.

Ship News &c. Carolina Coffee-House ——————— IH
D° Newman, New England Coffee-House ——————— NA
Letters, &c. Mr. Wall —————————————————— Edit.
Letters par[agraph]s &c. Charles Franklin a
                    Volunteer Correspond[en]t —— C.F.
P. C——y ———————————— Conway
A.   ———————————— Adams late reader
M.P. ———————————— Charles Stewart

The "W. H. Wynne" at the head of the list may contain an error in the first initial, for several poems signed "J. H. Wynne" appeared in the *Gazetteer* between 1778 and 1781.[33] "Guildhall Intelligence" consisted chiefly of reports of cases heard by the Lord Mayor and Aldermen of the City, and "Bow-Street Intelligence" concerned the activities of Sir John Fielding and his successor as magistrates and thieftakers. The "Court News" supplied by Mrs. Odell was of the royal household and consisted in part of accounts of balls and other assemblies. Possibly Mrs. Odell also furnished the accounts of fashionable entertainments at the Pantheon and at Vauxhall and Ranelagh gardens. The nature of contributions by Newman, Franklin and the editor Wall are obvious from the descriptions given. Conway, Adams, and Stewart were probably "collectors" who specialized in no single form of intelligence.

Records of expenditures in Owen's accounts show that besides these writers, several others were more or less regularly employed. A Mr. Cox who reported the weekly meetings of bankrupts' creditors received five shillings a week for his efforts. "East India Intelligence," consisting at least in part of reports of the company directors' meetings, accounted for payments by Owen of £30 6s. 6d. to "Mr. Nicol," "Mr. Cooke," and "W—— C——" between February 1781 and July 1782. For Parliamentary debates, Wall received two guineas per week in 1782, and a Mr. Stevenson (or Stephenson) who occasionally assisted him in that year[34] received the same stipend for a time; on 13 August 1782, however, Owen recorded that "Mr. Stevenson began at . . . [one guinea] pr week on Friday Aug 9." Whether the salary was for debate reporting is not indicated.

In addition to the correspondents in London, the accounts for 1780–83 indicate that a Mr. Marshall at Cambridge supplied the *Gazetteer* with intelligence from that city. Frequently during the period the publisher noted payments of three pence for postage on "Letter[s] from Cambridge," and annually from January 1782 until 1790 a payment of two guineas was made to Marshall for "Cambridge Intelligence." That such contributions were probably paragraphs or letters rather than copies of newspapers published at Cambridge is indicated by the entry for February 1784: "Paid Mr. Marshall Cambridge for Articles of Intelligence."

Newspapers were, however, second only to "live" correspondents in their importance as sources of news for the *Gazetteer*. During the period of Wall's editorship William Owen subscribed—for the *Gazetteer*—to no less than eleven weekly provincial papers in addition to several published in Scotland and Ireland. Besides the *Glasgow Mercury*, the Edinburgh *Caledonian Mercury*, and the thrice-weekly *Dublin Evening Post*, domestic news for the *Gazetteer* was garnered from papers published at Bristol (*Bristol Gazette and Public Advertiser*), Liverpool (*Gore's General Advertiser*), York (*York Gazetteer*), Bath (*Bath Chronicle*), Chester (*Adam's Weekly Courant*), Gloucester (*Gloucester Journal*), Newcastle (*Newcastle Chronicle*), Salisbury (*Salisbury and Winchester Journal*), and from unidentified Lewes and Canterbury papers.[35] The incompleteness of the accounts admits a possibility that there may have been others, particularly papers published on the Continent. The only foreign-language publications recorded as having been purchased, however, are the *Courier de L'Europe*, written in French but published at London twice weekly, and the *Amsterdam Gazette*.

A third source for the content of the *Gazetteer* under Wall was the periodical and pamphlet literature of the day. Among Owen's purchases for the editor were such publications as a "Court Kalendar" [36] and an unidentified "New Peerage," [37] the *Annual Register*, and the *Monthly Review*. At least two pamphlets purchased by Owen for Wall were reprinted in the paper: "A Letter from Lieutenant-General Burgoyne to his Constituents, upon his late Resignation," printed for John Almon and sold at one shilling, was obtained by Owen from the bookseller Thomas Payne (apparently at a discount of three pence) and reprinted in the *Gazetteer* of Tuesday, 9 November, where it occupied nine of the paper's sixteen columns; a "Narrative of the Siege of Gibraltar, taken from a lady's Journal who was present on the Spot" appeared in two installments in the *Gazetteer* on 15 and 16 August 1781, and Owen's ledger for 13 August contains the entry, "Siege of Gibraltar to Mr. Wall."

From the facts at hand a few conclusions may be drawn concerning the duties of the *Gazetteer*'s editor in the early 1780's. First,

C P — London

Num. 1.

The Daily Gazetteer.

MONDAY, JUNE 30. 1735.

No. 1.

The INTRODUCTION.

THE good Underſtanding which is neceſſary to be kept up between *Authors* and *Readers*, hath eſtabliſhed a faſhionable Correſpondence between them, and made it natural to introduce a *New Paper* with ſuch Accounts of the Deſign, and of the Perſons who undertake it, as may at once gratify every Man's Curioſity, and intereſt him in the Succeſs of the Undertaking.

THIS, which now offers itſelf to the Good-Will of the Reader, cannot have a better Recommendation, than that it is owing to the amicable Agreement of ſeveral Authors, who having, for many Years paſt, been embarked in the ſame Cauſe, have at length reſolved to unite in the ſame Paper, and by the moſt extenſive Circulation, to publiſh their faithful Endeavours in Support of the general Intereſt.

OF this Purpoſe I gave ſome Account in the FREE BRITON on the laſt *Thurſday*, intending to proſecute the Deſign of that Paper, on the *ſame Day*, every Week, in the Courſe of this. And the *Author of the* LONDON JOURNAL is likewiſe determined to proceed in this Paper every *Saturday*, as uſual. For the reſt, there are other Gentlemen, particularly thoſe of the DAILY COURANT, who will chooſe for themſelves, ſuch Days as may be convenient to them; and if there are any Vacancies, they will be ſupplied with ſuch Papers, as our Correſpondents ſhall be pleaſed to communicate to us.

FOR the Title, it hath been judged proper to give this Paper no other than what may relate to the Intelligence which it contains. Where ſo many different Hands are engaged, it will be equally impoſſible to preſerve any Form of Character upon the whole, as it muſt be to confine particular Perſons to the ſame Way of writing, or, which is ſtill more difficult, to the ſame Way of thinking. Every Gentleman will, according to his Fancy, ſubſcribe a Name to thoſe Performances which he would diſtinguiſh and anſwer for as his own; ſince every one, I preſume, can only be accountable to the Publick for himſelf, tho' I am perſuaded, that all will readily concur in giving the utmoſt Aſſiſtance to each other, and in promoting the great End of theſe Writings.

IT is not the Intention of this Undertaking to increaſe that Burden of *Weekly* and *Daily Papers*, which every *Coffee-Houſe* complains of, but to eaſe it as much as lies in our Power, by drawing the ſeveral Writers on the Subject of our Enquiry, within the Compaſs of *one Daily Paper*. And tho' the Article of publick Intelligence cannot fall within the Province of any who write amongſt us on Matters of higher Concern, yet I am authorized to ſay, that thoſe of our Friends, who have the beſt Opportunities of knowing the moſt early and moſt authentick *Foreign News*, will furniſh conſtant Supplies of it in this Paper; as alſo, that the *Domeſtick News* will be collected without ſparing Expence, and with the greateſt Care. Our Readers will have theſe Benefits from the Nature of this Inſtitution, that the Vindication of publick Authority will be regularly carried on, in one diſtinct Paper; that the Hands which contribute to this Work, will ſucceed to each other Day after Day; and that no more than one will require Attention on any particular Day. To this we may add, that whilſt we leſſen the Charge of our Readers, we increaſe their Entertainment, and, on the whole, we can have no Cauſe to doubt their intire Approbation.

THE frequent Opportunities which we ſhall have of obliging our Correſpondents, make us hope, that we ſhall have Aſſiſtance from every Gentleman, whoſe Affection inclines him, and whoſe Leiſure allows him, to join in the Defence of thoſe Principles, which every good Man ought to defend, and which every *Engliſhman* naturally holds moſt dear. The Apprehenſion of being moleſted by the Abuſe of Parties, if that can have any Effect on Men who are warm in the Defence of Truth, and brave in the Cauſe of Liberty; yet, in this Caſe, it can have no Influence, ſince any one may expreſs himſelf with as much Freedom as may be requiſite, without being known to more than he is pleaſed to confide in, and without being obliged to repoſe any Confidence at all.

THIS being the Nature of our preſent Undertaking, it is with particular Satisfaction that I can look back on more than *Seven Years* paſt; wherein, with the greateſt Zeal for the Cauſe of my Country, I have conſtantly appeared, in Vindication of our moſt happy Conſtitution, and of his Majeſty's mild and juſt Government, in Oppoſition to all who, from deſperate Deſigns againſt the one, have wickedly endeavoured to defame and miſrepreſent the other; and in Oppoſition to all who, from reſtleſs Ambition, or unreaſonable Reſentments, have blended their Intereſts with thoſe of a ruinous Faction, given Edge to their Weapons, and Strength to their Arm, whilſt they have taught even *Jacobites* to call themſelves *Patriots*, and to ſanctify the Cauſe of *Publick Deſtruction* with the Name of *Publick Virtue*.

THE Pleaſure which I have received, in the Courſe of this Vindication, hath been greater, not only from the Succeſs which the Force of Truth hath procured me, on various Occaſions, but likewiſe from the Acceſſion of other Hands to the ſame Service. When I firſt appeared in Defence of the Juſtice of this Government, I ſtood *ſingle* in the Field of Battle, and ſaw none but *Occaſional Writers* co-operate with me in the Cauſe. It hath been our common Advantage, that, from time to time, we have gained *new Aſſiſtance*; and it will, I hope, and aſſure myſelf, be our *greateſt* Advantage, that we have now aſſociated ourſelves for the more effectual Proſecution of our general Deſign.

THE preſent Situation of *Europe* in general, and of this Kingdom in particular, muſt awaken every Friend of Mankind, and call upon Him to think for the Publick, with all his Application. No Man can foreſee the Event of Things, or bound the Proſpect of Danger in the preſent State of them. And every Man ought to inſpire all around him with the tendereſt Affection for his Country, and the ſtrongeſt Reſolution to ſupport it, whatever may happen in the Viciſſitudes of Affairs. The Circumſtance of Power and perſonal Greatneſs is, in theſe Times, of all others, the laſt Condition to be envied. It is not for themſelves, that Miniſters can undertake the Care of the Publick, when infinite Difficulties muſt attend the Adminiſtration. There is no Solacement in great Employments, when all the World is involved in War and Confuſion; and any Man poorly gratifys his Spleen, if he attempts to diſtreſs thoſe whom for the Sake of himſelf, and of his deareſt Country he ſhould be moſt forward to help. It is the higheſt Intereſt of All to ſupport that Power which is neceſſary to the Protection of All. It is the Cauſe of Liberty to preſerve the Government in the Hands of Men who are the natural Friends of Liberty: And the Being of the Conſtitution depends upon our Care to exclude thoſe who have been the *Invaders*, and would be the *Deſtroyers* of the Conſtitution; who have actually been in *Arms* to overthrow the *Laws*, and can be in no Condition ſo dreadful to us, as in Power to deſtroy by the *Law* what they could not ſubdue by the *Sword*.

THE Cauſe which we have undertaken is, to vindicate Publick Authority from the rude Inſults of baſe and abuſive Pens: to refute the Calumnies, and the injurious Clamours, of factious diſhoneſt Men; to expoſe the Inſincerity of Mock Patriots the little Arts and mean Practices of which they are notoriouſly guilty, in ſeducing Mankind, and miſleading the People from their Duty to their Deſtruction: To ſet the Proceedings of the Adminiſtration in a true and faithful Light; to inculcate the moſt affectionate Zeal for the *Sacred Perſon* of the KING; the juſt Regard which every *Engliſhman* ought to have for all the Branches of his Illuſtrious Royal Family; and the moſt vigorous Reſolution to tranſmit the Crown in the *Proteſtant Line* to the lateſt Poſterity, as the only Security which we can have, under GOD, for our Religion and Liberty.

WE live in Times, when every thing ſacred to the *Britiſh Nation* hath been trampled under Foot; when the Ambition of the Unreaſonable hath made them forget the Foundation of their Happineſs, and when the Petulance of the Overbearing hath carried them into all manner of Licentiouſneſs. Our Allegiance hath been openly ſtruck at. Our King and common Father hath been aſperſed, in the Hearing of all his People. Our Obedience to the Laws of the Kingdom hath been diſputed; and the Fountain of the Laws, the Legiſlative Power, the Repreſentative Body of this Nation, hath been libelled by thoſe who unable to ſway their Reſolutions, or to awe their Proceedings, have moſt infamouſly miſrepreſented, to the People who choſe them, the great Guardians of our Liberties, as Betrayers of the Rights of their Country.

IF Practices of this Kind were to proceed with as great Succeſs as Impunity, and if the Indignation of Mankind was not ſome Reſtraint upon thoſe Enormities, which no other Penalty hath been ſufficient to redreſs, all Government muſt ſoon be at an End, and no Adminiſtration, even the moſt faithful, could ſubſiſt or be carried on. As the Malice and Violence of Factions will eternally be the ſame againſt a good Government as againſt the worſt; and even fiercer in Proportion, as bad Men are moſt diſſatisfied with the beſt Governors: As a vicious Invention will always ſupply abundant Matter for Complaint; and a warm Imagination will eaſily inſinuate into Multitudes, the ſtrongeſt Belief of Grievances which never had a Being: As Factions will ever employ their Wit, and their Abuſe to leſſen the Reverence for Majeſty, and the Reputation of Parliaments, knowing them to be the Source of that Authority which they oppoſe: The Conſequence muſt one Day be fatal, unleſs the good Senſe of Mankind ſhall interpoſe, for the Publick Preſervation, and the People reflect, that to gain exorbitant Power over them, is, the only End which ever made Factions ambitious to ſubdue the Government of their Country.

It is to the *Senſe of the People* that we muſt appeal, to their Intereſts, their Oaths, and their Conſciences, as they are *Free*, as they are *Proteſtants* and *Engliſhmen*, for the juſt Support of this Government, againſt the Ambition of thoſe who, *without the Excuſe* of Diſaffection, employ their Hands to overthrow that Eſtabliſhment which in their Hearts they approve; and, againſt the *leſs dangerous* Diſaffection of thoſe who, departing from the Love of Liberty, and blinded to the Happineſs of a lawful limited Government, (founded in the Rights of Subjects, and ſupported for their Protection) would introduce the moſt abſolute Tyranny, Civil and Religious, over the Lives, Eſtates, and Conſciences of Men.

FOR myſelf, I can promiſe always to abide by this Cauſe. I ſet out in the World as a WHIG, before I engaged in the Conteſts of theſe Times; and I have inviolably maintained, and defended, the *Whig Intereſt* on all Occaſions. For the Gentlemen with whom I am joined in this Service, the World who know them can teſtify to their Attachments, their Zeal for theſe Principles, and the Vigour and Succeſs with which they have aſſerted them. On *theſe Principles*, and on no other, we ground the Cauſe of this Adminiſtration, againſt their Enemies of all Complexions, and Oppoſition in every Shape. By theſe we ſubmit ourſelves to be tried; and from the Force of theſe we promiſe ourſelves to prevail.

FRA. WALSINGHAM.

Yeſterday arrived the Mail due from Holland.

Hanover, June 28.

ON the 25th the King went to Bernerode and reviewed the Troops which were aſſembled there, conſiſting of 10 Battalions and 15 Squadrons. M. de Chavigny, the Miniſter of France, arrived here the 26th, and went ſtrait to Herenhauſen, to pay his Compliments to the King, who the ſame Day made a Promotion of General Officers.

Frankfort, June 30. On the 25th the Count de Belliſle, with ſome General Officers and ſeveral Engineers, went with a Guard of 1500 Men, and took a View of the Ground near Ingelheim, which is but a League from the Rhine below Mentz, and on the 28th he decamped with his Body of Troops and took Poſſeſſion of the ſaid Ground. We are aſſured, that the Ma[illegible]

The marshaling of ministerial forces is announced: The first issue of The Daily Gazetteer, *30 June 1735, printed by Samuel Richardson for Thomas Cooper.*

The London Gazetteer.

FRIDAY, JUNE 15, 1753.

All Persons who chuse to take in this Paper, may be supplied early in the Morning, by giving Orders to any of the News-Carriers, or to W. OWEN, at *Homer's* Head, near *Temple-Bar*, where THIS PAPER is published, and Letters to the Author and Advertisements are received.

To the AUTHOR.

SIR,

 NOT long ago I was led by Curiosity, to peep into some of the Courts of judicature, established in your country, which you call the residence of the goddess *Freedom*. Happy for you, who can content yourselves with such chimeras. For my part, I must confess that I live under a despotic government, and am altogether as happy! We have men among us deputed by the higher powers, to take cognisance of all our inadvertencies, quarrels, and misdemeanours, full as well qualified, and as honest as yours, whom we love and reverence on account of their impartiality and justice; without regard to their full-bottom'd periwigs or other outward ornaments. If *reverence* is due to a person, of whose features we can see nothing but his *nose*; the rest being covered with borrowed hair, an old goat with a long beard, placed in the same high station, and in the same chair, had he as much gravity, would doubtless excite the courage of spectators, and at the same time divert the assembly. Pomp and attire, therefore, are ridiculous; because they may be ridiculed. When I reflect upon the odd dance of Judges and Bishops in the *Rehearsal*, I am fully convinced it ridicules none of them; because they never practice such oddities; but if these grave men was met and gambol'd together, as they do there, the ridicule upon them would be greatly enhanced; and Lorch Chancellor Hatton was remarkable for this kind of vagary.

It is a jest to expect *Reverence* from all men, for that which every individual may do, whether it consists in reading, repeating, wearing, or acting; nay it must certainly amount to a high pitch of impudence and imposture to do mean singular and vast respect in doing common things. It behoves us therefore in this Place, to give a true signification of the word *Reverence*, before I presume further to expatiate on so solemn a subject.

Reverence, if I rightly understand the true meaning of the word, signifies, a *solemn regard paid to the persons whose Gravity, Religion, and Authority, sets them in an awful sphere above their fellow mortals*. By these qualifications men are induced to treat; but when either pride, per onal interest, or the artifice of any one who has no real gravity, no real religion, or is an impostor, usurps a pretended or an awful authority, and would attract Reverence only to gross and grotesque names, it becomes as ridiculous to men of common sense, as it seems awful to such as have none.

Garments signify nothing; certainly it is the wearer that adorns them. Reason, Justice, and sound Judgment within, are the jewels I always prize. As to names and habits, the more grave they are, the more trifling and imposing are they as apt to make, if not worn by men of character and sobriety. Where is the difficulty, or merit, of saying certain words from a Roll-on, or making bows, of wearing a gown, surplice, short coat, or cravat, as the late Mr. *Pope* expresses it,

In selling arms and brandishing your hands?

Superior virtue, superior capacity, public actions and services done to mankind; a generous and benevolent heart, and a magnanimity of mind, are, with me, the true objects and sources of Reverence: but to claim respect and Reverence, to prating, to cuts and capers, to coloured dress and postures, is stupid, lazy, and ridiculous. This alphabet of a porter, is as good to me as that of a man of state, or even that of the present Pope of *Rome*; it being only artifice and conjuration to pretend that the same words pronounced by a Lay-man, would not have the same force as out of the mouth of a Cardinal or — p.

When any one of these candidates for *Reverence*, from the magic of their art remove a mole-hill, without the same instrument with which a poor labourer may do the same; can raise a dead insect, or kill a herretick by a charm; I am ready to bow down before them: but while I see them living like other Men, and doing nothing but what any man in the lowest station of life may perform as well, I must be excused if I look upon them only as seducers to fortune tellers, who cheat people out of their money, and fill their minds with worse terrors.

The ghostly train of the *Roman* augurs, which was practised for the ends of policy, made a far better use of their power; nay, what is still more remarkable, as far as I can find, had no revenues: I could willingly, for this very reason, pay them some respect, as they were great officers of the *Roman* state; but, had one of these augurs, demanded *reverence* of me on account of his whimsical dress, or long staff, his words, tricks, or divinations; I should have done laughed in his face; as I would in the face of any other man, who pretended to be my superior, or director, because I could see nothing but his *ass*, for the obumbration of a wig, or because his coat was longer or shorter than mine, or of a different colour; or because he uttered words, which I could utter as well, or played such pranks as a *Teates* or a *Maddox* could have played infinitely better, the latter of whom is certainly a prodigy. I will *reverence* no man, but for the good which he does, or is inclined to do; nor ought I for any other reason: but if, under this pretence, he can help despising him! If I find his intention really is to turn *religion* into *foolishness*, and that he has found out that fatal piece of chemistry of transforming it into gold, destroys morality, and practices every vice which he condemns; is he not lost to all modesty if he desire it; and how then should I pay him *reverence*?

If men would be upon their guard, and endeavour to preserve themselves from superstition, servitude, and folly, they would beware of *reverencing* names, accidents, and attire. In my country, a wise man never *reverences* his rulers for their *insignia*, or *titles*, but for their services done to the public, that is, to mankind in general; if they are faulty in this respect, he is apt to load them with infamy, which at length turns to honour. What should you *reverence* men for, but for the good actions which they possess, and the superior and useful offices by which they are distinguished? Now, if a man, in a great *post*, has not one good quality, or having such abuses them, and plays the devil in God's name; is it, if he gives me cause by his ill conduct to hate him, am I obliged to love him? None, but a madman, will offer to palm this contradiction upon me: none but a Fool, and the most notorious of our whole family, will venture to impose such an absurdity. But when people are taught to *reverence* robbers, cowards, and impostors, under the reverend names of rulers, to adore the *nose*, names, and persons of men, though their actions are like the actions of devils, where the servitude of the body is secured by the servitude of the mind, and oppression is fortified by deceit, as the life they live is the height of human slavery. 'Tis on this very account, that the *Turk*, and the *Pope*, hold their false *reverence*, and sanguinary authority. *Herod* was entitled to the same; but as you are soon likely to have a nation peopled with opulent *Jews*; in this point, *tace*, which I have heard some foolish *grammarians* term, in *latin* for a candle, may be the most proper word to conclude this epistle, for which I doubt not but to obtain an *encore*. But, mark ye! does not all *Europe* revere your senatorial or ministerial wisdom, or rather your unparalleled charity, in collecting a scattered nation together, to render them no longer contemptible, and to give them an opportunity of being admitted to that liberty, to purchase those lands, enjoy that trade, and banish that religion, which you seem to neglect, forget, and despise? Sir, you are a Fool, or you would think your country not worthy of preservation.

Yours, an unnaturalized Foreigner.

LONDON: Printed for W. OWEN, at Homer's Head, near Temple Bar, where ADVERTISEMENTS of a moderate Length, are taken in at Two shillings each.

The Gazetteer *in transition:* The London Gazetteer. *Note the page-one banner and imprint.*

This Day is published,
Price Four Shillings and Sixpence in Boards,
VARIOUS PROSPECTS of MANKIND, NATURE and PROVIDENCE.

Printed for A. Millar in the Strand.

This Day is published,
Price Four Shillings in Boards,
REMARKS on the LIFE and WRITINGS of PLATO;

Printed for A. Millar in the Strand; and A. Kincaid and Bell in the Strand.

This Day is published,
Price THREE SHILLINGS in Boards,
THE LIFE of JOHN MILTON,

By JOHN TOLAND.

London: Printed for John Darby, 1699. Reprinted for A. Millar in the Strand.

This Day is published,
HISTORICAL LAW TRACTS.

The SECOND EDITION, Corrected.

A MILITARY ESSAY, IN TWO PARTS.

By CAMPBELL DALRYMPLE, Esq;

Next Term will be published,

LEX CORONATORIA: OR, THE Office and Duty of CORONERS.

By EDWARD UMFREVILLE.

PECTORAL BALSAM of HONEY.

A New discovered Remedy for COUGHS and CONSUMPTIONS.

To the PUBLICK.

THE PROPRIETORS of the GAZETTEER having received frequent Intimations how agreeable an Amendment in Paper and Print would prove to their Readers...

An Account of the ceremony made use of at the coronation of the Monarchs of England...

Account of their Majesties Coronation.

The Gazetteer *approaches typographical maturity: The four-column makeup began with this issue. The other innovations promised were short-lived.*

The Gazetteer and *New Daily Advertiser.*

No. 15,669.

MONDAY, MAY 3, 1779.

"*Commercial Intelligence*" is emphasized by subtitle and proportion of front page given to advertisements. This makeup remained in use from 1776 until 1790.

No. 19,298.

The Gazetteer,

AND NEW DAILY ADVERTISER.

LONDON, TUESDAY, 12 OCTOBER, 1790.

Price Fourpence.

This new head was adopted in September, 1790. A rule between subtitle and date was added later.

The Gazetteer,
AND NEW DAILY ADVERTISER.

LONDON, SATURDAY, AUGUST 16, 1794.

Price Fourpence Halfpenny.

Black-letter title of 1794 suggests Gazetteer's *venerable antiquity and foreshadows obsolescent management that led to paper's failure in 1797.*

LONDON, *Published for the European Magazine by J. Asperne, 32 Cornhill 1ˢᵗ Oct. 1818.*

James Perry Esqʳᵉ

Engraved by Thomson from an original Drawing by Wivell.

James Perry, under whom the Gazetteer attained editorial distinction as the "paper of the people" from 1783 to 1790.

Specimens of Gazetteer manuscripts from the Public Record Office.
ABOVE: *W. Radcliffe's resignation as editor.*
BELOW: *A receipt for payment of stamp duty on advertisements by Mary Say Vint, last printer of the paper.*

as an editor properly so-called, Wall was much more limited in his responsibilities than Charles Say and Roger Thompson had been. He had, of course, no concern with the mechanical production of the paper. During the winter season the major portion of his labors would have been devoted to obtaining Parliamentary reports. A deadline would have existed at the printing office for the submission of his preliminary accounts of the debates that had taken place in the hours just before the paper went to press,[38] and the more detailed accounts which appeared a day later might have been drafted after the deadline and given to the compositors on the following day. Whether the editor was responsible, as Thompson had been,[39] for reading proof cannot be determined, but Owen's designation of one correspondent as a former "reader" may indicate that the function was still performed by employees of the printer.

Wall's most significant duty as editor was undoubtedly the selection of material submitted by correspondents both in pay and voluntary, and the perusal and selection of news from the London, provincial, and foreign newspapers, as well as from other printed sources. "Articles of intelligence being a mere matter of selection," he once wrote to a troublesome correspondent, "and perhaps one of the most nice and difficult parts of our duty, we hope that our *daily* correspondents . . . will . . . not pretend to judge as well as *write* for us." [40]

Finally, in addition to whatever original matter he may have written for the paper, Wall was responsible at least occasionally for a task which fell regularly to his successors, that of translating the foreign newspapers. On 16 November 1782 Owen paid him one guinea "for translating the mail." These functions, with the all-embracing one of synthesizing every day a wide diversity of materials, constituted the duties which, between 1780 and 1783, accompanied the relatively unaccustomed title "Editor of the Gazetteer."

It would be absurd to conclude that Wall made use of correspondents, printed sources, and editorial techniques not employed by previous editors of the *Gazetteer*, and it should be stressed that information relating to the period of his editorship, fragmentary as it is, survives only as a result of some unexplainable quirk in William Owen's bookkeeping. Later and more complete evidence will show, however, that what may be gleaned of editorial conditions under Wall remains generally valid for the ensuing fourteen years of the paper's life. Many of the same conditions certainly prevailed in the period before 1780. To Wall personally we may justly attribute only the changes observable in the *Gazetteer* itself between 1780 and 1783.

An innovation of 1780 was the setting aside daily of part of page 4, column 1, for a "Poet's Corner." Previous appearances of verse in the *Gazetteer* had been irregular, and in making poetry a daily feature the paper was following a practice inaugurated earlier by a number of its competitors. In the summer of 1780, a contest was held to select the best poem by a reader on the subject of recent British military successes, the winner to be awarded a silver medal. At the outset, the *Gazetteer* published several models by recognized poets for the guidance of contestants, and the competition was brought to a close with this announcement:

The Poems are come to hand, on the subject of our late successes in North America and in Europe, on the plan of *Fenton's Ode* to Lord Gower [one of the models previously published], yesterday being the last day. —The *prize* Poem will be inserted in this Paper on *Saturday;* and the copies will, if required, be left at the office for the unsuccessful candidates. —The successful candidate will receive the medal in a few days, through the same Channel.[41]

Accordingly, on Saturday, 19 August, the *Gazetteer* published the winning entry: "Ode in the Manner, but not in Imitation of Fenton's Ode to Lord Gower, on our late signal Successes by Sea and Land." The author, one "Pilumnus," was advised that he might "any day he may think most convenient after Thursday . . . send for the medal, which will be left at the office, to be delivered to the person who shall demand it in the same handwriting with the Ode."

The only previous feature comparable in popular appeal to such a contest was the legal advice given out to readers in 1771 by the "Attorney General to the Gazetteer." But popular appeal was not confined during Wall's editorship to a single feature. Again adopting a title from the other papers, Wall devoted part of a column to remarks "To Correspondents," and included the feature in the paper with greater frequency than it had ever before appeared. By this means readers were given a better understanding of the *Gazetteer*'s editor, his problems and policies. When in the summer of 1781 the editors of the *Morning Post* and *Morning Herald* were engaged in a dispute in which they attempted to involve the *Gazetteer*, Wall announced: "The *Editor* of this Paper, wishing earnestly to continue upon a friendly footing with the Gentlemen standing in the same situation with himself, trusts it will not be expected that he should become a party in their personal disagreements." [42] Partisanship in politics he also eschewed. His concern was for England, he declared, and he approved the political measures designed for her improvement, regardless of which party held them: "Once for all; we declare it to be our *fixed* resolution, that no public or private man, or body of men whatever, shall render this Paper an *instrument* of advancing their own interest, unless that interest is apparently calculated to promote the cause of virtue, or the 'public good.' " [43]

Of less profound matters the editor had also much to say. On the seasonality of "entertainment for . . . readers" he asserted: "We have hitherto endeavoured to avoid serving up *lamb* and *cucumbers* in July, when we have it equally in our power to treat our guests with *venison* and *turtle*." [44] Of anonymous and pseudonymous correspondents:

We shall be happy in receiving the future favours of this new correspondent, and shall pay the more respect to them if, like the present, they be signed with his real name. We perfectly coincide with him in opinion, that anonymous strictures are too often calculated to answer private purposes. . . .[45]

Even on so prosaic a matter as payment for political advertisements the editor expressed himself in a manner uncharacteristic of his predecessors: "We have no doubt that such of our correspondents as have sent Essays, Squibs, Paragraphs, &c. for or against certain candidates, upon observing that they have not been inserted . . . will conclude, that it is because they have not come *authenticated* in *such* a manner as to *prevent* any disagreeable notices being taken of them at the *Stamp*-Office." [46] When subjects unsuited to public explanation arose, Wall occasionally offered communications of a more private nature: "The author is desired to call or send any time this afternoon, after three o'clock, at the office, and he will receive a note from the Editor on the subject." [47]

Two more elements of the editorial personality which Wall imparted to the *Gazetteer* were really intensifications of characteristics visible at the close of the preceding decade. One was an emphasis upon the *Gazetteer*'s great age and long tradition of leadership, and it was expressed in a variety of ways. Of the Parliamentary reports, readers were reminded:

Regular debates in the public prints of what passed in Parliament were *unknown* till they first appeared in THIS PAPER, about *ten years* since, and . . . we have had a degree of good fortune which seldom falls to the lot of inventors, or introducers of new plans of public entertainment or instruction; that of *establishing*, and at the same time bringing our plan to a *state* of *perfection* hitherto unexcelled (if equalled) by any of our competitors. . . .[48]

Reference to the *Gazetteer* in the period of Sir Robert Walpole's domination could now, after forty years, be made with pride. In May 1780 the editor inserted in the paper "An Ode, presented to their Royal Highnesses the Prince and Princess of Wales (Parents of his present Majesty) in Richmond Gardens, on Thursday the 6th of May, 1736, on their Nuptials, and published in the *Gazetteer* on the Saturday following." [49] In the autumn of the same year Wall found occasion to state forcibly a policy which he claimed was traditional:

A person called at and sent to the office yesterday, and on Monday evening, in *expectation* that we would have given up an author's *name;* and, which is still *more* extraordinary, have delivered him the copy.

As well to set this person *right* in the present instance as to acquaint all others, who in future may think themselves authorized to come on a similar errand, we take this opportunity of informing them, that the *Gazetteer* has been now printed within a very *few weeks* of *fifty-two years;* and that a single instance, within that period, has not happened, in which the author or copy have been given up, unless with the author's own consent.[50]

The seven-year exaggeration in the paper's age was probably unintentional, for the issue containing the announcement, as a result of errors over the years, was numbered 16144. That number would have indicated to persons otherwise uninformed, or too young to have witnessed the paper's origin (as Wall must have been) that the *Gazetteer* had first been published in 1728.[51]

The second element of editorial personality which became more pronounced in the early 1780's was the tendency to discuss the news, in addition to merely transmitting it, and to provide readers with some description and evaluation of the sources whence it was gathered. In October 1780, for example, when there was a general rumor that England and Spain might conclude a treaty of peace which did not include France, the *Gazetteer* described matters thus:

A report was current yesterday on 'Change, that our Court was on the eve of entering into a treaty for a separate peace with that of Madrid.

It was much spoken of at the west end of the town likewise, but seemed to gain very little credit. —Whether there be any good ground for the report, or whether it is only an alley manoeuvre, stocks have certainly rose one and three-eighths. . . .

A correspondent assured us late in the evening, that what gave rise to the above report, was the arrival of Mr. Hussey, the Romish priest, from Madrid, with dispatches for our Cabinet. . . .

The editor was careful to conclude, however, with a general evaluation: "We have given the above reports as the mere rumours of the day, and by no means pledge ourselves to our readers even for their apparent probability, much less their truth." [52] Again, in 1782, Wall felt obliged to explain to readers the absence of a fully detailed report of an important debate:

The gallery doors being locked a little after twelve o'clock this day, and Members most scrupulously restrained from introducing more than one person each, the Gentleman who usually gives the Debates of this Paper, finding all his Parliamentary acquaintances previously engaged, was obliged for the above Abstract to a friend of his who had got early introduced. A more circumstantial Detail will be given in this Paper tomorrow; which, indeed, . . . we could not, in justice to the Speakers, and the importance of the Debate, wish to give sooner. [53]

The phenomenon which I have called editorial personality reached its full development in the *Gazetteer* some years later than in a number of that paper's rivals. In its development of the quality, therefore, the *Gazetteer* was following a trend of the times. Two factors were primarily responsible for its conformation to the trend. First, Charles Say, the "renowned printer and manager" of the paper, was dead. His successors, and particularly the editor Wall, were largely responsible for the changes that took place between 1775 and 1783. In contrast, *The Public Advertiser*, which had been most nearly comparable to the *Gazetteer* in the 1760's, continued under the editorial control of its printer, Henry Sampson Woodfall, and remained in the 1780's much as it had been during Say's lifetime.

More fundamental, however, was the powerful influence exerted by newly established competitors. In its efforts to compete with the *Morning Post* and the *Morning Chronicle*, the *Gazetteer* adopted some of the features and characteristics of those papers. Before 1779 Parliamentary reports received an almost exclusive emphasis; thereafter, and especially after the establishment in 1780 and 1781 of the *Morning Herald*, the *Aurora*, and the *Noon Gazette* brought the total number of daily papers published in London to ten, the *Gazetteer* itself, through the voice of its editor, became much more articulate. In special addresses to correspondents and to the public, first of all, and finally in leading articles at the head of the *London* column, the *Gazetteer* expressed for the first time after 1780 what its chief competitors had expressed for nearly a decade—policies and opinions for which it acknowledged itself fully responsible. There is no better example of this new editorial personality politically expressed than in the leading article which announced the resignation of Lord North's ministry on 21 March 1782. "That we have happily got rid of a *servile minion*, and a headless *Ministry*," Wall began, "must give every real intelligent friend to his country the most heartfelt pleasure . . . ." After a less strongly phrased discussion of the resignation, he concluded:

It is therefore to be hoped, that past experience will render Whigs and Tories what they ought to be, the *friends* of a *limited* Monarchy *circumscribed* by law, and that they will henceforth cordially shake hands, with hearts united, and determined equally to cut up by the roots that bane of all good and successful Government, corruption, and those *spurious pretensions* of governing by a *bribed* Parliament, or governing by *none!*

When such opinions came to be declared by "the Editor of the Gazetteer" rather than exclusively by "A Constitutionalist," "A True Briton," or some other pseudonymous correspondent, the paper had reached a state attained somewhat earlier by the *Morning Post*, the *Morning Chronicle*, and the *Morning Herald*, three papers which Stanley Morison has classified under the title "The Mature Eighteenth-Century Newspaper." [54]

In the years that followed, the *Gazetteer* was to proceed further in the direction it had taken during Wall's editorship. It was to be guided in its course by an editor recognized as one of the most brilliant journalists of his day, and one who conceived of the *Gazetteer*, politically and in other respects, as "the Paper of the People."

XI

PAPER OF THE PEOPLE

1783-1790

THE date of James Perry's appointment to the editorship of *The Gazetteer and New Daily Advertiser* cannot be determined precisely. If John Henley Wall of the Middle Temple is to be identified with the editor of the *Gazetteer* in 1781 and 1782, then the announcement of his death on 21 January 1783 marks the earliest date at which Perry could have succeeded him. If the extra meeting of the management committee on 18 January 1783 was an emergency meeting made necessary by Wall's final illness, the proprietors may have decided at that meeting to offer the editorship of their paper to Perry, who was then editor of the *European Magazine*. It is certain that by 22 January they had engaged a Mr. Stuart as a debate reporter to replace Wall, for on that date William Owen purchased two quires of copy paper for him and fifteen days later half a ream, besides twenty-five pens.[1] On 23 January a notice to correspondents announced that several letters were "under inspection"; Wall's phrase had been "under consideration."

There can be no doubt that by 30 January—two weeks after Owen's last payment to Mr. Wall and ten days after the death of John Henley Wall—James Perry was editor of the *Gazetteer*, for on that date appeared a leading article in the then unprecedented manner which was to become familiar during the eight years following. In a criticism of the Shelburne ministry the editor offered his readers philosophic consolation for recent misfortunes:

A new era now rises in the history of Britain: we are from this time to change our rank in the scale of nations, and descend from acknowl-

edged pre-eminence in power, commerce, and consequence, to a state
. . . of simple equality. The pride which accompanied our superiority
must be checked—we can no longer domineer over the ocean, nor
command foreign flags to lower themselves before the Majesty of
Britain—the name of an Englishman will now lose its terror among
distant people. All this is owing to the insolence with which we bore
ourselves; and the intoxication of a few weak and bad men, entrusted,
for the punishment of our pride, with the government of the state. . . .
Europe no longer will view us with alarm, and not desiring our extinc-
tion, they will protect our weakness. We must bring ourselves to bear
our degradation with the humility that becomes us; and as we shewed
no philosophy in our elevation, let us learn to be moderate in our decay,
and strive to seek for happiness where it is only to be found, in the
cultivation of our soil, in the support of our commerce, in the mainte-
nance of our Constitution, in the faith and purity of our national character, and not in the wild ambition of acquiring new territories by
conquest, in the low desire and the mad scheme of reducing fellow-
subjects or dependent states to slavery.

Never before had a conductor of the *Gazetteer* written so clearly
and forcefully, nor, perhaps, with such subtlety. The use of dashes
as full stops was to be a familiar characteristic by 1790; and the
leading article itself—in an early but recognizable form—was not
often absent from an issue of the paper after January 1783 when
the type size of the *London* heading was increased to call attention
to the editor's comments. There was a new tone, too, in the address
to correspondents on the following day:

In answer to the person who brought us a number of puffs in favour
of the Lord Lieutenant of Ireland, we inform him that we are the
servants of the people of England; and are not to be induced, by bribes,
to become the daubers of any Administration. We by no means intend
to outrage Royalty or even its Viceregent; but we shall steadily observe
the conduct of those who are either called to the service of their
country, or who aspire to be so; and in discharge of our duty to the
public, shall candidly approve or condemn them according to their deeds.

The packet of puffs in favour of the Earl of Shelburne, sent us by
an anonymous correspondent on Wednesday last, came under the same
determination. —They are ready to be delivered to the author, as they
may perhaps find admission into other prints.[2]

The new editor who wrote thus pointedly of puffs and bribes
and daubers had already achieved some reputation in the world

of London journalism, and he had accepted the editorship of the *Gazetteer* only after imposing on the proprietors a condition which was largely to determine the paper's policy throughout the decade.

James Perry was the son of a carpenter and builder known as Pirie. Born at Aberdeen on 30 October 1756, he had been educated at the grammar school there and had attended Mareschal College. After brief experiences as an attorney's clerk and as assistant in an Aberdeen draper's shop, Perry had spent a year with Booth's company of actors, leaving the troupe in 1774 when he was assured by the manager that his Scottish brogue was a hopeless impediment to a successful stage career. Three years as a clerk in Manchester had preceded his arrival in London at the age of twenty-one, in 1777.[3]

In applying for employment to the London publishers Richardson and Urquhart, Perry had acknowledged several anonymous contributions to the *General Advertiser*, of which they were then the principal proprietors. Through their influence he had subsequently been engaged to contribute regularly to that paper at a salary of one guinea a week, with an extra half-guinea for assistance on the *London Evening Post*. As a reporter his most noteworthy accomplishment had been to supply eight columns of matter daily to the *General Advertiser* during the trials of Admirals Keppel and Palliser in 1779. A penchant for oratory, possibly related to his earlier theatrical efforts, had made Perry a familiar figure at the Westminster Forum, the Lyceum, and other debating societies, and in 1782 the younger Pitt, then Chancellor of the Exchequer, "having had frequent opportunities of witnessing Perry's talent in public speaking, and particularly in reply . . . caused a proposal to be made to him of coming into Parliament . . . ."[4] But the young Scotsman preferred another path to recognition, and succeeding years brought him into sharp political conflict with Pitt.

In 1782 Perry had projected the establishment of the monthly *European Magazine,* and for the first twelve months of its publication he had served as its editor. Such experience must have proved valuable when, after Wall's death, "he was chosen by the proprietors of the *Gazetteer* to be the Editor of that respectable paper . . . ." Perry "undertook the editorship of the paper at a salary of four guineas per week," but he undertook it only "on the express condition that he was to be left to the free exercise of his political opinions, which were those asserted by Mr. [Charles James] Fox." Fox's ideas, "from their liberality in the cause of freedom, justice, and humanity, had made, on . . . [Perry's] first entering the gallery of the House of Commons, an impression that could not be effaced from his mind." So wrote a contemporary (or perhaps Perry himself) in 1818. "It is truly honourable to those Gentlemen [the *Gazetteer* proprietors]," the writer continued, "that, during the eight years in which he continued the Editor, they never endeavoured to influence his sentiments, but were pleased to express their unqualified satisfaction with his exertions."

The period of James Perry's editorship, from January 1783 to December 1790, is outstanding in the history of the *Gazetteer* for two reasons. First, the paper's makeup and content were in general more uniform during those eight years than during any earlier period of a comparable length. Secondly, a consistent and comprehensive editorial policy, previously lacking even during Wall's editorship, was for the first time clearly and firmly expressed. These factors make it profitable to depart from a mode of discussion based chiefly upon chronology, and to consider the paper in terms of those characteristics which are directly attributable to Perry's influence.

The keynote of James Perry's policy was contained in an address to readers of the *Gazetteer* at the opening of the 1783 session of Parliament, ten months after he had succeeded to the editorship:

On the commencement of a session which promises to be so interesting, it behoves us to say that we consider it as our duty to be more than ordinarily active in the service of the public. We have long flourished under their protection; and it shall be our pride, as we have felt it to be our interest, amidst all the involutions, changes, and coalitions of party, to preserve to the GAZETTEER the honourable and peculiar distinction of being the *Paper* of the *People*.

Perry's practice in this instance corresponded to that of his predecessor and to the accepted practice of the time. By 1783 most of the daily papers took occasion annually at the opening of Parliament to declare their zeal in serving the public, and designation of the *Gazetteer* as "the Paper of the People" implied a political impartiality often avowed by Wall. Perry refused to support any party out of blind allegiance. Instead he would, as he had announced in January, "observe the conduct of those who are . . . called to the service of their country, . . . and . . . candidly approve or condemn them according to their deeds." But in James Perry's opinion, it soon became manifest, the deeds of Charles James Fox all merited approval. The *Gazetteer* as "the *Paper* of the *People*" invited implicit association with Fox, who was called affectionately by his supporters, and jeeringly by his political opponents, "the Man of the People." Perry could not have foreseen, when he published this address on 11 November 1783, the ascendancy of William Pitt and the firm intrenchment of the Tory party, factors which soon brought him to an openly avowed support of the Whigs as the "party of the people"; but the name which he here applied to the *Gazetteer* proved singularly apt, politically and otherwise, throughout his tenure as editor.

The address to readers continued with an expression of the general principles by which he was to conduct the paper:

The Parliamentary intelligence will hold, as it ought, the first place in our daily miscellany; and we have made such arrangements for the important article, that we may confidently call the attention, and challenge the criticism of the public on its veracity and stile. We presume to do this, as we are honoured by the correspondence of two gentlemen of literary character, who, to the merits of accuracy and candour, will add those of composition and taste. They will make it their study to seize, as much as possible, on the manner of the Speaker as well as on the words, and to give a picture of his eloquence along with the report of his argument.

The debate reports were now to be considered as literary productions, an early indication of Perry's effort throughout his long career to impart a dignity to his profession.[5] "In our attention to the Debates in Parliament," he continued, "we shall not forget nor overlook our other duties":

The public may be assured of meeting in the daily productions of the Gazetteer, that pleasant variety of matter which is its acknowledged characteristic. Whatever engages the notice of the town, or deserves to engage it—Whatever swims on the surface of conversation, shall be caught and chronicled—We shall indulge ourselves in humor without pursuing it to farce—and we shall strive to be gay without daring to be licentious. —In short it shall be our aim so to conduct ourselves, that the public may continue to select the Gazetteer, from its contemporaries, not only as the most pleasant miscellany, but as the most authentic record.

The biographical article published near the end of his life, to which reference has several times been made, relates that as editor of the *Gazetteer* James Perry instituted a new method of obtaining Parliamentary reports by employing a group of reporters instead of only one, thereby making possible a more complete report of each night's proceedings in the paper of the following morning. The innovation was a significant one, and every historian of the English newspaper has given due credit to Perry for its introduction. H. R. Fox Bourne, however, may have overdrawn the matter somewhat when he stated that Perry employed "a staff of reporters" which "not only added greatly to the expense of production, but also necessitated much scheming to obtain admission for so many reporters to the parliamentary galleries . . . ." [6] Judging from all available evidence, Perry's staff of debate reporters seems to have consisted of himself and the "two gentlemen of literary character" mentioned in his address to the public.

William Woodfall of the *Morning Chronicle* was widely acclaimed the most accomplished Parliamentary reporter of his time.[7] Working alone, as Wall apparently had for the *Gazetteer*, Woodfall managed to give daily a report of the preceding night's debate sometimes extending, as Fox Bourne observed,[8] to eight, ten, or even more columns of type. Wall and the reporters for the other papers, less gifted, had been less copious, and undoubtedly their reports had suffered by comparison with those published in the *Morning Chronicle*. During the 1783–84 session of Parliament which followed Perry's first address to the public, the *Gazetteer* frequently gave accounts of the preceding night's debate extending to ten or more columns of the paper's sixteen and concluding with reports of adjournment sometimes as late as two, or even three-thirty, in the morning.[9] Reports of equal length continued to be published in the paper throughout Perry's editorship, and even afterwards, when the reporting staff certainly consisted only of the editor and two debate writers. Moreover, there were occasions on which the *Gazetteer* under Perry gave no more than three or four columns of Parliamentary proceedings, and although the length was determined chiefly by the importance of the proceedings themselves, there was at least one occasion, in 1790, when it was determined solely by the physical capacities of the reporters. A report of the significant debate on the motion for abolishing the Corporation and Test acts contained this note: "We have been unavoidably obliged to compress our account of the important debate of yesterday within very narrow limits, as the excessive crowd and consequent heat of the House exhausted us too much to go into it at adequate length." [10] Perry's staff at that time could not have been extensive.

The length of the accounts which might be published on the morning after a debate was determined almost entirely by the element of time. With only one reporter employed, the report had to be written after the House adjourned, and the setting of type by a number of compositors would proceed only as rapidly as the reporter could write or dictate. If William Woodfall, unassisted, could often compose a report ten or more columns in length between the adjournment of the House and the time his paper went to press, it would appear that James Perry (who had in 1779 filled eight columns of the *General Advertiser* daily with a report of Admiral Keppel's trial) could, with the assistance of no more than two reporters, consistently equal or surpass Woodfall's performance, as in fact the *Gazetteer* reports did. Under such circumstances it would have been seldom that more than one-third of the account had to be written up and set in type after the House had adjourned. Perry's inauguration of debate reporting by relays increased the quality of the *Gazetteer*'s accounts and the efficiency with which they were obtained, and it was not long before rival papers were following his example.[11] He deserves no less credit, certainly, for not having employed a greater number of reporters.

Parliamentary news was the feature most strongly emphasized by Perry as it had been earlier by Wall. The new system of reporting, while apparently never described to readers as such, was obviously a source of pride to him, as its success was undoubtedly a source of increased reputation for the *Gazetteer*.[12] Unlike Wall's reports, those published by Perry did not reveal obvious political bias. Perry maintained impartiality in the presentation of reports, he declared, so that the paper might "serve not only as a vehicle of intelligence for the day, but as a record for the future." [13] Editorial commentary on the debates was for the most part confined to leading articles, but occasionally Perry employed other means to convey his opinions. When the Duke of Richmond reminded the House of Lords in 1789 of the "general Licentiousness and profligacy of the newspapers, in their daily attacks on the most elevated and irreproachable characters," he was referring principally to attacks on the Prince of Wales by the Tory press. Lord Loughborough, a Tory, reprobated the Duke's insinuation, but he too "spoke in severe terms of the infamous and daring slanders of the Newspapers." Perry, incensed at the criticism, did not allow his resentment to intrude upon the account of the debate, but he appended this note to the report:

Indiscriminate Charges against the public Press, as they do not consist with truth, are unbecoming the dignity and justice of noble Lords to make. We are ready to confess that we have some meretricious Contemporaries, who chuse to feed that gross and vulgar appetite for Scandal which the learned Lord truly ascribed to the Public, and to which the licentiousness complained of should be referred. By disdaining the foul and scandalous practice we proudly disregard all general implications. We are as exempt from the accusation of licentiousness as from that of venality. Lord Loughborough will not find, either upon record or upon rumour, that we are SLANDEROUS, nor will Lord Cathcart that we are TO BE PURCHASED.

EDIT.[14]

The editor on this occasion came near to giving the lie direct, and such outspokenness might have been dangerous. Lord Loughborough was Alexander Wedderburn, Chief Justice of the Court of Common Pleas; as Attorney General in 1778 he had prosecuted Mary Say for the Libel on the Glorious Revolution.

One other method was employed by Perry to express his political sympathies by means of the debate reports. On the occasion mentioned earlier, when exhaustion resulting from the heat in the House of Commons limited the length of the *Gazetteer*'s report to seven columns, three of the columns were occupied by an account of the speech made by Charles Fox. The editor, to his apology for compressing the report "within very narrow limits," added this explanation: "The Speech of Mr. *Fox*, however, was too fine a piece of eloquence to be lost to our readers. We shall therefore endeavour, with our utmost care, to present it to the public." [15]

Perry's admiration for Fox was prominently displayed in the *Gazetteer* between 1783 and 1790, and it was openly acknowledged. While it would be unfair to conclude that the editor held the political opinions he did solely because Fox held them, it is certain that the *Gazetteer* throughout the period expressed support of Fox in every important issue on which he took a stand. The East India Bill which resulted in the fall of the Fox-North coalition in 1783, Fox's championship of the Prince of Wales in 1783 and in the Regency Bill crisis of 1788, the contested Westminster election of 1784, which deprived Fox of his seat for that constituency through two Parliamentary sessions, and the divergent views on the French Revolution which ended the friendship of Burke and Fox in 1790—these matters and many more evoked articles in which Perry espoused Fox's views.

On broad issues Perry wrote in general terms, attributing the principles he expressed to no individual and asserting his liberal views by an appeal not to the authority of Fox but to their intrinsic and (as he believed) self-evident justice. In defense of an article published in the *Gazetteer* which had criticized the monarchist editor of the *Courier de L'Europe*, Perry displayed as early as 1784 some of the republican sentiments with which he was to greet the beginning of the French Revolution:

To Frenchmen we have no objection—but to French politics, exposed to the public in a news-paper, under the conduct of a Gentleman, who declares himself to be by profession a lover of despotism, we shall at all times object; and it will make no difference to us, whether the author of such opinions is born in the kingdom of France or the county of Middlesex. Gentlemen may entertain in private the most slavish doctrines, uncensured by us; it is only when they inculcate them on the public mind, and endeavour to pervert the understandings of the people, that we think it our duty to raise our feeble voice against them, and reprobate doctrines so inimical to the Constitution.[16]

In November 1789 Perry took pleasure in the prospect of an event which was to shock many Englishmen and was to be partially responsible for Edmund Burke's most renowned piece of writing:

It must afford the highest pleasure to the true friends of the civil and religious rights of mankind, to inform them, that the celebrated Dr. Price intends, at the Anniversary of the Revolution Society . . . to move an Address of Congratulation to the National Assembly of France; a measure which, while it reflects honour on the mover, cannot fail to exalt the character which this country has hitherto maintained for liberality of sentiment in the opinion of all the civilized nations of Europe.[17]

Publication in the following year of Burke's *Reflections* and the split in the Whig ranks evoked from Perry a long leading article which revealed at once his views on Burke's theories and his adherence to the minority led by Charles Fox. An excerpt will illustrate the manner:

The argument, that no reform ought to be made because things go on very well as they are, might be applied to every case of apathy which ignorance or servility might engender. According to this doctrine, no opposition ought to be made to despotism, if the people are not made to groan under the yoke of the tyrant—and the superstition propagated by the Monks was harmless, while it produced a blunt obedience favourable to government. . . .

"We have been happy," say these advocates for despotism, "under our present system—moderation in those who had the power has done for us all that we could have received from a purer establishment. You shall still, therefore, depend for your happiness on the caprice of Kings and Ministers, and shall owe none of it to principle. You shall have no privileges of your own. Your condition shall be precarious,—like that of a house dog, it shall depend on the good will of your master.[18]

Such was the nature of Perry's more general political pronouncements. Expressions of his admiration for Fox, however, frequently took a more direct form. A year after his appointment as editor of the *Gazetteer*, he wrote:

Mr. Fox is alone the Minister of this country—In or out of place it is precisely the same with him—His influence in the Parliament is such, that he in truth is the source of every measure. When out of place he governs the Cabinet. They do not enquire how a new bill will affect the empire—how it will operate this way or that way—so much as how it will please Mr. Fox. His maxims in politicks are the most enlarged of any man in Parliament, and his powers without question the most extensive of any man's at this instant on the public scene— and yet in no moment of his life did he ever betray a notion that he was under the influence of self-opinion. Conceit and pride are weaknesses which never were imputed to Mr. Fox.[19]

And five years later:

The conduct of Mr. Fox, in regard to the Dissenters, was truly honourable and dignified. It manifested the greatness of a liberal mind, and the generosity of an enlightened understanding. That ungrateful race of men, in favour of whom he spoke, will, as usual, praise him for the part he acted, and do their utmost to hurt him in every part of the country.[20]

Last year, Mr. Fox proved his superiority in law, over all the lawyers in Westminster Hall: in his speech against the Test Act, on Friday, he evinced a knowledge of divinity, equal to that of the mitred fathers of the church.[21]

Of William Pitt the younger, Perry was of course generally critical, but his criticism was based on political principles and its tone was far from the scurrilous invective which he deplored in some of his "meretricious Contemporaries." Occasionally, as in March 1783 when Pitt at the age of twenty-three was invited by George III to form a ministry, Perry employed a comparatively inoffensive form of ridicule: "Mr. Pitt has very prudently declined the offer which was made him of the office of Prime Minister. . . . Though the Premiership has been hawked about, and sent a-begging through all the forms of Westminster school, not a stripling can be found forward enough to hazard himself in the seat." [22] Generally, however, Perry confined himself to criticism of the minister's political conduct and the motives on which it was based, as in his attempt in 1784 to prevent Fox's taking his seat for Westminster in the Commons—a deed which remains unjustified by historians most sympathetic to Pitt. [23] Another of Perry's favorite themes was Pitt's refusal to risk his office on the issue of electoral reform, a measure he had strongly supported before becoming Prime Minister.

Though diametrically opposed to Pitt politically, Perry was moved to acknowledge on occasion the minister's personal integrity. In 1784, when Pitt negotiated a public loan, Perry thought that he displayed "great manliness and integrity" in awarding the contract to the group of bankers who had submitted the lowest bid, rather than to "Mr. Harley, Mr. Atkinson, Mr. Drummond, and that particular corps who are in habits of intimacy with Mr. Pitt, and who were therefore looked to by the city as almost to a certainty the fortunate sett." [24] Of less importance, but still illustrative of Perry's manner, was his half-jocular rebuttal in 1790 of a scandalous rumor involving the minister:

The world, ever prone to be *censorious* on the slightest occasion, have circulated a *wicked* report, that the Minister has taken a *lady* into *keeping*. The circumstance on which this report is founded is laughable enough. It is no other than this—Mrs. Prettyman, the Bishop of Lincoln's Lady, borrowed the Minister's carriage to go a shopping, which being seen going from street to street, with, perhaps, *for the first time*, a Lady in it—it was said that it could be no other than the *Minister's Mistress*. [25]

Perry's own sentiments were openly declared, but he never excluded from the *Gazetteer* the opinions of his political opponents. "Our personal opinions," he once wrote, "we have never either changed or concealed"; but those opinions were not to "dam up the Paper against the writers on both sides. It is our duty to be for the people; and that they may be able to form a true judgment of public men and measures, we, as the Journalists of the day, ought to be impartial in our statements of facts, and liberal in our admission of commentaries." [26]

The *Gazetteer* in its "duty to be for the people" was considered by Perry a guardian of freedom, a quality found exclusively, he felt, in the principles of Whiggism. On New Year's Day 1790 he viewed conditions in France as preliminary indications of the millenium, and credited the *Gazetteer* throughout its fifty-five years of life with principles it had clearly expressed for only a decade:

At no period since the Gazetteer was first established by the Whigs, in the Ministry of Sir Robert Walpole, did it ever hail a new year so auspicious to the objects of its devotion as the present. It promises to accomplish, in every part of the world, the amelioration, if not the perfect deliverance, of mankind. Prejudices are encountered in every kingdom; and establishments, erected by tyranny, are surrendering to reason. We may be suffered to partake of the triumph, to which, as humble instruments, we have been zealous to contribute. Creditably to ourselves, but not so to the British press in general, we have been almost the only faithful organ of FREEDOM in the metropolis of its native country.

The early connection with the Walpole ministry had remained carefully unacknowledged for forty-eight years. Eight months after this address, Perry referred to the *Gazetteer* as "the *distinguished* ORGAN of the Whigs of England," [27] and in October 1790, when the *General Advertiser* ceased publication,[28] Perry declared with more spirit perhaps than accuracy: "While constitutional zeal and unbroken spirit remain in the country, the people shall hear their voice through the GAZETTEER—that from its outset in the cause of Whiggism no power has been able either to *silence or corrupt.*" [29]

Here, obviously, was the beginning of an attempt to create in the public mind a political tradition for the *Gazetteer* commensurate with its relatively great age. The device was a simple one, and it would almost certainly have succeeded under the continued impetus of Perry's forceful editorship. By 1790 the subsidization of newspapers by the government had left the *Gazetteer* with few allies in its dedication to Whiggism as represented by Fox.[30] Had James Perry remained in editorial control of the paper, it might have occupied by early in the next century the position of eminence as a great liberal daily to which Perry did in fact raise the *Morning Chronicle*. Only a month after he had made the ringing declaration last quoted, however, Perry resigned the editorship to assume editorial and proprietary control of the *Morning Chronicle*, and to announce that, thenceforth, that paper would be "the ORGAN of that honourable and temperate body, THE WHIGS, who are the great majority of the People of Great Britain." [31] Perry could not dignify the *Chronicle* by claims to a long if uncertainly derived tradition, but future events proved that he had no need to do so.

With his resignation there ended for the *Gazetteer* its period of greatest political significance as an independent newspaper. "The first object of our daily solicitation," Perry had written in 1785, "shall be Political Intelligence." [32] But his editorship of the *Gazetteer* deserves consideration for matters which, if less strongly emphasized, were at least equally interesting.

That political news and free expression of political opinion were the most important features of a newspaper was the first article of James Perry's journalistic creed. The second, more general in its application, was most succinctly stated in a 1784 notice to correspondents: "Miscellany is the soul of a newspaper . . . ." [33] And the third article—really an all-important qualification of the second—was that slander, invective, and scandal had no place in the columns of a respectable publication. The entire creed was summarized in this sentence which appeared in 1789: "The true business of a Newspaper is to give political intelligence, intermixed with literary and miscellaneous amusement, without sacrificing to the envy of the malicious, or propagating the tale of scandal." [34]

Of the literary amusement provided by the *Gazetteer* under Perry something will be said presently. Miscellaneous amusement and the pernicious nature of scandal were subjects upon which he expressed himself more directly. "Sensible that it is the miscellaneous quality of a News-Paper which recommends it to general acceptance," he wrote in 1785,

we shall not confine our efforts to the reports of Parliamentary Debates. . . .

The Gay and pleasurable pursuits of the fashionable world shall be equally the objects of our care; and in stating the various topics which may occur, we pledge ourselves to preserve the Gazetteer from the impurities of slander, and invective. Epithets of a coarse or scurrilous kind shall be applied to no public party, and tales of personal foible be related of no private individual. We wish to cultivate gaiety without licentiousness; and we announce to our Correspondents, both political and various, that we shall give admission to no article that is tinctured with illiberality.[35]

Four years later, in a discussion of the libel laws which threatened freedom of the press, the editor of the *Gazetteer* commented generally upon the growth of scandal in the newspapers:

The abuse of the liberty of the press has of late years become so great, that no character is safe — not even the retirements of domestic felicity remain undisturbed — the credit of the tradesmen, as well as the chastity of the female sex are assailed.

Such was not the case with the papers some years ago; the change took place when some needy adventurers thought that a fashionable Paper, that is, a record of private and public scandal, would suit the taste of the public, and fill *their* pockets better than a periodical detail of political information. . . .

The public *have been* to blame by encouraging such Papers. Many like the tale of scandal, which does not affect themselves — and the man of middling rank chuckled to read the amours and intrigues of Lords and Ladies, little thinking that his turn would one day come, his harmless actions be misrepresented, and his character be blasted in a paragraph.[36]

The chief objects of Perry's criticism were the so-called "West End sheets" of comparatively recent foundation: papers like the *Morning Post, Morning Herald,* and *World,* which specialized in "fashionable" intelligence but did not agree with Perry in its definition. The popularity which contributed to their success resulted from a factor only superficially described by Perry's reference to a public taste for scandal, for the readers who demanded such entertainment were much more numerous than those who in 1771 had shown a preference for the newspapers containing Parliamentary reports.[37] The growth of population and literacy had extended the newspaper-reading public beyond the group of the seventies which Professor Trevelyan has described as "intensely and intelligently political," [38] and Perry's "man of middling rank"—and the man's wife—were by 1785 probably almost as interested in nonpolitical or miscellaneous intelligence as they were in the speeches of Fox and Pitt. Indeed, the chief trend perceptible in daily journalism from about 1780 was toward a popularization conducive to the development of a new mass of readers. An increased reading public is clearly indicated by the foundation of nine daily papers at London in the decade of the eighties, even though a number of them proved unsuccessful.[39] The French Revolution was certainly responsible for the foundation of four in

1789, but readers were the first requisite, nevertheless, and readers alone made necessary the application of steam power and the rotary press to the production of daily newspapers early in the next century. The scandal retailed in the 1780's by the *Gazetteer*'s "meretricious Contemporaries" and the miscellaneous quality that Perry sought to impart to the *Gazetteer* were alike symptoms of the tendency toward mass appeal which had been revealed partially, I think, even in the development of that characteristic described in the last chapter as editorial personality.

The most obvious effects of Perry's editorial influence, apart from the political cast he imparted to the paper, were a simplification of the matter provided for readers' instruction and a diversification, as well as an increase in the quantity, of that provided for their entertainment. Both effects were embodiments of the trend which made the phrase "Paper of the People" applicable to the *Gazetteer* in a nonpolitical sense, and both were the results of conscious intent on the part of the paper's editor. Of the simplification, effected chiefly through interpretive articles in the *London* column, Perry wrote in 1789: "One of the real uses of the public papers is to give, in short plain statements, the true *outline* of such national matters as either from the length of time taken up in their discussion, or from the details incident to their process, have become too complex for the fair judgment of the public." [40] Of the increased and diversified content a brief general survey will give adequate indication.

The outstanding sign of increased editorial content, as distinguished from advertisements, was in the paper's physical makeup. Before 1783 the space devoted to essays and news had averaged about seven columns, or slightly less than half of the paper's total content. There had been exceptional issues, especially during Wall's editorship, when long debates had notably exceeded this average. During the period of James Perry's editorship, however, the average space allotted to advertisements decreased from nine to about five or six columns, and frequently it was even less. Most directly responsible for the decline in advertising space was the length of the Parliamentary accounts made possible by Perry's system of reporting. But even during the recesses of Parliament the *Gazetteer* under Perry almost consistently devoted less than half of its space to advertisements. Whether this resulted entirely from a decline in the number of advertising customers, brought about by a growing competition among newspapers, or whether it was due in part to a concept possibly held by Perry that advertisements were of less interest to readers than literary and miscellaneous amusement, cannot be determined.

Political essays by pseudonymous contributors were published less frequently during Perry's editorship than in any previous period of the *Gazetteer*'s history. Their rarity was determined partially, as in the past, by the emphasis placed upon the debate reports, but more directly responsible, probably, was the fact that James Perry was his own most valuable political correspondent. In articles which appeared directly under the *London* heading, and throughout the columns of varied intelligence which followed that heading, editorial opinions were voiced without apology. Moreover, contributions which might earlier have been published in the form of letters to the printer or editor were now included without distinction among these columns of miscellaneous intelligence. One result was that editorial remarks to correspondents—Perry labeled them simply "Notices"—were much less frequent between 1783 and 1790 than they had been during Wall's editorship.

A new feature of the paper's make-up for which Perry was probably less responsible than the example set by the more recently established daily papers was the use of subheads to divide and classify, at least roughly, the varied matter which fell generally within the scope of the *London* heading. Headings such as "Vienna," "Ireland," "Cambridge," and "Lewes" indicated Perry's frequent use of the foreign and provincial papers supplied by William Owen; and those (set in large and small capitals) like "Old Bailey Intelligence," "Westminster-Hall Intelligence," "Married," and "Died" classified portions of the paper's content which were more or less regular in their appearance. The variety and extent of the *Gazetteer*'s fashionable, miscellaneous, and literary intelligence is well indicated by these headings which appeared from time to time: "Parisian Dresses," "Richmond House," "Easter," "Political Conundrums," "Historical Anecdote," "Music," "Theatre," and (on 2 January 1788) "Remarkable Occurrences of 1787." The use of subtitles was one element in the general process of simplification visible in the *Gazetteer* at this period. It was carried over even into the Parliamentary reports, with topical headings descriptive of each subject debated: for example, "Trial of Mr. Hastings," "Scots Distillery," "Ordnance."

An element of content upon which Perry placed greater emphasis than had any of his predecessors—and for good reason—was news of conditions and events in France. In 1789 and 1790 part of a column immediately preceding the *London* heading was frequently labeled, in type of a size with it, FRANCE. NATIONAL AS-SEMBLY. But as early as 1784 Perry had informed his readers:

It is our design, in the accustomed mixture of the *dulce* with the *utile*, to enrich our publication . . . with an account of the State of the Arts, of the Literature, and Spectacles of Europe, and chiefly of France, which all men must acknowledge to be at present the seat of every thing that is great and enlightened — We shall communicate their various discoveries in science, their improvements in manufacture, and give rather a catalogue than a review of their splendid publications. Our limits are too brief for details; but we trust a short recital, such as may come weekly within our compass, will neither be unprofitable nor unpleasant to readers.[41]

The chief sources for such news were the French newspapers. William Owen's accounts for the period record annual payments to a Mr. Jackson of the Foreign Post Office for the *Journal de Paris, Le Courier d'Escaut,* and the *Journal d'Esprit,* as well as payments of half a crown on four occasions for "Foreign Postman del[iver]ing papers to Mr. Perry" and "Mr. Jackson's Porter." [42]

James Perry's promise to provide literary amusement for readers of the *Gazetteer* was well kept. Under his influence the paper devoted more space to literary matter than ever before, an indication of the editor's personal taste but also of an attempt to attract readers whose interests extended beyond politics and commerce. Perry's early experience as an actor does not appear to be reflected, as William Woodfall's was, in the pages of the paper that he edited. The emphasis upon theatrical intelligence which might be expected in the *Gazetteer* from 1783 to 1790 is not perceptible. In general, Perry's practice followed that of his predecessors. Reviews of the new plays were given; prologues, epilogues, and songs from plays were occasionally published; and puffs praising actors, actresses, and plays were inserted among the miscellaneous news as often as they were paid for by the theatres, and perhaps occasionally when they were not. In 1784 Perry wrote: "We are happy to insert fair and well written paragraphs respecting the theatres; we wish to second an animated and liberal contention between the two houses, but we will give our countenance to no article which obliquely tends to slander or uncandidly strives to raise the credit of one play or performer at the expence of another." [43] C. H. Gray, who made a comprehensive study of theatrical criticism published in the *Gazetteer* and other London newspapers, describes the paper generally in the period between 1781 and 1795. "New plays," he writes, "were regularly reviewed, at first lengthily and with care, but by 1788 in very short notes without critical power. . . . In 1792 even the reviews of new plays had degenerated into what look dangerously like mere puffs." [44] Gray's study concluded with the year 1795, so that he was unaware of reviews later contributed to the paper by the most eminent theatrical critic of the time. For the period now under consideration, however, I can only testify to the justice of his conclusion that the *Gazetteer*, in matters theatrical, was relatively without distinction.

Literary amusement, as distinguished from the dramatic, was much more plentiful. It was of three general types. The first, significant chiefly for the space devoted to it, consisted of matter reprinted in the *Gazetteer* from other sources and perhaps included on some occasions to fill up space when the quantity of news or advertisements was insufficient. Thus were published such varied items as "Account of the Egyptian Alme, or Dancing Girls," [45] "Virtue and Curiosity, an Allegorical Dream," [46] "The Knight and the Sword, an Heroic Tale," [47] "The Dean of Badajoz, A Tale. From the Abbé Blanchet," [48] "The Citizen of Abberville," and "The Voluptuary's Soliloquy." [49] All were inserted, apparently, only for their entertainment value. More edifying, probably, were offerings like a selection from Garrick's letters,[50] "Sketches Moral and Political, By Warren Hastings . . . Carefully Selected from various parts of that Gentleman's Works," [51] and essays reprinted from *The Lounger*, an Edinburgh periodical,[52] and from Thomas Monro's *Olla Podrida*, published at Oxford.[53] From the autumn of 1787 to the spring of 1788 William Owen recorded issues of the *Olla Podrida*, at 2½d. each, as having been purchased and "sent to Mr. Perry"; and on 16 April 1788 the purchases concluded with acquisition of the title page and preface to the periodical.[54] While entries are lacking for other items of this kind, it is probable that the proprietors authorized a number of similar purchases from funds at the printing office.

A second kind of literary entertainment, and that most frequently published, was poetry. Although Perry was merely following precedent in allocating a "Poet's Corner" on page 4, the inclusion of an isolated quatrain or epigram almost daily within the news columns of page 3 was an innovation. Of the latter a number were attributed to "T. N.," a signature frequently appended to longer verses in the Poet's Corner and occasionally found in front-page

essays of the period. In 1784 the writer was further identified as
"T. N., Esq; of Westminster," author of a complimentary epigram
on Dr. Johnson with which the doctor had declared himself
pleased.[55] He was possibly a regularly employed correspondent
whose poetic efforts had their original publication in the *Gazetteer*.
Not so, however, with much of the poetry published by Perry, for
the Poet's Corner often contained excerpts from the works of the
most popular poets of the day. Some of them, like William Collins [56] and Robert Burns,[57] have achieved permanent recognition
since the 1780's; others, notably Charlotte Smith [58] and Sir Samuel
Egerton Brydges,[59] have long since fallen into obscurity.

Probably the most obscure of all the *Gazetteer*'s poets was one
discovered by Perry three years after he assumed the editorship.
Early in 1787, when Robert Burns was achieving widespread recognition for the Kilmarnock poems published in the preceding year
and much was being made of Burns's supposed lack of education,
the *Gazetteer* offered its readers a rival to the "Ploughman" in
the person of William Hamilton Reid, "a day labourer in the
lowest circumstances." On Monday, 8 January 1787, a letter from
"Crito Sceptic" to the editor was published on page one of the
Gazetteer. "Instigated by the late representations relative to Burns,"
the writer asked permission to "offer a few hints on a more than
similar phenomenon."

Lately returned from the North, I confess I heard but little of Burns
at Berwick, and several places in Scotland, but what transpired through
the channel of your Gazetteer; but with many respectable circles that
read the London prints, I was witness to a general approbation and
liberal acknowledgments to the poetical performances of William
Hamilton Reid, (in the periodical publications) supposed to be an obscure
illiterate person. However, Sir, if this is the same person who signed
W. Hamilton, day-labourer, in the Gentleman's Magazine for June,
1786, I must say, that his painting of a Suicide and Modern Fanaticism
equally deserve the public attention with Burns, or any happier candidate. Can such lines as these, Sir, in his address to Humanity, be read
without the most sensible emotions from their fine pathos. . . . [Here
the writer quoted twenty lines from the poem referred to.] . . . This,
Sir, is not the style of a Plebeian, nor an uncultivated mind. I must
incline to scepticism; yet how far I may be impartial, I leave to the
determination of the discerning public: but from an immediate retrospective view, whilst I am turning over your papers for the last year, I
am the more confirmed in my sentiments, finding many descriptive

effusions highly poetic, and this last (Gazetteer, December 28) Elegy stands unequalled in any other daily print; but, Sir, there is so much caprice in the human system, that I must doubt these as the product of a day-labourer. Such a signature may be intended as a satire upon the credulity of such as can admit the possibility of a composition of elegant verses, by a man with a strong propensity to reading in a polished city. If this should not eventually be the case, every man of taste and sentiment must conclude with me, that W. H. Reid may claim the precedence of all the unlettered poets existing, and from the elevated taste of the age rise to the consequence his merit deserves. I hope, through the medium of your paper, for a gratification of this enquiry, which will oblige many, as well as your humble servant. . . .

Perry was delighted to comply. He fully shared the enthusiasm of his correspondent, only disagreeing with the specimen of Reid's poetry selected for quotation, and he testified from personal knowledge to Reid's unlettered condition:

We are happy that Crito Sceptic has noticed the productions of *W. Hamilton Reid*, as in resolving his doubts, we shall make known to the public this extraordinary man. W. H. Reid has communicated gratuitously to the Gazetteer various pieces of poetry, which, though not highly finished nor correct, had something better than the mere polish of art —they had warm passion and natural imagery. He described himself to us as an untutored writer, and submitted with extreme diffidence his effusions to the public eye. We have lately seen him, and we find he is what he represents, a *day labourer* in the lowest circumstances. He has read no poet save Thompson [*sic*], nor any other poetry except the fugitive productions of the day—and yet with a mind unstored by reading—with no knowledge of even the rudiments of Grammar, and with no corrector but his ear—he has produced stanzas burning with the genuine flame of poetry. Our correspondent Crito Sceptic has not done justice to the talents of this natural poet in the selection he has made. There are many more beautiful passages to be found in his late efforts. For instance, would it be believed that a description of night so truly poetical as the following could come from an undisciplined pen. . . . [Perry quoted four stanzas, of which I reproduce only the first.]

> The moon, emerging from the noiseless deep,
>   O'er ocean's bosom flings her silver veil;
> Still Eccho sits on yonder craggy steep,
>   And seems the sleep of nature to bewail.

Three months later "An Impartial Observer" wrote to praise Reid and to voice his distress that the poet, apparently in straitened circumstances, had as yet found no patron. "But," the Observer concluded, his "unfeigned desire" was that "the generosity of a discerning public may speedily obviate these apprehensions in the present case. . . ." [60]

Poetry by Reid, signed either in full or with his initials, was published frequently in the *Gazetteer* during the six years following Perry's discovery of him, and Reid's untutored state, if genuine, proved only temporary. In 1793 and 1794 he was a regular *Gazetteer* correspondent supplying paragraphs for the news columns,[61] and in November 1800 he contributed to the *Gentleman's Magazine* an essay upon the writings of William Law.[62]

The third variety of literary intelligence offered by the *Gazetteer* between 1783 and 1790 was less plentiful than the others but no less interesting. It may be classified generally as "biography and anecdotes of literary figures," but perhaps "Johnsoniana" would be more appropriate, since the great majority of items in this category concerned the doctor and were called forth by his death. The *Gazetteer* announced that event on 15 December 1784 with a regret untinctured by any political overtones: "With the truest concern we inform our readers, that at seven o'clock on Monday evening, the great and good Dr. SAM JOHNSON breathed his last, aged 74 years and three months." The account continued with details of the funeral preparations and the doctor's will, and it concluded by proposing the erection of a monument in Westminster Abbey "to the memory of a man who has not left an equal behind him." On the following day, the paper carried an anonymous "Sketch of the Life and Writings of Dr. Johnson," and a week later, so voluminous had been the anecdotes and expressions of grief in all the newspapers that Perry felt compelled to announce: "We shall be proud to register the tributary effusions of genius on the lamented death of Dr. Johnson, but we cannot add to the torrent of trash with which the press is inundated." [63] That declared, the *Gazetteer* gave a detailed description of Johnson's physical condition as observed by the embalmer.

Between New Year's Day and 10 January Perry published in several installments the "Biographical Sketch of Dr. Samuel Johnson" by Thomas Tyers which had appeared in the *Gentleman's Magazine* for the preceding month, and on the fourteenth he remonstrated sharply against the volume of Johnsonian matter submitted for publication: "The public are already sick of the quantity of nonsense published under the title of Memoirs, Anecdotes, and Bon Mots of Dr. Johnson, and of Epitaphs on him. What then would they have said if we had inserted all the trash with which we have been favoured?" [64] From that date until after the publication of Boswell's biography in 1791, however, the *Gazetteer* continued to publish anecdotes of Johnson as well as letters and paragraphs bearing upon the efforts of his biographers Hawkins, Mrs. Piozzi, and Boswell, and upon their disagreements.

Boswell and James Perry were to become well acquainted in the years preceding the biographer's death. John Taylor, a contemporary journalist, recalled "the elder Boswell" as an occasional member of the group including Perry, his brother-in-law Richard Porson, and Alexander Chalmers, which "generally assembled in the evening at the Turk's Head Coffee-house in the Strand." [65] And Boswell recorded in his journal what must have been an early meeting with his fellow Scot on 28 August 1790: "Dined at the house of Forbes, the great Coppersmith. . . . The company was all Scotch except one Barnes. . . . Perry and Gray, the Editors of the Gazeteer were of the Party. I was disgusted by the reviving in my mind of forward, coarse, north of Scotland manners. We drank a considerable quantity." [66] Gray was actually editor of the *Morning Chronicle,* and later a partner with Perry in that paper, but Boswell had probably overcome his confusion by October 1790, when he addressed the following letter to the editor of the *Gazetteer:*

SIR,

A considerable time ago I wrote you a letter, declaring that I would publish no paragraph whatever concerning my *Life of Dr. Johnson,* without putting my name to it.

Since that time there have been such a number written by friends, foes, and correspondents of all descriptions (of none of which I know or even suspect who the authors are) that I find it hard to be precluded from availing myself of any fair opportunity to meet them in their own way. I therefore intimate that this restraint is to last no longer, and that I hold myself at full liberty to throw into the prints whatever fancy may prompt.

I am, Sir, your most humble servant,
JAMES BOSWELL

London, Oct. 18.

To which Perry replied, "We assure Mr. Boswell, that we shall carefully attend to his communications." [67]

The editorial influence of James Perry in all of its manifestations is the main point of interest in the *Gazetteer*'s history between 1783 and 1790. Coincidentally, the period of Perry's editorship is the earliest for which there is considerable evidence to illuminate matters connected with the publication but unrevealed in the columns of the printed paper. The evidence is contained in two manuscript books: one is a volume of monthly general accounts kept by William Owen as treasurer from October 1783, ten months after Perry assumed the editorship; [68] the other, a volume of minutes taken at meetings of the proprietors from the spring of 1788, two and a half years before his resignation.

Owen's monthly accounts, submitted for inspection at each meeting of the management committee, were compiled for him by one Edward Bentley.[69] They record under general headings the expenditures for which the proprietors were considered indebted to Owen as treasurer, and the total sums received on account of the *Gazetteer* each month. A general summary of the items normally recorded, with some explanation of their nature, will indicate the financial and administrative details of the publication.

The debit page for each month contained first a list of the total number of copies of the *Gazetteer* printed on each day of publication, followed by the total number printed during the month. Next, the number of "blank" or unstamped *Gazetteers*, some two dozen of which were distributed daily to the proprietors, the editor and debate reporters, the printer, and a select group of advertising customers, was computed for the month and subtracted from the total number of papers printed. The remainder represented the number of papers upon which stamp duty had to be paid, and the expenditure for payment of that duty was duly recorded.

Following the stamp duty on papers, the quantity and cost of all paper used during the month was entered and then the amount of stamp duty due upon all the advertisements published. The next item of expenditure recorded was Mrs. Say's total monthly charge for printing. In 1783 daily printing charges were £3 19s. 9d. for the first thousand papers and 3s. 9d. for each additional token of 250. Ten years later a rise in compositors' salaries increased the basic charge to £4 6s. 6d. for the first thousand papers; the charge for additional tokens remained unchanged.

The monthly debits concluded with three items which are of

especial interest. The first was labeled "Say's Petty Expences," and the payments recorded ranged from £50 to £100 for each month. Another account book, for the period of the 1790's, contains itemized lists of these petty expenses or "incidents" and reveals that they consisted chiefly of disbursements relative to editorial functions: salaries of the editor and debate reporters, payments for paragraphs and such other news as "East India" and "Newgate Intelligence," subscriptions to foreign and provincial papers, fees for messengers, and many other expenses, regular and occasional.[70] Items of this kind recorded occasionally in William Owen's day-to-day accounts [71] have been noted earlier. The conclusion to be drawn from a comparison is that Mrs. Say the printer was still, as her husband had been, more directly concerned in the administration of editorial matters than was the publisher Owen.

Owen himself was the recipient of the next disbursement recorded in the monthly accounts, a payment of one guinea a week for "Keeping the accounts & collecting the Debts &c. Publishing." The final monthly expenditure was for "Owen's Petty Expences"; these consisted of the disbursements discussed in preceding chapters for proprietors' meetings, postage, newspaper subscriptions, occasional payments to contributors, legal costs, and other incidental expenses. Their total was invariably much less than the "petty expences" incurred by Mrs. Say.[72]

Monthly totals on the credit side of the treasurer's ledger consisted primarily of money due from advertisements, and of receipts from the sale of papers, at £10 per 1,000 from October 1783 until August 1789, £12 per 1,000 until June 1790, £14 per 1,000 until April 1794, and £16 per 1,000 thereafter. Occasional credits were entered also for such items as "Returns" of unsold papers to the Stamp Office (until August, 1789, when such credit ceased to be allowed by the government), sale of waste paper, and absences of proprietors from the general meetings, each of which resulted in a five-shilling fine.

The total receipts for each month were balanced against the total expenditures, and the difference constituted the proprietors' profit or loss. This amount was reported monthly at the meetings of the management committee, and the balance on hand at the end of each six months, entered on a separate page in the ledger, was reported to the general meetings at which, if conditions warranted, dividends were declared. The dividends on each of the sixteen shares in the paper during the eight years of James Perry's editorship averaged £22 9s. annually. Since each share was valued at £200,[73] this represents a yearly return of 11.2 per cent on each proprietor's investment, but relatively low circulation figures for the period suggest that the return must have been considerably higher in preceding years.

The average daily circulation of the *Gazetteer*, as distinguished from the number of copies printed each day, may be computed by dividing the total number of papers sold each month (recorded in the treasurer's monthly accounts) by the number of publication days within the month. In the winter of 1783-84, the earliest period for which there are records, the average daily circulation of the paper was 2,232 copies, or less than half of the daily average (5,300) printed during the first three months of 1772.[74] By the winter of 1789-90, the last during James Perry's very able editorship of the *Gazetteer*, the circulation had fallen by nearly 500 copies per day, or more than 22 per cent; yet in an announcement of 10 September 1789 Perry declared, "At this moment the GAZETTEER has avowedly the most extensive sale of any morning paper in London, the Daily Advertiser excepted," and there is reason for crediting his statement. A discussion of the problem makes necessary the consideration of a number of factors affecting circulation, and the efforts of the *Gazetteer* proprietors to offset the general decline.

The factor most directly responsible for a loss in circulation between 1772 and 1790 was certainly the increased competition which the *Gazetteer* encountered. In 1772 it had been one of six daily papers published in London; by 1790 it was one of fourteen.[75] The increased number of daily publications alone would account for a considerable decline in the paper's sale, but the relative popularity of the newspapers as determined by public preference does not appear to have been the only basis for competition in the 1780's. Two notices which appeared in the *Gazetteer* indicate that the hawkers who distributed the papers must have had a significant influence upon the success of those by which they were most liberally rewarded. Early in 1789 the *Gazetteer* announced:

We have received various complaints of the conduct of several of the Hawkers, who, from interested motives, hesitate to serve the Gazetteer, if they can, by misrepresentation and subtlety, prevail on their customers to accept some other paper in the room of it, to which they may happen to be attached. We shall take a decisive opportunity of correcting this breach of trust in the first glaring instance that we can possibly bring to legal proof. In the mean time we request such

Ladies and Gentlemen as may have been disappointed through this
abuse, and who wish to be served with the *Gazetteer* in preference, to
send a note of their address to the Printing Office, and their order
shall be given to some honest and fair-dealing person in the particular
walk, who will thankfully execute the commission.[76]

Nine weeks later the proprietors announced:

To counteract the very blameable conduct of many of the news
hawkers who obtrude other papers, in which they have peculiar interest,
for the *Gazetteer*, we beg leave to inform our readers at the West
End of Town, where this imposition has chiefly been practised, that
this paper will be regularly served by Messrs. *Shepperson* and *Reynolds*,
Oxford street; and Mr. Kerby, Stafford street, Old Bond street; by
whom also communications for the paper will be received.[77]

Another cause of the reduced circulation, not only for the *Gazetteer* but probably for every newspaper in England, was the additional halfpenny tax imposed by the government in August 1789.
By this law the total stamp duty on each paper sold was raised
from 1½d. to 2d., and as a result the price of nearly every daily
newspaper was increased from 3d. to 4d. The *Gazetteer* proprietors,
however, in an attempt to gain customers, resolved at a committee
meeting of 30 July 1789 "that the price of the Gazetteer be not
advanced beyond the new stamp duty of one halfpenny on each
paper." The results of their decision are clearly visible in the
accounts. In the summer of every other year for which there are
records, the average daily circulation for the month of July was
about 100 less than that for June, and the circulation for August
was still lower. In 1789 circulation of the *Gazetteer* declined from
1,566 for the month of June to 1,479 for the month of July; in
August, however, when a further decline would have been normal,
the paper was selling for a halfpenny less than most of its competitors, and its daily circulation increased by 240 copies. In the
following month, when Perry claimed a circulation second only
to that of the *Daily Advertiser*, an average of 1,753 papers were
sold daily at 3½d. each. The difference in price between the *Gazetteer* and its competitors lends credibility to Perry's claim.

An overproduction of stamped papers, for which credit was no
longer allowed at the Stamp Office, was probably responsible in
large measure for a loss in August 1789 of £95 8s. 4½d., and the
proprietors' profits for the six months ending in October were only
£25 19s. 11½d.[78] At a committee meeting in December it was resolved, "On account of the number of papers left on hand, unsold,

since . . . the new Act took place, . . . that no more papers be printed than the sale will take off. The Committee thinking it better to lose the probable sale of a few, rather than to sustain the loss of many being left on hand." [79]

From September 1789 to June 1790 the monthly profits ranged between £7 5s. 10½d. and £64 13s. 3d., and in the latter month the proprietors decided "to raise the price of the Gazeteer to 4d. which many of the Morning Papers have been raised to since August last." [80] The increase became effective on Monday, 21 June, with this announcement:

It is now almost twelve months since the Legislature imposed an additional duty on newspapers; at which time most of the other prints advanced their price on the public. Anxious to preserve unnarrowed the circulation of political intelligence we were willing to try, though at considerable risk to ourselves, whether a paper could not be conducted at the old rate of price under the new duty. We have been honoured by the most flattering support; but, after a fair trial, we find it utterly impossible from the many obvious additions to our expence, to furnish the requisite variety of information without charging the same price for the paper as our contemporaries. We therefore respectfully inform the public, that the price of the GAZETTEER will henceforth be four-pence.

Circulation of the *Gazetteer*, which should normally have suffered a seasonal decline from June to July of about 100 copies, fell from 1,702 to 1,340, a total of 362 copies, following the price rise; but the monthly profits for the six months following ranged between £34 16s. 4½d. and £102 9s. 8½d.

On 20 September 1790, three months after the increase in price, the *Gazetteer* displayed a striking typographical innovation. Partially in an attempt to justify the price rise, but more directly the result of the typographical influence of competitors [81] and of a desire to appeal to the eyes of prospective readers, new types were employed, and, for the first time in the paper's history, part of the title heading on page one was set in an open type. The subtitle, in italic capitals, was centered below "The Gazetteer" and followed in roman capitals by the word "London" and the date, both on a line with the issue number at the left and the price of the paper at the right. "We make no boast of the typographical improvements which the reader will this day observe in the paper," it was announced, "as every possible exertion on our part is no more than our own duty in grateful return for the very flattering distinction we enjoy through the favour of the Public." [82] The average daily

circulation for that month was 1,350; in the following month
(October) it increased to 1,425, and the editor declared:

The Gazetteer holds the highest and most reputable sale of any morning
paper in London. It goes into the BEST PLACES, and takes the most
EXTENSIVE CIRCLE. . . . It is selected for its fair and long-proved
consistency, as the organ of the popular voice by every independent body
of men in the three kingdoms, as the constant reports of every public
meeting transmitted to us from the country, and from Scotland and
Ireland, demonstrate: —And, if other proof were wanting, it may be
observed, that whenever contentions spring up among the journalists
themselves, they, who know the internal state of the papers the best,
make the Gazetteer the field of their hostilities, to secure the greatest
number of spectators to the combat. . . .[83]

In the absence of direct evidence on circulation of the other
papers at the time, the testimony of contemporary writers is the
only reliable indication of the *Gazetteer*'s success as measured
against that of its competitors. The Reverend Dr. John Trusler,
a shareholder in the *Morning Post* and a man of many contacts in
publishing circles, wrote in 1790, in a volume of advice for visitors
to London: "Of the morning papers, those most in circulation are
Daily Advertiser, Gazetteer, Ledger in the city and the *Herald,
Morning Post,* and *World* in the west end." [84] Thus, of the thirteen
daily papers which Trusler listed, the *Gazetteer* was considered by
him as at least among the first six in circulation. William Finey,
editor of the *Times* from 1788 to 1795, wrote in the latter year
that when John Walter had first engaged him "the Times sold
no more than 450 per day," [85] and John Watkins, who was to
succeed William Owen as publisher of the *Gazetteer*, declared
"from undoubted Authority" that the circulation of the *Morning
Chronicle* "was 800 at the Time Perry B[ough]t it" in December
1790.[86] That a sale of about 1,500 was sufficient to yield a reasonable profit is obvious from the *Gazetteer* treasurer's accounts. Thus,
while the paper's circulation was probably not the highest in London, there is fair indication that it was by no means lower than
the average. Moreover, James Perry's editorial abilities must
certainly have been acknowledged by the reading public. When
in December 1790 he purchased the *Morning Chronicle*, the retiring proprietors of that paper testified to the "consistency and
zeal" of their successor of which, they said, "the public has had
long experience and particularly for the last eight years as Editor
of the Gazetteer." [87] It is unlikely that they would have based

such a recommendation upon a reference to a paper of relatively small popularity.

The events surrounding Perry's purchase of the *Morning Chronicle,* after his efficient presentation of debates in the *Gazetteer* had done much to lessen the *Chronicle*'s reputation and sale, are comparatively well known. Financial assistance from a firm of London bankers as well as from a wine merchant who was caterer and doorkeeper to the House of Commons was augmented by the Duke of Norfolk's present of a house in the Strand which Perry converted into a new publishing office.[88] The circumstances of his resignation from the *Gazetteer,* however, have been inaccurately reported. W. P. Courtney stated in the *Dictionary of National Biography* that the *Gazetteer* "was purchased by some tories, who changed its politics, and Perry severed his connection with it." I have been unable to locate his source for the assertion, but the minutes of the proprietors' meetings for the period discredit it completely.

In the first place, the *Gazetteer* was not purchased by any group during the period of Perry's editorship. The proprietors of the paper in 1790 were, with the following exceptions, the same group who had contracted with Mary Say in 1775.[89] The share in the paper held by John Whiston had been divided at his death in 1780 between Benjamin White, his business partner, and Nathaniel (later Sir Nathaniel) Conant, his son-in-law; both were substantial London booksellers. The share of John Nourse had passed to his successor in business, Francis Wingrave, in 1780. Samuel Baker's share had passed to his nephew John Sotheby, first of the name in the renowned firm of auctioneers. The half-share of David Wilson had passed to his nephew George Nicol who succeeded to his business as bookseller; that of Wilson's partner, Thomas Durham, was held in 1790 by John Debrett, the Whig publisher and business successor to John Almon. The share of George Hayter, merchant, had been divided between the booksellers Thomas and John Egerton, the latter a son-in-law of Lockyer Davis. Finally, the share held in 1775 by John Twyman the ship broker was held in 1790 by Clement Strong, whom I have failed to identify. In all, five of the sixteen shares in the *Gazetteer* had changed hands since 1775. Another name unconnected with the paper until 1790 was that of Vint. In November 1787 Charles Say's widow had married Edward Vint, a calico printer, of Crayford. The name "Mary Say" had continued unchanged in the *Gazetteer,* however, until 5 March 1790, and even then the traditional association of the paper with the name of Say had not been relinquished; the new imprint read: "Printed by MARY VINT, (late SAY,)." [90]

Perry's relations with the proprietors, while they cannot be fully known, appear to have been harmonious. He attended the meetings of the management committee in 1789 and 1790 with considerable frequency, and the fact that succeeding editors attended only two such meetings between 1790 and 1797 seems to indicate that Perry's interest in the paper extended beyond his editorial duties, and that the proprietors admitted him more deeply into their confidence than they did any of his successors.[91] Meetings at the King's Head in Holborn were probably more pleasant when he attended, for Miss Mitford described him in 1813 as "a man so genial and so accomplished that even when Erskine, Romilly, Tierney, and Moore were present, he was the most charming talker at his own table." Charles Lamb, who characterized Daniel Stuart as "one of the finest tempered of Editors," considered Perry "equally pleasant, with a dash, no slight one either, of the courtier." Lamb had "worked for both these gentlemen." [92]

Co-operation between Perry and the proprietors was recorded on two specific occasions, one in July 1789 at a meeting "called in order to consider what steps may be proper to be taken upon the commencement of the new duty on Newspapers and Advertisements." Perry apparently participated in forming the decision to raise the price of the paper by only a halfpenny, and it was "Resolved that handbills be printed and dispersed announcing the . . . circumstance, under the care and direction of Mr. Perry and Mr. John Egerton." [93] Again, in December of that year, Perry attended a meeting at which "Mr. Conant and Mr. Nicol agreed, at the desire of the Committee, to meet Mr. Perry at the Printing Office on Friday next, in order to enquire into, & regulate, the time of publication, the lateness of which has been of late much complained of." [94] Perry's authority in this instance seems to have bordered on the administrative; he was co-operating with the proprietors to regulate a matter which almost certainly came within the province of the printer. The only recorded action of the proprietors which may imply dissatisfaction with one aspect of Perry's editorial policy was a direction given at the committee meeting of 18 February 1789. The editor was to be informed "that the interest of the Gazeteer having suffered much this winter from the rejection of Advertisements in order to make room for other matter, that everything shall for the future give place to Advertisements, except the Debates in Parliament on a great day." These instructions may indicate that literary and miscellaneous entertainment had been included in the paper by Perry's choice rather than as the results of advertisement shortages, but if the editor resented the direction, he left no record of it.

In June 1789 John Debrett wrote to the proprietors expressing a desire to sell his half-share in the paper,[95] and in September 1790 Perry, at a committee meeting, "desired that he might be admitted to purchase the said share." [96] Certainly he can have entertained no resentment of the proprietors at that time. At the general meeting of the following month "Mr Perry's desire to be permitted to purchase Mr Debrets 32d. share . . . was taken into consideration." It was resolved that Perry "be permitted to purchase the s[ai]d share, & be admitted a partner in the Gazetteer upon the payment of 100£ according to the present valuation." [97] At the next committee meeting Perry was in attendance and was informed of the resolution "respecting his admission to the purchase of Mr Debrets 32d share." [98] The decision, however, was announced too late. Perry had apparently been negotiating meanwhile for the purchase of the *Morning Chronicle*. Minutes for the committee meeting of 3 December 1790 record simply:

Mr Perry having signified by Letter, his determination of relinquishing the editorship of the Gazetteer, Mr. Beauchamp was desired to undertake the management for the present, & instructions were given him for that purpose.

Mr Perry's engagement ceased on Saturday, 27 Nov. last.

The proprietors' failure to display appreciation for Perry's abilities by presenting him with a share in the *Gazetteer* may have been a factor in determining the ultimate failure of the paper. Certainly a comparison of the *Gazetteer*'s progress through the next seven years with that of the *Morning Chronicle* justifies such an inference. But Perry himself would probably not long have been satisfied with less than the full rewards of his labor, and as proprietor and editor of the *Chronicle* (after a brief partnership with Gray, the former editor) he was able to exercise his talents with a freedom which would never have been possible in a connection with the *Gazetteer*. That independence and concentration of authority were important requisites for the development of outstanding journalists and great newspapers in the last decade of the eighteenth century is indicated by the success of Daniel Stuart and the *Morning Post*, John Walter II and the *Times*, and, most striking of all, perhaps, of James Perry and the *Morning Chronicle* —the new "Paper of the People."

XII

DECLINE

1791-1796

O N New Year's Day 1791 the *Gazetteer* was distinguished by
an unusual feature. It was an address to readers made not,
as was customary, in the name of the editor, but in the name of
the paper's proprietors, and it is of interest chiefly because it declared their intention to continue the paper in the policies inaugurated by James Perry.[1] Misled, apparently, as Wall had been
in 1780, by the paper's issue number for the day, the proprietors
took the opportunity, they said, "for the SIXTY-SECOND time" to
return their thanks to the public for its confidence and support.[2]
Reference to the proprietors' past conduct as revealed in the
Gazetteer could not be made, they were confident, without showing them to have been faithful in recording every event of foreign
and domestic importance, "and constantly watchful for the political and moral welfare of the community, for the interests of science,
and the progress of cultivated manners." Reference to the past must
further show, the address continued,

that the Gazetteer has been as it shall continue to be, a paper perma-
nently devoted to the CONSTITUTION, not to PARTY; to WHIGGISM,
rather than to OPPOSITION; to the PEOPLE, not to any set of political
LEADERS.

Yet, lest it should be misunderstood, or misrepresented, that this
general mention of an adherence to the Constitution is meant to countenance any deviation from the present principles of the paper, they
[the proprietors] think it necessary to go so far into an avowal of a

218

political creed, as to say that they consider the Gentlemen now acting under the name of opposition as the TRUEST FRIENDS TO THE CONSTITUTION, to WHIGGISM, to the PEOPLE; and further, that they believe Mr. Fox to possess a greater degree of EXPERIENCE, of INTELLECTUAL POWER, and of the NOBLE SPIRIT which renders a truly proud man independent of every consideration, but that of deserving well, and of the GENTLENESS of the BRAVE, than has ever been united in any person, whose conduct in Parliament has invited the notice of the Public.

Thus they announce *their* choice of MEN, and discover *their* opinion of MEASURES. . . .[3]

Having referred the public to its own past experience, the proprietors felt it unnecessary "to enter into promises for the future." They knew themselves to be "old favourites" with the public, they said, and they would

not now affect to practise the ceremonies of a first introduction. Their political resources are acknowledged to be extensive; and they hope to dwell, with equal information, upon the minuter, though pleasant topics of fashion, taste, amusement, and whatever forms "the exterior of polished life."

Of their rivals they are not very desirous to speak. They have, indeed, a pleasure in confessing that there are some with whom they shall be proud to continue a fair and ingenuous competition; but to others they can say, with some alteration of the antient reply — "All that you have said we have done."

The New Year's address may have been attributed to the proprietors in this instance because the paper was still, more than four weeks after James Perry's resignation, without an editor. How closely the *Gazetteer* adhered, in the years that followed, to Perry's political and journalistic policies as restated here will become apparent. That the address was made in the name of the proprietors, however, presages a general trend in the paper's management which was to become more and more pronounced in the remaining seven years of its life.

In the final two years and seven months of Perry's editorship, the earliest period for which records of the proprietors' meetings have been preserved, the *Gazetteer* management committee confined itself almost exclusively to a monthly examination of the paper's accounts. Rarely did the proprietors assert themselves in matters of day-to-day policy. Perry's abilities, as has been suggested, seem to have had their full confidence, and responsibility for editorial disbursements rested almost entirely with the printer. In the period following Perry's resignation, the committee minutes reveal a gradual increase in the proprietors' attention to policy and the details of publication. One reason for the change, undoubtedly, was that the partners never again acquired an editor of Perry's attainments. But for at least two years after he left their employ, their problems in this respect were relatively minor ones.

For nearly two months after Perry's resignation the *Gazetteer* had no editor properly so-called. The "Mr. Beauchamp" appointed to "undertake the management" of the paper in December 1790 had probably assisted in managing it for some years before. Minutes for the committee meeting of 19 January 1791 record that he was thereafter to be allowed a weekly salary of fifteen shillings instead of the half-guinea previously paid him. His relationship with the proprietors during the ensuing six years indicates that his position was equivalent to those of the modern production manager and make-up editor. From 1791 Beauchamp represented the chief link between the management committee and the printer, Mary Say Vint, and his duties embraced some of the functions known to have been carried out earlier by Roger Thompson. Like Thompson, he appears to have been a full-time employee of the printer, possibly supervising for her the production of the *Craftsman, General Evening Post*, and, after 1795, *The Selector; Or Say's Sunday Reporter*.

In January 1791 the proprietors appointed William Radcliffe "to the care of the Gazeteer in room of Mr Perry" and directed that he "be allowed three guineas per week for his care." [4] Radcliffe had taken a B.A. at Oriel College, Oxford, in 1785 [5] and two years later had married Ann Ward. Mrs. Radcliffe's later literary activities, it is said, owed their origin to her husband's nocturnal occupation as a journalist and their success, in some measure, to his encouragement.[6] Radcliffe had studied law for a time, and he may have taken to literary pursuits from economic necessity. In 1789 he had translated for the publisher George Kearsley *A Journey through Sweden*, "Written in French by a Dutch Officer," [7] and in the following year had produced another translation, this time of *The Natural History of East Tartary*.[8] Any previous experience he may have had as a writer for the newspapers is unrecorded, but his beginning salary of three guineas, compared to the four guineas Perry had received from 1783, probably indicates that his first editorial position was with the *Gazetteer*.

Commencement of Radcliffe's tenure as editor seems to have

been marred by some difficulty in the assertion of his authority. In mid-February he attended a meeting of the management committee with a complaint against a subordinate and was instructed by the proprietors "to inform Mr Oswald that his duty as a Reporter is not to exclude his assistance in other matters & that he is to apply to such other business as Mr Radcliffe shall point out." [9] Once this matter had been settled, Radcliffe apparently managed quite well. His only other application to the committee during the year was for authorization to cancel the *Gazetteer*'s subscriptions to the *Public Advertiser* and *Public Ledger* and to "take in their stead what Country Papers may suit his purpose." [10]

At the general meetings of April and October 1791 a dividend of £400 was declared, the first such in more than three years, and profits for the year totalled £774 13s. 4d. Although circulation continued in the gradual decline observable from the year 1785, the proprietors were sufficiently satisfied with the performance of the new editor to resolve, at their meeting of 18 January 1792 "that Mr Radcliffe be advanced to the sallary of the former Editor, viz four pounds four shillings per Week to commence from the first day of this Month."

In 1792, the second year of Radcliffe's editorship, the members of the *Gazetteer* management committee exerted their authority over details of the paper's publication with notably greater frequency than they had in the preceding four years. In February Radcliffe and John Sotheby suggested opening a distribution center for the paper at Bath, and on the fifteenth of that month the committee decided "that the hint of Mr Sotheby and Mr Radcliffe, for engaging a shop at Bath to dispose of the *Gazetteer*, be carried into execution, and, that Mr Sotheby (now at Bath) be requested to use his endeavours to procure such shop." Sotheby's efforts must have been successful, for the accounts record monthly debits averaging about £10 for "Papers sent to Bath" from March 1792 until February 1793.[11] This would indicate that only about 700 copies of the paper (at the wholesale price of £14 per thousand) were dispatched to Bath each month, for an average daily sale there of perhaps two dozen papers. In view of these figures it seems probable that the proprietors considered Bath circulation as an inducement to advertisers in London rather than as a profitable arrangement in itself.

And it was advertising with which the committee chiefly concerned itself. The same meeting at which the proprietors determined upon opening the shop at Bath passed a resolution "that Mr

Beauchamp be desired to pay a particular attention to the insertion of Advertisements and at all times to exclude such matter as may not appear to Mr Radcliffe and himself either immediately interesting or Pressing in favour of Advertisements." Minutes for the meeting of November 1792 record: "The Printer is desir'd to insert all Miscellaneous Advertisements that can with conveniency be done . . . Mr Newberry shoud be particularly attended to as he has complain'd." [12] In December, with Parliament in session and space at a premium, the proprietors recommended measures to curtail the space occupied by theatrical advertisements:

> Ordered that during the Winter Season the play bills be set as short as is at all Practicable & that the notices from the house added at the end of the advertisement be abridged as much as possible or wholly omitted if of small importance to the readers and no room taken up in any case for the more accomodation of the Theatres.
>
> Mr Beauchamp is also directed to try by composing both Theatres in one advertisement (after the manner of the *World* and some other papers) whether the Duty upon two advertisements may not be saved. [13]

Theatrical notices, as distinguished from reviews and criticism, had long been a staple of the *Gazetteer*'s content, and the proprietors' resolution of December 1792 is indicative of the basic change in policy which had taken place since September 1767 when Charles Say had announced: "The PLAYS and ENTERTAINMENTS at the THEATRES ROYAL of DRURY LANE and COVENT-GARDEN, will, for the future, be advertised, BY AUTHORITY OF THE MANAGERS, Both in THIS PAPER and the PUBLIC ADVERTISER." [14] From that date almost certainly—surviving records begin only seven years later—until the year 1782 William Owen had made annual payments of £50 to "Mr. Evans, Under-Treasurer of Drury Lane Theatre" and to "Mr. Carton" of Covent Garden. [15] In return the *Gazetteer* had received official notice each night of the plays to be given on the following evening, and the announcements had occupied the key position daily in column 1 of the paper's front page. In addition to these authorized playbills it seems probable that the *Gazetteer* (and the *Public Advertiser*) had received preference from the theatre managers when advance performances and benefit performances for individual members of the companies were to be advertised. A ledger of advertising accounts dating from 1786 [16] shows that after annual payments to the theatres had ceased (probably because increased competition from the other papers made them unprofitable), the *Gazetteer* still inserted the front-page announcements of daily performances on payment by the theatres of the advertising stamp duty alone. Advance notices and benefits were inserted at the standard advertisement rate of 5s. 6d. until 1789, and thereafter, when the stamp duty increased from 2s. 6d. to three shillings, at the rate of six shillings. Puffs and other announcements were also published at the standard advertisement rates, as is indicated by a 5s. 6d. ledger entry in the Drury Lane account for May 1787: "Mr Kelly deserving praise for his abilities &c. May 11 par[agraph]." [17]

The Haymarket Theatre, it appears, never received the same concessions accorded to Covent Garden and Drury Lane. Payments by the Haymarket's manager, George Colman, from 1786 were at the paper's regular advertisement rate, and in 1790 William Owen was compelled to retain an attorney for "proving Mr Geo Colmans debt . . . to the Gazetteer before a Master in Chancery." [18] That the Haymarket's patronage was valued, however, is clearly revealed by two series of expenditures in the interests of maintaining good public relations. From 1781 until 1791 Owen paid out one guinea annually for tickets to the benefit performances of William Jewell, treasurer to the Haymarket,[19] and annually at least from 1792 the proprietors were charged thirteen shillings in the printing office accounts for "serving *Gazetteer* to Mr Colman." [20]

The book which records deliveries of the paper to George Colman includes only the period in the *Gazetteer*'s history from February 1792 to April 1797, but it is in one respect the most interesting of all the accounts, for it is the only one containing detailed lists of the expenditures made at Mary Vint's printing office in Ave Maria Lane. If the book was not actually kept by an employee at the printing office, it was at least compiled monthly for the publisher from vouchers and receipts which had been forwarded to him from the office.[21] The book corresponds precisely to what would be expected from the clause in the 1775 contract requiring the printer to record all receipts and disbursements on account of the *Gazetteer* "and every thing incident thereto." [22] It records monthly receipts at the printing office from advertisements and sales of the paper, expenditures by the printer for stamp and advertising duties, charges for printing, and the monthly balance due either to the proprietors or (in months of low receipts at the office) from them to the printer. The most valuable entries, however, are those which fall within the contractual description of "everything incident thereto." They are headed, appropriately, "Incidents," and their total is identical to the single item listed in the treasurer's monthly accounts as "Say's [later Vint's] Petty Expences." [23] The individual entries under "Incidents" give the clearest view obtainable of editorial and production details. For this reason and because corresponding data survive, apparently, for no other daily paper of the period, it seems particularly desirable to consider a specimen of the Incidents as a general outline of the conditions prevailing within the printing office during the period of Radcliffe's editorship. The extract below is from the earliest surviving list of Incidents, that for the month of February 1792.[24]

Feb[ruar]y	Incidents	£	S	D
	Mr Radcliffe	16	16	0
	Mr Stables Court News	1	4	0
	[Mr Stables] Paragraphs	7	6	4
	Mr Adams [Paragraphs]	2	13	7
	Mr Kirkman [Paragraphs]		1	7
	Mr Walsh	2	2	0
	Mr Downes	1	11	0
	Mr Dixon Debates	10	10	0
	Mr Wilson [Debates]	10	10	0
	Admission for Mr Wilson		10	6
	East India Intelligence	1	1	0
	Newgate Intelligence	2	10	0
	Mr Reid Paragraphs	1	19	0
		58	15	10
	Mrs Vint	4	4	0
	W Watson	4	4	0
	Morning Papers	3	17	7½
	Evening Papers	1	6	0
	Proprietors Papers		14	0
	Old Woman Change Walk &c	2	2	0
	Playhouse Messenger		12	0
	Letters	7	5	0
	Gazettes		5	11
	Books		4	6
	J Beauchamp	3	0	0
	Extra Composing	10	7	0
	Extra Correcting	1	4	0
	Paper for Debate Writers		16	0
	Mr & Mrs Vint Expences on Arrest	5	15	6

Feb[ruar]y	Incidents	£	S	D
	Advertising for Paper		5	0
	Account Book Bound & Ruled		9	2
	Porterage of Stamps	1	6	0
	Stamp for Receipt			6

The first group of entries, totaled separately from the rest, may be considered as comprising those expenses which were exclusively editorial. Radcliffe, at four guineas, and the two regular debate reporters at £2 12s. 6d. per week (there was occasionally a third engaged temporarily to assist them), were the only regularly salaried writers. Reports of the Parliamentary debates, including those supplied by the editor, consistently made up about half of the total monthly charges for contributions to the paper. Later entries in the accounts reveal that the admission charges to both houses of Parliament, listed in this specimen only for Wilson, were four guineas for the editor and each debate reporter for a full session. This was paid, probably, in the form of a compliment to the doorkeepers.

Paragraphs contributed by Stables, Adams, Kirkman, Walsh, Downes, William Hamilton Reid, and later by their successors were paid for at the rate of a penny for every line of type they occupied. Each of the reporters submitted monthly an itemized statement containing the first line of every paragraph contributed, the date on which it appeared in the paper, and the number of lines it occupied. The total number of lines determined the amount of their monthly payment.[25] "Newgate Intelligence" was apparently purchased at the same rate, for the expenditures recorded were of varying amounts, as were those (not shown in the specimen) for "Guildhall" and "Old Bailey" intelligence. The charge for "East India Intelligence" was one guinea monthly through the year 1793, and thereafter it varied.

The second group of entries were more properly termed "Incidents." Mrs. Vint's weekly salary of one guinea was in compensation for her nominal supervision of the publication, her legal liability for the matter published, and her responsibility for receiving and disbursing cash on behalf of the proprietors. W. Watson was the *Gazetteer* clerk at the printing office whose duties included bookkeeping and receiving advertisements.

There was a regular monthly charge for morning and evening papers and for "Proprietors Papers"; and annual payments were recorded for provincial papers (specified by title) as they had been earlier in William Owen's accounts.[26] Payments for foreign newspapers were recorded only at irregular intervals.

The "Old Woman[,] Change Walk" listed regularly was identified by a memorandum prepared for the management committee in February 1795 as "A Person employed to go round to Coffee houses and other places, for Advertisements, &c.," [27] and the committee's minutes for 21 October 1795 identified the person further as a "Mr Bury (commonly called the Old Woman at the Royal Exchange)." [28] Presumably the Old Woman, who received a weekly salary of half a guinea, made daily rounds to pick up advertisements, letters, and articles of intelligence left at the establishments listed in the paper's imprint.

The committee memorandum referred to identifies the "Playhouse Messenger," who received sixpence a day, as "A Boy sent Every Evening for the Bills"—that is, for programs of the plays to be given on the succeeding night.

The item of "Letters" is defined in the same memorandum as including those "From Correspondents, Irish Papers, Oxford Paper &c." "Gazettes" referred to purchases of the *London Gazette,* from which extracts were published regularly in the *Gazetteer,* and the item for "Books," later altered to "Magazines and Reviews," included reference works for the editor and published materials which were reprinted in the paper.[29]

Charges for extra composing and correcting were made "for Over hours and extra Men" when there were "long Debates." [30] These and Beauchamp's salary, with the charge for porterage of paper to and from the Stamp Office, concluded the expenditures which were made regularly every month.

Charges for paper, as well as for ink and pens, for the editor and debate reporters, frequently appeared in the monthly accounts; the charge for a new account book, "Bound and Ruled," in the specimen above may have been for the one in which these particular accounts were kept.

The arrest of Mr. and Mrs. Vint referred to in the account of February 1792 was not, happily, a monthly occurrence. It is explained in an attorney's bill to the proprietors as having resulted from the insertion in the *Gazetteer* of an advertisement for an illegal lottery office. The consequences, apart from the proprietors' payment of £50 for legal fees, appear to have been negligible.[31]

Finally, the charge described as "Advertisement for Paper" was the result of an order by the management committee "that samples

of Paper, be procured by public advertisement and that Mr Beauchamp . . . undertake to inspect such samples and report to the
committee." [32]

While a number of the items appearing in the account reproduced were unique, hardly a month passed in which expenditures
of a nonroutine nature were not recorded. Some of them, like
those for a "Hawker's Feast" and a "Christmas Box," were annual.
Others, irregular or occurring only once, will be referred to as they
become relevant. Although general information on the organization and procedures at the Ave Maria Lane office which is derived
from the monthly list of Incidents is certainly valid only for the
period from 1792 to 1797, it may be assumed that, with some
variations, the conditions revealed were those which had existed
from a much earlier period in the paper's history.[33]

The *Gazetteer* itself, during William Radcliffe's editorship,
prominently displayed the effects of the proprietors' determination, expressed as early as 1789, to increase its advertising content.[34] In 1791 and 1792 advertisements consistently occupied
more than half of the paper's space except on those occasions when
particularly important debates displaced them; and Radcliffe's
editorial policy seems to have been directly influenced by the emphasis on advertising. In April 1791 he declared: "The face of this
paper, appropriated, in one part, to temporary intelligence of the
earliest nature, and in the other to advertisements, may convince
many very well-meaning correspondents, *that we have* not room
for the insertion of their letters." [35]

Radcliffe's policy differed most strikingly from Perry's in that
the paper under his direction displayed little of its editor's personality and opinions. Conspicuously absent were the regular articles
which Perry had composed. They were replaced for the most part
merely by paragraphs of news concerning the progress of the
French Revolution, having the superficial appearance of Perry's
editorials because they were set in leaded type. When Radcliffe
editorialized, which was infrequently by comparison with his predecessor, he usually did so by means of remarks appended to items
of news. The technique and the Whig sympathies expressed are
illustrated in this conclusion to a paragraph reporting a rise in
stock prices: "The rise in stocks—one of the circumstances which
in general imply the prosperity of Administration—is occasioned
by the confidence of the country not in *Ministry*, but in the wisdom and strength of Opposition." [36] On the whole, however, the
paper conformed to a resolution of which the editor reminded

correspondents in April 1792: "Several correspondents, who have sent letters upon different subjects, will understand, that they are rejected only in pursuance of a resolution, which we have frequently mentioned, to fill the paper with *facts*, rather than *opinions*. For authentic communications of facts, we shall always be thankful." [37]

Direct statements to readers, which in Perry's time had been distinguished for the variety of their subject matter, were concerned almost exclusively with calling attention to the merits of the paper itself, and their manner suggested that they were the pronouncements of a management committee rather than those of an editor. On 24 January 1791 this statement appeared in the *London* column:

When intelligence, conveyed through the medium of a daily Print, is confirmed by the authority of the State, it bespeaks no undue exultation to remind the public, by whom this intelligence was first laid before them. Our readers will, therefore, excuse us for mentioning that the accounts from India, in the Gazette of Saturday last, form only the confirmation of what was much more fully given in the Gazetteer of Monday, Tuesday, Thursday and Friday.

Two months later, the editor boasted of the *Gazetteer*'s priority on news of impending hostilities in Europe: "It may . . . be not impertinent," he said,

to remind the public, that, for several months past, WE have been particularly industrious to supply them with it. Under the heads "PREPARATIONS for WAR," and "PROGRESS of the INVASION of the TURKISH EMPIRE," the readers of the GAZETTEER have constantly received intelligence of all events relating to the hostilities then existing, and those which appeared to be amusing. . . .

We mention this circumstance only with the proper pride of having done our duty by a constant watchfulness for all circumstances which might inform or interest the public; a watchfulness which, now that the occasion for it is greater, will certainly rather increase than diminish.[38]

And on 15 June 1791 the proprietors presented an address to readers which closely paralleled that of the preceding January:

At the close of the Parliamentary Session, it is usual for the persons interested in Newspapers to address the Public; and we are induced to comply with this custom, not for the purpose of boasting our past labours, for we do not think so meanly of our duty, as to suppose, that we can have exceeded it, nor for that, of promising any thing to be done in future, for our rank in the public esteem is happily such, as to make promises unnecessary. Having served the public faithfully and industriously for more than *Sixty-two years* [*sic*], without adherence to party, otherwise than as it appeared to be our duty, and without desertion of principle, upon any occasion, we find ourselves rewarded by being considered as the GAZETTE of the WHIG CAUSE in England. . . .

The proprietors—or Radcliffe—apparently found this theme, which James Perry had largely improvised in the preceding decade, an attractive one. Its application to the paper in 1791, however, was far less appropriate than it had been in Perry's day. After a lengthy expression of gratitude for public support, the address continued in a manner also reminiscent of Perry. The proprietors expressed their intention

of presenting the readers of the GAZETTEER, during the summer, with the most accurate and early intelligence relative to . . . leading political circumstances . . . ; but it is not by politics alone that the GAZETTEER shall be occupied. We are anxious to provide for the public, a Miscellany of entertainment, as well as of information, and shall, therefore, attend, with almost equal eagerness, to the occurrences of fashionable life . . . the engagements of our Nobility and Gentry; the watering-places and scenes of summer resort; the places of elegant amusement, and the lighter productions of literature.

With these classes of information, and topics of comment, with abundant resources, with much serious attention, and, we hope, some pleasantry, it will be our endeavour to offer such a series of GAZETTEERS to the Public, as that those, who have been glad of our company in the winter, will not readily part with us in the summer.

The promise of a miscellany was not so faithfully carried out under Radcliffe as it had been under Perry. The proprietors' instructions to Beauchamp and Radcliffe in August 1792 give an indication of their interpretation of the term:

Resolved that during the Vacation whenever Mr Beauchamp finds a want of matter for the front Page that he insert under the Editor's inspection any letters of Correspondents and also that he procure a Column of Advertisement from any of the proprietors to be inserted when wanted in the manner they were last Year — and that any very popular advertisement which is thought desirable under such circumstances [be] adopted altho' not sent & paid for.[39]

Poetry and other literary entertainment was much less plentiful after 1790 chiefly, it appears, because of the renewed emphasis on advertisements. The "occurrences of fashionable life" were reported with comparative frequency in the winter of 1791–92, sometimes in a manner suggesting "a want of matter" for more than the front page. In January 1792, for example, a report of festivities on the queen's birthday occupied nine and one-half columns and was composed almost entirely of minute descriptions of the clothing worn by each lady present, and of that worn by a dozen or more of the gentlemen. "Her majesty's stomacher we have noticed," a typical paragraph ran: "The diamonds in her hair were solely three large pins in front, each two inches in diameter, in the center of one of which was a stone more than a quarter of an inch across." [40]

If Radcliffe's editorship seems now to have been far less dynamic than that of Perry, there is reason to believe that the proprietors found it entirely to their satisfaction. At a committee meeting of 17 October 1792, "it was agreed to raise Mr Radcliffes sallery from four guineas to five guineas per week the payment to commence on Saturday next." In that month the average daily circulation of the *Gazetteer* was 1,507; in November 1792 it was 1,546; in December it increased by more than 23 per cent, to a daily average of 1,904, previously unequaled since the year 1786.

The cause of the increase lay not in the efforts of the editor or proprietors. It was the result of a heightened public interest in the affairs of France during a crisis precipitated by the opening of the river Scheldt. Less than three months later, France and England were at war. That the crisis had a salutary effect upon the circulation of all the London papers can hardly be doubted. On 17 December 1792 the *Times* published an affidavit declaring its sales at more than 2,900 daily,[41] a thousand copies above the circulation of the *Gazetteer*.

On the last day of that month John Egerton brought important news to a committee meeting which might otherwise have been made pleasant by the prospect of increased circulation: "Mr Egerton informed the Committee, that Mr Radcliffe had acquainted him, that he had entered into a connection with another Paper; which would occasion him to relinquish his engagement with the Gazetteer, as soon as possible." Two days later the committee expressed its reaction to the news: "Resolved that Mr Beauchamp be directed to pay Mr Radcliffe up to Saturday Jan 12th and to acquaint him; that his *late professions* towards the Gazetteer, compared with his *present conduct;* render the Proprietors extremely desirous, of putting an end, to any further connection with him."

The date of Radcliffe's departure from the *Gazetteer* coincides generally with the beginning of a highly significant period in the history of English journalism. The war with France placed an unprecedented emphasis upon newspapers as the organs of public opinion and information. It brought about the development of new methods of obtaining foreign news, and its influence upon governmental policies had widespread repercussions. Measures designed to curtail the freedom of the press created on the one hand a system of Treasury subsidies unparalleled since the days of Sir Robert Walpole,[42] and on the other it gave rise to the group of liberal editors of which James Perry was an outstanding representative. In the years following Radcliffe's resignation, the *Gazetteer* remained editorially unaffected by these new influences. The proprietors applied the same techniques to the paper's management that they had applied, probably, in the 1770's, and the paper was without an editor of sufficient authority or talent to maintain it in successful competition with the other papers of the day. The result was inevitable. The history of the paper after January 1793 is almost exclusively the history of the proprietors' efforts to offset the decline in popularity which culminated in its failure.

The most immediate disadvantage experienced by the *Gazetteer* as a result of Radcliffe's resignation was the loss of his abilities as a translator, for the French newspapers had become the most important single source of the *Gazetteer*'s non-Parliamentary news. The proprietors instructed Beauchamp on 10 January 1793 "to engage Mr Wiley (who has offer'd himself) to translate the French Papers, and to furnish such other Paragraphs as may appear to Mr Beauchamp worthy of Insertion." In seeking a new editor, they decided that a "Gentleman recommended by Mr Kirkman" should be "requested, to furnish Mr Beauchamp with some specimens of his abilities as an editor; . . . the said specimens shall be inserted, or rejected, as Mr Beauchamp may determine." Beauchamp was to report on the candidate at the next meeting. Meanwhile, the partners resolved that "Mr Wilson the present Reporter, be requested (during the recess of Parliament) to give such assistance to the paper as Mr Beauchamp may think necessary."

Beauchamp apparently submitted a favorable report on the aspiring editor, for on 16 January the proprietors directed that "Mr Bourne be engaged for one month as a Tryal of his Abilities as Editor to the Gazetteer." But Bourne was in difficulties by the end of his first week, and there must have been talk of discharging him. A special meeting of the committee, called on 24 January, resolved "that Mr Bourne be continued as Editor for another W[ee]k with some particular Instructions being given him to alter his manner." Six days later George Nicol was instructed to apply to a "Mr MacDonald as an Editor to the Gazetteer." Bourne was to be retained on a weekly basis at a salary of three guineas until the new editor could take charge. In all, Bourne's editorship lasted for a period of three weeks.[43]

The name "MacDonald" mentioned in the minutes for 2 February 1793 continued to appear in the printer's accounts of Incidents until June, when it was altered to "Macdonnel." Since there was no indication of a change in editors to coincide with the change in names, it is certain that the editor engaged in February 1793 was the same D. E. Macdonnel who held the position (at four guineas per week) from June 1793 until December of the following year.[44] Macdonnel was more fortunate and more capable than Bourne had been.

On 22 March 1793 the proprietors voted "that the Business of the Translator be in the Editor as Usual and that Mr Wiley the present Translator be discharged from that Business . . . giving him the earliest notice." With continental news the item of greatest importance in all of the London papers, the new editor would have found the work of translation perhaps his most pressing duty. During the year 1793 the printer recorded expenditures of £23 13s. 6d. for French and other continental newspapers. Another source of foreign news was in the paragraphs supplied by a Mr. Barlow of the Post Office, to whom £15 9s. 6d. was paid in June.[45]

Allowance by the proprietors of an extra disbursement recorded by the printer only as "Mr. Macdonnel's Bill of Expences," and ranging from a few shillings to nearly three pounds monthly between June 1793 and the end of 1794 may indicate that Macdonnel was cultivating sources of foreign news in addition to the papers and the Post Office clerks, and the accounts for March 1794 record a payment of £3 2s. to an "Agent at Ostend." Macdonnel's most ambitious effort at obtaining news of the war, however, and one which, surprisingly enough, is not recorded in the minutes of the proprietors' meetings, was a journey to the continent which he undertook in the summer of 1794. Among Incidents for which the printer charged the proprietors in July of that year was an item of £15 16s. 1d. described as "Mr Macdonnel's Bill to the Continent." In the following month there was recorded an addi-

tional expenditure of £1 11s. 6d. for an "Assistant for J. Beauchamp during the Absence of the Editor on Continent."

Surviving files of the *Gazetteer* contain, unfortunately, only
four issues of the paper for the year 1794, so it is impossible to
determine what effect Macdonnel's travels produced on the quantity
and quality of foreign news published. A payment by the printer
of £6 18s. for "Forring Correspondance" in June of that year is
the last such expenditure recorded, but the publisher's accounts
for July contain entries for postage on half a dozen letters from
Macdonnel, and those for August record the receipt of several
"Foreign Letter[s] for Macdonnell" the postage on each of which
was 1s. 8d. It is probable, therefore, that one purpose of the editor's
sojourn was to arrange for correspondence from Continental cities.[46]

While I have been unable to adduce any general characteristics
which the paper in 1793 and 1794 may have owed to Macdonnel's
influence,[47] the minutes and account books leave no doubt of the
Gazetteer's condition during the period of his editorship. The increased circulation brought about by the crisis of December 1792
was but briefly maintained. Circumstances relative to England's
entry into the war in February 1793 created a public interest which
kept *Gazetteer* sales above normal, though declining, until late in
the spring. Average daily circulation for the first six months of the
year was as follows:

January	1,861
February	1,793
March	1,711
April	1,651
May	1,589
June	1,546

By May the average daily circulation had fallen below that for
the corresponding month in preceding years, and it continued to
decline steadily. The activities of the management committee
during the period clearly reveal the proprietors' conviction that
all was not well, though the paper continued to produce a monthly
profit until 1794, and a dividend of £320—the last on record—
was declared in April 1793.[48]

In February 1793 the committee found fault with conditions
in Ave Maria Lane:

It is the opinion of this Committee that the receiving office for advertisements &c. seems to be very much neglected by which means they often

miss insertion when there is often Complaint made of want of Advertisements from Mr Beauchamp — It is therefore desired that a proper person (& not the boy too frequently found alone there) be constantly attending at the office to give proper & satisfactory answers to persons applying on the business of the paper.

And in the following month the committee expressed with unprecedented emphasis, and at greater length than usual, its policy on advertisements—a policy which can hardly have failed to hasten the end of the paper's life:

The Committee observing that the profit of advertisements has lately fallen extremely short at this time of the year resolved that Mr Beauchamp be directed to insert more and leave out News or what is of small Consequence for their insertion, and that the paper should insert ever[yth]ing of Fact and lively intelligence that the Editor can procure not to hurt the profit of the paper by advertisements and that if a proper conduct can be managed by the persons taking the advertisements some matters on pressing occasions shoud be paid for more than Common as is done by every other paper.[49]

The proprietors seem to have been attempting a reversion to conditions of the 1760's, when the *Gazetteer* had entered into serious competition with the *Daily Advertiser*. They failed to realize, apparently, that the era of the "advertiser" as an end in itself had ceased, probably as early as the beginning of Parliamentary reports in 1771. Circulation was the principal factor in attracting advertisers, and readers of the 1790's demanded "Fact and lively intelligence" whether it "hurt the profit of the paper by advertisements," or not.

Another significant feature of the resolution quoted is characteristic of the proprietors' attitude throughout the years covered by the surviving minute books. Advertisement rates, they directed, were to be varied if a "proper conduct" could "be managed." The responsibility for executing the direction, apparently, was to fall on Beauchamp, to whom a copy of the minutes was to be sent. He, at a salary of fifteen shillings a week, was expected to attend faithfully to this and a thousand other details ranging from the selection of editors to "Straightening the Columns" of type in the formes "to the utmost of his Exertions."[50] The proprietors expected Beauchamp to perform every function carried out twenty years before by Charles Say or Roger Thompson, but the period of successful newspaper administration by a printer who was not the sole or principal proprietor had also passed. William Owen, whose accounts for the preceding twenty years show him to have taken a more active part in administrative matters than any committee of the 1790's, might have enlightened the partners in this respect, but age and illness had probably weakened his influence by March 1793, for he had then but nine months to live.

At the general meeting of April 1793 two other aspects of the advertisement problem were brought to light. There was, first, a matter of long-standing debts owed to the paper by advertising customers. Owen was authorized to pay a collector five shillings on the pound to recover all debts possible. Secondly, it was "represented to the Committee [by whom was not recorded] that extreme indifference is frequently expressed by the person attending at the office to take in Advertisements towards persons bringing temporary advertisements by which means many have been taken away." The proprietors attempted to solve this problem as they were to attempt the solution of many in the next three years—by formal resolution: "Resolved that no advertisements of a temporary and miscellaneous nature be rejected if there is time to compose the same, & that they be immediately inserted." [51]

Two factors which the proprietors found directly responsible for the paper's declining circulation during Macdonnel's editorship were poor typography and publication at too late an hour in the morning. Beauchamp, as has been noted, was directed to straighten the columns in May 1793. At the autumn general meeting of October 1794, "it was represented" that there had been "a great Falling off in the Printing," which had "occasioned a great Complaint & in some Instances . . . lost the Sale of the Paper . . . ." The proprietors resolved, consequently, "that it be recommended to Mrs Vint to make some Exertion to obviate these Objections, & for that purpose that she be requested to meet a Deputation of the Committee on a Day which shall be convenient for her to appoint." Three weeks later the committee requested the publisher "to inspect occasionally Specimens of the Gazetteer with a View to observe the Printing to be properly attended to." [52]

The problem of maintaining an early publication time was apparently universal. From at least as early as 1770 apologies to readers for late publication had been commonplace, and the excuse most frequently given had been the late hour at which the theatre programs were received nightly.[53] In March 1793 the management committee ordered, along with the curtailment of news in favor of advertising, that Beauchamp "be desired to take care of an Earlier publication." A month later the order was made more specific: "Resolved that measures be forthwith taken for an early Publication & that Mr Beauchamp do lay before the next meeting . . . a Statement of the hour of Publication on each day and on any late day the particular reasons that occasioned it and his opinion of the best way of avoiding same in future . . . ." At the same time Beauchamp appears to have placed the blame for the condition upon the debate reporters, with the result that the committee delegated to him part of the authority normally reserved for the editor: "Resolved that Mr Beauchamp be desired to arrange with the Gentlemen who take the debates some System Consistent with an early publication and the General business of the paper and that he Consider himself as having full power to this end." [54] Four months later the problem still existed, and the publisher requested an explanation from the editor. Macdonnel readily complied:

Sir

In answer to your letter of Friday I am to assure you that the occasional delays in publishing the Gazetteer neither rest with me, nor in my department. The men have been regularly provided with Copy, the last of which is sent in very rarely after *ten* o'Clock.

I find on enquiry that when the publication has been retarded it has been from the insufficiency of the persons employed as readers, two of whom have in consequence been dismissed.

I shall thank you to inform such of the Proprietors as have made the enquiry, that I shall in conjunction with Mr Beaucamp, use every effort to forward the Publication.

I am Sir
your most obed[ien]t Serv[an]t
D: E: Macdonnel [55]

At the end of 1793 the committee was still passing resolutions on the matter. On 18 December, Beauchamp was "ordered to *inforce* a more *early* Time of going to Press, & to look out for Men who will come sufficiently early for all purposes required."

By September 1793 the *Gazetteer*'s circulation had declined to a daily average of 1,396 copies. Accounts for the preceding month showed a loss of just over five pounds, the first since Macdonnel had become editor, and the committee considered it "requisite to call an early Meeting to be satisfied by what Means such Deficiency may have accrued." [56] At the next meeting, on 16 October, the committee gave evidence of its concern by imposing a fine of one shilling on every member absent thenceforth from a meeting, but it accomplished little else.

Edward Johnston had previously expressed a desire to dispose of his share in the paper, and the committee now authorized the treasurer to pay him £200 for it, an indication, at any rate, of their faith in the *Gazetteer*'s future. In the following month Johnston's share was offered for sale to the bookseller James Robson, who apparently declined to purchase it, and in November it was offered to T. Hookham, bookseller and proprietor of a circulating library. By 18 December, Hookham had "not returned any decisive answer." Johnston's share was finally acquired by John Watkins, an associate or partner of William Owen.[57]

Owen had died on 1 December 1793,[58] and the minutes reveal that his duties as treasurer, publisher, and secretary to the management committee had been carried out by Watkins for some time before that date. In December Watkins had agreed to purchase a share in the paper on the condition that he be appointed treasurer to succeed Owen, and at the general meeting of 15 January 1794 the proprietors formally elected him to the position with a vote of thanks "for his Attention to the Interests of the Newspaper during the Infirmities of the late Mr Owen." From that date management on behalf of the proprietors was virtually centered in Watkins. He had chosen an unfortunate time to assume the responsibility.

For only three months of the year 1794 did the treasurer's accounts show a profit, and monthly losses ranged between that for January of £3 16s. 3½d. and that for November of £65 5s. 4d. Average daily circulation declined from 1,353 in January to an unprecedented low of 918 in December. At the general meeting of April the committee voted to raise the price of the paper by a halfpenny to 4½d. and to allow the news vendors three extra papers in each quire instead of the two previously allowed. Judging from earlier practice, it was probably at the time of the price increase that a new head for the paper, with the title in black-letter, first made its appearance.[59] In the month following the increase, daily circulation declined an average of almost 9 per cent, from 1,209 to 1,101, and the venerable Thomas Payne was requested by the committee to call on a number of the principal advertisers. Beauchamp, as usual, was "desired to attend to the Insertion of Advertisements which on no Account should be protracted." [60]

The first unmistakable sign of alarm on the part of the man-

agement committee occurred on 18 September 1794, when it was
"agree'd to summon a General Meeting of the Proprietors to take
into Consideration the declining State of the Paper, & to propose
new Measures relative to the Management of the whole Concern."
At the resulting general meeting in September only one new
measure was proposed, but it seems to indicate a realization on the
proprietors' part that the condition of the paper required more
than an increase in its advertising content: "It was resolved (Nem.
Con.) to apply to Mr Radcliffe; to know of him, whether he can
again undertake the Office of being Editor to the Paper. This
Offer to be prepared by the Committee, & the Answer to be addressed to Mr Watkins who will communicate it to the Committee." [61]

Macdonnel, the incumbent editor, was not informed of the
committee's resolution, and someone must have remembered the
sentiments expressed on Radcliffe's departure in January 1792, for
when the committee met on Guy Fawkes' Day the proposal had
not yet been acted upon, and a more subtle approach to Radcliffe
was recommended. Beauchamp was to write the former editor "to
know if it would be agreeable to him to undertake the Editorship of
the Gazetteer provided there should be a Vacancy." Apparently,
Beauchamp could not discover Radcliffe's whereabouts, and Watkins wrote to Mrs. Radcliffe's father, William Ward, to inquire
of it. Ward replied on 18 November: "I believe my Son & Daughter are in Lancashire, but the Last Letter I Rec[eive]d from them,
my Daughter say'd they was going very soon into Yorkshire, to
viset some Relations they have their. I shall write to my Daughter
by this days post & dar[e] say you will hear from Mr Radcliffe
very soon." [62]

Meanwhile, Macdonnel had learned, possibly, of the negotiations, or had decided, perhaps, in view of the paper's condition, that
the only honorable move for him was to resign. He informed
Watkins of the decision on 13 November:

I shall not intrude upon you a detail of my motives; but shall simply
request of you to intimate, as soon as possible, to the Proprietors of the
Gazetteer, my desire, to relinquish the conduct of that paper.

I know not whether there is a time limited by precedent for a notice
of this description. I hold myself however too deeply indebted for the
friendship shewn by some of the Gentlemen & for the politeness of
all, to put them to inconvenience, by any abruptness on my part. A

person of more ability may easily be found; tho' certainly not one, I shall still presume to say, who can apply with more zeal or attention, to fulfill the trust reposed in him.[63]

A clue to Macdonnel's subsequent career is provided by John Taylor, who referred in his memoirs to the editor of the daily *Telegraph* in November 1795 as "an Irishman named M'Donnell." Taylor's "M'Donnell," who had previously "entered the Temple as a barrister," [64] and the editor of the *Gazetteer* are probably both to be identified with "D. E. Macdonnel of the Middle Temple" who later compiled a dictionary of popular quotations translated from French and Latin.[65]

If Macdonnel went directly from the *Gazetteer* to the *Telegraph*, the fact may explain John Watkins's apprehension that two of the reporters might resign with the editor. A message from Beauchamp reassured him:

I last night saw Mr. Walker, and asked him if he and Mr Wilson intended to remain with us as Reporters; he assured me they had not the most distant thought of leaving us, if it was the Proprietors will to retain them in their service. I am very sorry that I am not able to attend you, but I am so very ill, as not to be able to stir out of my Room[.] Macdonald spoke to me last night of his leaving me, and was for recommending two persons to my notice, Mr Gordon and Mr Skinner

> I am, Sir, Your humble Servant,
> J. Beauchamp.[66]

Macdonnel's recommendation seems to have had weight with the proprietors. On 19 November, Radcliffe still not having been heard from, Gordon, who had been employed as a reporter since June 1793, was appointed editor of the *Gazetteer* at four guineas per week; the committee's position relative to the editorial department became clear: a "Deputation of the Committee" was appointed to meet Gordon "& to explain to him the Nature of his Office as Editor at Mr Nicol's in Pall Mall." [67]

By 1 December Radcliffe had learned from his father-in-law of the proprietors' attempts to reach him. On that date he wrote to Watkins from Lincolnshire promising to wait there until "Saturday next, for the purpose of receiving any communication, which you may chuse to make . . . ." [68] The committee learned on 17 December that the proprietors had suffered a net loss in the preceding month of more than sixty-five pounds, whereupon it was resolved that a meeting be held to "examine the particulars of all Charges, & that the Monthly Expences be ascertained Article by Article, no Bills to be paid without Vouchers produced." At the meeting of 14 January 1795 "Minutes were made to retrench certain Expenses & to ascertain the Particulars of other Articles of the Printer's Bill," and "Particulars of the Charges of the Paragraph Writers" were to be "particularly ascertained." On 11 February, "The Queries of last Meeting relative to the Charges were examin'd & the Answers were minuted on the Paper of Enquiries."

John Watkins seems to have been entrusted with securing the information which the committee had desired, and the "Paper of Enquiries" on which answers to his questions were noted has survived.[69] Most of the information contained in it served merely to explain entries in the printer's monthly list of Incidents, and in that connection it has already been discussed. That such explanations were necessary at the beginning of 1795 seems to indicate, however, that for more than a year after William Owen's death none of the proprietors had a really adequate conception of details related to the production of a daily newspaper. Among questions asked which were designated as "not answer'd" were "What Printers in general charge for publishing the Papers they print," and "What Papers does the Editor receive?"

Most interesting of the items in Watkins' memoranda, and certainly the most revealing, were the notes taken of the committee's instructions in regard to various monthly charges. It was ordered, first, that sale of the *General Evening Post* which Mary Vint printed was "not to be suffer'd in the Gazetteer Office." The "Extra Correcting" charged for monthly in the list of Incidents was in the future "to be paid by the Printer." The charge for "Proprietors Papers" was "to be dropt." "All Covers of Letters" received at the printing office that did not "Contain Intelligence on the Other Side" were to be "sent to Mr Watkins with the Other Vouchers." More significant than these, however, were the orders given in relation to the *Gazetteer*'s secondary sources of news. "Country Papers" and "Foreign papers" were, without explanation, ordered "to be discontinu'd." A receipted bill to the proprietors by one G. de Boffe reveals that, in the latter part of 1794 at least, some of the foreign intelligence published in the *Gazetteer* had been taken from French newspapers *rented* for the editor at daily and hourly rates: [70]

The Gentlemen of the Gazetteer Office   To G. de Boffe

Moniteur from August 16 to the 31st both days
included the loan only for 2 hours at 1 sh per
paper —————————————————— 0 16 0

Moniteur from Sept 1st to November 10, to
be returned the next day at £2..2. per month —
when discontinued —————————— 4 18 0

£5 14 0

The final order noted by Watkins in February 1795 sounded more ominous than it really was: "Old Woman *must die.*" The reference was to Mr. Bury, and the printer's accounts indicate that his services terminated at the end of the third week in Febuary. At the general meeting in October the proprietors displayed their gratitude to the Old Woman by approving John Shepperson's motion "that Mr Bury (commonly called the Old Woman at the Royal Exchange) is entitled to a Reward for his long Services [and] that Five Guineas be allowed to him from the Fund." [71]

By 11 February 1795, the date of Watkins' report to the committee, William Radcliffe had returned to London. Thomas Payne and John Shepperson were requested to wait upon him and to "settle with him the Terms of his commencing Editor & Proprietor." Radcliffe replaced Gordon as editor on March first,[72] and on the eighteenth of that month the committee assigned him the task of improving the *Gazetteer*'s public relations. Radcliffe was requested "to make Application to the Principal Advertisers, & to direct Blanks [unstamped papers] to be sent to such persons as he shall think expedient in Acknowledgment of their Custom."

Radcliffe did not, after all, become a proprietor in the *Gazetteer*. Possibly he realized, after reassuming the editorship, that the paper could not long survive. The average daily circulation for March 1795 was 884 copies, and his applications to the "Principal Advertisers" would have shown the course things were likely to take in the future. The committee, so far as the minutes indicate, concerned itself less with editorial matters after Radcliffe's return, but there was still sufficient business to occupy its attention. In May, the paper's solicitor was instructed to use "Coercive Measures" for the collection of long-standing debts, and it was "observed that the Press-work" had been "very materially deficient." It was resolved that "Unless the Printers shall attend more carefully to that Point, that it is the Determination of the Committee to require the workmen to be discharged from any employ in this paper." [73]

By that time Radcliffe may have been convinced that his efforts would not avail to change the paper's fortunes, and ill health probably rendered those efforts less effectual than they might have been. The circulation continued to decline. In August it was down to a daily average of 741, and on the twenty-second John Watkins received the following letter from the editor:

Sir,

Having been advised, that the late hours, which are necessarily kept by the Editor of a Morning Paper, have been injurious to my health and are likely to be so, I am to intreat you to present my respects to the Proprietors of the Gazetteer and my thanks for their favours and civilities toward me, together with my resignation of my situation, which I make with the reluctance, due to their handsome conduct in my behalf and especially to their indulgence, during my illness.

I am, Sir
Your obliged and ob[edien]t humble Serv[an]t
W. Radcliffe [74]

The printer's accounts show that Radcliffe drew his salary to the end of the first week in September, after which he was succeeded by the reporter Wilson. On 10 September the proprietors were offered the services of William Finey, previously editor of the *Times*, who assured them of the justice of his assertion "that no Man is more capable of successfully conducting a dayly paper than I am." "My literary Talents are well known," Finey concluded, and "I am certain I can most essentially serve the Gazetteer; and, even to its long & reputable Establishment, add new Fame & increasing Profit." [75] Possibly an editor of Finey's experience and self-confidence might have had a salutary effect on the *Gazetteer* at the time, but there is no indication that the proprietors even acknowledged his letter of application. Wilson remained in the chair until the following May.

Throughout the autumn of 1795 monthly losses grew more formidable, and on 20 January 1796 the management committee decided that the situation had become hopeless. The average daily circulation of the paper was 675, and a loss of nearly sixty pounds was reported for the previous month:

It appears therefore on the Inspection of this, & of several of the late Monthly Accompts that the Loss appears to be so decidedly against the Interest of the Partners, that . . . [they are] determined to relinquish all Thoughts of continuing the Paper.

And that it be recommended to a general Meeting of the Partners to think of a Method to dispose of the whole Property.

In the mean time it is desired that Notices should be sent for a General Meeting of all the Partners to be summoned on Wednesday the third of February to consider of the Report of the Committee who recommend the Disposal of the Paper.

At this singularly inappropriate time, Beauchamp reported "that the Reporters of Parliamentary debates had suggested a demand of Payment during the present recess of Parliament." It may have been in connection with this demand that Watkins prepared a memorandum setting forth the procedure on other London papers:

The Oracle; pay the Debaters during the Recess, but expect them to write something per day.
Morning Post, pay, but calls on them for Par[agraph]s, and translating during the time
Herald, pay by the year round, and they report, give trials, &c
Publican's Advertiser nearly the same
True Briton, nearly the same[.] [76]

But the proprietors' reaction was briefly expressed, and hardly surprising: "Resolved that Mr Beauchamp do acquaint these Gentlemen that the present recess is considered . . . as of that length for which it has been the custom never to allow; and that they cannot think any payment due during that time."

On 3 February 1796 the committee was authorized to offer the paper for sale, but as all of the proprietors were not present at the general meeting it was deemed advisable a week later to send copies of the minutes to the absentees, requesting that they signify their "Assent or Dissent to the Treasurer." At the committee meeting of 12 March it appeared that the proprietors of six-sixteenths of the paper were not disposed to sell. There was a trace of sentiment, perhaps, in the refusal of Charles Kemp. "I never mean," he wrote to Watkins, "so long as there is the least possibility of retaining the paper, to give my assent for the disposal of it." [77]

Accordingly, a meeting was summoned of the ten proprietors who did wish to sell their shares for the purpose of deciding at what price their property should be offered to the remaining six partners. No record of the meeting is present in the book of minutes, but subsequent correspondence between George Nicol, who seems to have presided, and Watkins, who represented the prospective purchasers, throws considerable light on the negotiations. On 18 March 1796, the day after the meeting, Nicol wrote to Watkins:

D[ea]r S[i]r

I enclose you the Minutes that were made at our meeting on Thursday w[hic]h so fully explain themselves that I need add no Comment — You will therefore be so good as make the proposal, mentioned in the inclosed, to those Proprietors who wish to continue in the Concern, & have the goodness to favour me with their Answer; And, at the same time, return me the inclosed paper, which you will observe is the Original Minute

You will no doubt see, that in case of the remaining Partners refusing the offer, that we do not mean to injure the Concern, by sending 10/16ths to market at once. . . .

Nicol's enclosure has not survived, but a rough draft of Watkins' reply makes clear the nature of its content:

Sir—

I was last night favor'd with your Letter, inclosing the Resolutions of those Partners who intend to dispose of their Property in the Gazetteer, offering their Shares to the remaining Partners at the Sum of Eighty Pounds for each Sixteenth.

I beg Leave to inform you the remaining Partners cannot give any such Sum for the Shares — Permit me to Observe it is very extraordinary that the Valuation of a 1/16 shou'd be continu'd down to this day at the same price it was 14 Years ago when the Gazetteer was regularly paying Dividends — this Observation presses very forcibly on my mind, because that Valuation seems the Basis on which you form your present high Price.

Respect[in]g the Sale of the Shares I cannot conceive but it is the Interest of *all* Parties to bring the whole to Market immediately — The Sale of the Gazetteer Property is now universally known — in Consequence of which it daily falls being now considerably under 700 — what it may be a Week hence I will not pretend to say — clearly in its present State there is no one can properly come forth to take an active Part — In Consequence of this delay, & its present derang'd State of finances I am sorry to inform you that there must be a Call on the Proprietors to make Deficiencys good at the Close of the Business.

For in fact this Matter has been in Agitation more than 6 Months

— wavering, without coming to any decided point on the Business to the great Injury of the Property at large. . . .[78]

Here the details end. There is no further record of the transaction until 8 June, when it was finally completed. At a meeting on that date:

The Report of Messr[s] Payne & Nicol was rec[eive]d that they had disposed of 10–16th of the Gazetteer as they were authorized to Mr Watkins for £250 —

Mr Watkins laid before the Partners the following Acc[oun]t of the State of the paper up to the 31st of March last which closes the original concern —

In the Treasurers hand —	£363	3	10
Debts due —	642	12	2
	£1005	16	—
Due to Mrs Vint —	£789	5	10½
to Flower the Stationer	195	—	
	£984	5	10½
	21	10	1½
	£1005	16	—

Which Balance of £21 . . 10 . . 1½ The Company present think will be exhausted by a former & the present Reckoning & other expences incurred by Mr Watkins —

Watkins was asked to pay the £250 to Nicol, whose receipt was to constitute "a full discharge to Mr Watkins & the other remaining proprietors of the Gazetteer."

Having thus purchased ten shares of the paper at one-eighth of the nominal value which had for so long been carried on the books, Watkins proceeded, with the help of Mrs. Vint, to acquire five new partners in the *Gazetter*. These were formally admitted on 17 June 1796. They were William Williams, William Dalmeida, Thomas Hattam, Walter Watkins, and Benjamin Watkins. Dalmeida is designated as "of the India House" in subsequent legal documents, and the printer's accounts show that he had previously contributed "East India Intelligence" to the *Gazetteer*, along with other occasional paragraphs. It was he who interested Williams in becoming a proprietor, and each paid thirty pounds for a sixteenth share—a profit to the concern of five pounds per share.[79] Hattam and the Watkinses, Walter and Benjamin, are designated only as "Gentlemen"; it is not improbable that the latter were related to the treasurer, John Watkins. Proprietors remainding from the old group were, besides the treasurer and the printer, John Sotheby, George Whiteside, son-in-law of the late William Owen, Joseph Walker, an Oxford vintner who had acquired Francis Wingrave's share by litigation,[80] and Charles Kemp of Evesham.

In a conversation with William Dalmeida before his purchase of a share in the paper, Mary Vint, the printer, had declared that the *Gazetteer*'s decline was a result, simply, of mismanagement. She had no doubt, she told Dalmeida, that if the paper were properly managed "and the proprietors would take some pains relating thereto a considerable profit would arise in a short Time . . . ."[81] Subsequent measures by the new proprietors indicated their willingness to take pains, but the strength of their resources did not, it soon became apparent, match that of their good intentions.

XIII

LAST YEARS

1796-1797

From the end of March until 17 June 1796, when the five new proprietors were formally admitted to partnership in the *Gazetteer*, John Watkins and Mary Vint shared full responsibility for the paper's management. The printer's accounts show that the duties of Wilson, Radcliffe's successor as editor, terminated at the beginning of May, and Watkins seems to have offered the position to a Mr. Price. A letter to the treasurer dated 11 April 1796 set forth the terms on which Price would accept the editorship, and it revealed an awareness on the prospective editor's part of the necessity for cultivating circulation in order to attract advertisers:

Mr Price's Compliments to Mr Watkins, will be happy to undertake the conducting of the Gazetteer, provided he can be excused the attendance on the House of Commons, & will readily accept of a less salary, or will engage to pay a competent person to perform that service in his stead.

Or if his proposal is incompatible with the determination of the Proprietors, Mr Price will be ready to give such assistance as his present engagements will permit, & will, if agreable, furnish them daily with such *Literary Intelligence* both Foreign & Domestic as cannot fail to secure an additional number of readers, whose pursuits lead them to search for such information & which will also command an increased number of advertisements.[1]

It appears that Price's proposal was, at length, considered "incompatible with the determination of the Proprietors." Or possibly he demanded a salary higher than they were willing to pay. At any rate, the editorship was held from the beginning of May by a John Kent, who received only £2 12s. 6d. a week for his labors.[2] If Kent composed the notice published on 17 May which announced that the *Gazetteer* was under new management, then his wages were possibly commensurate with the quality of his prose.

The first part of the announcement was relatively clear, assuring readers of the new proprietors' determination to provide "fresh spirits, increased powers, and more accumulating resources" in the collection and presentation of political, "fashionable," and commercial news, and promising the speediest accommodation to prospective advertisers. When politics came to be discussed, the writer first seemed to repudiate the policies inaugurated by James Perry and occasionally professed by the *Gazetteer* after his resignation in 1790. It was the determination of the new proprietors "to mould, *as much as possible*, the *whole* of our diurnal labours into a *'form* and *pressure'* generally acceptable to any reader, even in despite of the bias which his public and private principles may have taken." Having declared this, the announcement assumed a tone perhaps intended as a veiled appeal for Whig patronage. Proud and somewhat exaggerated reference to a long Whig tradition dating from the time of Sir Robert Walpole had become by 1796 a relatively familiar theme; the metaphorical elaborations of this announcement, however, made it a bit difficult to recognize:

Much farther back than its *Contemporaries* may the GAZETTEER turn to enjoy a retrospective investigation of the period when it chearfully *repaired* to the STANDARD *of the* PUBLIC! At first, a *young* and *raw* RECRUIT, it served, with inexperienced, but with firm and cordial attachment, those by whom (not dropping the metaphor) it was *glory* to be *commanded.* The crouded series of its *campaigns* has brought it into *tried* and *honourable Discipline.* Now, grown a *Veteran of sixty-seven* [*sic*], yet, as eager as in the prime of youth, to prove the *foremost in the action,* without a dread of being *sent upon the forlorn hope,* where is the probability that, disgracing its favourite *colours,* it can become guilty of DESERTION?

At the first meeting of the new proprietors, a month after this announcement appeared, the feeling was general that with careful and active management the paper could rise again to its former prominence. There seems to have been an intense determination to make a fresh start. The new management committee, appointed at the first meeting, was to consist of the five new proprietors, besides

Sotheby and John Watkins. A new volume of minutes was begun.[3]
The first resolution made is indicative of the prevailing spirit:

Resolv'd that great inconvenience having been experienc'd from want
of proper Accomodation at the printing Office of the Gazetteer it is
expected that a Convenient room to meet in and consult with the
Editor upon the Interest of the Paper be fitted up and prepared by
Mrs Vint the Printer for the time being at her own expence against
the next Monthly Meeting.

It is significant not only that the new committee intended to meet
frequently with the editor, but also that the status of Mrs. Vint
was carefully defined as temporary. Later difficulties seem to have
been foreshadowed in the resolution, and Mrs. Vint seems to have
ignored it, for the majority of committee meetings were held
thenceforth, probably in the interests of economy, at John Watkins'
place of business, formerly William Owen's, No. 11 Fleet Street.

The most significant decision taken at the meeting of 14 July
1796 concerned the procurement of early foreign news. To enable
the *Gazetteer* to compete on an equal basis with the other daily
papers, it was resolved that the French newspapers should be obtained by express from an agent at Dover, and that William Williams should travel to that city at the proprietors' expense in order
to arrange for their transmission. Six days after the meeting Williams wrote to the treasurer reporting success in his mission. The
letter is highly informative:

Dear Sir
    I arrived . . . on Monday last, and found it extremely difficult to
get a person to undertake the business, & the person I was recomended
to engaged for the Morning Post, & very fairly declined to be concerned for us for that reason, but recommended the person whose name
you have with the inclosed & he is reported here to be a man of
Character & Worth. Mr Elgar spoke of in London is concerned for
the Telegraph Times Morning Chronicle Courier &c. & not in very
high reputation here, so after much treaty, thinking it better not to
appear anxious about the matter I send you his terms &c. he will send
some papers immediately indeed you may expect them tomorrow, as
the wind is fair and the Sea Smooth, you may at any time revoke the
agreement if better terms can be obtained. . . .[4]

The person of "Character and Worth" engaged by Williams was
J. D. Debaune, who undertook to supply "5 Setts of Papers 2 of a

sort making 10 Papers daily" at the rate of three guineas per week plus express charges from Dover to London.[5] Debaune's charges, he wrote to Watkins, consisted of the subscription costs of the papers at Paris, commissions to agents at Calais and Dover, and "all other Expences . . . (excepting those to be incurr'd from Dover to London, Boat hire to sea after the Papers or Horse Hire to Ramsgate or elsewhere after them) . . . ." [6]

There appears to have been a strong rivalry at Dover between the agents of the various London newspapers for obtaining priority in their deliveries, and the expenses of boat and horse hire mentioned by Debaune were possibly to be incurred in efforts to excel his rivals. On at least one occasion he was able to supply the *Gazetteer* with exclusive intelligence, and the editor was grateful. "I am glad the *unique* Paper answered your purpose," Debaune wrote to Kent; "Fuller of the Morning Post wrote to his agent here concerning it, which was full of invectives against the *Gazetteer*, but shall be happy in vexing them a little more, whenever I can possibly find an Opportunity." [7] Watkins, too, expressed his gratification, and apparently requested more favors of the kind. Debaune, however, was not optimistic: "I certainly will avail myself of any Opportunity I may find in securing you priority but I am fearful it may seldom fall to my share." In the same letter was a postscript which is typical of the intelligence he occasionally supplied: "As Capt. Radcliff of the Princess Augusta has been waiting it is supposed, for those who may be going officially to Paris to treat for Peace, should his Freight come here I shall immediately inform you thereof." [8] Twice Debaune requested of the treasurer a concession generally made to such correspondents, "the favor of a Newspaper daily . . . as the agents here are generally favored with one . . . ." [9] The London papers were of use, he explained, "to send as occasion might require to my . . . friends at Dieppe, Dunkirk, Boulogne, &c. benefit of which you shall reap when invoices of French Papers from them may come . . . ." [10]

The proprietors' attempt to compete with the other papers in supplying foreign news was commendable, but it was made too late in the course of the paper's decline, and the expense proved insupportable. Debaune's bill for the first month of his services totaled £18 15s., and the proprietors seem to have realized even before they received it that they could not profitably continue the arrangement. At the committee meeting of 12 August it was suggested that the *Gazetteer* obtain permission to make use of one of the *Morning Post*'s sources of Continental news, a "Mr Wright of the Ship," an inn at Dover, and William Dalmeida was authorized to negotiate with the proprietors of the *Post*. At the meeting of 7 October he reported "the result of his conference with the Proprietors of the Morning Post . . . by which it appeared that no engagement could with propriety be enter'd into with that Paper for a joint concern in the expences attending foreign expresses." The committee therefore decided—"having taken into mature and very serious consideration the present critical state of affairs on the Continent"—that "the contract for foreign intelligence with Mr De Baume [*sic*] be continued." Three weeks later, however, Watkins wrote to the Dover agent that "the very great Expence attending the Expresses, without receiving any material Benefit from them" made necessary the termination of his services.[11]

The decision proved only temporary, for without adequate foreign news no daily paper in London could have hoped to survive in 1796. In December, Watkins was offered the services of William Elgar, who supplied French papers to the *Times, Telegraph,* and *Herald,* and who had been "informed" that the *Gazetteer* had canceled its agreement with Debaune "on acc[oun]t of the Expence." "Thinking from my having several commissions I could lessen the expence I have presumed to trouble You," Elgar wrote.[12] But Debaune apparently called on Watkins at about the same time, and his terms matched those offered by Elgar. On 28 December, the treasurer wrote to Debaune authorizing him to supply three French papers at three guineas per month (one-fourth of the expense under the previous contract), "as early Communication is so anxiously look'd for by the Public & so interwoven with the Interest of the Paper . . . ."[13]

An effort to provide early reports of Continental developments was not the only sign of initiative displayed by the new proprietors. In October 1796 they became dissatisfied with the performance of the editor, John Kent, and resolved that "as that Gentleman does not find it convenient to take a part in the Debates of both Houses . . . they shall be under the necessity of dispensing with his Services."[14] On 4 November the committee voted "that Mr Franklin be appointed sole Editor of the Gazetteer at a Weekly Salary to be hereafter settled by any three of the Proprietors." Franklin, it appears, had been recommended by the *Gazetteer*'s former editor, D. E. Macdonnel. His letter of application was addressed to Beauchamp at the printing office, and it was forwarded to Watkins for consideration:

Sir

As I understand my friend Macdonnell has mentioned my name to
you respecting the arrangement which I find is to take place in the
Gazetteer, before any person is entrusted with the care of so weighty
a concern, I think it is necessary that he should state his pretensions.
I should thank you to mention a few particulars to the Proprietors, who
are probably unacquainted with my character or pursuits. I was three
years concerned with the Morning Herald in various departments, and
had repeatedly the approbation of Mr Dudley, and was never in any
one instance charged with neglect. I have for the last year conducted the
Morning Post, but with little pleasure to myself as the intemperate
politics of the Proprietors, were always at variance with my opinion,
as I knew consistent with the temper of the Times that such would
mar the best exertions, and finally prove detrimental to the Property.

It may not be improper to remark that neither Printer nor Proprietor
have ever been involved in a prosecution by me or my writings. As to
abilities, though humble they may be useful, but zeal and attention are
in the power of every man to Command.

The Gentlemen at the Herald & Mr Macdonnell with whom I was
for years a fellow labourer will not I believe discredit me by their
report, and those who know the Character or the Ability of Mr Gray
of the Morning Chronicle will I believe hold his opinion in some
estimation; the latter I mention because he offered me his recommendation to such of the Gentlemen as he knew.[15]

Notwithstanding his impressive references and the proprietors'
resolution of 4 November, Franklin did not become sole editor.
From 29 October 1796 until April of the following year, he and
Gordon, who had served briefly as editor in the preceding year,[16]
performed the dual functions of debate reporters and joint editors,
receiving one guinea a week extra in consideration of their editorial duties.[17]

Two significant changes in policy were made at the general
meeting of 4 November 1796. First, by unanimous resolution the
editor was "directed to prevent all partial statement of debates[,]
it being the earnest wish of the Proprietors to render the Gazetteer
independent of all Party considerations." Secondly, the partners
decided to abandon the subtitle "New Daily Advertiser" which
the paper had borne for thirty-two years. The latter resolution
may have indicated a desire to decrease the emphasis on advertising and to stress the paper's news content; but if that was the
case, other resolutions passed at the same meeting tended to vitiate

the effort. With the accounts showing a loss for the preceding six
months of £277 10s. 4d. the partners resolved that "the Paper be
conducted upon the most economical principles and that no charge
be in future admitted on paragraphs furnished by Messrs Bridgeman and Reid—the Court and Old Bailey News to be continued
as usual." The only morning papers to be purchased in the future
were the *Times*, *Morning Herald*, and *Morning Chronicle*, "and
the only evening Paper the Courier — and one of the best of the
Scotch and Irish Papers." Furthermore—and this was perhaps the
most imprudent of their efforts to economize—"unless Mr Beauchamp, were able to "give sufficient reason for the charge of £3 a
Month extra," it was to be "no longer admitted."

 Although the November meeting voted to cut the expenditures
for paragraphs submitted by reporters, a letter addressed to William Dalmeida and referred by him to John Watkins reveals that,
at least during December 1796, the *Gazetteer* enjoyed the services
of the most distinguished reporter of the time, Memory Woodfall.
After leaving the *Morning Chronicle* in 1789, Woodfall had
founded a new daily paper, the *Diary*, in which, with his phe-
nomenal ability at reporting debates, he had attempted to compete
with the system instituted by James Perry and generally adopted
among the London dailies by 1790. *The Diary* had failed in 1793,
and Woodfall was apparently earning his living by occasional contributions to a number of the papers.

 The letter reveals that his contributions to the *Gazetteer* included dramatic criticism and accounts of debates at the East India
House, the latter based in part, it would appear, upon notes supplied by Dalmeida. It is of particular interest for its revelation of
Woodfall's own estimate of his ability to write rapidly, and for a
description of the circumstances under which he must often have
composed his reviews of theatrical performances:

Queen Street, Westminster Dec[embe]r 26
1796

Dear Sir

 I am preparing a Report of the Debate at the E. India House of
Wednesday last, but as I was determined to clear my Mind of as much
of the Parliamentary Debates as possible, previous to my sitting down
to it, I did not open your packet of Minutes till this Evening, and
consequently did not before see the Letter enclosed in it. I was not at
all offended at the omission of my Theatrical Article the next day after
the performance, because I was conscious it could not reach the Office

till a very late hour, though as I sent it from the *Oracle Office* at *one*, it ought to have come nearly three quarters of an hour earlier than you state. The reasons why it was sent so late by me were these: The Pantomime was not over till just *twelve;* in the Box Lobby I met Boaden and Stuart,[18] who said they had not seen the performance, having been in the Ho: of Commons, and at their desk, the whole of the afternoon, and till that time, they would therefore be greatly obliged, if I would favour them with an account of half a Column. I immediately hastened to Young Slaughter's Coffee House, where for the sake of convenience, (as it is on my way here) I generally write the Articles I send of such representations as do not take place on a Saturday Evening. Though few men write faster than I do, it was near *One* before I had scribbled both articles, and when I called for the Porter to carry them, he was unfortunately gone to bed. Disagreeable as it was therefore, I was obliged at that late hour to run myself to the Oracle Office where the first thing I said to Peter Stuart was, that he must instantly dispatch a Messenger *currente calce* to the Gazetteer Office; I saw him deliver my Packet into the hands of a friend, (I believe his brother) who promised to go with it immediately and went down Stairs for that purpose. I was at home here long before *Two.*

In God's name let Beauchamp place my Articles where it is most convenient to the Paper, I care not a doit about their locality; I wish however the Reader were a little more attentive to correctness. He suffered the last article to appear very negligently—for the *anvil* of the Blacksmith of Gretna Green, he suffered the *arrival* of the Blacksmith &c to be substituted, and a few other errors equally egregious. The reason why I did not send an Account of the new *Orestes*, was solely because I did not see it. It was, you will recollect, the day of the Debate at the India House, and having been there from Twelve till the Court rose, I had my hands full of business on my return home.

I am Dear Sir
Yours sincerely
W Woodfall.

There are no copies of the *Gazetteer* extant for the period at which this letter was written, but several theatrical reviews had appeared in the paper during April and May 1796 over the signature "W.," and all had been received, according to editorial notes, from "a most respectable Correspondent." On Monday, 2 May 1796, the *Gazetteer* published a review of a "Musical Romance" entitled *Mahmoud* to which this note was appended:

Not only the respectability of our Correspondent, who has chosen to sign his favours with the initial of *W*. but his long and universally acknowledged preeminence in all dramatic criticism (a truth to which we heartily subscribe) are motives why, although conceiving ourselves still bound to insert another account also, from a quarter of some importance, we seize the first opportunity of giving place to the following.

There can be little doubt that the dramatic critic "W." was William Woodfall.

Woodfall's contributions to the *Gazetteer* probably ceased not long after the date of his letter to Dalmeida. In January 1797 the average daily circulation of the paper was 587 copies; in February it was 588, and the proprietors, at a meeting on the fourteenth of that month, proposed more stringent measures for economy. The most distressing treasurer's report, certainly, in the paper's history revealed a loss for the final three months of 1796 totaling £359 14s. 11½d. Resolutions made at the preceding meeting were reaffirmed, and a number of charges for paragraphs by Bridgeman and Reid were disallowed. Beauchamp's salary was definitely done away with, and Mrs. Vint was given notice "to discharge Mr Gray from being Clerk to the Paper and that Mr Hewerdine be appointed to that situation . . . on Monday the 27th Ins[tan]t."

It would be interesting to know how the proprietors came to consider Hewerdine as a candidate for the position of clerk. He is probably to be identified with William Hewerdine, author of a collection of odes and epigrams "against the Whigs," [19] who received £345 from the Treasury between 1790 and 1793 for "writing in the papers." [20] If the proprietors held an unexpressed desire to form a connection with the Treasury in a last effort to save the *Gazetteer*, they were destined to be disappointed, for Mrs. Vint "sent a Verbal Message by Mr Beauchamp stating that she would not dismiss Mr Gray or employ Mr Hewerdine as Clerk to the Paper." [21]

By mid-February the enthusiasm of the new proprietors, perceptible in the early months of their association with the paper, had vanished. Desperation had replaced it. At the same meeting which proposed the employment of Hewerdine, a strong dissatisfaction was expressed with Mary Vint's management:

The Committee having taken into mature deliberation the present state of the Paper and the necessity of submitting to the proprietors at large the losses that have and must eventually be annexed to each share they think it their duty to call a Special General Meeting on the 16 Day of March . . . then and there to submit the necessity of removing the printing of the Paper or of taking the general management into their own hands or ultimately to take such measures as they shall think most conducive to the Interests of the Proprietors . . . either by private or public Sale.

Mrs. Vint seems to have been equally dissatisfied with the proprietors. She had mastered some of the tactics of her first husband, and she was not to be dealt with easily. On 4 March, the committee sent her the following letter:

Madam

The Treasurer of the Gazetteer having receiv'd several Verbal Messages thro' the Medium of Mr Beauchamp & others—intimating that shou'd the Gazetteer be remov'd from Ave Maria Lane you were determin'd to print a Gazetteer No 1 & as the Proprietors wou'd wish to act upon equitable as well as legal ground They now transmit you a Copy of the Clause in the Original Deed which totally precludes you from publishing any other Paper independent of the Gazetteer than Says Craftsman & General Evening Post which Article they Conceive you have infring'd upon by printing Says Selector & which Clause farther empowers ¾ of the Proprietors to remove the Printing at any General Meeting.

The Committee being determin'd not to Continue the Gazetteer in its present Situation will be extremely willing to pay Attention to any Proposal made by you which they request may be transmitted in writing previous to or on the day of the next General Meeting to be held . . . the 16 March Instant.[22]

The meeting of the sixteenth was attended by all the proprietors except Charles Kemp and Mary Vint herself. The lady had ignored the committee's letter of the fourth, and Sotheby, Whiteside, and Williams were delegated to wait upon her on Monday the twentieth. A letter was dispatched to prepare her for the visit, but it failed to produce the desired effect. The report of the delegation, composed shortly after the encounter, is unusually expressive. John Sotheby, who drafted it, appears to have been too angry to concern himself with syntax:

The Gentlemen appointed by the Meeting of Proprietors on Thursday last report as follows That in obedience to their directions, they waited on Mrs Vint with an intention to offer the property in the Gazetteer but she appeared so unreasonable, that she hardly permitted an offer to be made to her finding her disposition averse to enter into any conversations with her on the measure proposed that [they?] did not conceive it necessary to continue the subject—we whose names are hereunto affixed are of opinion that it becomes necessary to call a Meeting of the Proprietors as soon as possible, that in the mean time Mr Watkins be empowered to State a Case by Mr Mainstone of Essex Street for the opinion of Counsel as to what steps will be proper to be persued to take the printing of the Gazetteer from Mrs Vint, and for any other measures that may be most conducive to the General Interest of the Proprietors . . . .[23]

Three days later Whiteside and Dalmeida were authorized to "conclude a treaty with the Proprietors of the Courier for Printing the Gazetteer—or to resort to any other Printer that they think eligible for that purpose . . . ."[24]

On 28 March, the committee received estimates from several printers which deprived them of all hope of continuing the paper, and they resolved, as the quickest means of disposal, once more to offer "the exclusive Property in the Gazetteer" to Mrs. Vint, "to whom from local circumstances it appears particularly advantageous." The offer to sell "upon the Terms lately accepted by certain new Proprietors" was communicated in a letter which threatened, if the printer failed to reply within a given time, either to dispose of the property elsewhere, or to remove the printing from her charge. But Mrs. Vint had anticipated the proprietors. A letter written on the same date as that of the proprietors and signed by John Nichols, who was to represent Mary Vint throughout the transactions, informed them that she intended to cease advancing money for the payment of stamp duties. The proprietors countered with the assurance that if she did so, they "must be under the Necessity of resorting to that Redress the Law affords them."[25]

By the end of the month the attitudes of both parties had become less antagonistic. Nichols met with the proprietors on 31 March and assured them that Mrs. Vint "had no objection to treat the matters in dispute in an amicable way."[26] On 4 April the committee received a note from the proprietors of the Courier "declining to undertake the printing of the Gazetteer." Nichols again waited upon them, and a letter was sent to Mrs. Vint offering her a clear title to the whole of the property together with an assignment of "all the debts due and owing to the said paper," in return for a discharge "of all the demands you may conceive the proprietors liable to."[27] Three days later Nichols reported that Mrs.

Vint "was not inclined to treat on the terms proposed," but he asked that the proprietors fix a price at which they would part with their shares and present it for her consideration.[28] On 10 April they offered the property and all "Debts incurred under the new proprietors" for £300. Mrs. Vint announced through Nichols that she would give £200.[29]

In the meantime the proprietors of the *Morning Post* had become interested in purchasing the copyright of the *Gazetteer*. By 17 April Watkins and the partners were more anxious than ever to be relieved of financial responsibility for further losses. Watkins was authorized to treat "absolutely and finally" with Mrs. Vint, Fuller of the *Morning Post*, "or any other person inclinable to treat for the purchase of the Copy Right, the Parties so concluding the Bargain to pay the Purchase Money down Mrs Vint excepted— & in case no person shall offer more than £200, Mrs Vint to have the Preference . . . ."[30] On the same day the proprietors of the *Morning Post* made a formal offer to Watkins of £250 for the *Gazetteer*:

Sir,

In compliance with your request, I now state to you in writing, the proposition I have to make respecting the purchase of The Gazetteer.—

I would give considerably more for The Gazetteer than The Telegraph, even admitting that the Gazetteer sells no more in point of number. The day previous to The Telegraph being united with The Morning Post it sold 310 of which we have kept about half. For this we paid to Mr Parry of The Courier £100. Mr Parry having purchased the Lease of the House (valued at £200) the materials of Copyright & every thing of Mr Robinson for £400.

Admitting The Gazetteer to sell only 310, we will then give £100 for the Copyright, & so on in proportion. If it sells 600 we will give £200 for the Copyright.

But as The Gazetteer is a more respectable Paper than The Telegraph, as we should preserve its Name, & as we should probably derive some benefit from its advertisers, on these Considerations we will give £50 more, making in all £250 if the Paper sells about 600—tho' even this Sum might possibly be increased, could the Copyright be made over without opposition from any Quarter.

We are ready to meet you on the subject and I remain
Sir
Your very obed[ien]t Serv[an]t
J: Fuller [31]

On 18 April Watkins apparently acquainted Mrs. Vint with Fuller's proposition, for a letter of that date from Nichols was considered by the committee on the nineteenth. It matched the £250 offered by the *Morning Post*, and a resolution was immediately passed "that the Property be vested in Mrs Vint solely from this Day." [32] Sometime on that day Watkins must have received another letter dated 18 April, this one from Daniel Stuart:

Sir

In the absence of Mr Fuller and by his desire I now state to you that we will give 300£ for the Copy right of the Gazetteer under the following Conditions.

1st: That the daily sale of the Gazetteer is (exclusive of extra days) 600 stamped Papers per day

2 That Mrs Vint does not set up any other Morning Paper either under the title of the Gazetteer or otherwise, to oppose the Union of the Gazetteer with the Morning Post: But that the Gazetteer shall be united without opposition or impediment of any sort in the same way that the Telegraph was.

3 £100: to be paid on the 3d day after it shall appear that the Gazetteer is made over as above, and united with the Morning Post. The remainder to be paid by Bills of 50£ at 2—4—6— and 8 Months.

You will observe that the whole value of the Property to us will be destroyed if Mrs Vint sets up another Paper, since, on the uniting the Gazetteer with the Morning Post it is most probable that the Gazetteer's Customers would return to Mrs Vint. You will therefore see the necessity of either making Mrs Vint sign the Agreement, or of carrying the Gazetteer away from her some time before uniting it with the Morning Post, in order that it may be decided whether Mrs Vint will set up another Paper; and if she does, whether it is probable she will continue it.

I am Sir
Morning Post Office   Your humble Serv[an]t
335 Strand   D Stuart [33]
April 18

Whether Stuart's letter arrived too late for consideration, or whether the committee felt that it could not guarantee to prevent "opposition or impediment" from Mary Vint there is no indication. The *Gazetteer* minutes end with the resolution of 19 April, and the accounts close with the entries for 22 April.

There are, so far as I have been able to determine, no extant copies of the *Gazetteer* for the period during which Mrs. Vint controlled it exclusively. It is altogether probable, however, that Beauchamp assumed the conduct of the paper on her behalf, since John Watkins gave the joint editors, Gordon and Franklin, "a fortnight's notice" on 22 April.[34] In view of the paper's final disposition it is safe to assume that it fared no better during the summer of 1797 than it had in the previous year. In July the stamp duty was increased to 3½d., and the price of the *Gazetteer* must have been raised, probably to sixpence, thus further discouraging its relatively few remaining purchasers. The death of the *Gazetteer* was announced in the *Morning Post* on Monday, 20 September 1797:

The Proprietors of the Morning Post having purchased the Copy Right of the Gazetteer, the oldest established Morning Newspaper in London, feel it their duty thus early to announce, that after the 30th of this Month, the two Papers will be united into one . . . . The Morning Post will now have as extensive a circulation, as any of its Contemporaries, a Circumstance well worthy the attention of Advertisers.

Ten days later, the epitaph appeared: "In consequence of the new arrangements made by the Proprietors of this Paper, . . . our Readers are respectfully informed, that it will, on Monday next, assume the title of The MORNING POST and GAZETTEER."

The cares of John Watkins and his partners in the *Gazetteer* did not all vanish with the transfer of the copyright to Mary Say Vint in April 1797. In May of that year they received a statement for £436 0s. 5d. from the stationer William Flower for paper, and a letter in which Flower threatened suit if a payment were not made within fourteen days.[35] In October of the following year collections of outstanding debts not having been sufficient to meet the bill for paper, each of the partners was assessed to make up the balance, and the account appears to have been later settled without recourse to the law.[36]

Financial affairs between Mrs. Vint and her former partners were not so simply adjusted. Watkins received a number of letters from the printer's solicitors in 1797 and 1798 threatening legal action if the former proprietors' account was not settled. In a surviving draft of an answer to one of them the treasurer declared that "the Partners have not the smallest objection to pay Mrs Vint the Balance that may appear justly due," but he explained that the amount of the balance had to be "settl'd by a general Meet[in]g of all the Partners," and that "some are at this time out of town." [37]

The final treasurer's account, that of 22 April 1797, showed a balance due to Mrs. Vint of £847 6s. 1½d.[38] This would indicate that after deducting the £250 received for their shares in the *Gazetteer* the proprietors owed her a sum of just under £600, but the situation was apparently too complex for such simple solution.

In January 1799 Mary Vint and her husband exhibited a bill of complaint in Chancery stating that the proprietors were indebted to Mrs. Vint for a net total of £742 1s. 11d. In their answers to the bill the partners expressed a complete willingness to settle with the printer, but they disagreed as to the amount of the debt, declaring that Mrs. Vint had not allowed for unused paper stocks left in her possession, that she had charged them with bad debts incurred by herself in giving credit to news vendors, and that she had unjustly debited them "with various considerable sums of Bad Silver and Halfpence" received by her from sales of the *Gazetteer*.[39]

The suit was hardly well under way before death claimed two of the defendants. In April 1799 the Vints were forced to amend their complaint to include Jeremiah Watkins, brother of Walter Watkins and administrator of his estate. John Watkins died early in March of the following year, and a bill of revivor was filed against his widow, Elizabeth.[40]

In February 1801 the court decreed that all surviving account ledgers relative to the *Gazetteer* be referred to a Master in Chancery who would determine the amount of the proprietors' debt to Mrs. Vint.[41] John Sotheby and George and Elizabeth Whiteside declared in an affidavit that all documents concerning the paper which had been in the possession of Mrs. Whiteside's father, William Owen, had been turned over to John Watkins in 1793.[42] In January 1802 Watkins' widow delivered to the court all of the accounts and documents relative to the *Gazetteer* which had been in the possession of her husband at the time of his death.[43] Thereafter little action appears to have been taken.

Two years after the accounts had been surrendered to the court, in January 1804, the Vints filed a bill of revivor against the administrators of the estate of William Williams, who had "lately departed this Life."[44] In the bill it was stated: "No general report hath yet been made." And none, apparently, ever was made. It seems highly probable that the delays and expenses involved in the litigation finally induced Mrs. Vint, the surviving partners, and the heirs of those deceased to compromise in reaching a private settlement of the debt. Mary Say Vint, a second time widowed, died in February 1831, in her ninety-third year.[45]

XIV

THE *GAZETTEER* AND THE ENGLISH NEWSPAPER

THE sixty-two–year span of the *Gazetteer*'s life falls naturally into a number of individual periods, each of which corresponds generally to a stage in the development of the daily newspaper during the eighteenth century. The limits of these stages are by no means sharply defined; there is a constant overlapping between them. But each is recognizable, nevertheless, as embodying in a more pronounced manner than any of the others a single major trend.

Thus the period of the *Gazetteer*'s origin was for the newspaper press an age of government subsidization on a scale unprecedented, and the foundation of the paper itself by consolidation of the three leading organs of the Walpole government was uniquely symptomatic of the conditions prevailing. The economic support provided by the Treasury in the forms of guaranteed circulation and subsidized contributions by ministerial writers had to be replaced somehow after the fall of Walpole in 1742, and the means by which this was undertaken is clearly revealed in the subtitle "London Advertiser" which the paper assumed about 1746.

The *Gazetteer* entered what may be conveniently termed an "age of advertisers" eighteen years after the foundation of Jenour's highly successful *Daily Advertiser* and four years behind the paper which ultimately became Woodfall's *Public Advertiser*. At mid-century advertising had become the chief economic factor influencing the success of a daily newspaper, as is indicated by the foundation of the short-lived *London Daily Advertiser* in 1750 and by the almost contemporaneous emergence of the *Public Ad-*

vertiser (1752) and the *Gazetteer and London Daily Advertiser* (1753).

For a decade thereafter, the nature of the *Gazetteer* remained essentially unchanged, but in the 1760's two new forces began to influence its development. The first was the foundation in 1760 of the *Public Ledger*. Increasing to five the number of daily newspapers published in London, it produced a heightened spirit of competition which resulted not only in striking changes of the *Gazetteer*'s makeup, but in a new initiative manifested by the expensive monopolies on police news and advertisements and on theatrical notices which the *Gazetteer* acquired jointly with the *Public Advertiser* later in the decade. The second and more significant influence of the sixties was the political ambition of the new king, George III. His efforts to govern through a personally dominated cabinet provoked a widespread and vociferous opposition which in turn called forth a defense of monarch and ministry. The views of both critics and apologists found expression, to a large extent, in the pages of newspapers which were, unlike those of the 1730's, basically independent in their politics. The *Gazetteer*, and probably most other papers as well, flourished as a consequence of the new public interest engendered in this age of political essayists. It was an age culminating in the productions of Junius, and it was distinguished by a number of government prosecutions which served ultimately to secure increased protection for the liberty of the English press.

Attainment in 1771 of the freedom to publish with impunity accounts of the proceedings in Parliament marked the beginning of a new era in British journalism. Daily reports of the Parliamentary debates displaced in significance the productions of political essayists and remained until the time of the French Revolution the most important and extensive form of intelligence published in the newspapers.

Throughout the four stages of development that have been summarized—the periods of government subsidization, of increasing emphasis upon advertising, of political essayists, and of Parliamentary debates—the organization by which the *Gazetteer* was controlled and the essential character which it presented to readers were, so far as the evidence indicates, typical of the daily newspaper of the period. Proprietorship was organized on the same joint-stock principle widely employed for publication of single works in which the copyright was held by several booksellers. Surviving contracts and records of meetings between the shareholders of copyright in individual books [1] bear a close resemblance to similar *Gazetteer* documents for this and a later period.

Editorial administration was entrusted almost exclusively to the printer of the daily newspaper, with a part of the responsibility falling upon the publisher in cases where one person did not perform both functions. If the printer was not himself the editor or conductor of the paper—as he certainly was not in the early years of the *Gazetteer*'s life—that office was held by a person directly responsible to the printer. He was customarily known to the public either by a pseudonym or simply as "The Author," and the character or individuality displayed in his writings was, for the reading public, the character of the newspaper itself.[2]

After the appearance of the *Public Advertiser* and the *Gazetteer and London Daily Advertiser* the printer himself evolved as the editorial head of the daily newspaper, either in fact or in the minds of readers. Essays and correspondence previously addressed "To the Author" were consistently published as having been addressed "To the Printer" and, in many instances, to "Mr. Woodfall" or "Mr. Say." These were the men, also, who assumed legal liability for everything published in their papers, and who more than once faced public prosecution as a result. Documentary evidence makes it certain that they were directly responsible for the selection and preparation of the matter published daily.

The *Gazetteer* at the height of its success, from about 1765 to 1773, is in many ways an ideal specimen of the London daily newspaper as it had thus far evolved. Specializing in political and commercial intelligence—the latter, of course, including advertisements—it was controlled largely by a printer who, although he held no greater share in the property than any of the other proprietors, had yet the most to gain financially from its success. Editorially the paper professed to be politically impartial. It served ostensibly as a forum for the writers of all parties, imposing only such limitations on their writings as were necessary to maintain ordinary standards of decency and a legal immunity for the printer. Direct editorial expression by the printer was confined to nonpolitical observations upon the correspondence received, including apologies for some of the letters rejected and criticism of others upon moral or stylistic grounds.

The *Gazetteer* and the *Public Advertiser*, the two leading daily papers in London about 1770, never completely developed beyond this stage of exclusive control by the printer. That the *Gazetteer* seems to have altered more radically in character than the *Public*

Advertiser in the last twenty years of their respective lives is due in part to the absence after 1775 of the personal influence of the printer Charles Say. From the date of Say's death until the paper's failure twenty-two years later, however, the *Gazetteer* displayed consistently, except during the eight-year interval of James Perry's editorship, a conservatism—journalistic rather than political—which considerably retarded its development along lines taken by the daily papers founded comparatively late in the century.

Influenced by competition from newly established rivals, the paper gradually abandoned the neutral impersonality character-istic of the printer-dominated publications to become fully articu-late only in 1780. Thereafter in utterances of a publicly acknowl-edged editor it provided commentary upon political affairs and Parliamentary measures the news of which it had earlier professed only to transmit. Between 1783 and 1790, under James Perry, the paper reached the height of its editorial power. Perry was sensitive to the currents of the time, and he seems to have been indulged by the proprietors in the free exercise of his political and journal-istic ideas to an extent never permitted in his successors. One result was the introduction of a new and more efficient system of debate-reporting.

Equally important, perhaps, as Perry's forthright declarations of adherence to the causes of Fox and Whiggism were the results of his tendency to popularize the content of the *Gazetteer* in an effort to appeal to a wider reading public. A forthright expression of political allegiance was one aspect of this process, but it is more readily observable in his practice of abstracting and attempting to simplify the most important political issues of the day. The process of popularization is revealed, too, in the greater variety of subject matter which Perry provided for readers—in his increased em-phasis upon "literary" and "fashionable" intelligence.

"Fashionable" news in the form of personal scandal had become a feature in several of the daily newspapers before 1783, and while Perry frequently expressed an abhorrence for scandal, he yielded far enough to the obvious preferences of the time to insert such items in the *Gazetteer* as this paragraph describing a soiree at which the Prince of Wales was present: "The entire complexion of the meeting indicated devotion to *Bacchus*, rather than *Le Dieu de danse*. Lady A. C. and Miss H—— both were *carried home*. The Duchess of C. Lady A——, &c staid; and for their entertainment some *curious catches* were sung, which the Ladies had *never heard before*." [3]

Typographically the *Gazetteer* of the eighties and nineties was obsolescent. The aesthetic improvement of an ornamental title head which was introduced by a number of the daily papers founded in those decades, and the added convenience and attractiveness of a title and dateline at the head of the *London* column, were adopted late at Ave Maria Lane, and on the whole they were adopted unsatisfactorily.

It may be surmised that the paper's typographical conservatism was intentionally maintained to accord with the dignity of the *Gazetteer*'s age—an attribute which in the final fifteen years of publication was perhaps overemphasized. It seems more probable, however, that after Perry's resignation the phrase "old established paper" became a somewhat too convenient substitute for the new techniques and practices inaugurated by the more progressive newspaper conductors of the time.

Certainly events in the last seven years of the *Gazetteer*'s existence indicate that the system of management employed was then wholly inadequate, however successful it may have been twenty years before. Mary Say Vint was a less able manager than Charles Say had been, and J. Beauchamp was not a Roger Thompson. But the responsibility for recognizing this and taking steps to remedy it rested solely with the proprietors. Perhaps the fact that no effort to obtain Continental newspapers from Dover was made before the end of 1796—or that William Owen, after more than thirty years' association with the *Gazetteer*, could refer to its most dynamic editor, Perry, in a ledger entry of 1783 as "the Author" [4]—indicates a lack of awareness on the proprietors' part that the years were passing. Or it may have been that control by a management committee, no matter how efficiently applied, had become obsolete—that proprietorship in a daily newspaper could no longer be successfully treated merely as a profitable sideline to the business of bookselling. The examples of the most outstanding newspapers of the period seem to bear this out. The profession of journalism had come of age.

APPENDIX

NOTES

BIBLIOGRAPHY

INDEX

APPENDIX

A. The Numbering of Issues

IT WILL be noted that throughout the text and references single issues of the *Gazetteer* have been designated by their dates only, rather than by their issue numbers. The justification for this practice lies in the carelessness with which numbering was performed by the several printers of the paper. The inconsistencies which resulted make it practically impossible to estimate with any accuracy the length of time between the first publication of the paper under a given title and the earliest surviving issue under that title. For the purpose of such an estimate a working average of 313 issues of a daily paper per year (365, minus 52 Sundays) may be taken as sufficiently accurate. Thus a thousand issues occupy a period of just over three years and two months. But most attempts to apply such a method fail completely. For example, the issue of the *Daily Gazetteer: or, London Advertiser* for 31 July 1747 is numbered 3201; however, the number of the issue for 15 April 1748 is 7374, which would make it appear that the *Gazetteer* had been first published more than 23 years before, or about 1725. Similarly, the issue of the *London Gazetteer* for 29 January 1753 is 1238, while that of the *Gazetteer and London Daily Advertiser* for 1 January 1756 is 4459, a difference of 3,221 which would imply an interval of ten years. In vain one seeks a solution in the hypothesis that the *Gazetteer and London Daily Advertiser* continued its numbering from the *London Daily Advertiser* after the merger of November 1753, since the issue of that paper for 21 July 1753, three months before the merger, is numbered 738.

The inconsistencies in numbering which occur seem to have been entirely the result of compositors' errors. It is virtually certain that the heading of the paper, containing the title and issue number, was left standing from day to day like the imprint, and that only the appropriate digits of the issue numbers were changed. If proofs of the text were taken, then, before the type was locked into the forme, the numbering of issues would not have been checked by proofreaders. Two clear examples of compositors' errors occur in the early years of the *Gazetteer*'s publication. The issues of the *Daily Gazetteer* for 26 and 27 November 1736 are numbered 443 and 445 respectively, number 444 having been omitted. On 23 August 1737 the issue was numbered 676; the following day a transposition occurred, and the issue for 24 August, which should have been number 677, was numbered 667. Consequently, the following nine issues of the paper duplicated numbers already published.

As the issue numbers became larger, the magnitude of any errors due to transposition in the first digits would have increased, but the realization of this provides no solution to the problems raised by the errors. Transposition and omission were responsible for some of them; for others, probably, only a misplaced piece of type in the case. Such an error passing for a day undiscovered was probably perpetuated by daily addition until, if it were noticed, correcting it would have caused more confusion than allowing it to stand.

B. Proprietors' and Printers' Contracts

1. B.M. Additional MSS., 38729 (fols. 126–27)

Copy of the Articles of Agreement assented to and concluded upon this Fifth Day of December in the Year of our Lord One thousand seven hundred forty Eight, by and between the several and respective Parties whose Hands and Seals are hereunto subscribed and affixed in Manner and Form following.

In the first place, It is agreed for the mutual Benefit and at the respective Risques of the several subscribing and contracting Parties, to print and publish a certain Daily News Paper, to be entituled the London Gazetteer, for one year from the Day of the Date of these presents, and so to continue joint Proprietors in the said paper from Year to Year, so long as all or any of the said parties shall be content. And as to such as shall chuse to relinquish at any of the said periods, they shall be released on giving Notice of such their Intention, at the Quarterly Meeting next preceeding the Conclusion of each Year, and paying what, if any Thing, shall be due from them, to the Treasurer for the time being, on account of the present Engagement.

Secondly. That the Property of the said Paper shall be divided into Twenty Shares, of which each subscribing Party shall only be entituled to One; and so many of the said Shares as remain unsubscribed, or shall at any Time become relinquish'd, or forfeited, shall be at the Disposition of the Majority of the Quarterly Meeting next following such relinquishing or Forfeiture, and the Money arising by the Disposition of such Share or Shares shall be paid into the Hands of the Treasurer, and go as and for the Common Joint Stock or Fund for carrying on the said News Paper; but no more than one Share shall be disposed of to one Person.

Thirdly. That a Treasurer shall be chosen annually by the majority of the Proprietors at such Quarterly Meeting, to whom all Dividends shall be paid, and to whom the printer and Publisher for the time shall be accountable, And the said Treasurer account over to the Proprietors at each Quarterly Meeting.

Fourthly. That at the Time of signing these Presents the first Quarterly Meeting shall be appointed, and so on successively; and at which Meetings so from Time to Time appointed, — the Majority of the subscribing Parties present, may settle and allow the Treasurer's Accounts, and make such Orders as may by them be deemed beneficial, whether the same regard the Methodizing or Management of the said Paper, calling in for Dividends from the respective subscribing Parties, the chusing of new Proprietors, or otherwise however relative to the Support and Conduct of the same. And by which Orders, being regularly signed and entered in a Book for that purpose to be kept in the Custody of the Treasurer for the Time being, all Parties shall be bound; and either of them refusing to pay such Dividends as may by such Order or Orders be allotted them, to the said Treasurer within thirty Days after Notice in Writing by the said Treasurer to be given to them or either of them, shall forfeit all their Share, Right and Interest in the said Undertaking.

Fifthly. That any of the said subscribing and contracting Parties who shall be concerned as a Proprietor in any other Daily Paper, are hereby agreed and declared to forfeit all their Right, Title and Interest in these Articles, or in the said Paper which they are intended to establish.

Sixthly. That no Person to whom any Proprietor may dispose of his Share or Interest herein, nor the Executor or Administrator of any Person dying, shall be entituled to interfere in the Conduct or Management of the said Paper, unless first admitted with the Consent of the Majority of the remaining Subscribers at a general Quarterly Meeting, and the same enterd in the Book of Orders & signed by the Majority so consenting.

Seventhly. That upon any Proprietor's quitting this Paper, with due Notice as above mentioned, his full share of the Profits shall be paid him by the Treasurer.

Eighthly. That no more than one Guinea shall be expended or allowed at the general Quarterly Meeting out of the Common Stock.

Ninthly. That each Proprietor, at the Time of Signing of these Presents, shall pay into the Hands of the Treasurer Ten Guineas, as a Fund or Joint Stock towards carrying on and supporting the said Paper. And whereas several Persons, subscribing Parties hereto, were and are concerned in another Daily paper, entituled the Daily Gazetteer or London Advertiser, and which, for the better carrying on of the said London Gazetteer, they have agreed to lay down, It is therefore hereby mutually consented to and agreed, that all such Sum or Sums of Money that they or either of them shall appear to have been out of Purse on Account of the carrying on and supporting the said now declined Paper, shall, before any general Dividend be made of the profits arising by the Sale of the said London Gazetteer, be first paid and refunded their several and respective Disbursements in due Proportion, and after such Proprietors shall be fully paid and satisfied as aforesaid, the Treasurer for the Time being shall yearly account with & pay to the several subscribing Parties hereto their respective Shares of the real Produce which shall arise by the said News Paper called the London Gazetteer.

Lastly. It is agreed that Mr. Robert Wilson, stationer, and one of the subscribing and contracting Parties, shall be the Treasurer for the Year ensuing. And that John Griffith, of Green Arbour Court in the Little Old Baily London, shall print and publish this Paper, so long as a Majority of the Parties subscribing and continuing shall think proper, and on such Terms as shall be between him and them agreed upon, to be ascertained by an Entry in the Order Book signed by a majority of the Subscribing Parties. And the said John Griffith is to deliver in to the Treasurer his Accounts Monthly, in the Form of Debtor and Creditor, which the said Treasurer is to examine and produce at the respective Quarterly Meetings, in order to be adjusted and allowed with his other Accounts.

In Witness whereof we the several and respective contracting Parties have hereunto subscribed and set our Hands and Seals the Day and Year first above written.

[Unsigned]

2. B.M. Additional MSS., 38729 (fols. 128–29)

Articles of Agreement made and Confirmed by and between the Underwritten Persons, as Partners in a Daily Paper called the Gazetteer and London Daily Advertiser, which Partnership Commenced actually November 1:st 1753.—

Whereas the underwritten Parties are hereby acknowledged to be equally Interested in the Twenty Shares of the Daily Paper called the Gazetteer and London Daily Advertiser. It is hereby Covenanted and Agreed by each of them severally for himself in manner following.

1st That no person shall have more than one share in this Paper, and shall not in any manner be Concerned in Printing or Publishing any other Daily Paper whatsoever; while he is a Partner in this Paper under the Penalty of immediately forfeiting his Share in this Paper called the Gazetteer and London Daily Advertiser.

2^{d} That a General Meeting of the Proprietors of this Paper shall be held twice in the year at least without one Month after Lady day, and one Month after Michaelmas Day, and at the said Meetings shall appoint a Committee, Sign their Accounts then Ballanced, make a Valuation of the Shares in the said Paper, Alter the present Articles of Partnership or add new ones as to a Majority of the Partners then present shall seem Convenient.

3^{d} That the said General Meetings have Power to raise Money upon the Partners in equal Proportions, for the use of the said Paper, to be paid to a Treasurer by them Chosen, and to declare Dividends of Profit, in such manner as the Gain Arising from the said Paper will fairly Permit: and any partner refusing or neglecting to pay within one Month, his proportion of the Money so Called for, shall forfeit his share in the said Paper, and be immediately excluded from any property therein.

4th That the Publisher shall Summons the General Meetings, and always give two Days Notice to each Partner, under the Penalty of Five Shillings for every Partner neglected to be Summoned; and any Partner neglecting to attend the General Meeting, according to his Summons shall forfeit two shillings and Six pence if he is not there within one Hour by the House Clock, of the Time named in the said Summons, and five Shillings if he doth not attend by Ten of the Clock at Night, and that all Penalties be Applyed to the Encrease of the General Fund.

5th That the Committee shall meet the last Wednesday in every Month, or oftener if they find Occasion, to transact Business relating to the said Paper, and shall be allowed for those who Attend, for their Expences, out of the General Fund.

6th That the present and future Committees have power to Contract for Paper, to print the said Gazetteer upon, To regulate the Prices of Advertisements, to Contract with the Author, Collectors, Printer and Publisher, and Summon them to Attend, and to examine their Accounts, and to call a General Meeting, and to report to the General Meeting the State of the Paper, and offer such Alterations or Matters, as to the said Committee shall seem Conducive to the interest of the Paper.

7th That the present Committee, which shall Continue to Act till the General Meeting next after Lady day next; shall Consist of the Ten following Persons (seven of whom must be present to do Business) viz:^t Daniel Browne, Thomas Osborne, Robert Wilsonn, John Nourse, John Whiston, Samuel Baker, Thomas Trye, Lockyer Davis, John Ward, and William Owen But that all future Committees shall Consist only of Seven Persons, three of which at least, shall be from out of the Eight Persons, who represent the Partners, that were formerly concerned in the London Daily Advertiser and Monitor, and five of the Committee being present may transact Business.

8th That the Publisher do regularly Summon every Member of the Committee to meet and do Business at such place as they shall Appoint, by Eight o'Clock in the Evening the last Wednesday in every Month from Lady day to Michaelmas, and at Seven from Michaelmas to Lady day, or oftener if any three Members shall Direct him. And any person neglecting to Attend, by the Time mentioned in the Summons according to the House Clock where they meet, shall forfeit one Shilling for every such Neglect. And the Publisher omitting to summon any Person on the Committee shall forfeit One Shilling for each Person so Omitted.

9th That Charles Green Say be the Printer, and William Owen the Publisher of the said Paper called the Gazetteer and London Daily Advertiser, untill removed by the Vote of the Majority of Partners, present at a General Meeting, who shall in such Case immediately Appoint another Printer and Publisher.

10th The Printer and Publisher shall be respectively and separately Answerable to the Partners for All Advertisements inserted in the said Paper, and shall not Trust any Person on the said Account, but at their own respective Risque and shall well and truly Account for all Paragraphs or Letters that shall be paid for to be inserted in the said Paper.

11th And the Printer of the said Paper shall bear one half of the Expence of any Prosecution, arising from any Letter Paragraph or Advertisement inserted in the said Paper, Unless such Letter Paragraph or Advertisement be signed by Two of the Committee to some of whom he shall Apply for Advice upon any Doubt. But it shall be in the power of a General Meeting by a Majority, to remit this Penalty on the Printer, when they shall see fit.

12th That no Partner in the said Paper shall sell his Share without leave of the Majority of Partners at a General Meeting, to whom also it shall be first offered, at the Price fixed by the last General Meeting. But upon their refusal to buy, he may Sell to whom he will.

13th That if any Person dye possessed of a Share in this Paper, It shall fall into the General Stock, the Partnership paying to the Executor or Administrator, the Sum which his share was valued at by the last General Meeting Preceeding his Death, and the Dividend if any was due, after deducting such Debts as were due from him to the said Paper, which Share shall be kept or disposed of, as a Majority of Partners at a General Meeting shall think Proper.

14th That the Minutes of the Proceedings and Resolutions, both of the Committees and General Meetings, shall be fairly

Entered in Books for that Purpose provided, and be Signed by the Partners present, The Committee Book to be kept in the Possession of the Senior Person of the Committee, and the Book relating to General Meetings by the Chairman of the said General Meeting, who shall at each Meeting be Chosen by Ballot.

The Eight Persons who represent the Partners that were Concerned in the London Daily Advertiser are M.ʳ Richard Ware, M.ʳ Daniel Browne, M.ʳ Charles Davis, M.ʳ John Whiston, M.ʳ Samuel Baker, M.ʳ Lockyer Davis, M.ʳ John Ward, M.ʳ Thomas Payne.

In Witness of our Agreement before Recited we have hereunto Set our Hands and Seals, and Do hereby Declare it binding to ourselves, Executors, Administrators and Assigns. This Seventh Day of November 1753.

[Unsigned]

3. P.R.O. C104/68

Articles of Agreement Indented had made concluded and agreed upon this twenty seventh day of July in the year of our Lord One thousand seven hundred and seventy five Between John Twyman of Saint Catherines Court near the Tower of London Ship Broker Robert Wilson of Lombard Street London Stationer George Hayter of Pancras Lane London Merchant William Johnston of Ludgate Street London Bookseller John Whiston of Fleet Street London Bookseller Benjamin White of the same place Bookseller William Owen of the same place Bookseller Lockyer Davis of Holbourn in the said County of Middlesex Bookseller John Nourse of the Strand in the said County of Middlesex Bookseller Samuel Baker of York Street Covent Garden in the said County of Middlesex Bookseller David Wilson of the Strand in the said County of Middlesex Bookseller Thomas Durham of Cockspur Street in the said County of Middlesex Bookseller Thomas Payne of Castle Street Leicester Fields in the said County of Middlesex Bookseller Paul Vaillant of Pall Mall in the said County of Middlesex Esquire Thomas Gardner of Craigs Court Charing Cross in the said County of Middlesex Gentleman and James Fletcher of Oxford in the County of Oxford Bookseller of the

one part and Charles Kemp of Evesham in the County
of Worcester Gentleman and Mary Say of Ave Maria
Lane London Widow of the other part —
Whereas by Articles of Agreement bearing date on or about the
seventeenth day of December One thousand seven hundred and
seventy one and made or mentioned to be made Between the said
John Twyman Robert Wilson Charles Kemp of the parish of Saint
Mary Islington in the County of Middlesex Gentleman now
lately deceased the said George Hayter William Johnston John
Whiston Benjamin White William Owen Lockyer Davis John
Nourse Samuel Baker David Wilson Thomas Durham Thomas
Payne Paul Vaillant Thomas Gardner Charles Green Say of Ave
Mary Lane London Printer now also lately deceased and the said
James Fletcher Reciting that the said several parties were jointly
concerned and interested in a Certain periodical News paper called
the Gazetteer and New daily Advertiser in the proportions therein
mentioned It is witnessed declared and agreed between all the
parties thereto and they did thereby severally Covenant with each
other that the said partnership should subsist from the day of the
date of the said Articles for so long time as the said News Paper
should continue to be printed by Virtue of the said Articles and
Subject to the several Covenants thereinafter mentioned And that
the profits which should arise from the publication and Sale thereof
and of the several matters inserted therein should belong to and
be the property of the said parties their Executors Administrators
and Assigns in the several proportions in the said Articles specified
And that all Costs Losses and Damages which should arise by
reason of printing or publishing the said Paper or of any matter
therein contained should be borne and answered by the said
several parties in proportion to their respective Shares therein and
for the more orderly proceeding in and carrying on the said Undertaking and for the security of the several persons who then
were or thereafter should be interested therein it was Covenanted
and Agreed as aforesaid to stand to and abide by and well and
faithfully observe perform fulfill and keep the several Rules Orders Regulations and Agreements thereinafter particularly mentioned and expressed of and concerning the same And Whereas
since the Execution of the said Articles the said Charles Kemp is
dead and the said Charles Kemp party hereto is his personal
Representative and the said Charles Green Say is also dead and
the said Mary Say is his personal Representative And the said
Charles Kemp party hereto and the said Mary Say are thereby

become entitled to the Shares belonging to the said Charles Kemp deceased and Charles Green Say respectively Subject to the several Covenants and Conditions contained in the said herein before recited Articles and to the several Rules Orders and Determinations heretofore made fixed upon and resolved or hereafter to be made fixed upon and resolved at any of the General Meetings of the said proprietors And Whereas the said Mary Say hath been on the day of the date of these presents appointed by a General Meeting of the said proprietors Printer of the said News Paper Now these Presents Witness that in Consideration thereof she the said Mary Say doth hereby for herself her Heirs Executors and Administrators Covenant promise and agree to and with all and every other of the proprietors or partners of and in the said News paper their several and respective Executors Admors and Assigns and every of them that she the said Mary Say shall not nor will at any time or times hereafter during such time as the said News paper shall continue to be printed by or in the name of her the said Mary Say or in the Name or names of any Person or Persons whomsoever by her Consent change or alter the Title Form Face or Appearance of the said News paper without the Consent of the Majority of the Proprietors or Partners of and in the same at a general Meeting to be holden for that purpose And further that she the said Mary Say shall not nor will during the time aforesaid do any other act or thing whatsoever whereby the said joint Property may be injured or to occasion the Proprietors or Partners of and in the said News paper to remove her the said Mary Say from the Employment of Printing the same And further that she the said Mary Say shall not nor will during the time aforesaid sell or dispose of her property or Share in the said News paper by way of setting herself at liberty to become the Printer or Publisher of any other Morning News Paper And further that she the said Mary Say shall not nor will during the time aforesaid undertake directly or indirectly by any Evasive means whatever the printing or be in any other manner or wise concerned in Printing any other News paper whatsoever during the Continuance of the said undertaking or partnership concern Save and Except two certain News Papers both of which the said Mary Say is at this time the Printer (Vis^t) the one intitled The Craftsman or Says Weekly Journal while the same shall continue to be published only one day in the week the other intitled The General Evening Post while the same shall Continue to be published only on Tuesdays Thursdays and Saturdays And further that she the said Mary Say shall not nor will during the time aforesaid assign or make over the profits of printing the said Gazetteer or Print the same in the Name of any Person or Persons but by Consent of a Majority of the Proprietors or Partners of and in the said Gazetteer first had and Obtained under their Hands And further that she the said Mary Say shall and will from time to time and at all times hereafter during the time aforesaid duly attend all and every the General Committee and other Meeting and Meetings of the Proprietors or Partners of and in the said News paper if thereto required And further that she the said Mary Say shall and will also from time to time and at all times hereafter during the time aforesaid fairly enter into one or more Proper Book or Books to be provided and kept by the said Mary Say for that purpose a true and particular Account of all and every the Sum and Sums of Money by her received paid laid out or expended for or on Account of the Printing the said News Paper and every thing incident thereto and shall and will Produce such Books of Account which shall also contain the true Names Places of abode and Professions of all and every such Person and Persons as she shall employ to write for the said Gazetteer unto the said General or Committee Meeting of the Proprietors or Partners of and in the said Gazetteer when and so often as she the said Mary Say shall be required to do the same And moreover that she the said Mary Say shall and will once at least in every Month during such time as she shall be printer of the said News paper well and truly Pay unto the Treasurer for the time being appointed or to be appointed by or on the behalf of the Proprietors of the said News Paper all such Sum and Sums as upon the Ballance of such her Account shall appear to be due from her to the said Proprietors And Lastly that she the said Mary Say shall and will from time to time and at all times hereafter also well and truly pay or Cause to be Paid all and every such Forfeiture Sum and Sums of Money as a General Meeting of the proprietors or Partners of and in the said Gazetteer shall and may from Time to Time Order and direct and inflict as a Punishment for her Non Attendance as Printer of the said Gazetteer And Whereas by Bond or Obligation bearing even date with these presents the said Mary Say hath become bound to the said William Owen Paul Vaillant and Lockyer Davis in the Penal Sum of Two thousand pounds Conditioned for the Payment of the said Sum of Two thousand Pounds on the day next following the date of the said Bond or Obligation Now these Presents farther Witness and the said William Owen Paul Vaillant Lockyer Davis and Mary Say do hereby severally and respectively declare acknowledge and agree that such Bond hath been so Entred into for the Purpose only of securing and enforcing a due Observance and Performance of the Covenant hereinbefore contained on the part of the said Mary Say And the said William Owen Paul Vaillant and Lockyer Davis do hereby for themselves severally and for their several and respective Heirs executors and Administrators Covenant Promise and Agree to and with the said Mary Say her Executors Administrator[s] and Assigns that in Case the Covenant hereinbefore contained on the Part and Behalf of the said Mary Say shall be in all things duly observed and performed They the said William Owen Paul Vaillant and Lockyer Davis shall and will deliver up to the said Mary Say her Executors and Administrators the Bond aforesaid to be Cancelled. In witness whereof the said parties to these Presents have hereunto interchangeably set their Hands and Seals the Day and Year first above written—

Sealed and delivered by the said
William Owen Lockyer Davis and   [signed] W:^{m} Owen
Mary Say in the presence of
[signed] Joseph Baldwin
Sealed and Delivered by the said
Paul Vaillant in the Presence of   [signed] Paul Vaillant
[signed] Danl Battiscomb Clk to M:^{r} Baldwin
                                             [signed] Lockyer Davis
                                             [signed] Mary Say

NOTES

Chapter I

[1] By the *Daily Advertiser,* which had been founded in 1730, five years earlier than the *Gazetteer.*

[2] Laurence Hanson, *Government and the Press 1695–1763,* p. 110. Hereafter designated as Hanson.

[3] Italic and roman types have been transposed in the citation. Hanson appears to have overlooked this announcement. *The Daily Courant,* he says, "seems to have been subsidized . . . down to the fall of Walpole, although precise details of the sums paid or of the numbers distributed are not to be found among the Treasury papers."

[4] For a full discussion of this development, see Stanley Morison, *The English Newspaper,* p. 103.

[5] *The Craftsman,* 1726–27; continued as *The Country Journal; or The Craftsman,* 1727–47, published weekly, on Saturdays, "By Caleb D'Anvers, of Gray's Inn, Esq." 'D'Anvers" was the pseudonym of Nicholas Amhurst, founder and conductor of the paper. *The Craftsman,* which expressed the views of the opposition to Walpole, was perhaps the most influential political journal of the period. Its most eminent contributors were Bolingbroke and the two Pulteneys, Daniel (until his death in 1731) and William.

[6] Hanson, pp. 112–13; *DNB;* "An XVIIIth Century Journalist," *TLS,* 16 August 1923.

[7] *A Critical History of the Administration of Sir Robert Walpole,* p. 518; for Ralph's possible connection with the *Gazetteer* see Hanson, p. 120, and James Sutherland, ed., *The Dunciad* by Alexander Pope, Twickenham Edition, 1742 version, Book I, line 216 and note.

[8] *Dunciad,* ed. Sutherland, p. 311n.; Hanson, p. 111.

[9] *Craftsman,* Saturday, 12 July 1735.

[10] Morison, *The English Newspaper,* p. 126.

[11] A note to the 1742 *Dunciad* pushed the application to an extreme. *The Daily Gazetteer,* it explained, "was a title given very properly to certain papers, each of which lasted but a day."—*Dunciad,* ed. Sutherland, Pope's note on Book II, line 314.

[12] Sir Richard Steele held the office from 1707 to 1710; Samuel Buckley, who had conducted the *Daily Courant,* was gazetteer from 1714 to 1741.

[13] Hanson, p. 115, says Arnall died at this time. The *DNB* gives his dates as "1715?–1741?"

[14] The copy of the *Gazetteer* for 12 May 1738 in B.M. Burney 326.b. has the Courteville signature; that in Burney 327.b. contains the same letter signed "R. Freeman." The two copies are otherwise typographically identical.

[15] *An Historical View of the Principles, Characters, Persons, &c. of the Political Writers in Great Britain* (London, 1740), 56 pp.

[16] *An Historical View,* pp. 52–53. It is an interesting coincidence that the description would have been applicable to William Murray (later Lord Chief Justice Mansfield), who became K.C. and Solicitor General in 1742.

[17] *An Historical View,* p. 54.

[18] William M. Sale, Jr., *Samuel Richardson: Master Printer,* p. 65. Chapter III ("Richardson and the Periodical Press") contains a full discussion of the evidence for Richardson's connection with the *Gazetteer.*

[19] He was also printing Aaron Hill's semiweekly *Prompter* and the *Weekly Miscellany.* Cf. Sale, *Samuel Richardson,* p. 73. On 21 February 1739 Hill assured Alexander Pope that the views expressed by the political essayists in the *Gazetteer* by no means represented Richardson's own. "There should be nothing imputed to the *Printer,* which is impos'd *for,* not *by* him, on his *papers,* but was never impress'd on his mind."— *The Works of the late Aaron Hill, Esq.,* II, 68.

[20] Cf. *Dunciad,* ed. Sutherland (1742 version), Pope's note on Book II, line 314.

[21] *Dunciad,* ed. Sutherland (1742 version), Book I, lines 231–32 and note.

[22] *Champion,* 5 February 1740, quoted in Hanson, p. 117.

[23] *Calendar of Treasury Books and Papers, 1739–1741* (London, 1901), p. 269.

[24] By an act of 1712, a tax of ½d. had been imposed on every paper printed on a half-sheet or less, and a tax of 1d. on every newspaper larger

than a half-sheet, but not exceeding one full sheet. A double *Gazetteer*, printed in four quarto pages, occupied only a half of the large folio sheets on which most newspapers were to be printed after about 1760. Cf. Collet Dobson Collet, *History of the Taxes on Knowledge* (London 1899), Ch. II; Graham Pollard, "Notes on the Size of the Sheet," *Library*, 4th ser., XXII (1941), 105–37.

The only double issues which I have seen are those for the year 1741 in the B.M. Burney 354.b. Throughout that year each double copy was numbered as a single issue, but the practice appears to have been instituted only a short time previously. For example, the double issue for January 5[–6] was No. 1729, while the single issues for those dates were Nos. 1731 and 1732 respectively. It appears, then, that No. 1727 of both impressions would have fallen on the same date, i.e., Wednesday, 31 December 1740. Several specimens of double *Gazetteers* issued in 1735 are held by the University of Texas Library.—Powell Stewart, *A Descriptive Catalogue of a Collection at the University of Texas: British Newspapers and Periodicals 1632–1800*, p. 34.

25 By Professor Sale (*Samuel Richardson*, p. 65), who points out that 3,000 double *Gazetteers* at 2*d*. each (the price previously paid for double *Daily Courants*) would total approximately the £900 quarterly average of the Treasury payments to Walthoe.

26 Ellic Howe, *The London Compositor* (London, 1947), p. 95.

27 Two variations in the procedure outlined would have been possible. First, pages 1 and 2 of the double issue might have been printed on the half-sheets on Monday, and pages 3 and 4 added on Tuesday. But this would have entailed exactly twice the amount of labor by pressmen. Secondly, the folio imposition could have been made after Tuesday's paper had been set in type but before the single issues for Tuesday morning were printed. This, however, would have been pointless in view of the mail schedule; moreover, an interval of twelve hours between the setting of the daily issue and its printing for morning publication seems incredible, despite the general lack of urgent or last minute news in the *Gazetteer* at this time.

The practice of printing double issues of a daily paper on alternate days, for distribution to the country, appears to have been inaugurated in 1702 by Samuel Buckley of the *Daily Courant*. On 26 November 1702 he advertised: "*The* News *of every* Post-Day's Courant *is printed on the Back of the* News *of the* Day *before, upon a whole Sheet of* Writing-Paper, *a* Blank *being left for the Conveniency of sending it by the* Post."

28 Reproduced, dated and discussed in James R. Sutherland, "The Circulation of Newspapers and Literary Periodicals, 1700–1730," *Li-*

brary, 4th ser., XV (1934), 110–24. *The Daily Courant* advertisement in the preceding note is cited in this article.

[29] *The London Journal* continued to run until 1738, but without its well-known author, James Pitt, and without government subsidies.

[30] *An Historical View*, pp. 52–53.

[31] The work was reprinted in book form in the following year.

[32] *Daily Gazetteer*, 4 January 1738.

[33] *Daily Gazetteer*, 5 July 1738; 21 July 1738.

[34] Hill to Richardson, 6 July 1738. *The Correspondence of Samuel Richardson*, ed. Anna Laetitia Barbauld, I, 15–17.

Chapter II

[1] *Daily Post*, Saturday, 6 March 1742.

[2] *Craftsman*, Saturday, 13 March 1742.

[3] *Common Sense; Or, The Englishman's Journal* was a weekly paper written, like the *Craftsman*, in opposition to Walpole. Its contributors included the Lords Chesterfield and Lyttleton, and William Guthrie, a writer pensioned by the Pelham ministry in 1743.

[4] There are references to contributions by Hill of literary and dramatic criticism and of two odes in the unpublished Hill-Richardson correspondence at the Victoria and Albert Museum. Forster MSS., XIII, 23, 40.

[5] For example, on 11 September, with the fever of "the '45" running high, the *Gazetteer* reprinted on page 1 Addison's *Freeholder* No. 9, an answer to the declaration of the Old Pretender in 1715.

[6] Hill to Richardson, 13 June 1746. Forster MSS., XIII, 41.

[7] A copy of the issue for Friday, 15 April 1748, is in B.M. Burney 427.b.; the *CBEL* lists issues for 26 October 1746 and 27 June 1748 which I have been unable to locate. Copies of 24 of the 27 issues for July 1747 are at present in my possession.

[8] *The London Daily Post and General Advertiser*, founded in 1734, was the second. It became in 1744 the *General Advertiser*, and in 1752 the *Public Advertiser*.

[9] The writer of the humorous *Advice to Editors of Newspapers* (London, 1799) speaks (p. 19) of "advertisements, or, as they are technically called, *Ads*."

[10] *The Fool: Being a Collection of Essays and Epistles, Moral, Political, Humourous, and Entertaining. Published in the Daily Gazetteer* (London, 1748), two volumes. The last essay in this collection is No. 93 for Wednesday, 25 February 1747; the *Gazetteer* for 15 April 1748 contains No. 280, and that for 26 March 1751, No. 738.

[11] *The English Newspaper,* p. 126.

[12] *Catalogue of a Collection of Early Newspapers and Essayists formed by the late John Thomas Hope, Esq.,* p. 73.

[13] B.M. 522.l.33.

[14] See Appendix A.

[15] The assumption that at least some of the publishers of this collection were proprietors in the *Gazetteer* in 1748 is supported by a parallel instance in the case of the *London Daily Advertiser.* In 1753 a similar collection of John Hill's "The Inspector," which had originally appeared in that paper, was published. Of the eight booksellers who appear in the imprint of that collection, four are conclusively proved to have been proprietors of the *London Daily Advertiser* by the *Gazetteer* partnership contract of 1753. See below, p. 34.

[16] Especially during February and March, when his advertisements sometimes occupied as much as two columns. In July 1747 he advertised more extensively in the *Gazetteer* than any other bookseller.

[17] B.M. Addit. MSS., 38729, fols. 126–27. The full text of the agreement will be found in Appendix B.

[18] *The English Newspaper,* p. 145.

[19] *The Case Between the Proprietors of News-Papers, and the Subscribing Coffee-Men, Fairly Stated* (London, 1729), pp. 17–19.

[20] *Whitehall Evening Post* from Thursday, 4 January, to Saturday, 6 January 1750.

[21] P.R.O. *SPD* 36/112.

[22] P.R.O. *SPD* 36/112.

[23] The Say family is treated in two articles by L. G. H. Horton-Smith: "The Old City Family of Say, and its Connexion with Essex," *The Essex Review,* January, 1948, pp. 37–44; and "The Press and Bookselling: Some Memories of the Past," *Publisher and Bookseller,* 4 March 1932, pp. 491–93. Mr. Horton-Smith's interest was primarily genealogical, but I am indebted to the latter article for references to Public Record Office documents which contain vital information on the *Gazetteer* for the years 1770–74.

[24] P.R.O. C24/1686/21 (*Crowther et al.* v. *Mechell*).

[25] The talents and activities of this remarkable individual were first brought to light by Mr. Stanley Morison in an appendix to *The English Newspaper.* Notable among eighteenth-century newspapers displaying blocks by Hoffman were the *Post-Man, Post-Boy,* and Mist's *Weekly Journal.* There is no mention in Morison's treatment of the *London Gazetteer* factotum.

[26] Henry Sampson Woodfall's accounts for 1774 show a payment of fifteen guineas to "A person to go daily to fetch in Advertisements, get

Evening Papers, &c." First published in F. Knight Hunt, *The Fourth Estate*, II, 191. The *Gazetteer*'s payments for the same duties, at least during the 1790's, were somewhat more liberal. Cf. p. 226, below.

[27] He was probably best known for the paper which bore his name, *Owen's Weekly Chronicle* (1758–68). Among numerous other periodicals "printed for W. Owen" were *The Spectator*, a twice-weekly essay paper inaugurated in 1753 with an humble apology for reviving the name (B.M. Burney 46.b); *The Remembrancer* (1748–51); and *The General Magazine* (1764–?).

[28] *London Gazetteer*, Friday, 15 June 1753. The names of Brown and Say are to be found in the imprint as late as 20 October 1752.

Chapter III

[1] *The London Daily Advertiser*, first published in March 1751 as *The London Advertiser and Gazette*, was continued from April 1751 as *The London Daily Advertiser and Literary Gazette*, the subtitle being dropped in November 1751. It was published by R. Griffiths in St. Paul's Churchyard. The paper's only claim to distinction seems to have been Sir John Hill's essay series "The Inspector" (1751–53).

[2] Timperley, *Encyclopaedia;* H. R. Plomer, G. H. Bushnell, and E. R. McC. Dix, *A Dictionary of the Printers and Booksellers Who Were at Work in England, Scotland and Ireland from 1726 to 1775.*

[3] B.M. Addit. MSS., 38729, fols. 128–29. The full text of the contract will be found in Appendix B. This manuscript volume contains many author-bookseller contracts to which John Nourse was a party, making it seem probable that the copies of the 1748 and 1753 *Gazetteer* agreements preserved therein may have belonged to him.

[4] *The New Morning Post* of 9 December 1776 referred to Say as the *Gazetteer*'s "late renowned printer and manager"; the *Gazetteer* of 12 December acknowledged the "great justice" of the designation. Similarly, H. S. Woodfall is styled the "manager, publisher and printer" of the *Public Advertiser* in Morison's *The English Newspaper*, p. 126.

[5] James Boswell, *Life of Samuel Johnson*, ed. G. B. Hill, revised by L. F. Powell (Oxford, 1934–50), I, 351. The letters are reprinted in most editions of Johnson's works. Copies of the *Gazetteer* issues in which they first appeared have not, so far as I have been able to determine, survived.

[6] *Gazetteer and London Daily Advertiser*, Monday, 1 January 1759, hereafter abbreviated as *G&LDA*.

[7] The date of the *Craftsman's* origin is given by Pollard in *CBEL* as "June 1758?" based apparently on a computation from the issue

number of the earliest extant copies, those for 1771 (B.M. Burney 583.b.). My quotations are from an advertisement for the *Craftsman* which appeared in the *Gazetteer* of Thursday, 30 December 1762. Pollard seems to have been unaware of the original subtitle, which referred to the series of forty-nine essays contributed by Arthur Murphy (under the pseudonym "Joseph D'Anvers") between October, 1752, and September, 1753. See Howard H. Dunbar, *The Dramatic Career of Arthur Murphy* (New York, 1946), pp. 4–5, 9n.

[8] Now composed of printer's flowers. The Hoffman block was apparently replaced in 1758; I have found no copies of the paper for that year.

[9] The best general discussion of the development of Parliamentary reporting is in Frederick Seaton Siebert, *Freedom of the Press in England, 1476-1776* (Urbana, 1952), Ch. XVII, pp. 346 ff.

[10] For a time there had even been difficulty about this. Around the turn of the century the patentees of the King's Printing Office had instituted several actions in Chancery against newspaper printers for publishing speeches from the throne and abstracts of the acts of Parliament which injured the sale of the official publications. See Robert Haig, "New Light on the King's Printing Office," *Studies in Bibliography*, VIII (1956), 163.

[11] *House of Commons Journals*, XXVIII, 741, 745.

[12] For a list of them see Alexander Andrews, *The History of British Journalism*, I, 205–6.

[13] Advertisement in the *Public Advertiser*, 5 July 1757.

[14] *The English Newspaper*, p. 151.

[15] D. Nichol Smith, "The Newspaper," in *Johnson's England*, ed. A. S. Turberville, II, 331–32.

[16] R. Leslie-Melville, *The Life and Work of Sir John Fielding*, p. 9.

[17] The issue of September 1 is the earliest known for 1760.

[18] So far as I can determine, it was the first established paper to adopt the *Ledger*'s form. The *St. James's Chronicle* appeared in sixteen columns from its first publication in 1761. Cf. Nichol Smith in *Johnson's England*, II, 331–32.

[19] *G&LDA*, Wednesday, 29 November 1760; Wednesday, 3 December 1760; Monday, 15 December 1760. On Massie, see the *DNB*.

[20] A list of these publications with dates is given in *CBEL*, II, 715–16. The *Gentleman's Magazine* included a monthly list of prices from its first publication in 1731.

[21] The original notice was set in italics.

[22] The only issues of the *Gazetteer* for 1761 in the Burney Collection are those for 17 March and 25 May. The "Commercial Register" had

been continued on the original plan as late as 31 December 1760 when
No. 53 appeared. The practice of numbering each issue of the Register
was discontinued at some time between that date and 17 March 1761.

[23] *Memoirs of John Almon, Bookseller, of Piccadilly*, pp. 14–15. The
narrative is written throughout in the third person.

[24] *A Review of Mr. Pitt's Administration* (London, 1762). B.M.
E.2053.(5.).

[25] This admonition appeared on Thursday, 9 September 1763, after
a letter extending to four columns; it is typical of others.

[26] *G&LDA*, Wednesday, 1 June 1763.

[27] *North Briton*, No. XV, Saturday, 11 September 1762. The text
is that of the folio collected edition "with Several useful and explanatory
Notes" printed for W. Bingley, 1769.

[28] The issue for 1 June 1762 is the earliest known surviving copy
for the year. The heading was already in use at that time.

[29] On 28 December 1762 the location of the office changed to "John's
Coffee-House, the Corner of Swithin's Alley, Royal Exchange."

[30] Almon was at Wilkes's house on the morning of Saturday, 30
April, for a part of the time that the king's messengers were present—
Memoirs of John Almon, p. 15. But no copy of the *Gazetteer* for
Monday, 2 May, which might reveal effects of the coincidence, is
known to have survived.

[31] *Memoirs of John Almon*, p. 16.

[32] *G&LDA*, Tuesday, 23 April 1765, and Thursday, 16 May 1765
(page 1 advertisements by Kearsley); Saturday, 11 May 1765 ("The
Contrast," No. LVIII).

[33] The announcement of this collection was prominently displayed
below the playbills on page 1 of the *Gazetteer* for Wednesday, 17 June
1767.

[34] *G&LDA* (advertisements), Saturday, 15 October 1763; Monday, 2 April 1764.

Chapter IV

[1] The *Gazetteer* was still employing this device as late as 10 September
1789, and *The Times* also made use of it during its early years. Cf.
The History of "The Times," I, 35.

[2] For example, D. Nichol Smith, "The Newspaper," in *Johnson's
England*, II, 331–67; Arthur Aspinall, *Politics and the Press c. 1780–
1850*, p. 6 and note; *The History of "The Times,"* I, 24.

[3] *History of "The Times,"* I, 26–27.

[4] As though to celebrate the innovation an issue number was omitted.

The Gazetteer and London Daily Advertiser for Thursday, 26 April 1764, was numbered 10958; *The Gazetteer and New Daily Advertiser* for the following day was 10960. Cf. Appendix A.

[5] *Gazetteer and New Daily Advertiser*, Saturday, 2 June 1764. Hereafter abbreviated as *G&NDA*.

[6] The notice was printed in italics except for the word I have italicized, which was in roman type. Future typographical alterations of this nature are indicated by an asterisk (*) in the note.

[7] For some time after its establishment in April 1769 *The Middlesex Journal* (a thrice-weekly evening paper, founded by William Beckford the "patriot" Lord Mayor, to which Chatterton was an occasional contributor) employed the *Gazetteer* style of double rules.—*The English Newspaper*, p. 154.

[8] *G&NDA*, Tuesday, 15 January 1765.

[9] Quoted, from Stuart's defense of himself in the *Gentleman's Magazine* (1838), by Wilfrid Hindle, *The Morning Post 1772–1937* (London, 1937), p. 83.

[10] The subtitle was changed twenty-four days after the announcement began to appear.

[11] After 19 May 1764 the words "as also in the Public Advertiser" were dropped. The same notice appearing in the *Public Advertiser* from 4 April contained a similar reference to the *Gazetteer*. R. Leslie-Melville (*The Life and Work of Sir John Fielding*, p. 72) points out that Fielding began advertising in the *Public Advertiser* in 1754.

[12] A similar notice had appeared in the *Public Advertiser* on 17 December 1764. Cf. Leslie-Melville, p. 77.

[13] Leslie-Melville, pp. 75–76; 285–86.

[14] *The Fourth Estate*, II, 190–91.

[15] *The History of British Journalism*, I, 192.

[16] P.R.O. C104/67, Book M. See Bibliography, Manuscripts.

[17] *Public Advertiser*, Tuesday, 1 January 1771.

[18] Cf. pp. 44–45 above. They became rare after the alterations of October 1760 and remained so until the decade of the 1780's.

[19] *G&NDA*, Wednesday, 9 May 1764*; Wednesday, 30 May 1764; Wednesday, 18 June 1766.

[20] On page 39.

[21] Friday, 22 July 1757. The introductory address to the public in this issue contains a valuable general discussion of foreign news sources.

[22] Cf. p. 148, below.

[23] Plomer, *Dictionary* . . . *1726–1775*; cf. p. 47 above.

[24] *G&NDA*, Monday, 7 October 1771.

[25] *Lloyd's Evening Post*, Friday, 22 July 1757.

[26] *The History of British Journalism,* I, 220.

[27] *The Tuner, A Periodical Paper on Popular Topics,* No. 1: "On the Most Popular of Popular Subjects, News-Paper Abuse." This publication (B.M. Burney 46.b.) is undated. Graham in *CBEL* dates the first number, for unspecified reasons, 21 January 1754. This date cannot be correct, since (1) the first issue contains an advertisement referring to *Junius,* whose letters began appearing in 1769; (2) the poem from which I quote contains references to the "Lying Ledger" (i.e., the *Public Ledger,* founded in 1760), Lord "B[ut]e" and the Duke of "G[rafto]n." A much more probable date is that given by Timperley (*Encyclopaedia,* p. 721) for the first issue: 9 December 1769.

[28] A notable exception was the group of letters on American affairs contributed by Benjamin Franklin at irregular intervals between December 1765 and April 1774 over such signatures as "N.N.," "A.B.," "Homespun," etc. See Verner W. Crane, ed., *Benjamin Franklin's Letters to the Press, 1758–1775* (Chapel Hill, 1950), pp. 38–258, *passim.*

[29] A few may have employed the services of one William Wardlaw, "Scrivener and Translator," who described himself in the *Morning Chronicle* for 6 July 1776 as ready to undertake "every Branch of LITERARY BUSINESS . . . upon very equitable terms," including "Letters, Memorials, Petitions, Essays, Advertisements, &c. . . . composed upon all subjects, and in all languages. . . ." Characters, Wardlaw suggested, which had been injured in "malicious publications" might be vindicated through his efforts "by properly stating those facts, a favourable exposition of which may tend to remove unmerited prejudice, and to fix the stigma of infamy upon real guilt."

[30] *G&NDA,* Friday, 27 April 1764.*

[31] *G&NDA,* Wednesday, 19 September 1764.

[32] *G&NDA,* Wednesday, 25 April 1764.

[33] *G&NDA,* Wednesday, 23 May 1764.

[34] *G&NDA,* Thursday, 24 May 1764.

[35] *G&NDA,* Tuesday, 31 December 1765.

[36] *G&NDA,* Thursday, 7 June 1764.

[37] *G&NDA,* Tuesday, 18 September 1764.

[38] *G&NDA,* Tuesday, 4 June 1764.

[39] *G&NDA,* Wednesday, 7 November 1770.

[40] *G&NDA,* Wednesday, 6 June 1764.

[41] *G&NDA,* Wednesday, 11 July 1764.

[42] *G&NDA,* Friday, 13 March 1767.

[43] *Journals of the House of Lords,* XXX, 508, 511. Hereafter referred to as *Lords Journals.*

⁴⁴ *Lords Journals*, XXXI, 214–15.

⁴⁵ *Lords Journals*, XXXI, 463.

⁴⁶ *G&NDA*, Tuesday, 15 March 1768.

⁴⁷ *House of Commons Journals*, XXXI, 580, 584, 596. Hereafter designated as *Commons Journals*.

⁴⁸ *Commons Journals*, XXXI, 603.

⁴⁹ *Commons Journals*, XXXI, 606, 610, 612–13.

⁵⁰ John Wilkie, who had published a similar advertisement in his *London Chronicle* and was unable, after "diligent inquiry," to discover its source, received the traditional reprimand, kneeling, and was discharged on payment of fees.—*Commons Journals*, XXXI, 617, 621.

⁵¹ *G&NDA*, Saturday, 2 April 1768.

⁵² H. R. Fox Bourne, *English Newspapers: Chapters in the History of Journalism*, I, 193.

⁵³ *G&NDA*, Monday, 2 January 1769.

⁵⁴ B.M. Addit. MSS., 38169.

⁵⁵ *G&NDA*, Thursday, 6 December 1770.

⁵⁶ P.R.O. C12/901/33 ("The further answer of Charles Green Say . . . ," dated 9 July 1773). Say had been ordered to pay over one-eighth of the profits from printing the *Gazetteer* during this period. His statement of the number printed was to serve as the basis for determining the amount of the payment. He would not, therefore, have exaggerated in making that statement.

⁵⁷ 1772 was a leap year the first day of which fell on a Wednesday. There were fourteen Sundays between 1 January and 6 April.

⁵⁸ *Commons Journals*, XXXII, 451. There is no record that the committee ever submitted a report on the matter.

Chapter V

¹ *G&NDA*, Saturday, 7 January 1769.

² *The Constitutionalist* was written, according to Andrew Kippis (*Biographia Britannica* [London, 1784], III, 13–16), by James Burgh (1714–75).

³ Letter of John Wilkes to Junius, 12 September 1771.—*The Letters of Junius*, ed. C. W. Everett, p. 340. The reference is to Arthur Lee (1740–92). Cf. *DAB*. Letters on American affairs by Junius Americanus appeared in the *Gazetteer* almost daily in the latter half of January 1771 and frequently thereafter.

⁴ Letter of Junius to John Wilkes, 6 November 1771. *Junius*, ed. Everett, p. 355.

⁵ *G&NDA*, Wednesday, 21 November 1770.

⁶ *G&NDA*, Thursday, 20 September 1770.

⁷ P.R.O. MS. Calendar of Treasury Solicitors' Papers, Vol. III, 1753–1820.

⁸ The proceedings are set forth at large in the *State Trials*, Vol. XX; the results are clearly summarized in Frederick Seaton Siebert, *Freedom of the Press in England*, pp. 385–88.

⁹ P.R.O. TS. 11/836 (2897). I am indebted to the Treasury Solicitor for permission to inspect these documents, granted by a letter dated 2 May 1952.

¹⁰ *Calendar of Home Office Papers of the Reign of George III* (London, 1881), II, 39.

¹¹ *Junius*, ed. Everett, p. 118, note.

¹² *G&NDA*, Thursday, 22 November, and Friday, 23 November 1770.

¹³ Cf. the references to Say in *Parliamentary History*, XVI, 1130, 1139, 1148–49.

¹⁴ The most important documents in the case of *Thompson* v. *Say* (1772–74) preserved in the Public Record Office are C12/901/33, consisting of Thompson's original "Bill of Complaint" and Say's "Answer" (with two supplements), and C24/1814, consisting of depositions by thirty witnesses who were either directly concerned in the *Gazetteer* or well acquainted with Say and Thompson. The depositions were discovered by L. G. H. Horton-Smith, who referred very briefly to them in "The Press and Bookselling: Some Memories of the Past," *Publisher and Bookseller*, 4 March 1932, pp. 491–93. Since there is a single reference number for both Thompson's Bill and Say's Answer, and another for all of the depositions, citations of the individual documents will be descriptive of each, without repetition of the P.R.O. reference. Thus, the reference for all depositions is P.R.O. C24/1814, but my first citation of each will contain only the name of the witness and some indication of his occupation or connection with the *Gazetteer*.

In quotations from these documents, legal contractions have been expanded, and capitalization, a matter largely arbitrary with the law-scrivener who engrossed them, has been normalized.

¹⁵ Information supplied from records at Stationers' Hall by Mr. R. T. Rivington, Clerk of the Company.

¹⁶ P.R.O. C12/901/33. Thompson's Bill of Complaint and Say's Answer are in basic agreement on these facts. The differences arise in their interpretation.

¹⁷ Deposition of Miles Penfold, goldsmith, of Newgate Street, sworn 30 April 1774. Penfold had known Say for about ten years in 1770.

[18] Depositions of James Dixwell, printer, of St. Martin's Lane, sworn 5 May 1774, and William Phillips, tobacconist, of Newgate Street, sworn 11 April 1774.

[19] It was really two houses according to the parish rate-books as cited in the deposition of Edward Cheney, parish clerk of Christ Church, London, sworn 4 May 1774.

[20] Deposition of Mary Morris, spinster, of St. John Street, Clerkenwell, sworn 23 April 1774.

[21] Say's Answer to Thompson's Bill of Complaint.

[22] Thompson's Bill of Complaint. The name of the daughter is not specified, but it was probably either Mary, who would have been 19 at the time, or Ann, who would have been 17. Both were the children of Charles and Grace Say, his first wife. By 1770 he had married for a second time.—*The Registers of Christ Church, Newgate Street, London, 1538–1754*, ed. W. A. Littledale (London, 1895), pp. 180, 184, 186.

[23] Plomer, *Dictionary* . . . *1726–1775, s.v.* "Say, Edward"; Horton-Smith, in *Publisher and Bookseller,* 4 March 1932, pp. 491–93.

[24] Deposition of Mary Morris.

[25] Thompson's Bill of Complaint.

[26] Deposition of John Cooke, clerk in the *Gazetteer* office, sworn 29 March 1774.

[27] Deposition of Edward Cheney, parish clerk.

[28] Thompson's Bill of Complaint.

[29] Deposition of George Abraham, printer and senior apprentice to Say in 1770, sworn 8 June 1774.

[30] Depositions of John Gibson, printer, sworn 12 April 1774, and William Brinkworth, printer, sworn 20 April 1774.

[31] Say's Answer to Thompson's Bill of Complaint.

[32] *Memoirs of John Almon,* p. 119.

[33] Say's Answer to Thompson's Bill of Complaint.

[34] *Memoirs of John Almon,* p. 119.

[35] *G&NDA,* Monday, 26 November 1770.

[36] For example, on Saturday, 1 December 1770 a correspondent wrote: "Having seen, in your paper of yesterday, an account of the debates in the Lower Room of the Robinhood Society, in order to fill up a leisure hour, I shall inform you of the principal topics which were agitated in the Upper Room on the same evening, between those who are in office, and those who would gladly turn them out. . . ."

[37] See note 15.

[38] Deposition of Edward Benson, printer, sworn 19 May 1774.

Benson appears to have been in direct charge of the typographical side of the publication though subordinate to Thompson.

[39] Depositions of John Gibson, and of Thomas Ferebee, apprentice to Say in 1771 and compositor on the *Gazetteer*, sworn 13 May 1774.

[40] Agreement signed 2 April 1771, cited in Thompson's Bill of Complaint.

[41] Deposition of Mary Morris.

[42] Deposition of George Abraham; corroborated by that of John Cooke.

[43] *The English Newspaper*, pp. 60–61.

[44] Say had an interest in Miller's paper, then, when Almon began contributing his Parliamentary reports; that he "printed and published" it is unrecorded elsewhere.

[45] At least on the part of the proprietors. I have found no copies of the *General Evening Post* published by Thompson for the period.

[46] If Charles Say was the printer of the *London Evening Post* early in 1769, it must have been during the first four months of the year, for his father died sometime between May first, the date of his will, and May sixth, when the will was probated. Cf. Horton-Smith in *Publisher and Bookseller*, 4 March 1932, pp. 491–93.

[47] *G&NDA*, Tuesday, 9 July 1771.

[48] B.M. Addit. MSS., 38729, fol. 130.

Chapter VI

[1] *Sir Henry Cavendish's Debates of the House of Commons, during the Thirteenth Parliament . . . commonly called the Unreported Parliament . . . 1768–74*, ed. by John Wright (London, 1841–43), II, 257–60. Cavendish's reports were taken down in shorthand during the actual debates and are thus fuller and more reliable than the reports of contemporary journalists, who were forbidden to make notes. In editing the original manuscripts (B.M. Egerton MSS. 215–62), Wright omitted some details and supplied a few speeches, unrecorded by Cavendish, from contemporary newspapers. The paragraph read by Onslow, for example, is not transcribed at large in the manuscripts, but the text given in Wright's edition agrees, except in a few matters of punctuation, with the original paragraph in the *Middlesex Journal* for 7 February 1771. For convenience, I have employed the published text (abbreviated as *Cavendish's Debates*, ed. Wright) except where the manuscript has unprinted details.

[2] Advertisement by the society in *G&NDA*, Monday, 11 March 1771.

[3] *G&NDA*, Saturday, 26 October 1771. Wheble's statement is reprinted from his own paper of Thursday, 24 October.

[4] *Cavendish's Debates*, ed. Wright, II, 311–12.

[5] Cavendish's Debates, B.M. Egerton MS. 225, p. 38.

[6] *Cavendish's Debates*, ed. Wright, II, 321–22.

[7] Cavendish's Debates, B.M. Egerton MS. 225, p. 159.

[8] *G&NDA*, Friday, 1 March 1771.*

[9] Cavendish's Debates, B.M. Egerton MS. 225, p. 38.

[10] *Ibid.*, p. 291. The error in recording the name of Roger Thompson lay neither with the deputy Serjeant at Arms nor with Sir Henry Cavendish in his account of the deputy's report. Stamp Office records for the period, published by Professor A. Aspinall ("Statistical Accounts of the London Newspapers in the Eighteenth Century," *EHR*, LXIII [April, 1948], 201–32), designated the printer and publisher of the *Gazetteer* as "Robert Thompson." The Chancery depositions in *Thompson* v. *Say* all concur with the records at Stationers' Hall in giving the name as Roger, but Mr. Horton-Smith, who discovered the depositions, referred to the printer as "Ralph."—*Publisher and Bookseller*, 4 March 1932, pp. 491–93.

[11] *Cavendish's Debates*, ed. Wright, II, 323–24.

[12] *G&NDA*, Saturday, 26 October 1771.

[13] They were Miller of the *London Evening Post*, Bladon of the *General Evening Post*, Wright of the *Whitehall Evening Post*, Baldwin of the *St. James's Chronicle*, Evans of the *London Packet*, and W. Woodfall of the *Morning Chronicle*.

[14] *G&NDA*, Monday, 19 March 1771. Baldwin's statement to the House, if accepted as true, appears to contradict John Almon's specific designation of the *St. James's Chronicle* as the second paper to undertake publication of the proceedings. Cf. above, p. 90.

[15] B.M. Addit. MSS., 30871, fol. 69. I am indebted for this reference and the one following to Professor Robert R. Rea.

[16] B.M. Addit. MSS., 30871, fol. 70.

[17] *G&NDA*, Friday, 12 March 1771.

[18] P.R.O. Index 4,626 contains applications for rewards promised in royal proclamations of the period and records of payment. A search has failed to reveal Carpenter's name.

[19] *Memoirs of John Almon*, p. 119.

[20] H. R. Fox Bourne (*English Newspapers*, I, 211), following the *Parliamentary History*, XVII, 95–98, dates Miller's arrest as 16 March, the day after Wheble's, but the *Gazetteer* published early on the morning of 16 March reported both arrests as having occurred "yesterday."

[21] *G&NDA*, Monday, 18 March 1771.

[22] *G&NDA*, Friday, 15 March 1771.

[23] Letter of John Wilkes to Junius, Wednesday, 15 January 1772.— *Junius*, ed. Everett, pp. 358–59.

[24] *Memoirs of John Almon*, p. 120.

Chapter VII

[1] *G&NDA*, Thursday, 25 July 1771.*

[2] *G&NDA*, Thursday, 1 June 1771.

[3] *G&NDA*, Thursday, 15 August 1771.

[4] *G&NDA*, Thursday, 26 September 1771.

[5] *G&NDA*, Monday, 23 September 1771.*

[6] *G&NDA*, Thursday, 3 October 1771.

[7] W. T. Laprade, "The Power of the English Press in the Eighteenth Century," *South Atlantic Quarterly*, XXVII (October, 1928), 434.

[8] *G&NDA*, Thursday, 18 July 1771.

[9] See p. 105, above.

[10] Letter of Junius to H. S. Woodfall, 6 August 1769. *Junius*, ed. Everett, p. 299.

[11] *G&NDA*, Monday, 27 May 1771.

[12] *G&NDA*, Friday, 20 November 1772: "To our obliging correspondent L. —We never find fault with our brother printers, which apology, for not inserting his letter, will, we hope, be kindly accepted." Cf. *G&NDA*, Tuesday, 24 October 1775.

[13] *G&NDA*, Friday, 13 September 1771. The practice of calling attention to new type (always Caslon) was continued throughout the life of the paper. The average life of a font ranged from two to three years.

[14] P.R.O. C24/1814 (*Thompson* v. *Say*). Deposition of William Brinkworth, sworn 20 April 1774.

[15] Deposition of Thomas Ferebee, sworn 13 May 1774.

[16] *G&NDA*, Friday, 13 September 1771.* At the same time, Thompson estimated that it might be "reasonably supposed," that the paper was actually "read by upwards of 50,000 people" daily.

[17] Depositions of Joseph Dunball (whence the quotation) and Samuel Turlington, both sworn 19 May 1774.

[18] Deposition of John Cooke.

[19] *G&NDA*, Thursday, 23 May 1771: "Our Constant Customer is informed, that Drury-lane and Covent-garden Theatres will be shut in a few days, and then he may depend on having our paper as early as he wishes." Cf. *G&NDA*, Friday, 23 October 1772. Such statements were commonplace in the paper after 1770.

²⁰ Deposition of Richard Birtles, sworn 8 June 1774.

²¹ *G&NDA*, Wednesday, 1 January 1772.

²² Deposition of William Haynes, printer, sworn 4 June 1774. Haynes was one of the compositors so employed, as was Richard Birtles. The weekly sum of £7 13s., if Haynes's figure is accurate, probably means that a total of six extra compositors were employed at £1 5s. 6d. each, for as late as 1795 regular compositors on the *Gazetteer* were receiving only £1 11s. 6d. per week.—P.R.O. C104/68, memorandum by the publisher, [1795].

²³ Deposition of Thomas Ferebee.

²⁴ Above, p. 79. Several witnesses expressed a belief that the circulation of the weekly *Craftsman* also increased under Thompson's management. Between 1 January and 6 April 1772 the average number of the *Craftsman* printed was 6,314 for each issue.—P.R.O. C12/901/33, Say's Answer to Thompson's Bill of Complaint.

²⁵ At the rate of 250 sheets per hour (cf. Ellic Howe, *The London Compositor*, p. 95). Mr. Arthur Brown informs me that experiments performed on the press at University College London indicate that, even with an iron platen which would allow one pull to a forme and the employment of "flies" (cf. Timperley, *Encyclopaedia*, p. 647) to remove the sheets from the press, it is doubtful whether such a rate of production could have been maintained.

²⁶ *History of "The Times,"* I, 35.

²⁷ Depositions of Dryden Leach and William Palmer Davis, both sworn 28 April 1774.

²⁸ In January 1770, the proprietors of the *London Packet* had resolved to offer shares in that paper to Charles Say among others. Apparently Say had declined the offer. B.M. Addit. MSS., 38729, fol. 165.

²⁹ Cited in Thompson's Bill of Complaint. Say's answer confirmed the terms of the agreement.

³⁰ Deposition of James Dixwell.

³¹ Thompson's Bill of Complaint. It is only fair to state that, according to Say, the initiative was taken by his daughter, who, considering Thompson's behavior to her father improper, wanted no more to do with him. Say admitted that he had sent the girl into the country to prevent Thompson "from having access to her and to prevent the renewal of his addresses and his visits to her." He also stated, however, that he had refused to allow the marriage, which may imply that some willingness on his daughter's part remained.

³² Deposition of William Carter, of Newgate Street, sworn 31 May 1774.

³³ Thompson's Bill of Complaint.

[34] Deposition of Edward Benson.

[35] Deposition of John Cooke.

[36] Depositions of John Russel, sworn 25 April 1774, and Charles Surmont, sworn 28 April 1774.

[37] Depositions of Mary Morris and George Abraham.

[38] Depositions of John Russel and Charles Surmont.

[39] Deposition of George Abraham.

[40] Deposition of Mary Morris.

[41] Depositions of John Russel and Charles Surmont.

[42] Deposition of John Gibson. Gibson, a *Gazetteer* workman, had rushed downstairs at the sound of "a bustle in the house" in time to see Abraham attempting to eject Thompson.

[43] Depositions of John Russel and Charles Surmont.

[44] Thompson's Bill of Complaint. Say's Answer does not contradict the Bill on any of these points.

[45] Say's Answer to Thompson's Bill of Complaint.

[46] Deposition of Jabez Goldar, sworn 7 May 1774.

[47] Depositions of John Cooke, Jabez Goldar, and Charles Surmont.

[48] Say's Answer to Thompson's Bill of Complaint.

[49] Cf. p. 116, above.

[50] Deposition of Richard Birtles.

[51] Deposition of George Abraham. Cf. Abraham's important role in the violence of 10 December 1771, above, p. 129.

[52] Say's Answer to Thompson's Bill of Complaint.

[53] I have found no reference to Thompson in connection with the newspaper press after the removal of his name from the *Gazetteer* imprint.

Chapter VIII

[1] P.R.O. C24/1814 (*Thompson* v. *Say*), deposition of Nevil Maud, gentleman, of Ave Maria Lane, sworn 19 May 1774.

[2] *G&NDA*, Thursday, 16 February 1775.*

[3] "One evening when the House of Commons was going to adjourn, . . . [Wilkes] begged permission to make a speech 'for,' said he, 'I have sent a copy to the 'Public Advertiser' and how ridiculous should I appear if it were published without having been delivered.' "— John Taylor, *Records of My Life* (London, 1832), I, 114.

[4] Postponement of letters was often necessary; e.g., *G&NDA*, Thursday, 18 February 1773: "The length of the Debates in the House of Commons obliges us to postpone the favours of our other correspondents."

[5] *G&NDA*, Friday, 30 October 1772.

[6] *G&NDA*, Thursday, 24 December 1772.*

[7] Cf. pp. 71–74 ff., above.

[8] *G&NDA*, Tuesday, 15 September 1772.

[9] *G&NDA*, Thursday, 4 June and Wednesday, 10 June 1772.

[10] *G&NDA*, Monday, 11 January 1773.

[11] The general theme of these articles, though it was common enough at the time, suggests the possibility that they may have been inspired or written by the political economist Joseph Massie (cf. pp. 48–49, above). Letters signed by him appeared in the paper at irregular intervals throughout the seventies, and his deposition in the *Thompson* v. *Say* suit (sworn 4 June 1774) displays a fairly intimate knowledge of the conditions surrounding publication of the *Gazetteer*.

[12] Pp. 44–45, 66, 289 *n*.18 and note, above.

[13] Deposition of William Haynes.

[14] No issues of the paper between these dates are known to be extant.

[15] He had become publisher in December 1764. Cf. p. 64, above.

[16] See p. 32, above.

[17] P.R.O. C104/67, Book M (see Bibliography, Manuscripts). The entries in this book commence in June 1774. They are in Owen's handwriting.

[18] *G&NDA*, Saturday, 14 January 1775.

[19] The notice was set in italics.

[20] The notice was set in italics.

[21] News of the encounter appeared in the Massachusetts papers only from three days to two weeks after it had occurred. See Allen French, *The Day of Concord and Lexington* (Boston, 1925), p. 283.

[22] The italics are mine.

[23] *Morning Chronicle*, Friday, 2 June 1775.

[24] Reprinted in *G&NDA*, Wednesday, 31 May 1775.

[25] *G&NDA*, Wednesday, 14 June 1775.

[26] *G&NDA*, Friday, 11 August 1775.

[27] *G&NDA*, Friday, 13 December 1776.

[28] See p. 82, above.

[29] *G&NDA*, Wednesday, 18 December 1776; *G&NDA*, Thursday, 13 February 1777. The offending advertisement was reprinted at length in the news columns of the former issue, ostensibly as part of the report of the trial. A. Andrews (*History of British Journalism*, I, 217) erroneously dates the advertisement as having appeared in June 1776.

[30] P.R.O. TS 11/1079 (5385–86). I am indebted to the Treasury Solicitor for permission to inspect these documents, granted in a letter of 3 May 1952.

[31] *Literary Anecdotes*, III, 737.

[32] P.C.C. 289 Alexander, Somerset House, London.

Chapter IX

[1] The contract is preserved among other documents relating to the *Gazetteer* in P.R.O. C104/68. For a general description of this group of documents see the Bibliography, Manuscripts. The full text of the 1775 contract will be found in Appendix B.

[2] See p. 34, above.

[3] Plomer, *Dictionary* . . . *1726–1775*; Timperley, *Encyclopaedia*, p. 811.

[4] Plomer, *Dictionary* . . . *1726–1775*.

[5] Of the accounts which she was required to keep, the only ones surviving cover the period from 1792 to 1797. They are discussed in Chapter XII.

[6] P.R.O. C104/67, Book M. Hereafter designated as MS. Book M. A key to the abbreviated designations of the *Gazetteer* documents in P.R.O. C104/67–68 will be found in the Bibliography, Manuscripts.

[7] Such outings were apparently popular among newspaper proprietors. Cf. George Colman, *The Spleen, or Islington Spa* (London, 1776), Act II:

RUBRICK (a bookseller): "Thursday I am engaged to eat a buck with the proprietors of Lloyd's Chronicle, at the Long Room, in Hampstead."

On 9 July 1800, the proprietors of the *Whitehall Evening Post* reached an agreement "that the annual dinner in the country be held at the Ship at Greenwich." B.M. Egerton MSS., 2236.

[8] See p. 83, above; Timperley, *Encyclopaedia*, p. 646.

[9] See p. 64, above.

[10] On 23 April, 30 July, and 29 October 1776.

[11] This reply by "Regulus" also appeared as a two-shilling pamphlet printed for J. Williams. The title page is undated, but the British Museum Catalogue places its publication in 1775. If this is correct, the *Gazetteer* was simply reprinting the pamphlet in installments.

[12] The Mr. Davis to whom the payments were made is otherwise unidentified in the publisher's account book, and the commonness of the name itself is hardly worthy of remark. It seems probable, however, that had he been other than Owen's partner in the *Gazetteer* Lockyer Davis, bookseller to the Royal Society and one of the nominal printers of the votes of the House of Commons, Owen would have made some kind of distinction. While I am hesitant to suggest that Lockyer Davis

was the author of "Regulus," two considerations make such an identification at least partially tenable. First, the Mr. Davis of the account book was very possibly Regulus himself. Of the six entries recording payments to him, five are phrased "Regulus by Mr. Davis" and the sixth "Mr. Davis for Regulus." From other entries in Owen's book, it seems probable that had Davis been merely the agent through whom the publisher transmitted money to Regulus, the record would occasionally have described the payments as made "by the hands of" Davis. Secondly, Lockyer Davis is known to have written occasional pieces for the newspapers. "He had read much, and to the purpose," John Nichols said of him (*Literary Anecdotes*, VI, 436–37). "Some little matters he had written; but they were principally, I believe, *jeux d'esprits*, arising from temporary circumstances and dispersed in the public papers, particularly 'The St. James's Chronicle.' The only volume of which I recollect his having acknowledged himself the editor was a valuable collection of the 'Maxims of Rouchefoucault, 1774.' . . . Few men, however, knew more of books or of the world . . . ."

[13] The collected edition was first advertised in the *Gazetteer* on Thursday, 20 November 1777.

[14] Owen's entry for 22 December 1779 reveals that the proprietors received sixpence from John Bew for each volume sold. Their cash receipts, then, represent a sale of 528 copies; this figure with the 127 books they received indicates an edition of perhaps 700 copies.

[15] *G&NDA*, Tuesday, 29 August; Wednesday, 30 August; and Thursday, 21 August 1775.

[16] *G&NDA*, Saturday, 23 September 1775 contains a summary of these proceedings up to that date; subsequent developments are reported in the issues of the paper for Monday, 25 September and Thursday, 28 September 1775.

[17] *European Magazine*, LXXIV (1818), 187–90. H. R. Fox Bourne (*English Newspapers*, I, 250n.) believed this article to have been "either written or inspired by Perry himself."

[18] See pp. 90–91, above.

[19] The memoir is printed in Nichols, *Literary Anecdotes*, III, 151–56.

[20] Cf. *G&NDA*, Tuesday, 6 August 1776, in the column headed *London:* "A ministerial writer in this paper of Thursday, has with a kind of superficial argument, endeavoured to stamp a degree of reputation upon the proceedings of Administration with respect to the American war . . . ."

Occasional poems signed "J. H. W——NE" appeared in the *Gazetteer* during 1777, and from 1778 to 1781 odes signed in full "J. H.

Wynne" were published annually on New Year's Day and on the royal birthdays.

[21] The statements are pasted to the flyleaf of MS Book M.

[22] *G&NDA*, Tuesday, 24 October 1775.*

[23] The head of the paper was also changed. Previously "The Gazetteer and" had been set in upper and lower case roman, "*New Daily Advertiser*" in italic. In the new head "GAZETTEER" appeared in roman caps, and the remainder of the title in upper and lower case, to the exclusion of italic types. For reasons unspecified, the head reverted on 9 September 1776 to its old form.

[24] *G&NDA*, Friday, 5 July 1776.

[25] For an account of this short-lived publication, see Wilfrid Hindle, *The Morning Post* (London, 1937), pp. 13–14.

[26] *G&NDA*, Thursday, 12 December 1776.*

[27] *G&NDA*, Friday, 6 June 1777.

[28] *G&NDA*, Monday, 27 October 1777.

[29] Thus, for example, Wynne's[?] verses on the death of Foote were reprinted in the *Morning Chronicle* on the day after they appeared in the *Gazetteer*.

[30] The information, Mary Say's memorial, and a copy of the *Gazetteer* inscribed "Bought at Say's John Boult's young Man" are in P.R.O. TS 11/424/(1340). I am indebted to the Treasury Solicitor for permission to inspect these documents, granted by a letter of 3 May 1952.

[31] P. 88, above.

[32] P. 135, above.

Chapter X

[1] See Ch. IV.

[2] Hindle, *The Morning Post*, Ch. III, " 'West End Sheet': 1772–1795."

[3] Fox Bourne, *English Newspapers*, I, 218 ff.

[4] *European Magazine*, LXXIV (1818), 188.

[5] "The essays of the political writers," Professor W. T. Laprade observes, "were removed from the position of importance on the front page which they had been wont to occupy to make room for the sayings and doings of political leaders."—"The Power of the English Press in the Eighteenth Century," *South Atlantic Quarterly*, XXVII (October, 1928), 433.

[6] *G&NDA*, Monday, 13 November 1775.*

[7] *G&NDA,* Thursday, 20 November 1777.*

[8] *G&NDA,* Friday, 13 February 1778.

[9] *G&NDA,* Thursday, 17 April 1777.

[10] *G&NDA,* Thursday, 20 March 1777.

[11] *G&NDA,* Wednesday, 25 November 1778.

[12] *G&NDA,* Monday, 19 July 1779.*

[13] *G&NDA,* Friday, 19 November 1779.*

[14] *G&NDA,* Thursday, 2 December 1779.*

[15] *G&NDA,* Wednesday, 7 July 1779.*

[16] *G&NDA,* Thursday, 25 November 1779.

[17] *G&NDA,* Tuesday, 30 May 1780.*

[18] *G&NDA,* Wednesday, 29 December 1779.

[19] *G&NDA,* Thursday, 10 June 1779.

[20] *G&NDA,* Wednesday, 24 November 1779.*

[21] *G&NDA,* Tuesday, 31 October 1780.

[22] *G&NDA,* Friday, 27 April 1781: "The following Papers have been put into our hands by a very respectable Member of the Legislature . . . ." Cf. the reference to a "respectable correspondent," p. 167, above.

[23] MS. Book M. The entry is dated 5 October 1780.

[24] Page 90, above.

[25] In 1779 the *Gazetteer*'s debate reporter spoke of having had "nine years experience" (p. 174, above). This may have referred to the length of his reporting experience as well as to his experience of the North ministry.

[26] *European Magazine,* LXXIV (1818), 187–90.

[27] *Register of Admissions to the Middle Temple* (London, 1949), I, 377.

[28] See p. 160, above.

[29] *G&NDA,* Saturday, 22 March 1777; cf. pp. 167–68, above.

[30] See p. 175, above.

[31] Hansard, *Parliamentary Debates,* XVI, 33, 34.

[32] The list is pasted to the inside of the lower cover of MS. Book M. A number of abbreviations have been expanded and superior letters lowered in the transcript which follows. It should be noted that so far as I have observed none of these private signatures was ever appended to any letter published in the *Gazetteer,* although a "D. G." who contributed several long letters to the paper in September and October 1777 may have been "D Gunstan," the Guildhall reporter. Such highly questionable identifications are without value, however, except perhaps as exercises in observation, and they are hereafter left unrecorded.

[33] See pp. 301–02, note 20, above.

[34] MS. Book M., 6 June 1782: "Paid Mr. Stevenson, by order of Mr. Wall, for assistance in Lords Debates . . . ."

[35] This list has been compiled from Owen's scattered entries recording payments for the papers. In most cases, the entries specify only the place of publication and the name of the printer or publisher (e.g., 13 April 1780: "Pd. Mr. Monk for Chester Paper"). H. G. Pollard's bibliography of eighteenth-century newspapers in *CBEL,* which names many of the printers and publishers of the papers listed, is my source for the titles given in the text.

[36] MS. Book M, 5 September 1780. The reference is probably to the annual *Court and City Register* (1742–1814) or to the *Royal Kalendar* (1767–1893), both of which contained lists of office-holders, governing boards, etc. Cf. Stanley Pargellis and D. J. Medley, eds., *Bibliography of British History: The Eighteenth Century,* p. 246.

[37] MS. Book M, 23 September 1780. This may have been Arthur Collins' *The Peerage of England,* which went through many editions between 1709 and 1812.

[38] There is evidence that as early as 1776 the presses were stopped on occasion for the insertion of late Parliamentary news. The House of Lords had sat until nearly one o'clock on the morning of Wednesday, 6 March 1776, before dividing for a vote. The *Gazetteer* had gone to press sometime before that hour, but the presses were stopped and the numbers of the division inserted so that they appeared in some copies of the paper published that day. On the following day, after a full account of the long debate two nights previously, this note appeared: "As the House sat till between twelve and one o'clock, debating the above important business, it was impossible to insert the division in all our papers of yesterday; we therefore now repeat it . . . ." *

[39] See p. 88, above.

[40] *G&NDA,* Wednesday, 2 August 1780.* One item copied into the *Gazetteer* from another paper in 1781 produced some unpleasant consequences. On 19 January 1781 John Almon's *London Courant* carried a paragrapph which, purporting to be news, declared of the Russian Ambassador at London: "The Ministry have reason to suspect his excellency to be little better than a *spy* . . . ." The printer of the *Courant* and those of six other papers (including the *Gazetteer*) which copied the item were convicted of libel. Six printers were fined £100 each and sentenced to prison for a year. Mary Say, in consideration of her sex, was fined £50 and received a six-month prison sentence. The convictions were reported in the *Gentleman's Magazine,* LI (July, 1781), 340. Cf. Fox Bourne, *English Newspapers,* I, 237.

The index to the MS. Calendar of Treasury Solicitor's Papers at the Public Record Office contains an entry recording that the libel was published in the *Gazetteer* for 20 January 1781, no copy of which appears to be extant. Documents of the case formerly preserved among the Treasury Solicitor's Papers are listed in the calendar as missing. MS. Book M records expenditures by William Owen in 1781–82 for coach hire for the "R Ambass. Chaplain" and for "Mrs. Say's bill in the cause of the Russian Ambassador." I have been unable to discover further details of the affair.

[41] *G&NDA*, Thursday, 17 August 1780.*

[42] *G&NDA*, Friday, 8 June 1781.

[43] *G&NDA*, Saturday, 8 July 1780.*

[44] *G&NDA*, Monday, 10 July 1780.*

[45] *G&NDA*, Tuesday, 17 August 1780.*

[46] *G&NDA*, Saturday, 9 September 1780.*

[47] *G&NDA*, Monday, 16 October 1780.*

[48] *G&NDA*, Thursday, 2 November 1780.

[49] *G&NDA*, Friday, 12 May 1780.*

[50] *G&NDA*, Wednesday, 25 October 1780.*

[51] For a discussion of the errors in numeration see Appendix A. H. R. Fox Bourne, who must have employed the same method as the editor Wall in dating the paper's origin, was undoubtedly misled also by the issue numbers. He stated that the *Gazetteer* was founded in 1728.— *English Newspapers*, I, 193.

[52] *G&NDA*, Tuesday, 17 October 1780.

[53] *G&NDA*, Thursday, 21 February 1780. *The Public Advertiser* had experienced the same difficulty: "The Avenues to the House were so crowded, that no person could be admitted to the Lobby . . . the Gentleman, who gives this report, could not gain Admittance at One o'Clock. We are therefore compelled to give such a short Account of the Debate as could be acquired by Hearsay." The account given was not the same as that published in the *Gazetteer*.

[54] *The English Newspaper*, Ch. X.

Chapter XI

[1] MS. Book M, 6 February 1783. By 9 April, Stuart required twenty-five more "best pens" and half a ream of fools cap.

[2] *G&NDA*, Friday, 31 January 1783.*

[3] The most valuable source of biographical information on Perry before 1790 is the previously cited article in the *European Magazine*, LXXIV (1818), 187–90. It was the only account published during

Perry's lifetime, and it constituted the basis for later memoirs like those in *Bell's Weekly Messenger* for 9 December 1821, and the *Gentleman's Magazine*, XCI (1821), 565–66. Quotations otherwise unidentified are from this article.

⁴ *European Magazine*, LXXIV (1818), 189. It may be pointed out that this statement, if it was not based on information supplied by Perry, appears never to have been contradicted by him. An essay published in the *Gazetteer* of Thursday, 27 July 1777, the year of Perry's arrival in London, was entitled "Thoughts on Disputing Societies" and was signed with the initials "J. P." This may have been one of Perry's earliest contributions to the London newspapers.

⁵ See Arthur Aspinall, "The Social Status of Journalists at the Beginning of the Nineteenth Century," *RES*, XXI (July, 1945), 216–32.

⁶ *English Newspapers*, I, 253.

⁷ John Nichols reported that when Memory Woodfall went to Dublin in 1784 to report debates in the Irish Parliament, "so great was his fame, crowds followed him through the streets eager to catch a glimpse of a man whom they considered as endowed with supernatural powers." —*Gentleman's Magazine*, LXXIII (1803), 792, reprinted in *Literary Anecdotes*, I, 303–4.

⁸ *English Newspapers*, I, 252.

⁹ I have encountered reports as long as thirteen columns in the issues of the *Gazetteer* for January 1784.

¹⁰ *G&NDA*, Wednesday, 3 March 1790.* On 29 March 1787 the *Gazetteer* was compelled to publish a report at second hand: "The gallery having been unexpectedly filled at an hour unusually early, we are indebted for the preceding short sketch of the debate to the friendly communication of a Member."

¹¹ As early as January 1784 the *Morning Herald* occasionally published reports as long as those of the *Gazetteer*.

¹² Surviving files of the *Gazetteer* for 1783–90 are not entirely complete, but addresses to the public pointing out the superiority of the paper's reports at various times during the period make no claim to a unique or novel system of obtaining them. Cf. *G&NDA*, Monday, 24 January 1785; Thursday, 4 December and Friday, 28 December 1788; Wednesday, 24 November 1790.

¹³ *G&NDA*, Monday, 24 January 1785. During a part of the period in which Perry served as editor of the *Gazetteer* he also edited a number of volumes of the Parliamentary debates published by John Debrett, one of the original publishers of the *European Magazine*.

¹⁴ *G&NDA*, Saturday, 24 January 1789.* Lord Cathcart had re-

ferred to rumors that "certain persons" were purchasing newspapers in an attempt to establish their popularity. The reference was probably to the Prince of Wales, who purchased a share in the *Morning Post* in order to silence its criticism. See Hindle, *The Morning Post*, pp. 54–56.

[15] *G&NDA*, Wednesday, 3 March 1790.*

[16] *G&NDA*, Thursday, 8 January 1784.*

[17] *G&NDA*, Monday, 2 November 1789.* On Tuesday, 22 December 1789, Perry published a part of Price's celebrated sermon on the revolution. "We are proud," he declared, "to have the merit of adding to . . . [its] publicity."

[18] *G&NDA*, Saturday, 6 March 1790.

[19] *G&NDA*, Monday, 26 January 1784.

[20] *G&NDA*, Monday, 11 May 1789.

[21] *G&NDA*, Wednesday, 13 May 1789.

[22] *G&NDA*, Saturday, 1 March 1783.

[23] *G&NDA*, Wednesday, 9 June 1784.

[24] *G&NDA*, Thursday, 1 July 1784.

[25] *G&NDA*, Friday, 20 August 1790.

[26] *G&NDA*, Tuesday, 9 March 1784.*

[27] *G&NDA*, Wednesday, 11 August 1790.

[28] It had been conducted by John Almon for some years, and partially subsidized by the opposition. See A. Aspinall, *Politics and the Press*, pp. 271–72.

[29] *G&NDA*, Monday, 18 October 1790.

[30] Aspinall, *Politics and the Press*, Ch. III: "Government Subsidies (England)."

[31] *Morning Chronicle*, Monday, 13 December 1790.

[32] *G&NDA*, Monday, 24 January 1785.

[33] *G&NDA*, Monday, 10 September 1784.*

[34] *G&NDA*, Monday, 7 December 1789.

[35] *G&NDA*, Monday, 24 January 1785.

[36] *G&NDA*, Monday, 7 December 1789.

[37] Cf. Henry Baldwin's statement to the House of Commons, p. 110, above.

[38] G. M. Trevelyan, *English Social History*, 3d ed. (London, 1946), p. 412.

[39] *The Morning Herald* (1780); *Aurora, Noon Gazette* (both 1781); *Times* (1785); *World* (1787); *Argus, Diary, Star,* and *Oracle* (all 1789). *CBEL*, II, 709.

[40] *G&NDA*, Thursday, 5 February 1789.

[41] *G&NDA*, Tuesday, 24 August 1784.

[42] MS. Book M. The payments referred to occur in the entries for January 1784, 1785, and 1786; January and April 1787; January 1788 and 1789.

[43] *G&NDA*, Wednesday, 1 December 1784.* Puffs were charged for as advertisements and were subject to the advertising stamp duty, as were obituary notices containing eulogies on the dead. (*G&NDA*, Friday, 1 June 1775: *"All encomiums upon deceased friends are charged at the Stamp-office."*) Cf. pp. 222–23, below, and *History of "The Times,"* I, 48.

[44] Charles Harold Gray, *Theatrical Criticism in London to 1795* (New York, 1931), p. 251. For full discussions of the theatrical criticism published in the *Gazetteer* from its beginning, refer to the index of Gray's work. Commercial relations between the *Gazetteer* and the theatres are taken up in Chapter XII of this study.

[45] *G&NDA*, Thursday, 4 January 1787.

[46] *G&NDA*, Saturday, 6 January 1787.

[47] *G&NDA*, Saturday, 7 October 1786.

[48] *G&NDA*, Saturday, 9 September 1786.

[49] *G&NDA*, Monday, 16 October 1786.

[50] *G&NDA*, Saturday, 9 September 1786.

[51] *G&NDA*, May 1786, *passim.*

[52] *G&NDA*, October 1785, *passim.*

[53] *G&NDA*, Tuesday, 25 December 1787.

[54] MS. Book M, 9 October 1787 to 16 April 1788, *passim.*

[55] *G&NDA*, Monday, 20 December 1784.

[56] *G&NDA*, Friday, 4 April 1788.

[57] *G&NDA*, Monday, 29 January 1787.

[58] Sonnets by "Miss Charlotte Smith" were occasionally published in the *Gazetteer* between July and December 1788, the year before her *Elegaic Sonnets* reached a fifth edition.

[59] A number of poems by "Egerton Brydges, Esq." appeared in the paper during the first half of 1785, the year in which his *Sonnets and Other Poems* went through two editions.

[60] *G&NDA*, Monday, 2 April 1787.

[61] See p. 225, below.

[62] *Gentleman's Magazine*, LXX (1800), 1038–39.

[63] *G&NDA*, Tuesday, 21 December 1784.*

[64] *G&NDA*, Friday, 14 January, 1785.*

[65] Taylor, *Records of My Life*, I, 248; II, 340.

[66] *Private Papers of James Boswell from Malahide Castle*, prepared for the press by Geoffrey Scott and Frederick A. Pottle (n.p., privately printed, 1928–34), XVIII, 91–92.

[67] *G&NDA*, Wednesday, 20 October 1790. I have been unable to locate in extant issues of the *Gazetteer* the earlier letter to which Boswell referred, though he had written to the editor in August 1785 to thank him for favorable comment upon Boswell's "Letter to the People of Scotland."—*G&NDA*, Monday, 1 August 1785.

[68] P.R.O. C104/67, Book H, hereafter designated as MS. Book H. See Bibliography, Manuscripts, for key to abbreviations.

[69] MS. Book M records annual payments to Bentley for keeping the accounts.

[70] P.R.O. C104/67, Book F, hereafter designated as MS. Book F.

[71] MS. Book M.

[72] Owen's "petty expences," when discussed, are consistently cited from among the day-to-day entries in MS. Book M where they were first recorded. An account book labeled "Owen's Petty Expences" (P.R.O. C104/68, Book E) for the period 1784–97 is composed of extracts from MS. Book M, and it apparently served as an intermediate account between the rough entries of that book and the totals given in Book H discussed above.

[73] The valuation of £200 was declared at each general meeting from 1788 to 1796 and had apparently remained at that figure from a considerably earlier period. In 1778, however, Thomas Durham had sold his half-share for £200, indicating a valuation at that time of £400 for a full share.—P.R.O. C104/68, assignment of $\frac{1}{32}$ share from T. Durham to W. Owen, dated 20 July 1778. P.R.O. C104/68, Book C, contains minutes of committee and general meetings from April 1788 to March 1796; Book A continues the minutes through April 1797. In future references these books will be designated simply as "Minutes" and the date given of the meeting under discussion. In my transcriptions, superior letters have been lowered; words or phrases stricken out in the MS. have been omitted and those substituted for them reproduced, unless otherwise indicated in the notes.

[74] See p. 79, above.

[75] Morison, *The English Newspaper*, p. 197.

[76] *G&NDA*, Wednesday, 28 January 1789.*

[77] *G&NDA*, Friday, 3 April 1789.*

[78] Minutes, 28 October 1789.

[79] Minutes, 16 December 1789.

[80] Minutes, 16 June 1790.

[81] Compare, for example, facsimiles of the *Times, World,* and *Star* in Morison, *The English Newspaper*, pp. 178, 186, 188.

[82] *G&NDA*, Monday, 20 September 1790.*

[83] *G&NDA*, Wednesday, 6 October 1790.* The final sentence re-

ferred to a dispute between Captain Edward Topham and Charles Este concerning property in the *World*. The *Gazetteer* at this period was publishing frequent and lengthy letters by the two men. Cf. Charles Este, *My Own Life* (London, 1787).

[84] *The London Adviser and Guide*, 2d ed. (London, 1790), quoted in Morison, *The English Newspaper*, p. 197n. For Trusler, see *DNB*.

[85] P.R.O. C104/68, Finey to the proprietors of the *Gazetteer*, 10 September 1795. For the full text of the letter, see "William Finey and 'The Times,'" *TLS* correspondence, 4 April 1952.

[86] P.R.O. C104/68, J. Watkins to G. Nicol [19?] March 1796.

[87] *Morning Chronicle*, Tuesday, 7 December 1790.

[88] Fox Bourne, *English Newspapers*, I, 261–62.

[89] See p. 148, above.

[90] Shareholders of the period about 1790 are listed on the first leaf of MS. Book M, with transfers of individual shares noted. Signatures in the minute book for 1790 identify the proprietors at that date. Professions and family relationships have been supplied from Timperley, *Encyclopaedia*, and Plomer, *Dictionary . . . 1726–1775*. The marriage of Mary Say was reported in the *Gentleman's Magazine*, LVI (1787), 1023. Vint's occupation and Christian name are given in P.R.O. C12/251/39, *Vint v. Sotheby et al.*

[91] The minutes for each meeting contain a list of those in attendance.

[92] A. C. L'Estrange, *The Life of Mary Russell Mitford in a Selection from her Letters* (London, 1870), III, 254; Lamb's essay, "Newspapers Thirty-Five Years Ago," is in *The Last Essays of Elia*, all editions.

[93] Minutes, 30 July 1789.

[94] Minutes, 16 December 1789.

[95] Minutes, 17 June 1789.

[96] Minutes, 15 September 1790.

[97] Minutes, 20 October 1790.

[98] Minutes, 16 November 1790.

Chapter XII

[1] Another feature of that date, the addition of the paper's title to the heading of the *London* column, was a step in the evolution of the modern masthead in which the *Gazetteer* was again following the example of competitors. Inclusion of the current date in that position, which had been common practice in the other papers for nearly a decade, did not take place until February 1793.

[2] See p. 184, above. The issue for 1 January 1791 was numbered 19367, indicating an origin for the paper in the year 1729. Cf. Appendix A.

[3] Compare this statement of political policy with the assertion in *DNB* that James Perry left the *Gazetteer* when it was "purchased by some tories, who changed its politics."

[4] Minutes, 19 January 1791.

[5] Joseph Foster, ed., *Alumni Oxonienses* . . . *1715–1886* (Oxford, 1887–88), III, 1170. A. Andrews (*The History of British Journalism,* I, 196), describes Radcliffe as having "edited the *Englishman* in 1762, . . . numbering Edmund Burke among his staff." Obviously, this would have been chronologically impossible.

[6] C. F. McIntyre, *Ann Radcliffe in Relation to her Time* (New Haven, 1920), pp. 12–15.

[7] Advertised in *G&NDA*, Thursday, 7 January 1790.

[8] McIntyre, *Ann Radcliffe*, p. 12.

[9] Minutes, 16 February 1791.

[10] Minutes, 16 November 1791.

[11] MS. Book F. Fragmentary accounts in William Owen's ledger (MS. Book M) indicate that the paper had previously been distributed at Bath from 1784 to 1786 and at Southampton for a time in 1783.

[12] Minutes, 21 November 1792.

[13] Minutes, 19 December 1792.

[14] *G&NDA*, Saturday, 12 September 1767.

[15] MS. Book M. The payments were always made in the months of June or July.

[16] P.R.O. C104/67, Book K. Hereafter designated as MS. Book K.

[17] MS. Book K.

[18] MS. Book M, 30 March 1790.

[19] MS. Book M.

[20] MS. Book F.

[21] This is established by the correspondence between entries in the book (MS. Book F) and a number of loose receipts and vouchers in P.R.O. C104/68.

[22] See p. 149, above.

[23] See p. 210, above.

[24] MS. Book F. Obvious mispellings have been corrected, superior letters lowered, and bracketed entries indicate the use of ditto (D°) in the original.

[25] P.R.O. C104/68 contains a number of such statements, several of them submitted by William Hamilton Reid. Some employee, probably the *Gazetteer* clerk at the printing office, must have checked the first

lines quoted in the reporters' bills against marked copies of the papers. A memorandum of this period in P.R.O. C104/68 lists the initials of "Writers employed on the Gazetteer as set down on the marked Papers" (including Walsh, Stables, Wilson and Reid), and William Owen's ledger (MS. Book M) records annual payments of four shillings for "Sewing Marked Papers in blue Paper for the year."

[26] See p. 180, above.

[27] The memorandum is among papers in P.R.O. C104/68.

[28] Cf. p. 31, above.

[29] Cf. p. 180, above.

[30] Memorandum in P.R.O. C104/68.

[31] P.R.O. C104/68, statement to the proprietors and receipt by one Mainstone, an Essex Street attorney. Payment of the bill is recorded in MS. Book M, 17 January 1793.

[32] Minutes, 15 February 1792.

[33] Elimination of part of the editorial staff—the editor and debate reporters, certainly, and perhaps some of the paragraph writers—might yield an approximate view of the organization prevailing twenty-five years earlier, in the time of Charles Say, John Almon, and Roger Thompson.

[34] See p. 216, above.

[35] G&NDA, Monday, 25 April 1791.*

[36] G&NDA, Thursday, 14 April 1791.

[37] G&NDA, Saturday, 28 April 1792.*

[38] G&NDA, Thursday, 31 March 1791.

[39] Minutes, 15 August 1792.

[40] G&NDA, Thursday, 19 January 1792.

[41] History of "The Times," I, 35. Gazetteer circulation figures are from MS Book H.

[42] Aspinall, Politics and the Press, Ch. III.

[43] This may have been the Bourne concerned in the Sunday Observer in 1794, mentioned in a letter from W. H. Bourne of Dublin to Evan Nepean, a Treasury Secretary and dispenser of patronage for Pitt's government. W. H. Bourne was offering the Observer, apparently conducted by his younger brother, for sale to the government.—P.R.O. H.O. 42/31.

[44] He is to be identified, probably, with the "D. E. Macdonnel of the Middle Temple" who compiled A Dictionary of Quotations in Most Frequent Use, . . . Chiefly from the Latin and French . . . , printed for G. Wilkie and J. Robinson (5th edn., London, 1809). Cf. p. 239, below.

[45] MS. Book F. On foreign intelligence supplied by the Post Office clerks, see History of "The Times," I, 96–97.

[46] P.R.O. C104/67, Book I, hereafter designated as MS. Book I. It is a continuation of the accounts in MS. Book M.

[47] Extant issues for the year 1793, comprising about two-thirds of the total number published, are undistinguished.

[48] MS. Book H.

[49] Minutes, 22 March 1793.

[50] Minutes, 15 May 1793.

[51] Minutes, 17 April 1793.

[52] Minutes, 15 October and 5 November 1794.

[53] Cf., for example, above, p. 296 n.19.

[54] Minutes, 17 April 1793.

[55] P.R.O. C104/68, Macdonnel to J. Watkins, 12 August 1793.

[56] Minutes, 18 September 1793.

[57] Other new proprietors since 1789 were John Shepperson, Oxford Street bookseller, who had purchased John Debrett's share in 1791, and Charles Davis, who apparently inherited the share of Lockyer Davis in 1791 and succeeded him as virtually a permanent member of the management committee.

[58] Timperley, *Encyclopaedia*, p. 781. Owen's share in the *Gazetteer* passed to his daughter Elizabeth and was subsequently administered by her husband, George Whiteside, a linen draper. P.R.O. C12/251/39.

[59] Minutes, 23 April 1794. The earliest surviving issue containing the new head is that for 26 June 1794. The change had certainly been made since the end of 1793. The printer's Incidents for February 1793 included a five-guinea charge for "New Head for Gazetteer," indicating that the change had been long anticipated.

[60] Minutes, 21 May 1794.

[61] Minutes, 25 September 1794.

[62] P.R.O. C104/68, W. Ward to J. Watkins, 18 November 1794.

[63] P.R.O. C104/68, D. E. Macdonnel to J. Watkins, 13 November 1794.

[64] Taylor, *Records of My Life*, II, 272-77.

[65] See note 44, above.

[66] P.R.O. C104/68, J. Beauchamp to J. Watkins. The letter is undated, but it was folded within Macdonnel's letter of resignation. The condition of these documents when I first inspected them gave no reason to believe that they had been rearranged by the Master in Chancery into whose custody they had come in 1802. The monthly accounts of Incidents in MS. Book F show both Wilson and Walker to have been employed as reporters at this time.

[67] MS. Book F; Minutes, 19 November 1794.

[68] P.R.O. C104/68, W. Radcliffe to J. Watkins, 1 December 1794.

[69] P.R.O. C104/68. The memorandum, in John Watkins' hand,

is undated, but it corresponds to the description given in the minutes for 11 February 1795.

[70] P.R.O. C104/68. Other statements among these documents indicate that the Leyden and Brussels *Gazettes* had been obtained from D. Braithwaite, a stationer.

[71] Minutes, 21 October 1795.

[72] MS. Book F.

[73] Minutes, 20 May 1795.

[74] P.R.O. C104/68, W. Radcliffe to J. Watkins, 22 August 1795. Radcliffe later purchased *The English Chronicle, and Universal Evening Post.* The imprint of that paper in March 1796 declared that it was "Printed by J. NORRIS for W. RADCLIFFE."

[75] P.R.O. C104/68, William Finey to the proprietors, 10 September 1795. The full text of the letter is printed in *TLS* correspondence, 4 April 1952.

[76] P.R.O. C104/68, undated memorandum in John Watkins' hand.

[77] P.R.O. C104/68, C. Kemp to J. Watkins, 11 March 1796.

[78] P.R.O. C104/68, G. Nicol to J. Watkins, 18 March 1796; and J. Watkins to G. Nicol, [19?] March 1796.

[79] P.R.O. C12/262/43, statement of William Dalmeida and William Williams in answer to a Bill of Complaint by Edward and Mary Vint.

[80] P.R.O. C104/68, J. Walker to J. Watkins, 15 February 1796.

[81] P.R.O. C12/262/43, statement of William Dalmeida in answer to a Bill of Complaint by Edward and Mary Vint.

Chapter XIII

[1] P.R.O. C104/68, "Mr. Price" to J. Watkins, 11 April 1796.

[2] MS. Book F.

[3] P.R.O. C104/68, Book A. The first meeting was on 17 June 1796.

[4] P.R.O. C104/68, W. Williams to J. Watkins, 20 July 1796.

[5] P.R.O. C104/68, J. D. Debaune to J. Watkins, 22 August 1796.

[6] P.R.O. C104/68, Debaune to Watkins, 19 July 1796.

[7] P.R.O. C104/68, Debaune to John Kent, 4 October 1796.

[8] P.R.O. C104/68, Debaune to Watkins, 11 October 1796.

[9] *Ibid.*

[10] P.R.O. C104/68, Debaune to Watkins, 2 January 1797.

[11] P.R.O. C104/68, Watkins to Debaune (rough draft), 29 October 1796.

[12] P.R.O. C104/68, W. Elgar to John Kent, 12 December 1796.

[13] P.R.O. C104/68, Watkins to Debaune, 28 December 1796.

[14] Minutes, 7 October 1796.

[15] P.R.O. C104/68, A. Franklin to J. Beauchamp, undated.

[16] See p. 239, above.

[17] MS. Book I. From October 1796, John Watkins paid the salaries of Franklin and Gordon besides that of a third debate reporter, thus apparently removing editorial matters entirely from Mrs. Vint's control.

[18] James Boaden and Peter Stuart, "Conductors and Proprietors" of the *Oracle*, according to the imprint of that paper. Woodfall's letter to Dalmeida is in P.R.O. C104/68.

[19] B.M. pressmark 11622. ee. 4.

[20] Aspinall, *Politics and the Press*, p. 165. John Taylor described Hewardine admiringly as a "very extraordinary character who used to join the literary and social set at the Turk's Head." Taylor considered him "the most perfect master of what is called slang that I ever knew," and was "fully convinced that if he had been brought properly forward in public life, with the advantage of a good education and regular connections, he would not have submitted to being . . . dependent upon any man. . . ."—*Records of My Life*, I, 249–52.

Mary Wells the actress referred in her memoirs to a magazine report of 1807 which "put me under the protection of a Mr. Hewerdine." "Who the gentleman is I cannot say," she continued, "nor did I ever see or hear of such a person, but rather fancy he is the offspring of the editor's brain."—*Memoirs of the Life of Mrs. Sumbel, late Wells . . .* (London, 1811), III, 11. Mary Wells's intimate connection with London journalism through Edward Topham and the *World* makes it likely that the Hewerdine with whom her name was linked is to be identified with Taylor's acquaintance of the Turk's Head.

[21] Minutes, 4 March 1797. On 15 April 1796 John Watkins had been granted an appointment with one H. Hodgson to solicit Navy Office advertisements for the *Gazetteer*. On 11 May 1796 Hodgson wrote to Watkins (P.R.O. C104/68): "I am happy to inform you that Directions will be given for the Insertion of the Navy Office Advertisements in the Gazetteer—" This is the only indication I have found of any financial relations between the *Gazetteer* and the government after 1742.

[22] Minutes, 4 March 1797.

[23] Minutes, 20 March 1797.

[24] Minutes, 23 March 1797.

[25] Minutes, 28 March 1797.

[26] Minutes, 31 March 1797.

[27] Minutes, 4 April 1797.

[28] Minutes, 7 April 1797.

[29] Minutes, 10 April 1797.

[30] Minutes, 17 April 1797.

[31] P.R.O. C104/68, J. Fuller to J. Watkins, 17 April 1797.

[32] Minutes, 19 April 1797.

[33] P.R.O. C104/68, D. Stuart to J. Watkins, 18 April 1797.

[34] MS. Book I.

[35] P.R.O. C104/68, W. Flower to J. Watkins, 17 May 1797.

[36] P.R.O. C104/68, receipts of W. Flower to the proprietors, 15 October 1798; letter of Flower's solicitors to Watkins, 2 November 1798; C104/67, book N, receipts of Flower to the proprietors, 1789–98.

[37] P.R.O. C104/68, J. Watkins to G. Farquharson (20 October 1798).

[38] P.R.O. C104/68, Book B.

[39] P.R.O. C12/251/39, *Vint* v. *Sotheby et al.*

[40] P.R.O. C12/262/43.

[41] P.R.O. C33/514, fols. 449–51.

[42] P.R.O. C120/539.

[43] They are preserved at the Public Record Office in two bundles, C104/67 and 68, and are the materials upon which much of Chapters XI, XII, and XIII of this study are based.

[44] P.R.O. C13/494, *Vint* v. *Williams*.

[45] John Nichols, *Illustrations of the Literary History of the Eighteenth Century* (London, 1817–58), VIII, 503.

Chapter XIV

[1] B.M. Addit. MSS., 38730 contains a number of such documents.

[2] This generalization does not, of course, apply to the period of the *Gazetteer*'s government connection, during which readers encountered a successive cycle of such "characters" as "Fra. Walsingham," "R. Freeman," and "Francis Osborne"; the paper's conductor, the enigmatic "W——ly" of Gray's Inn, may have been responsible either to the government or to the *Gazetteer*'s printer, Samuel Richardson.

[3] *G&NDA*, Saturday, 13 February 1783.

[4] MS. Book M, 29 March 1783.

BIBLIOGRAPHY

THE sources most extensively employed in this study have been the files of the *Gazetteer* and a group of manuscript materials, most of which have not been known previously to writers on eighteenth-century journalism. In the following bibliography I have listed in detail the principal manuscript sources and have attempted to describe generally the extent of surviving *Gazetteer* files. The use of bibliographical references throughout the text precludes the necessity for a detailed listing of the books consulted, but I have included a full list of the most important bibliographies and newspaper catalogues—to most of which reference has not been made in the notes—and a selected list of other works which are of particular importance to the student of eighteenth-century English journalism.

I. Manuscripts

British Museum

Addit. MSS., 38729, fols. 126–27, *Gazetteer* proprietors' contract, 5 December 1748; fols. 128–29, *Gazetteer* proprietors' contract, 1 November 1753.

Addit. MSS., 30871, fols. 69–70, letters of Roger Thompson and Robert Morris to John Wilkes, 13 March 1771.

Addit. MSS., 38728, fols. 130, 133; 38729, fols. 165, 166, minutes of meetings of the proprietors of the *London Packet*, January 1770 and January 1773.

Addit. MSS., 38169, general monthly accounts of the *Public Advertiser*, 1765–71.

Egerton MSS., 215–62, notes of debates in the House of Commons, 1768–74, by Sir Henry Cavendish.

Egerton MSS., 2236, minutes of the meetings of the proprietors of the *Whitehall Evening Post*, March 1795–February 1802 (incomplete).

Victoria and Albert Museum

Forster MSS., XIII (48.e.7), fols. 14, 23, 35, 40, 41. Correspondence of Samuel Richardson and Aaron Hill, 1743–46.

Somerset House

P.C.C. Alexander 289. Will of Charles Green Say, proved 22 July 1775.

Public Record Office

State Papers Domestic, 36/112. Letters: T. Curtis to the Duke of Newcastle, 10 January 1750; Sir Michael Foster to same, 11 January 1750.
Chancery Town Depositions. C24/1686/21, *Crowther et al. v. Mechell*, 1757; C24/1814, *Thompson v. Say*, 1774.
Treasury Solicitors' Papers. TS 11/836 (2897), information against Charles Say for publishing Junius' letter to the King; TS 11/1079 (5385–86), informations against Charles Say for publishing John Horne's advertisements for the Constitutional Society, 1775; TS 11/424 (1340), information against Mary Say for publishing "An Honest Man," 1778.
Chancery Proceedings. C12/901/33, *Thompson v. Say*, 1772; C12/251/39, *Vint v. Sotheby et al.*, 1799; C12/262/43, *Vint v. Watkins*, 1800; C13/494, *Vint v. Williams*, 1804.
Chancery Decrees and Orders. C33/444, fols. 1, 130, 560, 572, *Thompson v. Say;* C33/514, fols. 449–51, *Vint v. Sotheby et al.*
Chancery Masters' Papers. C120/539, *Vint v. Sotheby et al.*
Chancery Masters' Reports and Certificates. C38/885, *Vint v. Sotheby et al.*
Cancery Masters' Exhibits. C104/67–68, *Vint v. Sotheby et al.* These bundles contain account books and other documents relative to the *Gazetteer* from 1774 to 1797. Loose correspondence, memoranda, receipts, statements, and vouchers are in bundle 68. Individual documents cited are described in the text and notes as reference is made to them.

Account books in both bundles were each labeled with a letter of the alphabet by an official of the court. Although the resulting alphabetical sequence is inconsistent with the chronology and nature of the books themselves, I have employed the letter designations to facilitate brief and more specific references in the notes than would otherwise have been possible. Following is a list of the books by their alphabetical designations, with a descriptive note on each.

C104/68 BOOK A. Minutes of *Gazetteer* proprietors' committee and general meetings, June 1796–April 1797. A continuation of Book C, below.
—BOOK B. "General Account of the Gazetteer," April 1796–April 1797. This book continues Book D, below. Entries from April 1796 to March 1797 are found in both.
—BOOK C. Minutes of committee and general meetings, April 1788–March 1796. Continued by Book A, above.
—BOOK D. "General Account," April 1787–March 1797. Cf. Book B, above.
—BOOK E. Treasurer's "Petty Expences," March 1784–April 1797. Com-

posed of extracts from Books M and I, below, hence not cited in the notes.
C104/67 BOOK F. Printer's monthly accounts to proprietors, February 1792–
April 1797. A specimen extract from this account is given in Chapter XII.

—BOOK G. Monthly treasurer's accounts to proprietors, April 1796–April
1797. A continuation of Book H, following.

—BOOK H. Monthly treasurer's accounts to proprietors, October 1783–March
1796. This and the preceding book (G) contain records of the total number of papers sold in each month as distinguished from the number printed,
making it possible to ascertain the average daily circulation of the *Gazetteer*
for any given month during the period.

—BOOK I. Cash book, recording daily receipts and disbursements of the
treasurer and publisher, January 1794–April 1797. A continuation of Book
M, below.

—BOOKS K, L. Advertising accounts, 1786–97. One or more pages are
devoted to the account of each regular *Gazetteer* advertiser over the eleven-
year period. The first few leaves of each volume contain an index to the
accounts in the volume.

—BOOK M. Cash book, recording daily receipts and disbursements, January
1774–January 1794. Several memoranda relative to writers for the paper,
receiving stations for advertisements, and shareholders in the *Gazetteer*
copyright are attached inside the upper and lower covers. Continued by
Book I, above.

—BOOK N. A volume containing twelve leaves of prepared stamped receipts,
eight of which are filled by receipts issued to the treasurer by stationers
and others, 1789–98.

II. Printed Sources

Newspapers *

The Daily Gazetteer. London, 1735–[46?].
The Daily Gazetteer: Or, London Advertiser. London, 17[46?]–48.
The London Gazetteer. London, 1748–53.
The Gazetteer and London Daily Advertiser. London, 1753–64.
The Gazetteer and New Daily Advertiser. London, 1764–96.
The Gazetteer. London, 1796–97.

* My study of the printed paper has been confined exclusively to the holdings
of the Burney Collection at the British Museum. This collection includes by far
the most extensive file of the *Gazetteer* in existence. Of the approximately 19,500
issues of the paper published (at an average of 313 issues annually) during its
sixty-two–year life, the Burney Collection, catalogued, unfortunately, only in a
unique manuscript volume, contains nearly 11,000, or about 56 per cent of the
total. For the most part, the gaps in the Burney file of the *Gazetteer* are chronologically diversified, so that at least a representative number of issues is present
for almost every year of the paper's life. The most serious lack of surviving
issues is for the early period of the *Gazetteer's* independence from government
control. Thus, for the years 1746–47, 1750, 1753–55, and 1758 there are no

Bibliographies, Catalogues of Newspapers

Catalogue of a Collection of Early Newspapers and Essayists, formed by the late John Thomas Hope, Esq. Oxford, 1865.

Crane, R. S., and F. B. Kaye. *A Census of British Newspapers and Periodicals, 1660–1800.* Chapel Hill, N.C., 1927.

Gabler, Anthony J. "Checklist of English Newspapers and Periodicals before 1801 in the Huntington Library," *Huntington Library Bulletin,* II (November 1931), 1–66.

Milford, R. T., and D. M. Sutherland. *A Catalogue of English Newspapers and Periodicals in the Bodleian Library, 1622–1800.* Oxford, 1936.

[Muddiman, J. G.]. *"The Times" Tercentenary Handlist of English and Welsh Newspapers, Magazines, and Reviews.* London, 1920.

Pargellis, Stanley, and D. J. Medley. *Bibliography of British History: The Eighteenth Century, 1714–1789.* Oxford, 1951.

Pollard, H. G. Bibliography of The Newspaper, 1695–1800, in *The Cambridge Bibliography of English Literature,* ed. by F. W. Bateson, Vol. II. Cambridge, 1939.

Roupell, Marion G. *Union Catalogue of the Periodical Publications in the University Libraries of the British Isles.* London, 1937.

Stewart, Powell. *A Descriptive Catalogue of a Collection at the University of Texas: British Newspapers and Periodicals, 1632–1800.* Austin, Texas, 1950.

Weed, Katherine Kirtley, and Richmond P. Bond. *Studies of British Newspapers and Periodicals from their Beginning to 1800: A Bibliography.* Chapel Hill, N.C., 1946.

Selected Books, Pamphlets, and Articles

Almon, John. *Memoirs of John Almon, Bookseller of Picadilly.* London, 1790.

Andrews, Alexander. *The History of British Journalism.* 2 vols., London, 1859.

Aspinall, Arthur. *Politics and the Press, c. 1780–1850.* London, 1949.

issues in the Burney Collection; for the year 1752 there is one issue; and for each of the years 1748, 1751, and 1757, only half a dozen. The same conditions apply, though less extensively, to the final years of the paper's life. There are four issues for each of the years 1794 and 1795, and none for 1797.

Gazetteer holdings in American libraries and in British libraries other than the British Museum, as catalogued in the bibliographies listed below and in the Library of Congress Union Catalogue, have been, for the purposes of this study, negligible. Very rarely is even a single issue of the paper to be found for years unrepresented in the Burney Collection. Where external evidence (such as that of the "Bristol affair" described in Chapter II) makes it desirable to examine particular issues not found in the British Museum, the deficiency is in no instance supplied by the holdings of other libraries.

References in the text and notes to newspapers other than the *Gazetteer* are based upon personal inspection of the papers unless otherwise specified.

Bourne, Henry Richard Fox. *English Newspapers: Chapters in the History of Journalism.* 2 vols., London, 1887.

Calendar of Treasury Books and Papers, 1735–1745, prepared by William A. Shaw. 3 vols., London, 1900–1903.

The Fool: Being a Collection of Essays and Epistles, Moral, Political, Humourous, and Entertaining published in the Daily Gazetteer. 2 vols., London, 1748.

Gray, Charles Harold. *Theatrical Criticism in London to 1795.* New York, 1931.

Hanson, Laurence. *Government and the Press, 1695–1763.* Oxford, 1936.

Hill, Aaron. *The Works of the Late Aaron Hill, Esq.* 2d edn. 4 vols., London, 1754.

Horton-Smith, Lionel G. H. "The Old City Family of Say, and Its Connexion with Essex," reprinted from *The Essex Review,* January 1948, pp. 37–44.

———. "The Press and Bookselling: Some Memories of the Past," *Publisher and Bookseller,* 4 March 1932, pp. 491–93.

Hunt, F. Knight. *The Fourth Estate.* 2 vols., London, 1850.

Junius. *The Letters of Junius,* ed. with an Introduction by C. W. Everett. London, 1927.

Laprade, W. T. *Public Opinion and Politics in the Eighteenth Century, to the Fall of Walpole.* New York, 1936.

Leslie-Melville, R. *The Life and Work of Sir John Fielding.* London, 1934.

"Marforio." *An Historical View of the Principles, Characters, Persons, &c. of the Political Writers in Great Britain.* London, 1740.

Morison, Stanley. *The English Newspaper: Some Account of the Physical Development of Journals printed in London between 1622 and the Present Day.* Cambridge, 1932.

[———]. *History of "The Times."* Volume I: "The Thunderer in the Making." London, 1935.

Nichols, John. *Literary Anecdotes of the Eighteenth Century.* 9 vols., London, 1812–16.

Plomer, Henry R., G. H. Bushnell, and E. R. McC. Dix. *A Dictionary of the Printers and Booksellers Who Were at Work in England, Scotland and Ireland from 1726 to 1775.* Oxford, 1932.

[Ralph, James]. *A Critical History of the Administration of Sir Robert Walpole, Now Earl of Orford.* London, 1743.

Richardson, Samuel. *The Correspondence of Samuel Richardson,* ed. Anna Laetitia Barbauld. 6 vols., London, 1804.

Sale, William M., Jr. *Samuel Richardson, Master Printer.* Ithaca, N.Y., 1950.

Savage, James. *An Account of the London Newspapers, and of the Manner in which They are Conducted.* London, 1811.

Siebert, Frederick Seaton. *Freedom of the Press in England, 1476–1776.* Urbana, Illinois, 1952.

Smith, David Nichol. "The Newspaper," in *Johnson's England,* ed. Arthur S. Turberville, 2 vols., Oxford, 1933. II, 331–67.

Sutherland, James R. "The Circulation of Newspapers and Literary Periodicals, 1700–1730," *The Library*, 4th ser., XV (1934), 110–24.

——, ed. *The Dunciad*, by Alexander Pope. Twickenham Edition, London, 1943.

Taylor, John. *Records of My Life*. 2 vols., London, 1832.

Timperley, C. H. *An Encyclopaedia of Literary and Typographical Anecdote*. London, 1842.

Index

[The name of the *Gazetteer* is abbreviated throughout by *G*.]

London Evening Post: comments on
G, 16; G copies story from, 75;
debate reports published in, 90;
C. Say prints, 96; J. Perry works
for, 189; mentioned, 28, 82, 94–
95, 99, 102, 112, 117, 145, 146
London Gazette: foreign news
sources, 6; published by authority,
7; G publishes extracts from, 66;
proclamation published in, 107,
109; G payments for, 226; men-
tioned, 142, 143
London Journal, 4, 11
London Magazine, 40
London Museum, 82
Lords, House of. *See* House of Lords
Loughborough, Alexander Wedder-
burn, Lord, 193–94
Lounger, 204
Lyceum debating society, 189

M'Alpin, Roderic, 152, 161, 164
Macdonnel, D. E.: journeys to conti-
nent, 232–33; editorship of G,
232–39; resignation from G, 238–
39; editor of *Telegraph,* 239;
recommends editor to G, 251–52
Mahmoud, 254
Mainstone, Mr. (attorney for G),
257
Manchester, 189
Mansfield, Lord. *See* Murray, Wil-
liam
Mareschal College, 189
"Marforio," 7–8, 12–13
Marks, J., 158
Marshall, Mr. (G contributor), 179–
80
Massie, Joseph, 48–49, 145, 299n11
Mawby, Sir Joseph, 114
Merchants: and Spanish war, 14–15;
and G, 16, 21; appeal of *Public
Ledger* to, 43; comment on "price
current" by, 49
Meredith, Sir William, 79–80
Middlesex Election of 1768, 77
Middlesex Journal, 102–18 *passim,*
125

Milborne Port, Borough of, 76–77
Miles, William Augustus, 63
Miller, John: prosecuted for Junius
letter, 82; publishes debate reports,
90; C. Say's son-in-law, 90; ar-
rested on Speaker's warrant, 112–
13; prepared to defy House of
Lords, 117; ejects R. Thompson
from printing house, 129; directs
removal of G printing equipment,
132–33; prosecuted for libel, 145;
C. Say's bequest to, 146; mentioned, 84, 94, 114, 116, 128,
130, 134
Mineral Water Warehouse, Owen's,
152–53
Mitford, Mary Russell, 216
"Modestus," 84
Monitor, 38
Monro, Thomas, 204
Monthly Review, 180
Morison, Stanley, 21, 186
Morning Advertiser, 243
Morning Chronicle: debate reports
in, 166; J. Perry and, 198–99,
217; circulation, 214; mentioned,
58, 110, 136, 140, 141, 144, 160,
165, 168, 177, 186, 192, 249,
252, 253
Morning Herald: dispute with
Morning Post, 182; and scandal,
200; circulation, 214; mentioned,
58, 177, 186, 243, 251, 252, 253
Morning Post: purchases G, 3, 258–
60; specializes in "fashionable intelligence," 165; and scandal, 171,
200; dispute with *Morning Herald,* 182; circulation, 214; payment of debate reporters, 243;
mentioned, 58, 62, 136, 140, 141,
160, 178, 186, 217, 249, 250,
251, 252. *See also New Morning
Post*
Morris, Mary, 87–89 *passim,* 92,
128, 129
Morris, Robert, 110
Motte, Benjamin, 30
Murray, William, first Earl of Mansfield, 109, 282

Walsingham, Francis. *See* Arnall, William

Walthoe, John, 8, 9, 19

Walter, John II, 217

Ward, John, 34, 35

Ward, William, 238

Wardlaw, William, 290n29

Ware, Richard, 34

Watkins, Benjamin, 245

Watkins, Elizabeth (wife of John), 261

Watkins, Jeremiah (brother of John), 261

Watkins, John: succeeds Owen as *G* treasurer, 214, 237; negotiations with editors, 238, 242, 247, 251–52, 260; duties as treasurer, 243; and sale of *G*, 244–45, 258, 260; solicits Navy Office advertisements, 315n21; death of, 261; mentioned, 246, 253, 257

Watkins, Walter, 245, 261

Watson, W., 224, 225

Wedderburn, Alexander, First Baron Loughborough: prosecutes *G* printer for libel, 162; criticizes newspaper slander, 193–94

Westminster election of 1784, 194

Westminster Forum, 189

Westminster Journal, 30

Whatley, Stephen, 8

Wheble, John: summoned before House of Commons, 102, 106; invited to defy House of Commons, 104–5; royal proclamation issued against, 107–8; warned by Wilkes, 108; arrested, 111–12; mentioned, 109, 110, 125, 156

Whigs: *G* and, 198, 229

Whiston, John, 34, 35, 148, 215

White, Benjamin, 148, 215

Whitehall Evening Post, 27

Whiteside, Elizabeth Owen, 261

Whiteside, George, 246, 256, 257, 261

Whitworth, Richard, 110, 105–6, 122

Wiley, Mr. (translator for *G*), 231, 232

Wilkes, John: solicits printer's allegiance, 108; communicates with *G*'s printer, 110–11; voids arrest on proclamation, 111–12; plans defiance of House of Lords, 117; supplies speeches to newspapers, 135, 136, 298n3; criticized in *G*, 154–55; mentioned, 51, 52, 54–55, 75, 77, 104, 109, 113, 114, 116, 157

Wilkie, J., 40–41, 145

William III, 161

Williams, William, 245, 249–50, 256, 261

Wilson, David, 148, 215

Wilson, Mr. (reporter and editor of *G*), 224, 231, 239, 242, 247

Wilson, Robert, 23, 26, 34, 35, 148

Wingrave, Francis, 215, 246

Withy, Robert, 76

Woodward, Thomas, 8

Woodfall, Henry Sampson: printer of *Public Advertiser*, 66, 109, 160, 165, 185, 262, 264; prosecuted for Junius letter, 82, 84

Woodfall, William: arrested by House of Lords, 110; takes over *Morning Chronicle*, 165; renowned for memory, 166; as editor and debate reporter, 177, 192, 193; and theatrical news, 203; contributions to *G*, 253–55; on speed of composition, 254; mentioned, 160, 167, 168

World, Fashionable Advertiser, 58, 200, 214

Wright, Mr. (Dover agent for *Morning Post*), 250–51

Wynne, John Huddlestone, 156–57, 160–61, 164, 178, 179

York Gazetteer, 180

Young Slaughter's Coffeehouse, 254